LEADING WOMEN

LEADING WOMEN

PLAYS FOR ACTRESSES II

EDITED BY *Eric Lane*

AND *Nina Shengold*

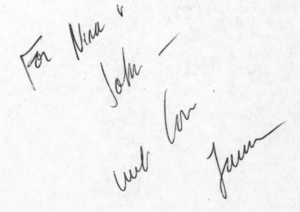

VINTAGE BOOKS

A DIVISION OF RANDOM HOUSE, INC.   NEW YORK

A VINTAGE ORIGINAL, AUGUST 2002

Copyright © 2002 by Eric Lane and Nina Shengold

Library of Congress Cataloging-in-Publication Data
Leading women : plays for actresses II / edited by Eric Lane and Nina Shengold.
    p. cm.
  ISBN 0-375-72666-7
    1. American drama—20th century. 2. Women—Drama. 3. Monologues.
I. Lane, Eric.   II. Shengold, Nina.
PS627.W66 L43 2002
812'.50809287—dc21   2002022852

Book design by Debbie Glasserman

www.vintagebooks.com

Printed in the United States of America
10 9 8 7 6 5 4 3 2 1

CONTENTS

INTRODUCTION

One of the first things you learn in drama school is that there are more roles for men than for women. This is a wonderful thing to learn because it is true of the real world as well.
       —from *Medea* by Christopher Durang and Wendy Wasserstein

Actresses deserve better roles. This was our premise four years ago when we edited the Vintage anthology *Plays for Actresses,* a collection of seventeen plays with all-female casts. The response was overwhelming. The book became an instant bestseller among actresses. Teachers ordered it as an acting class text and monologue sourcebook. Most gratifying of all were the letters from playwrights, who told us about the new productions the anthology sparked—many mounted by groups of actresses who had banded together to produce plays that showcased their talents.

We're thrilled to be publishing this brand-new collection. You'll find an abundance of plays with all-female casts, along with a few that have one or more male roles but center on strong female leads. We selected the plays with an eye to variety, including works by award-winning authors and cutting-edge newer voices, with challenging roles for women of various ages and ethnic backgrounds. There are full-length and one-act plays, dramas and comedies, two-handers and ensemble pieces. We've also added a monologue section, which offers wonderful audition material and a sneak peek at even more plays for actresses.

The characters who populate the seven full-length plays in this book represent an amazing cross section of female experience: girl gang members, Southern debutantes, pilots, teachers, traffic reporters, rebel teenagers—and, of course, authors and actresses.

Jane Martin's screwball farce *Anton in Show Business* goes

behind the scenes of a regional theater production of Chekhov's *The Three Sisters* as it spins wildly out of control. Its seven-woman cast plays multiple roles, ranging from a silicone-filled TV star to a gay male director to audience members who never shut up. In *Collected Stories,* Pulitzer Prize—winning playwright Donald Margulies examines the shifting relationship between a celebrated author and the grad student protégée who idolizes, then betrays her.

The Black and Latina gang members of Kia Corthron's *Breath, Boom* speak a raw and immediate street poetry that lights their bleak lives like the fireworks its heroine dreams of creating. The ensemble cast includes juicy roles for as many as eighteen women. In *Five Women Wearing the Same Dress,* by *American Beauty* Oscar winner Alan Ball, the Southern bridesmaids stuck in identical taffeta gowns are one-of-a-kind individuals, as is the lone male who joins them.

Julia Jordan's *Smoking Lesson* and Diana Son's *Stop Kiss* are an acting class bonanza, filled with scenes for young actresses. *Smoking Lesson* takes place under the railroad trestle where three Midwestern girls once found a drowned child. Every year, the girls return on the anniversary, and tonight, their fifteen-year-old leader will tempt fate with the older male drifter accused of the crime. The multilayered *Stop Kiss* alternates two story lines, which take place before and after its central event. In the first, we watch two hip and witty young women, who both see themselves as straight, tentatively exploring the bounds of their friendship; in the second, we witness the aftermath of the brutal gay bashing spurred by their first kiss.

Tongue of a Bird, by actress/playwright Ellen McLaughlin, is a striking theatrical portrait of a female search-and-rescue pilot. In her obsessive search for an abducted teenage girl, she comes face-to-face with her own ghosts.

For actresses looking for shorter scripts, we've included four ten-minute plays. To paraphrase Spencer Tracy's description of Katharine Hepburn: There's not much meat on them, but what's there is choice. Durang and Wasserstein's hilarious take on *Medea* is joined by two equally lunatic comedies: Laura Shaine Cunningham's "Happy Talkin'," in which a lonely woman is pursued by a tribe of surreal telemarketers, and Mary Louise Wilson's "Lost," a portrait of two aging friends who can't remember a thing. In Nina Shengold's ten-minute drama "No Shoulder," a childless woman discovers an unforeseen bond with a teenage hitchhiker.

Actresses looking for solo material will find an extraordinary range of women's voices in our new monologue section. Three of these excerpts are from one-woman shows: Eve Ensler's taboo-breaking hit *The Vagina Monologues;* Claudia Shear's *Blown Sideways Through Life,* an exuberant hymn to temporary employment; and *Rose,* Martin Sherman's portrait of a feisty Jewish widow whose life spans three continents and most of the twentieth century.

Warren Leight's *The Princess of Babylon* and Michelle Carter's *Hillary and Soon-Yi Shop for Ties* shed light on two teenagers best known from the tabloids: Amy Fisher and Soon-Yi Previn. Both pieces were first performed in anthology evenings of monologues, scenes, and (in Carter's case) songs by their authors.

The six remaining monologues are excerpted from full-length plays with many strong female roles. These include Lynn Nottage's *Crumbs from the Table of Joy,* a memory play about an interracial marriage; Jenny Lyn Bader's quick-witted romantic comedy *Manhattan Casanova;* Migdalia Cruz's *Miriam's Flowers,* a searing look at a teenage girl driven to self-mutilation; Eric Lane's *Times of War,* a lyrical trilogy that follows one woman's journey over fifty years; Sherry Kramer's *What a Man Weighs,* a highly original study of love and compulsion; and Margaret Edson's Pulitzer Prize–winning *Wit,* whose scholarly heroine battles with cancer. If any of these monologues speaks to you, go out and read the entire play. (Contact information for productions appears at the back of this book.)

Finding the plays for this book was a joy and privilege. We hope *Leading Women* will introduce readers to some of the finest writers working today. Their plays are complex, funny, tragic, and always original. We also hope that actresses frustrated by the lack of roles in the marketplace will find ways to bring these characters to life. Put together an evening of scenes, rehearse a staged reading, produce your own showcase or production. You'll find audiences all over the world who long to see plays about women's lives, just as actresses everywhere long to perform them. Go out there and find one another. The words are right here.

Nina Shengold and Eric Lane
May 2001

ACKNOWLEDGMENTS

Many individuals generously contributed to the creation of this book. We'd like to thank the literary managers, agents, and publishers who helped us find such a wealth of material and secure the rights for this collection. In particular, we wish to acknowledge Michael Bigelow Dixon at the Guthrie Theater; Linda Karland at Samuel French; John McCormack; Ian Morgan at The New Group; Terry Nemeth, and Ben Sampson at TCG; Carol Christiansen at Dell Publishing; and Patricia Flynn at Villard Books. Much gratitude to Martha Banta, Sarah Bisman, Steven Corsano, Chris Karczmar, Joe Reeder and the Rondout Valley Drama Club, David Robinson, Werner Schnackenburger, and Martin Sherman. As always, we wish to thank our family and friends for their support.

Special thanks to our agents, Phyllis Wender and Susie Cohen, whose invaluable guidance made this collection possible. Also to our editor at Vintage Books, Diana Secker Larson, for all her assistance and for the opportunity to publish this book. And most of all, to the playwrights for their wonderful plays and to the actresses who bring their works to life.

FULL-LENGTH PLAYS

ANTON IN SHOW BUSINESS

A COMEDY

by Jane Martin

Anton in Show Business premiered at the Humana Festival of New American Plays in February 2000. It was directed by Jon Jory with the following cast:

T-ANNE, ANDWYNETH, DON BLOUNT	Saidah Arrika Ekulona
LISABETTE	Monica Koskey
CASEY	Gretchen Lee Krich
KATE, BEN, JACKEY, GATE MANAGER	Annette Helde
RALPH, WIKÉWITCH, LOLA, JOE BOB	Chick Reid
HOLLY	Caitlin Miller
JOBY	Stacey Swift

and the following production staff:

SCENIC DESIGNER	Paul Owen
COSTUME DESIGNER	Marcia Dixcy Jory
LIGHTING DESIGNER	Greg Sullivan
SOUND DESIGNER	Martin R. Desjardins
PROPERTIES DESIGNER	Ben Hohman
STAGE MANAGER	Deb Acquavella
ASSISTANT STAGE MANAGER	Amber Martin
DRAMATURG	Michael Bigelow Dixon
ASSISTANT DRAMATURG	Ginna Hoben
CASTING	Laura Richin Casting

CAST

T-ANNE:	The Stage Manager—also playing: Airport Announcer; Andwyneth; Don Blount, Gate Manager
ACTRESS 1:	Kate, Ben, Jackey
ACTRESS 2:	Ralph, Wikéwitch, Joe Bob
CASEY:	Thirty-six years old; tall, lean, plain
LISABETTE:	Twenty-four years old; charming and energetic
HOLLY:	Thirty years old; a drop-dead gorgeous TV star
JOBY:	Twenty-six years old; a recent graduate with an MFA in dramaturgy

The play is performed by women in roles of both sexes.

SETTING

Various locations in New York and San Antonio in the present. There is one intermission.

DIRECTOR'S NOTE

It is possible to use a bare stage and minimal furniture. Many costumes must be rigged for quick change. You need six female scene changers/dressers, who handle the furniture moves and quick changes. Costume changes were full and were not done in sight. All changes were possible with the given text. I strongly suggest that you have the scene changers in several rehearsals prior to tech. Actors continued to play during scene changes. Have fun!

ACT ONE

A bare stage. In the darkness, rolling thunder and then suddenly cutting across it, lightning. The flashes illuminate a mysterious cloaked figure. Thunder. A special. The figure speaks.

T-ANNE: The American theatre's in a shitload of trouble. (*Flash, crash.*) That's why the stage is bare, and it's a cast of six, one nonunion. (*Flash, crash.*) I'm T-Anne, the stage manager, but I'm also in the play. (*Flash.*) Like a lot of plays you've seen at the end of the twentieth century, we all have to play a lot of parts to make the whole thing economically viable . . . (*Crash.*) . . . HOMAGE TO THORNTON WILDER. (*Flash, crash. She drops the cloak. She wears blue jeans, a T-shirt, many keys at her belt.*) The date is (*date*), just before noon. Well, I'll show you a little bit about how our profession is laid out. Up around here are the Broadway theatres, sort of between Forty-second and Fifty-second street, we like to think that's the heart of everything. City of New York, State of New York, United States of America, the world, the universe, the galaxy. Down over here is Greenwich Village, around there we do off Broadway, that's good too. Now Tribeca, SoHo, Lower East Side, we call that the "downtown scene," off-off stuff. An incredibly colorful group of people who despise realism and have all won the Obie Award . . . that's good too. Beyond that, radiating out in all directions for thousands of miles is something called "regional theatre," which I understand once showed a lot of promise but has since degenerated into dying medieval fiefdoms and arrogant baronies producing small-cast comedies, cabaret musicals, mean-spirited new plays and the occasional deconstructed classic, which everybody hates. After that, moving west, we reach the burning, uninhabitable desert and its militias who don't go to plays, and beyond that, singing a siren call, the twin evil kingdoms of Flic and Tube, the bourne from which no traveler returns. Now back to New York, thank God. Let's see, the Empire State Building, the Statue of Liberty and the Actors' Equity offices . . . that's our union. They make sure no more than eighty percent of our membership is out of work on any given day. And over there . . . yes, right over there is where we worship, yes sir, *The New York Times.* Well, that's about it. Now, with a short subway ride we get to one of the audition studios where producers and theatres come to find actors for their plays. Here's the front door, elevator up to the fifth floor, Studio C, where the San Antonio, Texas, Actors Express has come to the big city to cast *The Three Sisters* by Anton Chekhov. He's Russian. At noon, you can always hear the actors doing their vocal warm-ups.

(*Vocal warm-ups can be heard.*)

Aya—there they are. Not much happens before noon. Theatre folks sleep late. So, another day's begun. There's Lisabette Cartwright walking into Studio C. She graduated from the SMU (*Southern Methodist*) drama department and began teaching third grade. Then she was invited all the way to New York for an audition because the producer once had her appendix removed by one of her uncles. Lisabette's really excited, and her mom, who is at this moment canning okra, is too. Over there is Casey Mulgraw, the one dressed in the skirt/pants, skirt/pants thing, a lot of people call her the Queen of off-off-Broadway. She's a little hung over because she just celebrated the opening of her two hundredth play without ever having been paid a salary. She also has a yeast infection that is really pissing her off. In our town, we like to know the facts about everybody.

(*NOTE: All scene and costume changes are done by six female "changers," dressed in a variety of contemporary styles but all in black. T-Anne, the stage manager, moves to a small out-of-the-way table where she sits and follows the script. Three folding chairs are placed to create the waiting room of Studio C. Casey, a woman of 36, waits. Lisabette, 24, enters. She has a rolling suitcase.*)

LISABETTE: Hi. (*Casey nods.*) Is this the Studio C waiting room for Actors Express? (*Casey nods.*) *Three Sisters* audition? (*Casey nods.*) Oh, my heavens, it's so humid! I feel like I'm oiled up for the beach or something. I surely admire your fortitude in wearing both skirt and pants. Bet you're auditioning for Olga, huh?

CASEY: Why? Because Olga is older and homely and a spinster and has no life of her own and thus has assumed the role of caregiver to her brother and it's usually thought to be the least interesting acting role of *The Three Sisters.* Would that be it?

LISABETTE: Well, no, I . . .

CASEY: It's what you meant.

LISABETTE: I think I'll just start over. (*She does.*) Hi.

CASEY: Hi.

LISABETTE: I'm Lisabette Cartwright, from La Vernia, Texas. Graduated SMU but then I taught third grade for two years, bein' scared of an actor's life, and Maple Elementary loved me and wants me back anytime, but in a dream the Lord himself reaffirmed my calling so I made my comeback in *Fiddler on the Roof* but this is my first New York audition and I'm so jumpy my breasts bob even when I walk real slow. What's your name?

CASEY: Casey Mulgraw. One of my breasts had to be surgically removed because of a malignancy and I seem to be in remission but who knows how long that will last.

LISABETTE: Oh, my G-o-o-d-d-d!

CASEY: Want to do one more take?

LISABETTE: No, I would like you to forgive me for bein' such a dipshit, pardon the language, Jesus. I'm real sorry for your troubles and it looks to me like they did a real good match.

CASEY (*chuckles*): And yes. I'm reading for Olga for the obvious reasons.

LISABETTE: Really, I think Olga is the most spiritual of all the sisters.

CASEY: Good try. You don't have a smoke by any chance?

LISABETTE: Ummmm, I don't.

CASEY: Cough drop?

LISABETTE: Beef jerky.

CASEY: No thanks.

LISABETTE: I'm auditioning for Masha.

CASEY: The dark, passionate, amoral poetess. I feel dark; men call me passionate; I'm definitely amoral, and I've actually had several poems published but they never, never, never let me read for that part.

LISABETTE: Because you're a little plain?

CASEY: Thank you for speaking the unspeakable.

LISABETTE: I did it again, huh? I'm, oh my, very nervous but that's just no excuse. I would like to say I'm in way over my head and could I have a hug?

CASEY (*not unkindly*): If it's absolutely necessary.

(*They hug. The stage manager enters to speak to the actors. A rolling door might divide the spaces. Behind her, a table with three chairs is set up as the audition room. Ralph Brightly, an English director, and Kate, the producer, are at the table. In a third chair, to the side, sits Holly Seabé, a TV goddess who is cast as Irina and is helping audition.*)

STAGE MANAGER: Ms. Todoravskia is ready to see you both.

CASEY: Both?

STAGE MANAGER: Both. Hustle it up, we're running behind.

LISABETTE (*still in the anteroom, to Casey*): Do they usually see actors in groups?

CASEY: No. And we're not a group.

(*Casey and Lisabette enter the audition room.*)

KATE (*rising*): Hi. I am Katrina Todoravskia, Producing Director of Actors Express. And you are?

LISABETTE: Me?

KATE: You.

LISABETTE: I'm sorry, I forgot the question.

CASEY: Your name.

LISABETTE: Oh, Lisabette Cartwright.

(*Kate kisses Lisabette's hand extended for a shake.*)

KATE: You are devastatingly beautiful. (*Turns to Casey.*) And I gather you're here to audition for Olga?

CASEY: How'd you guess?

KATE: You look like an Olga.

CASEY: Thanks.

KATE: This is the play's director, Ralph Brightly; he runs the Toads Hall Rep in London.

RALPH (*shaking hands*): Well, a stone's throw outside, really. (*Shakes Lisabette's hand.*) Charmed. (*Shakes Casey's hand.*) Pleased.

KATE (*gesturing toward Holly*): And this is . . .

LISABETTE: Oh my G-o-o-d-d, you're Holly Seabé. I can't believe it! Holly Seabé. I love your TV show! Your character is so kooky and glamorous. You have such great timing. I've learned practically everything I know about foreplay from that show. You are so liberated!

HOLLY: Thanks.

LISABETTE: Oh my God, pardon me Jesus, are you going to be *in* the play?

HOLLY: Irina.

LISABETTE (*clapping her hands*): She's going to be *in* the play. This
is way cool! (*To Casey*) Isn't that cool?

CASEY: (*smiling but a bit reserved*): Yes, cool.

HOLLY: Thanks.

LISABETTE: I am so stoked!

RALPH: Yes, well, off we go then. *Three Sisters,* as you know, by
Anton Pavlovich himself. I'll just drop some bread crumbs
along the path before we hear you . . .

KATE: Running forty minutes behind.

RALPH: Right. Straight along. Give you the gist in five words.
Funny, funny, funny, funny, tragic.

CASEY: We're referring to *Three Sisters?*

RALPH: *The Three Sisters,* yes.

CASEY: Funny, funny, funny, funny, tragic?

RALPH: *Funny,* funny, funny, *funny,* tragic.

CASEY: Okay, I can do that.

LISABETTE: Do what?

CASEY: Show him that in our auditions.

LISABETTE: Gee, I didn't think it was funny.

RALPH: Precisely, that's to be our little revelation.

KATE: Forty minutes late.

RALPH: Right then, on we go.

JOBY (*a young woman in the audience rises and says*): Excuse me.

RALPH: Let's get cracking.

JOBY: Excuse me.

(*The actors glance up, confused. The "director" tries to go on.*)

RALPH: It's Chekhov, don't you see, so we're certainly not ready
    to do text . . .

JOBY (*from the audience*): Excuse me.

(*The actors stop. They look to Kate.*)

KATE: Yes?

JOBY: Is the director . . . ummm . . .

RALPH (*supplying the character name*): Ralph.

JOBY: Right, Ralph. Is it supposed to be a man played by a
    woman?

KATE: Yes. (*To Ralph*) Go on.

JOBY: How come?

RALPH: You mean why am I playing a man?

JOBY: I mean what's the point?

RALPH: Could you possibly sit down and let us act?

KATE: Wait. (*To Joby*) Hi.

JOBY: Hi.

KATE: What's your name?

JOBY: Joby. But I . . .

KATE: Joby, we want to thank you for coming to the theatre; we
    need young audiences.

RALPH: But—

KATE: Shhhh. Now you'll understand this as a woman, Joby—

RALPH: Could she please—

(*Kate silences Ralph with a look.*)

KATE: Eighty percent of the roles in the American theatre are played by men, and ninety percent of the directors *are* men. The point of having a male director played by a woman is to redress the former and satirize the latter. How's that?

JOBY (*after a brief pause*): Okay.

(*She sits down. Kate nods at Ralph.*)

RALPH: Right. Onward and upward, eh? (*He looks at Casey.*) What I'd like you to do, sweetie, is use only the word "tiddlypee" as text. . . . (*He looks at Lisabette.*) And you, dear, will say only "tiddlypoo." With these words, we will now play the scene where Masha tells Olga she's leaving her husband Kulygin and leaving town with the soldier Vershinin.

CASEY: But there is no such scene.

RALPH: Yes, precisely.

CASEY: So why?

RALPH (*sweetly*): You don't wish to audition?

CASEY: That's the answer to "why?"

RALPH: Look, dear—

(*Lisabette, trying to circumvent the oncoming conflict, goes into the improvisation.*)

LISABETTE: (*You wished to see me?*) Tiddlypoo, tiddlypoo?

CASEY: (*Is it true you and Vershinin are in love?*) Tiddlypee, tiddlypee, tiddlypee . . . tiddlypee?

LISABETTE: (*I am leaving Kulygin and going away with Vershinin.*) Tiddlypoo, tiddlypoo . . . tiddlypoo . . . tiddlypoo, tiddlypoo, tiddlypoo, tiddlypoo.

CASEY: (*If you go, what will happen to me?*) Tiddlypee . . . tiddlypee, tiddlypee, tiddlypee?

LISABETTE: (*You'll be fine.*) Tiddlypoo, tiddlypoo.

CASEY (*to Ralph*): How am I supposed to know what she's saying?

RALPH: Well, that would be the heart of the audition, wouldn't it?

(*Casey tries once more.*)

CASEY: (*If you go, we'll be left with Natasha!*) Tiddlypee, tiddly-pee . . . tiddlypee, tiddlypee. (*She stops.*) Look, this is ridiculous.

RALPH (*coolly*): Really?

CASEY: Well, yes, really. Can't we just do a scene using the script? I mean that would be sensible, right?

RALPH: Perhaps to an American actress, dear.

CASEY (*not happy*): Ummmmmm . . .

LISABETTE: Oh, but this is fun. Don't you think it's fun? It's kind of interesting.

CASEY (*slow burn*): American actress.

LISABETTE (*feeling the tension*): Just really, really, really, really fun!

CASEY (*burning*): You know, Ralph . . . dear . . . you Brits are arrogant, pompous, chauvinistic, smug, insufferable boors who take jobs from American actors and directors because of the toadying of the American press and the Anglophile American rich, and I've seen Chekhov done in London that really smelled up the place with its stiff-upper-lip, overpractical, no-self-pity-or-despair-here-darling style that has nothing to do with Russian passion or spiritual darkness, so—

JOBY: Excuse me.

CASEY (*still on the emotional high*): What?! What do you want?

KATE: Easy.

JOBY: Isn't this all just a little self-referential?

KATE: I'm sorry, Joby, but we are trying to perform a play and—

JOBY: I mean it's all just about the theatre. Isn't that a little precious?

KATE: Why?

JOBY: Well, theatre people talking about theatre.

KATE: As opposed to theatre people talking about the international monetary fund or the cloning of sheep?

JOBY: Well, is theatre culturally important enough to be the subject of a play?

RALPH: Nice of you to buy a ticket.

JOBY: Actually, they're comps.

RALPH: Ah.

JOBY: I'd think your only hope is to work on a deeply personal and profoundly emotional level.

CASEY: Well, the thing about the Brits is very emotional.

RALPH: And plays aren't ordinarily deeply personal until after the exposition.

JOBY: Oh.

CASEY: Later on, the play takes hold, and there is devastating loss and a lot of really profound metaphors that will knock your socks off. I mean, *knock your socks off!*

JOBY: Oh.

CASEY: Okay?

JOBY (*a brief pause*): Fine. (*She sits down.*)

CASEY (*going back*): . . . with its stiff-upper-lip, overpractical, no-self-pity-or-despair-here-darling style that has nothing, nothing to do with Russian passion or spiritual darkness. So don't give me that American actress crap!

(*A tense moment.*)

RALPH: Right. Nicely done. I think I've seen more than enough. Thanks ever so for coming in.

LISABETTE: We're finished?

RALPH: Lovely work, sweetie. (*Turning to Casey, smiling*) And I quite agree with you, dear, when Americans do Chekhov, it's just awash in self-pity.

(*Casey gives him the finger and stalks out.*)

LISABETTE: Well, anyway, this was my first professional audition, and it was really a lot of fun, and I want to thank you for calling me in and I really hope to work for you someday and . . . (*she begins to cry*) and I'm sorry I'm crying. I didn't mean to cry, and I've never even been to London but . . . she's right, you're a real jerk.

(*She runs out, leaving Ralph, Kate, and Holly alone.*)

RALPH (*ironically*): Well, that was a breath of fresh air.

KATE: Ralph, I want to apologize to you as an American—

RALPH: No, no—

KATE: I've seen hundreds, thousands of auditions, and I never—

RALPH: No need, sweetie—

KATE: I mean, who do they think they are?

RALPH: Made their beds, haven't they? Fat chance they'll be getting any work from this old British fairy.

(*Kate laughs appreciatively.*)

HOLLY: I liked them. (*They turn to look at her.*) I've been treated like dirt in situations like this, but now I'm rich and famous and you need me so you're sort of shit out of luck, huh? So here's the deal: I liked them and I'm bored with auditions so they're over and those two are in our play.

RALPH: Miss Seabé, they do not have the requisite talent.

HOLLY: Well, neither do I so maybe nobody will notice. (*She starts to exit.*) One thing, though. The little sweet one from Texas should play Irina, and I'll play Masha. Oh, and the Olga . . . well, she's Olga. Tiddlypee, tiddlypoo.

RALPH: So, Kate, love, I gather that's the horse that pulls our custard wagon, eh?

KATE: Well . . .

RALPH: Not to worry. In the kingdom of the barbarians, shit tastes like veal.

(*Lights change. Furniture is removed as Casey and Lisabette move into two specials, where they talk to their mothers on the "phone."*)

LISABETTE: Ma? It's me, Lisabette . . .

CASEY: Mother, okay, don't go ballistic . . .

LISABETTE: I got it! I got it! I got it! I got the part!

CASEY: Yes, I know I'm thirty-six years old, and I still have forty thousand dollars in student loans . . .

LISABETTE: Ma, Ma, wait, no, there's more . . .

CASEY: Yes, I would have to leave my day job . . .

LISABETTE: I'm gonna act with a TV star!

CASEY: Okay, the real deal . . .

LISABETTE: Holly Seabé! Yes! Me and Holly Seabé; can you believe it?

CASEY: Yes, it's kind of a crappy part; it's some hick town in Texas; the salary is like pesos; I'll lose my job; you won't have anybody to abuse but, lest we forget here, I'm supposed to be an actress!

LISABETTE: Ma, it's Chekhov!

CASEY: Mother . . .

LISABETTE: He's a Russian.

CASEY: Mother . . .

LISABETTE: No, it's beautiful and wise and sad, and I get to be a real professional!

CASEY: Screw you! Mother!

LISABETTE: Love you, Ma!

CASEY (*hanging up*): Damnit!

LISABETTE (*hanging up*): Yes!

(*Two connected plane seats are brought on. Lisabette and Casey move to sit in them. We hear an airport announcement.*)

GATE ANNOUNCER: Flight number two-seventy to San Antonio, Texas, gate twenty-seven B, boarding is now complete. Flight number two-seventy. All passengers . . .

CASEY: My dad's great. I worked weekends for a thousand years in his hardware store.

LISABETTE: You are kidding!

CASEY: What kidding?

LISABETTE: My dad has a hardware store.

CASEY: Yeah?

LISABETTE: You sorted screws?

CASEY: Oh yeah. (*They smile.*) Your dad want you to run it?

LISABETTE: Me? No. He sold it. He works in a community center.

CASEY: Well, my dad wants me. I dream I take it over and I wake up, stapled to three-quarter-inch plywood, screaming. Okay, the hardware connection.

LISABETTE: You're not married, right?

CASEY: I'm not married, right. You?

LISABETTE: I can't abide sex.

CASEY: Oh.

LISABETTE: Well, temporarily. I've kinda had some bad luck.

CASEY: Doesn't hold me back.

LISABETTE: I was kinda doin' it with my high school boyfriend
in the back of his car, an' we were hit from behind by a
drunk in a pickup.

CASEY: Ouch.

LISABETTE: They said they'd never seen that kind of whiplash.

CASEY: Sorry.

LISABETTE: Meanwhile, back at school I was kind of bein' forced
into an affair by my history teacher an' just after that I was
sort of halfway raped by a plumber.

CASEY (*horrified*): Jesus.

LISABETTE: No, it wasn't too bad really. I had to deal, y'know?
The only bad part was for three years I couldn't touch a
man, even like a handshake, without throwing up. Projectile
vomiting, so there were some awkward moments at parties.

CASEY: You're kidding me, right?

LISABETTE: No, really, it wasn't so bad. I'm over it, except really,
really occasionally when I first meet people. How about
your relationships?

CASEY: A lot of casual sex.

LISABETTE: Really.

CASEY: A lot. Always with members of the cast. And I've done
two hundred plays off-off.

LISABETTE: Wow.

CASEY: Outside of rehearsal, I'm actually a virgin.

LISABETTE: Wow.

CASEY: Of course, I'm always in rehearsal.

LISABETTE: Oh, I really respect that. I'm a virgin too. Except for being harassed, whiplashed, and on New Year's Eve.

(*Holly enters from first class.*)

CASEY: Hi.

LISABETTE: Oh my God.

HOLLY: I saw you guys when you came through first class.

LISABETTE: We walked right by you!?

HOLLY: No problem. I was enjoying some brain surgeon hitting on me.

LISABETTE: Excuse me, but . . . shoot . . . I just want to say that when Kate, the producer person, made me the offer . . . well . . . she said you had put in a word for us—me and Casey, Casey and I—God, I am such a hick, pardon me Jesus, anyway . . . thank you, thank you, thank you!

CASEY: It was really nice.

HOLLY: Well, hey, yeah I did, thanks but, you know, I was like nobody once too. Really down on the food chain like you guys . . . ummm . . . I won't even tell you the stuff I went through. Well, okay, the easy stuff was being told I had no talent like that director piranha said about you, right? And my deal was that talent isn't the point here . . . I mean, we're going to whatever Texas or wherever. Like, nobody who is anybody will see us or care. Maybe excepting my manager who has time for one client, me, and who would not care diddly dick if you guys had talent or not. (*A brief awkwardness.*) But the point is . . . you didn't think I meant you had no talent, did you?

CASEY: No, no.

LISABETTE: No, no.

HOLLY: Because you can understand I have no way of knowing that. I mean . . . tiddlypee, tiddlypoo.

LISABETTE: Right.

CASEY: Right.

HOLLY: My point is you guys were disrespected and he had to pay.

CASEY: You mean . . .

HOLLY: I mean, once they said you had no talent, I had to see you were hired.

LISABETTE: Wow.

HOLLY: Because I had that pulled on me, and now that *will not happen* in my presence. Like I'm the respect police.

CASEY: Thanks.

HOLLY: No problem. So I just wanted to shed a little light.

LISABETTE: That is really so nice.

CASEY: Just think, all of us have been told we have no talent.

HOLLY: Exactly!

CASEY: Well, that's something to build on.

HOLLY: Yeah, that's the other thing. We have to stick together down there in . . .

CASEY: Texas.

LISABETTE: Oh absolutely.

HOLLY: Because I have this intuition it's going to be like combat, but we stick together, we make them pay.

LISABETTE: Like we were three sisters.

HOLLY: That is so sweet and so right. That like zaps my guts.

CASEY: There's an empty seat.

HOLLY: Nah, I got to go back—I don't eat pretzels.

LISABETTE: We're talking about guys.

HOLLY: Them I eat. See you later.

(*Holly leaves. Three folding chairs are set, facing two other chairs for the next scene. Please remember the changes are cinematic. We never stop or take the lights out for a change.*)

T-ANNE: Please place your seats and tray tables in an upright position; we are beginning our descent into San Antonio.

(*We are now in the rehearsal room on the first day. Kate, T-Anne, Casey, Holly, Lisabette and the new director, an African American woman named Andwyneth Wyoré.*)

KATE (*addressing them*): Actors Express. Get it? Express? We are a serious theatre. We are unique. What is our artistic policy? Well, I can state that policy clearly. We live these ideas. At Actors Express, we call them the Seven Virtues. Number one, we do plays that . . . (*She makes a complex gesture.*) Two: our style is surgically defined as . . . (*A series of sounds.*) And only that. Fourthly, multicultural new works from the classical repertoire that say to the audience . . . (*An even more complex gesture.*) So that, in summation, or seventh, we can say . . . (*She stares at the ceiling, thinking.*) and we say that with no fear of being misunderstood. Oh, I know, this policy makes us controversial. We offend, we pique, we challenge while at the same time bringing together, healing, and making our community one. In a nutshell. This unique mission has made us essential to San Antonio, not because— Is there something out the window?

CASEY: Sorry.

KATE: Not because I have the best education money can buy . . .

LISABETTE: Wow.

KATE: Stanford, Harvard, Yale, but because . . . (*Holly is doctoring her lipstick.*) Holly, if you give this a chance, I think you'll find it's crucial to our work.

HOLLY: Stanford, Harvard, Yale . . .

KATE: Precisely.

HOLLY (*pointing at herself*): Biddyup High, Biddyup, Nebraska.

KATE: But because—hear this—contemporary relevance.

CASEY: Contemporary relevance.

KATE: Contemporary relevance.

CASEY: Yes.

KATE: Our raison d'être! Does anyone find what I said moving? (*Lisabette raises her hand.*) Because I am moved, and it is central to our aesthetic. (*Lisabette applauds.*) Now I wanted to meet with you, our three sisters, before the rest of our cast arrived, to bond as sisters and to achieve a . . . It's now my pleasure to introduce our director, Andwyneth Wyoré, Artistic Director of San Antonio's Black Rage Ensemble. We're involved in an exciting cultural exchange with Black Rage.

HOLLY: Doesn't that happen between countries?

KATE: Excuse me?

HOLLY: Cultural exchange?

ANDWYNETH (*chuckling*): You got that right, girl.

KATE: Interestingly enough, Andwyneth also went to Stanford, Harvard, and Yale.

ANDWYNETH: 'Course I went free.

CASEY: What happened to the Brit?

KATE: Well, there were—

KATE, ANDWYNETH, and HOLLY: Artistic differences.

ANDWYNETH: Uh-huh.

KATE: And I came to feel a sister—

ANDWYNETH: Girl, I'm not your sister. My momma see you, she faint, girl. She smack my daddy with an iron skillet! Huh-uh, baby, we got a little mutual use goin'. How about that? Down here in San Antonio you get some black people, some white people in the same room, there's always some foundation goes orgasmic. (*Cries deep in the act of sex*) Multi-cultural! Multicultural! Yes! Yes!! Multicultural!! (*Back to her own voice*) Pay a little rent, right? Suck a little green. Hey, I never did no white play, dig? Y'all a mystery to me, but I tell you one thing on Brother Chekhov, he just talk, talk, talk, talk, talk! Lord have mercy!

KATE: Well yes, but—

ANDWYNETH: Whine, whine, whine. Man, he got the self-pity diarrhea! Gushin' it out all over! Cut all that shit, X it out! Get down on the race question, down on the poverty question, get down on abuse of power, baby! No more, "Whine and dine with Brother Chekhov." Huh-uh. We gonna heat this sucker up! No script, huh-uh. I don't do script. Hell with that! What I see is a little white-sisters thing, an' a black peasants thing. Little dance drama thing, little street corner doo-wop. (*Holly raises hand.*) S'up, girl?

HOLLY: I'm doing the script

ANDWYNETH: You didn't follow the conversation?

HOLLY: Yeah, I can follow it, but I'm not doing that.

ANDWYNETH: Who the hell are you, girl?

HOLLY: You watch TV?

ANDWYNETH: Hell no, colored people all live in a cave.

HOLLY: I'm a big TV star.

ANDWYNETH: Well girl, you just pat yourself right on the back.

HOLLY: They begged me to come down here to wherever Texas to do a classic-style play. I don't give a shit about the race question or the poverty question. I don't have those problems. I got the film problem. I need to do film. No film, no respect. It's kind of like the race problem only in show business.

ANDWYNETH: You crazy, huh?

HOLLY: Yeah. So the rap is, you do TV you can't act. So my manager says to go backdoor. Get a little respect. Chekhov, Shakespeare, that stuff gives you shine. So like then you're a classical actress with fabulous breasts, and you can segue into sci-fi, action, cop-schlock, meet-cute or any genre.

ANDWYNETH: Let's cut to the bottom line, sister.

HOLLY: I'm saying every syllable Chekhov wrote, slow and clear.

ANDWYNETH: See, you are so far from my trip I can't even find you on the map.

HOLLY: Ms. Wyoré, the real difference between the two of us isn't what you think.

ANDWYNETH: Well, little thing, you bring it on.

HOLLY: The real difference is, you're fired.

(*Andwyneth looks at Kate.*)

KATE (*at a loss*): Well . . .

HOLLY: Trust me.

ANDWYNETH: You are one straight-up, no kiddin' around, in-your-face, don't-misunderstand-me bitch.

HOLLY: Sometimes, things just don't . . . work out.

ANDWYNETH (*focusing on Kate*): What are you, invisible?

KATE: Ummmmm . . .

ANDWYNETH: She's the deal, or you're the deal?

(*Holly also focuses on Kate.*)

KATE (*finally, to Andwyneth*): She's the deal.

ANDWYNETH: You get me down here, whip up a little money on my color, cast a buncha white girls an' then blow me off 'cause this prime-time toots shows up? (*To Kate*) I'm gonna pin "racist" to your ass, Momma. They gonna burn you in the public square to get right with my people. There won't be nothin' left of you but little snowy white ashes, dig? You an' Chekhov is both toast!

(*She exits.*)

KATE: Ummm . . . if you'll excuse me.

(*She exits to talk to Andwyneth. The sisters are silent for a moment.*)

CASEY: Anyone want some Skittles?

LISABETTE: You just fired the director in front of the producer without asking.

HOLLY: I am saying the lines.

CASEY: She's saying the lines.

HOLLY: Directors are a very gray area for me. It has been my experience that they actually like to be fired because they suffer from severe performance anxiety. They have these pushy little egos but hardly any usable information, which makes them very sad and time-consuming. I wouldn't worry because after you fire them, they usually find successful careers on cruise ships where they are completely harmless.

LISABETTE: But to do that, is that ethical?

HOLLY: Lisabette, I like you. I do. You seem like a very nice person. I'm not a very nice person, but I can still appreciate one when I see her.

LISABETTE: Thanks.

HOLLY: In college plays, community stuff, arty nowheresville professional gigs like this, there is probably something called ethics, but up where the eagles fly and the wolves run, up where American presidents screw the actresses, there is only power. The ethics thing is a little foggy. Power, on the other hand, is clear, it's clear, it's understood. For a very short time, Lisabette, here in wherever-it-is Texas, you will fly with an eagle. Say whoosh.

LISABETTE: Whoosh.

HOLLY: Enjoy.

(*At this moment, Ben Shipwright, a craggy actor, enters. He is playing Vershinin.*)

BEN: Hello, ladies.

LISABETTE: Hi.

CASEY: Hi.

HOLLY: Hi.

BEN: Ben Shipwright. Gonna play Vershinin.

CASEY: Olga, the boring sister.

LISABETTE: Masha. But I can't shake your hand right now. I'll explain later.

HOLLY: Masha.

LISABETTE: You're playing Masha?

HOLLY: We'll talk. Where are you from, Ben?

BEN: Right around here. I do some acting but I actually make my living singing country.

LISABETTE: Oh my God, you're Ben Shipwright?

BEN: Yeah.

LISABETTE: Oh my God, I love your records!

HOLLY: You record?

BEN: Little bit.

LISABETTE: Little bit? This week he has two singles in Top 50 Country!

HOLLY: Really?

CASEY: Mazeltov.

BEN (*to Holly and Casey*): You girls from New York?

CASEY: Yeah.

HOLLY: L.A.

BEN (*to Lisabette*): Now I know *you're* a home girl.

LISABETTE: *How* do you know?

BEN: Well, you talk San Antonio and you listen to a bunch of no-good pickers like me.

HOLLY: Ben?

BEN: Yes ma'am.

HOLLY: This relationship thing that goes down between Masha and Vershinin? We probably should get together and talk that out.

BEN: Be my pleasure. I'll let y'all get settled. (*He starts to exit.*)

HOLLY: Dinner?

BEN: I'm sorry, you speakin' to me?

HOLLY: I was speaking to you.

BEN: Well . . . ummm . . . I don't believe I caught your name.

HOLLY: Holly Seabé.

BEN: Well, Miss Seabé, I got me a couple of kids want me to barbecue some ribs tonight. (*Starts to exit.*)

HOLLY: Drink later?

BEN: Well, ummm, no ma'am. No ma'am, I can't. No offense intended.

HOLLY (*smiling, but not pleased*): Really?

BEN: No ma'am, I better not. My wife . . .

HOLLY: How old are your kids?

BEN: Four and seven. Seven and a half.

HOLLY: Won't they be asleep?

BEN (*They regard each other.*): Just no can do, ma'am. (*Shakes her hand.*) Real pleased to meet you. Lookin' forward to rehearsal. Catch y'all later.

(*He exits.*)

LISABETTE: I don't think he knew who you were! Can you believe that? I mean, you are on the cover of *TV Guide!*

HOLLY: I'll have to buy him a copy.

LISABETTE: But, am I right or am I wrong, he is really cute!

CASEY: My take is if you (*She indicates Holly.*) come on to a guy, looking the way you do, and he stiffs you while talking about his kids, he is *really* unavailable.

HOLLY: If I come on to a guy—and I'm not saying I did—that guy can kiss his previous life good-bye for as long as I find said guy entertaining. And on this I would be willing to wager some fairly serious money.

CASEY: I think serious money to me and serious money to you could be seriously different.

LISABETTE: But what about his wife and kids?

HOLLY AND CASEY: Shhh.

HOLLY: Okay, forget the money thing. We'll bet hair. Loser shaves her head.

LISABETTE: Wow.

CASEY: You can't afford to shave your head.

HOLLY: I won't have to.

CASEY: The guy's straight from Norman Rockwell.

HOLLY: I could screw anybody Norman Rockwell ever drew.

LISABETTE: This is so yeasty!

CASEY: Let's get it on.

(*She holds out her hand. Holly shakes it.*)

HOLLY: He's going down.

LISABETTE: You aren't Baptist, huh?

HOLLY: Hey, Lisabette?

LISABETTE: Uh-huh?

HOLLY: I'm going to play Masha because it's the best part, and the most powerful person plays the best part. That's one of Hollywood's ten commandments. You'll play Irina, because I say so, but also because she's the youngest and you're the youngest and you would be really good doing her because you have yet to become a completely calcified diva.

LISABETTE (*not at all upset*): Okay.

HOLLY: Everything's copacetic. Hey, let's go to the apartment hotel and get settled in fleabag hell and then find some cowboy dive with pine paneling and get unbelievably plotzed before tomorrow's first rehearsal, because I need to be hungover to face whatever director she digs up next.

(*A scene change starts. Eventually, there will be two single beds, two chairs, and a rolling door in place. This scene is played during the change.*)

JOBY (*from the audience*): Excuse me. (*Scene change continues.*)
    Excuse me.

T-ANNE: What?

JOBY: Well, I . . . didn't you—

T-ANNE: Hey, spit it out; I'm busy.

JOBY: Well, didn't you consider that role offensive?

T-ANNE: Did you notice we're doing a scene change?

JOBY: Golly, as a person of color . . .

T-ANNE: You're a person of color?

JOBY: No, you are.

T-ANNE: Ooooo, I hate it when I forget.

JOBY: But, wasn't that (*whispers*) stereotyped behavior?

T-ANNE (*again stopping her work*): Listen, I have to— All right, okay . . . listen, Babyface, I would like to do something, almost anything, where nice white people like you didn't feel like they had to defend me. Particularly (*whispers back*) in the middle of a scene change. (*Goes back to work.*)

JOBY: But it satirizes your political—

T-ANNE: Got to go.

JOBY: But, aren't you—

T-ANNE: No, I'm not. Want to know why?

JOBY: Oh, I do.

T-ANNE: 'Cause if I didn't do the plays that offended my color or politics or sex or religion or taste, I'd be shit out of work. Lights!

(*She exits. The scene light snaps on. Joby is still standing.*)

CASEY (*to Joby, not unkindly*): Sit down, Joby. (*Starting the scene*) I am *leveled* by that last drink. I am, as my beloved father would say, schnockered. (*Sings*) Tell me I can't sing karaoke?

HOLLY: You can't sing karaoke.

LISABETTE: This is so amazing, it's like a pajama party.

HOLLY (*patting her knee*): It is a pajama party.

LISABETTE: I mean, here I am, just out of drama school, and I am completely drunk, talking with real actors in a real way, including a great actress of the stage and a great actress from TV, and it just makes me want to cry.

HOLLY: Don't cry. Where did the vodka go?

LISABETTE: Holly, can I ask you a question?

HOLLY: Here it is. (*Pours herself another drink.*)

LISABETTE: It's something about acting.

HOLLY: I don't know anything about acting.

LISABETTE: Okay then, have you had breast implants?

HOLLY: Yes.

LISABETTE: Yes?!

HOLLY: Yes.

CASEY: That actually makes me feel better.

HOLLY: I have had seventeen separate surgical procedures to make me the completely natural beauty you see before you. They have even reshaped my toes because I do a lot of swimsuit.

LISABETTE: Those are artificial toes?

HOLLY: They are not artificial, they have been slimmed.

CASEY: How much?

HOLLY: Altogether?

CASEY: For the toes?

HOLLY: Seventeen thousand dollars.

LISABETTE: Wow.

CASEY: How much would it take to make me beautiful?

HOLLY: You're serious?

CASEY: Yeah.

HOLLY: Take off the sweatshirt.

(*She does.*)

LISABETTE: But beauty is subjective.

HOLLY: Not in Hollywood. Stand up and turn around. Over here. Over here, over here. (*Casey does.*) Look at the ceiling. (*She does.*) Hold your arms out like wings. Look left. Look right. Okay. I could be off ten, even fifteen percent here depending on bone and muscle structure, but my estimate would be six hundred thousand.

CASEY: Go ahead, flatter me.

HOLLY: Oh, there are divas who have paid more, and the kicker is even then there's no guarantee the camera loves you.

LISABETTE: Oh my God.

HOLLY AND CASEY: Pardon me Jesus.

CASEY: I'm giving it one more year.

(*Refreshes her drink.*)

LISABETTE: Give what?

CASEY: This. I don't have to put up with this hellish life. I have other skills.

HOLLY: Let me guess . . .

CASEY: For six years I worked in a slaughterhouse.

LISABETTE: No.

CASEY: Yeah.

LISABETTE: No way. You worked in your dad's hardware store.

CASEY: That was earlier. Where's the chocolates?

HOLLY (*handing her the box*): There's only creams left.

CASEY: I took the slaughterhouse job because it paid more than
waitressing, and I could cut the pigs' throats at night, which
left my days free to audition.

HOLLY: Was there a lot of blood?

CASEY: Gouts.

HOLLY: I hate blood.

LISABETTE: I faint. I fainted the first time I had my period.

CASEY: I mean, look at us. Holly's the Frankenstein monster.
You teach third grade. I support myself as a murderess from
midnight to dawn so I can do godawful plays for free in
black box theatres built into linen closets in welfare hotels.
This is a career in the arts in America.

LISABETTE: But now we get to do Chekhov! It's like lacework.
It's beautiful and delicate and demands everything. Everything! It's unbearably sweet and sad and painful, just like our
lives.

HOLLY: Don't you love her.

CASEY: Plus I get a paycheck so my mother will think acting is
actually a job.

LISABETTE: No, but it's Chekhov!

CASEY: As long as it pays the bills.

LISABETTE: That's so cynical.

CASEY: Lisabette, sweetie, I'm not cynical. Look at me. I'm like a
beating heart you can hold in your hand. I just happen to
live in a country where they give people who do what I do
endless shit.

LISABETTE: But why can't it be beautiful? I want it to be beautiful.

CASEY: Lisabette, you're drunk.

LISABETTE: I am, I'm really drunk. But the three of us are so sad, right? I mean, I'm sad because I'm hopelessly naïve and have absolutely no idea what will become of me, like I'm running down the railway tracks and the train is coming. (*To Casey*) And you're sad because you're hoping against hope when you really probably know there is no hope. (*To Holly*) And you're sad because . . . Why are you sad, I forget?

HOLLY: I am sad because that beautiful country singer dissed me, and now I'm going to have to make him pay, and that'll make me feel bad about myself, and that'll put me back in therapy which means I have to switch therapists because my last one is too busy writing screenplays.

LISABETTE: See, Chekhov knows us.

CASEY (*nodding*): 'Fraid so.

LISABETTE: To Chekhov.

(*There is a knock at the door.*)

LISABETTE: Who is it?

KATE (*outside*): Lisabette? It's Kate. Kate Todoravskia. I wondered if you would like to drink red wine with me and make love?

LISABETTE (*sotto voice to the sisters*): Oh my God.

KATE: I find you unbearably beautiful. I can't think, I can't eat. I want to produce *Romeo and Juliet* for you.

LISABETTE (*to the sisters*): What do I do?

(*Holly beckons her over and whispers.*)

KATE: I just want to hold you. You could move into my apartment. I have a satellite dish.

LISABETTE: Kate?

KATE (*still outside*): Yes?

LISABETTE: It's a little awkward because I'm in here having sex with Holly.

(*She mouths "Pardon me Jesus" to the ceiling.*)

KATE: With Holly?

HOLLY: With Holly.

KATE: Oh . . . never mind . . . good-bye.

(*They wait as Kate's footsteps recede.*)

CASEY: Now that's Chekhov.

LISABETTE: Thank you, thank you, thank you!

HOLLY: No problem.

LISABETTE (*turning to Casey, meaning Kate's crush*): Did you know that?

(*Casey indicates yes.*)

HOLLY: Hey, Lisabette.

LISABETTE: What?

HOLLY: In my world, you'd be right there looking at her satellite dish.

(*A change now moves from the apartment to a circle of folding chairs. It takes place during the opening half of Kate's speech.*)

KATE: Dearest friends. Dearest, dearest actors. You may wonder why at this our first rehearsal I have spoken of my childhood for three hours. Why, I have told you of my Mother, the only American killed by prairie dogs, of my Father whose love of literature inspired him to inscribe three chapters of Tolstoy's *War and Peace* on the convex side of a single contact lens which was then tragically lost at Daytona Beach. These then are the threads with which I wove my love of the Russian Classics and then carried in my heart here to San Antonio . . . San Antonio is to Houston as rural Russia is to Moscow. The sisters of San Antonio, their hearts beat with this play. We know what it is to be isolated, vulgarized, *we know* what it is to work! This play runs in our veins. Its pain is our pain. The pain of the women of San Antonio. So I say to you, on the brink of rehearsal, the final lines of Chekhov's Texas play, *The Three Sisters,* "In a little while we shall know why we live and why we suffer!"

(*Applause from those gathered.*)

CASEY: But that's not the final line, right?

KATE: I was speaking metaphorically.

CASEY: Because the final line is, "If only we knew."

KATE: Yes, Casey, that is the final line. Thank you.

CASEY: Said twice.

KATE: I'd like to move on if that's all right?

CASEY: Hey, it's your theatre.

KATE: Thank you. Thank you. And now it is my extraordinary pleasure to introduce our fabulous director, Wikéwitch Konalkvis, a fellow Pole and recent émigré who has directed seventy-one Chekhov productions and—

WIKÉWITCH: Seventy-two.

KATE: . . . seventy-two productions and—

WIKÉWITCH: No, you are right, seventy-one.

KATE: . . . seventy-one productions and—

WIKÉWITCH: Every one jewel. Make beating heart of Chekhov.

KATE: . . . and I just want to say—

WIKÉWITCH: Make beautiful from the pain of love this life which is like some—

KATE: . . . he is so—

WIKÉWITCH: You, I know, will play Olga. You have pain. Have loss. Radiating of loss. Good. Good Olga.

KATE: I just want to say, and I'm likely to get a little emotional—

HOLLY: Could we go around the room and meet the other actors?

KATE: Oh.

HOLLY: So we like know who we are. Like we were beginning a *process.*

KATE: Absolutely.

HOLLY: Holly Seabé, which probably goes without saying, Masha.

CASEY: Casey Mulgraw, radiating of loss, Olga.

LISABETTE: Lisabette Cartwright, Irina.

(*Now T-Anne moves from chair to chair, being all the other actors.*)

GUNTHER: Gunter Sinsel, Solyony.

ALLEN: Allen Greif, thrilled to be Andrey.

JAMES: James George, the hapless Tusenbach.

WIKÉWITCH (*ferocious*): Not hapless!

JAMES: The definitely-not-hapless Tusenbach.

(*T-Anne indicates it would take too much time to do every introduction.*)

T-ANNE (*on book*): Talk, talk, talk, talk, talk, talk, talk, talk, talk. Introductions over.

WIKÉWITCH: Okay, now I talk—

KATE: Could I . . .

WIKÉWITCH: You are going to speak of deep love you feel for Chekhov . . .

KATE: Yes, because when I was fifteen—

WIKÉWITCH: Stop! This love for Chekhov is like American fantasy. You make God from Chekhov. You say Chekhov, bullshit, Chekhov, bullshit, Chekhov, bullshit, bullshit, bullshit. From God we can't make play. From God we make worship. Worship makes boring play. You want to know in this room who is God? Who is God here?

LISABETTE: (*a guess*): You are?

WIKÉWITCH: This is very intelligent young actress. God in theatre is interpretation of play. I, Wikéwitch, make interpretation . . . In this room, in this time, I, Wikéwitch, will be God.

JOBY: Excuse me.

WIKÉWITCH: This is audience. Audience is talking!

JOBY: I mean, this is driving me crazy! This is the whole problem with twentieth-century theatre. This is part of the reason nobody wants to buy a ticket. We used to get stories; now we get "interpretations." The director is not God!

WIKÉWITCH: I am God.

JOBY: You are not God!

CASEY: Joby . . .

JOBY: *What?!*

CASEY: A character is talking.

JOBY: I know a character is talking, so?

CASEY: Who says it's the author's view?

WIKÉWITCH (*triumphantly*): You are making interpretation!

JOBY: I don't care whose view it is, it's pernicious.

WIKÉWITCH: You are being God. Who gave you this position?

JOBY: I have a ticket!

WIKÉWITCH: If *I* do not make interpretation, you cannot make interpretation of my interpretation. You are secondary! I am artist! I fuck you with my art and you cry out.

JOBY: What the hell are you talking about?

WIKÉWITCH: Sit down, little audience, I give you *Three Sisters*. From big soul.

CASEY (*trying to calm her*): Joby—

JOBY: I have never heard such unadulterated—

CASEY: Joby—

JOBY: Sit here and listen to—

CASEY: Joby! (*Joby stops talking.*) Not now.

JOBY: Then "now" what?

CASEY: You are the audience, Joby. If you talk to us all the time, you become an actor, and then you would have to come down here. Do you want to come down here?

(*Joby, still upset, stands in silence for a moment, then, making a decision, sits back down. Don Blount enters.*)

KATE: Don!

DON: Running a little late.

KATE: Don Blount, everybody, Vice President for Grants and Contributions at Albert & Sons Tobacco, our wonderful corporate sponsor.

DON: Don't mean to interrupt. Please go on with the Art.

KATE: Thanks Don. Now, we have the opportunity to make Chekhov with (*indicating Wikéwitch*) this fine artist—

WIKÉWITCH: Great artist.

KATE: Great artist, and I feel deeply, even profoundly, that—

DON (*back in the scene*): Could I just say a couple of things . . . (*Taps watch.*)

WIKÉWITCH: Okay. I pee now.

DON: . . . because, uh . . . well, I'm not part of your world . . . I'm a businessman. I actually have things to do.

KATE: Oh, Don, absolutely. Don Blount, everybody. Our underwriter.

DON: This is really a . . . revelation . . . for me to get to see what art's really all about. It's just that, uh . . . (*Taps watch.*) So I wanted to say that Albert & Sons Tobacco is really pleased to make this gift to the community of . . . *Four Sisters* (*Casey holds up three fingers.*) *Three Sisters*. Sorry. Because Albert & Sons Tobacco International . . . we're in one hundred and thirty countries, but we feel our role in this community is to—

CASEY: Kill people.

DON: Excuse me.

CASEY: Your role is to kill people, to target children and African Americans and to seek profit independent of any ethics or morality.

KATE: Oh dear.

CASEY: And by involving yourself in the arts who have no money and have no alternative to taking your minuscule handout, you hope to give the impression that you are on the side of life, when actually you are merchants of death.

DON (*pause*): Thank you so much for the feedback. Albert & Sons respects others and their disparate and useful points of view. But in closing, I will say to you personally that if you take money from us it is disingenuous to make a pretense of morality and that historically, insofar as I understand it, actors were traditionally pickpockets, whores, and parasites on the body politic. Of course, given that your very profession is pretense, I still have the pleasure of enjoying your morality as entertainment. (*Taps watch.*) Got to go. Good luck with however many sisters you've got.

(*He leaves. There is a stunned moment. Lights down.*)

ACT TWO

The act opens with a bare stage, one folding chair, and an inch-high, two-foot-square box that Holly stands on while being fitted for her dress as Masha.

JACKEY (*the costume designer*): Baby-Darlin'-honey-dear, your luscious body is a costume designer's dream! You have proportions goin' on like Greek statuary on a good day! Oh, my goodness! Your "out arm center back to wrist bent" is a world-class pisser. Your "shoulder point to mid-bust to center waist" is to die for, and your "depth of crotch and nipple to nipple" would turn Cleopatra mauve with envy. Golly-goodness-gracious, darlin', you are Masha the bomb!

HOLLY: But this is like, "Why have a body?"

JACKEY: Well, a little draggy, but 1901, if you see what I mean?

HOLLY: I am not going out there dressed up like a funeral cake. This would be, in fact, a good dress for somebody ugly. I mean, Olga might look like this, sure.

JACKEY: Au contraire, my goddess, au contraire. Every man in that audience is gonna hafta keep his program over his lap.

HOLLY: Ugly does not enhance luscious. People who wear ugly become ugly. Are we trying to make me ugly? I am not here to suffer the revenge of the ugly Texans. And I am not beautiful in this dress!

(*Wikéwitch enters.*)

WIKÉWITCH: Okay, okay. So. Masha is great beauty, yes? But is hiding. Hide-and-go-seek Masha.

HOLLY: The West Coast, we don't hide it. All right, a slit—waist to floor—let a little leg out.

JACKEY: 1901, honeydoll, no tits, no slits.

WIKÉWITCH: Repress. Very constrict. Very dark. This is sex for brain peoples.

HOLLY: Brain peoples. Reality check, all right?

JACKEY (*working*): Ooooo, reality, I don't live there.

HOLLY: I spent a hundred and fourteen thousand dollars on my legs. I was in rehab for three months with animal, killer, monster rehab nurses in the Dominican Republic. An Internet survey shows that my legs alone, without the rest of me, have nineteen million fans. I either have legs or I walk. (*Jackey has his head in his hands.*) Jackey, will you stop crying. Every time we have a fitting, you weep.

JACKEY: You think I want to make women ugly because I'm a gay man.

HOLLY: Oh, please.

JACKEY: You think I'm hostile because you make millions, and I do consignment store windows.

HOLLY: Okay, all right. I'm going to try something completely new for me. I'm going to try compromise.

WIKÉWITCH: No compromise.

JACKEY: I *love* compromise.

HOLLY: Everybody listening? Floor length/see-thru.

WIKÉWITCH: I am in madhouse.

JACKEY: Well, lil' darlin', you would look delicious, but I keep rememberin' what you said the day you got here as to how

the play was about like a tidal wave of vulgarity sweepin'
everything good and beautiful away, which just made me
bawl like a baby, and how the vulgarity of the rich was not
to see the desperate need of the poor, and how the vulgarity
of the poor was to be blind to beauty, and the vulgarity of
the intellectual was to separate thought from action. So that
everyone in the play was as different as they could be but in
this funny way they all shared the same despair.

HOLLY: When did I say that?

JACKEY: Well, it was such a pretty thought, you are such a talk
diva, baby love. But it made me think maybe Masha could
be this little simplicity in the sea of vulgarity and get all the
attention, an' reviews, an' applause, applause, applause.

HOLLY: Well, if I said that, that's what we should do.

WIKÉWITCH (*to Jackey*): You are God in other form.

JACKEY (*sweetly*): Well, she said.

HOLLY: No more talking!!! The dress rocks. I gotta book to
make rehearsal.

(*The scene now transitions into rehearsal. At first we see only the director because Holly has a costume change.*)

WIKÉWITCH: Okay. Okay. Please stopping. Good. Okay. Leave
brain. Brain no more. Brain outside, art inside. What you are
doing in this time? Hah? Okay, good. Is very clear, is very
smart, is very beautiful, is very *professional*. But is not *art*. No
more professional. No good to Chekhov, this professional.
No, no, no, no, no, no, *no!* Peel off skin. Rip open body.
Lungs, liver, spleen. Okay. Begin.

HOLLY/MASHA: "I don't know. I don't know. Of course, being
used to something means a lot. For example—"

WIKÉWITCH (*interrupting*): You say line.

HOLLY/MASHA (*confused*): I did.

WIKÉWITCH: Yes, you *say* "you don't know."

HOLLY/MASHA: I know the line.

WIKÉWITCH: You don't know!

HOLLY/MASHA: I just said it!

WIKÉWITCH: Saying is not being.

HOLLY: What are you talking about?

WIKÉWITCH: Look, little television actress, Masha say, "I don't know," but you don't know what this is not to know, so you just say line. So this little thing, this "I don't know" is dead, and more you say, you go from corpse to corpse over this dead Chekhov. You make graveyard of scene by just say lines. No good. Okay. Her father, military man, is dead. Real corpse, not acting corpse. Since that moment, this Masha lives, imbeciles all around, peasant idiots, animals, mud, stupidity. Peasant thirsty for drink, they spit in hand, like spit for drink. Only soldiers, like father, have brain. She is thirsty for brain. She says soldiers honorable, educated, worthwhile. Vershinin is soldier. His soul is dead. He knows soldier is animal too. He says this. How can she bear this? This is break her heart. He says this before scene. It is like stone. Like stone. You understand? She says, "I don't know." Yes! This is heart bleeding. Yes! Now you say.

HOLLY: I don't know.

WIKÉWITCH: No.

HOLLY: I don't know.

WIKÉWITCH: No!

HOLLY: What the hell do you want?

WIKÉWITCH: I want you to *be* line, not *say* line!

HOLLY: I don't know!

WIKÉWITCH: No.

HOLLY: I don't know.

WIKÉWITCH: No!

HOLLY: You think I know what the hell you mean but I'm telling you *I don't know!*

WIKÉWITCH: Yes! *Now* you know!

HOLLY: What?!

WIKÉWITCH: What you don't know! Chekhov is back from dead!

(*A pause.*)

HOLLY: Okay, I get it.

WIKÉWITCH: You get it.

HOLLY: Yes.

WIKÉWITCH: One line. Twenty minutes. You get one scene, I'm dead from old age.

HOLLY: I really get it.

WIKÉWITCH: Enough. Rehearse. Say "I don't know."

HOLLY: *I don't know.*

WIKÉWITCH: Okay. Next line.

(*There are now a series of short Ben/Holly scenes with minimal furniture being brought in and out during a continuous flow.*)

BEN: Hey.

HOLLY: Hi.

BEN: Ummmm.

HOLLY: Ummmmm?

BEN: Coffee?

HOLLY: Sure.

(*Chairs are placed under them and a table between them.*)

BEN: I held that kiss too long.

HOLLY: I noticed.

BEN: That was unprofessional.

HOLLY: Nice tongue, though.

BEN: Ma'am, I never meant . . .

HOLLY: You did.

BEN: I have to go.

(*He moves away from the table.*)

HOLLY: Ben?

BEN: Yeah?

HOLLY: You kiss your wife like that?

(*They meet outside rehearsal.*)

HOLLY: What the hell's going on in rehearsal?

BEN: Please don't call me at home.

HOLLY: When we're doing the scene, don't avoid the kiss and then say "kiss-kiss over." I feel like I'm in middle school.

BEN: That scene is driving me crazy.

HOLLY: Why is that?

BEN: You know perfectly well why.

HOLLY: Yeah. I do.

BEN: I am married. I have two kids.

HOLLY: I have a live-in lover.

BEN: My wife is ill.

HOLLY: My lover's an ex-convict.

BEN: The kids are waiting for me to come.

HOLLY: Me too. All right, Ben. Come over in the morning.

(*A rolling door moves on. Ben knocks. Holly opens it. He steps in and immediately kisses her. They start ripping off clothes. Dialogue along this vein ensues.*)

HOLLY: My neck. Yes. Yes! My mouth.

BEN: Oh God.

HOLLY (*while being kissed, she is trying to undo his belt*): Belt.

BEN: Belt.

(*She keeps trying.*)

HOLLY: Can't. Ouch. Hate that belt.

(*She steps back and takes her blouse off over her head. He is working on the belt.*)

BEN: Beautiful. Goddamnit, you're beautiful!

HOLLY: I know. (*Trying to undo his buttons*) Hate these buttons.

BEN: Boots.

HOLLY (*pulling his pants down*): Screw the boots!

JOBY: Excuse me.

BEN (*freezes, pants around his ankles*): Yes, Joby, we've missed you.

JOBY: I don't think this love story is necessary.

HOLLY: Does anybody have any Tylenol?

(*T-Anne brings her some.*)

BEN: The Ben/Holly relationship is a crucial parallel to Masha and Vershinin in *The Three Sisters*.

JOBY: I never read *The Three Sisters*.

HOLLY: Shut up. I'm a character, and you're a character, and I'm cutting your character's lines!

(*He kisses her more roughly. They freeze. The lights change. It's now postcoital. Ben pulls up his pants.*)

BEN: You were incredible.

HOLLY: Lots of practice.

BEN: What in the hell did you say that for?

HOLLY: Because it's true. It doesn't mean I didn't like it.

BEN: I'm not kidding around here, Holly.

HOLLY: Okay. It was my first time.

(*The scene breaks up. Two period chairs and a standing lamp become the set for rehearsal.*)

HOLLY/MASHA: What a noise the stove's making. The wind was . . . line?

T-ANNE (*prompting*): Moaning in the chimney.

HOLLY/MASHA: moaning in the chimney just before Father died.

T-ANNE: The same sound exactly.

HOLLY/MASHA: The same sound exactly.

BEN/VERSHININ: Are you superstitious?

HOLLY/MASHA: Yes.

BEN/VERSHININ: Strange. (*Kisses her hand.*) You magnificent, magical woman. Magnificent, magical! It's dark in here but I can see the shining of your eyes.

HOLLY/MASHA: There's more light over here . . .

BEN/VERSHININ: I'm in love, I'm in love, I'm in love . . .

(*He stops.*)

T-ANNE (*prompting*): In love with your eyes, with the way you move.

BEN (*out of scene*): I don't want to do this.

HOLLY (*out of scene*): Are you?

BEN: Am I what?

HOLLY: In love?

T-ANNE (*prompting*): In love with your eyes, with—

HOLLY: Can it, okay? You are or you aren't.

BEN: I have a real life. I can hurt real people here.

HOLLY: And what am I, animation? You think I'm not susceptible? Hey, man, three years ago, I'm involved with a guy
commits suicide jumping off the Golden Gate Bridge in a
wedding dress. Two years ago, the guy I'm living with
whacks me, breaks my jaw so I couldn't work for three
weeks and they almost pulled the show. Right now, as we
speak, my significant other is an actor who has an immobi-
lizing drinking problem mainly because in high school he
murdered his prom date and served eleven years. You see
why I might be susceptible to some ordinary, straight-up
guy? Okay, it's mutual.

(*Light comes up on Joby. Holly sees it.*)

JOBY: Excuse me.

HOLLY: Don't even think about it!

(*Holly leaves. Furniture is struck. An Exercycle and some mats become
the gym.*)

CASEY: So, the casting agent says to me, "You're not right for it;
you're a character woman." I die. My blood congeals. Fis-
sures appear. It's the actresses' death knell. I go through
menopause in five seconds. All fluids dry. I become the
Mojave Desert. Character woman! I, who have screwed
every leading man on the East Coast, become their mother.
Vertigo. I scream out in a silent, unattending universe: "I'm

too young to be a character woman!" and the echo replies, rolling out of infinite space: "They want to see you for the funny aunt at the wedding!"

(*She ritually disembowels herself. Holly enters in exercise clothes. All three begin to work out; Holly particularly exercises fiercely.*)

CASEY: Bad day?

HOLLY: Bad day.

LISABETTE: Bad day.

CASEY: Bad day.

(*They exercise.*)

CASEY: Why does every actor in America go to the gym?

HOLLY: Because it's a beauty contest, not a profession.

(*They exercise.*)

LISABETTE: Damn it to hell! (*She drops the weights.*) Wikéwitch called me dense as a turkey, an' I'm a lot smarter than a turkey. An' then he picked on me for three hours an' I cried an' he patted me on my shoulder an' I threw up all over him. Then I ran out an' tripped over the doorjamb an' cracked a tooth an' I could just spit fire an' eat broke glass.

CASEY (*exercising*): He called you a turkey?

LISABETTE: He didn't call me a turkey. He said I had the brain of a turkey.

HOLLY: Wikéwitch is a tyrannical, woman-hating buttwipe, but he seems to know what he's doing.

(*They exercise.*)

HOLLY: Meanwhile, my boyfriend has just been arrested for sexually soliciting a seven-foot transsexual on Hollywood Boulevard who turned out to be a policewoman on stilts, so *People* magazine called me for a quote.

(*They exercise.*)

CASEY: What'd you say?

HOLLY: I said it just showed he missed me.

(*They exercise.*)

CASEY: Play's going pretty well. (*They exercise.*) Whattayathink? (*They exercise.*) Play's going pretty well.

HOLLY: I wouldn't know, I've never done a play.

(*Casey and Lisabette stop exercising.*)

CASEY: You are kidding? Are you kidding?

HOLLY: From high school to TV . . . well, I was in one play, but I had to leave to get an abortion. One play and one porn flic.

LISABETTE: You didn't do a porn flic!?

HOLLY (*still exercising*): Yeah.

CASEY: Tell.

HOLLY: Actually I got fired.

LISABETTE: How do you get fired from a porn flic?

HOLLY: I came. Joking. I got fired because I started crying uncontrollably on camera. It depressed the porn divas so they dumped me.

LISABETTE: Why were you crying?

HOLLY: Because I came. First time. Consider those implications.

(*They all exercise.*)

LISABETTE: What if it were good?

CASEY: What?

LISABETTE: You know.

CASEY: Our little Russian skit? The Sisters Three?

LISABETTE: I mean, what if it were *really* good? Really. Really, really good. Could we? You're good. You're both good. We could do something good. Could we do something good? It could be good. It could be really, really good. Could it? Be good?

CASEY: I once believed I could be very good. I wanted to be so concentrated, so compressed, so vivid and present and skillful and heartfelt that anyone watching me would literally burst into flame. Combust.

LISABETTE: That *kills* me. I *want* that. Did you ever do it? Did it ever happen?

CASEY: No.

LISABETTE: But maybe we could do that? What would happen if we did that?

HOLLY: Nobody would care.

LISABETTE: That's so cold. How can you say that? It could change people's lives.

CASEY: God love you, Lisabette, two months later the audience can't remember the name of the play.

LISABETTE: *I don't believe that. I don't believe that.*

CASEY: Has anybody you know to be a sentient being ever walked up to you and said the play changed their life?

CASEY: No, fine, okay. You know who is changed by Chekhov? Me. I finish a play, it's like, "Get me an exorcist!" He eats my life. He chews me up. He spits me out. I'm like bleeding from Chekhov. The audience? Who knows what their deal is? They come from the mists; they return to the mist. They cough, they sneeze, they sleep, they unwrap little hard candies, and then they head for their cars *during* the curtain call. And once, once I would like to step out and say to the ones who are up the aisles while we take the bows, "Hey! Excuse me! Could you show a little mercy because I just left it all out here on the stage and even if you don't have the foggiest notion what it was or what it meant, could you have the common courtesy to leave your goddamn cars in the garage for another forty seconds and give me a little hand for twenty years of work!

JOBY: That is unmitigated hogwash!

HOLLY: Oh, please . . .

JOBY: I don't cough or sleep or unwrap little candies, I come to feel. (*She taps her head and chest.*) Here and here. Because if I'm ever going to understand my own life, it will have to be through feeling, and my own life and experience isn't big enough so I come for enlargement. Plus I want the highest-quality moments for my life I can get, and you're supposed to provide them, though you usually don't, so when I write my review—

CASEY: Hold it.

JOBY: . . . I need to point out whether there is any enlargement—

HOLLY: Your review?

JOBY: . . . to be had by the audience—

CASEY: You're a critic.

JOBY: . . . in this particular experience!

CASEY: You have been interrupting us all night—

JOBY: I am part of the process.

CASEY: After the play, not *during* the play.

JOBY: After the play I'm not part of the process. After the play you revile and dismiss me. Some of you claim you don't even read reviews, which is a complete joke!

CASEY: I don't read reviews.

JOBY: You do.

CASEY: Don't.

JOBY: Do.

CASEY: Don't.

JOBY: Do.

CASEY: Okay, sometimes.

JOBY: Hah!

CASEY: Look, we only put up with you because half our audience is three months from the nursing home.

HOLLY: I can't believe it—a critic!?

JOBY: Well . . .

HOLLY: How are we doing so far?

JOBY: Well, it's definitely interesting, sometimes amusing, well paced, but a very uneasy mix of—

LISABETTE: Stop! Not while we're doing it! Critics are gods to me. I completely measure my self-worth by my reviews.

HOLLY: Who do you write for?

JOBY (*a pause*): I don't want to talk about it.

(*She sits down.*)

CASEY: That is completely unfair. We have to go on here. Do we have to be afraid of you or not?

JOBY: It doesn't matter who I write for; it matters what I perceive.

CASEY: Joby, even you don't believe that. Don't tell me there isn't a critical hierarchy when you would poison your colleagues for the six best jobs.

JOBY: Not my job.

CASEY (*turning back to the stage*): *Who do you write for,* Joby?

JOBY: *Bargain Mart Suburban Shoppers Guide.*

CASEY (*turning back to the stage*): She's nobody, let's act.

JOBY: I am *not* nobody!

CASEY (*referring back*): I didn't mean you personally, Joby.

(*Joby sits down. The actresses exercise.*)

LISABETTE: What was wrong with your day, Casey?

CASEY: Forget it.

LISABETTE: We told you.

CASEY: Forget it.

LISABETTE: We're not important enough to tell?

(*They exercise a moment in silence.*)

CASEY: I felt a lump in the shower. I saw a doctor. She wants to
    do a biopsy.

HOLLY: When?

CASEY: On the day off.

LISABETTE: Oh my God.

(*Casey exercises. Lisabette is frozen. Holly stops exercising, stands and
walks over to Casey, who keeps working out.*)

HOLLY (*standing above her*):   Stop. (*Casey does. Holly puts out her
    hand.*) Get off. (*Casey does.*) Hug me. (*Casey does.*)

BEN: Excuse me?

LISABETTE: Yes?

BEN: It's Ben.

HOLLY: Come in.

(*He does.*)

BEN: I left my wife.

(*A moment.*)

CASEY: Well, either way I lose my hair.

(*Holly and Casey exit. The gym is struck and a desk and two chairs are brought on for Don Blount's office.*)

DON: Don Blount of Albert & Sons Tobacco calling for Martha Graham. Then why is it called the Martha Graham Dance Company? Oh. No, I knew that. Little joke. Listen, the grant's in the mail. Yes. Well, it's our pleasure to support a dance company of your caliber, and if you might find an opportunity to mention to the chairman of your board that we'd be thrilled if she'd tell her brother the congressman to stop sodomizing the tobacco industry just because he's personally in the pocket of the HMOs, I think you'd find your grant is definitely renewable. My pleasure.

(*Don hangs up the phone, picks it back up, and dials.*)

Mom, it's Don. Your son Don. I need the favor, Mom. I know we did it yesterday, but I'm feeling a little alienated . . . a little remote. Wonderful. Good. I knew I could count on you, Momma. Ready? All right, light it up. Mom. Inhale, Mom. Would I encourage you to smoke if there was any danger? That's right, I wouldn't. I would never harm my mom. I must be a good person if I would never harm my mom. If I'm a good person, it must be all right to do what I do. Thanks, I feel a lot better. Put it out now, Momma. Everything's all right. I feel damn good. Go back on the oxygen, Ma. See you Sunday.

(*Kate enters Albert & Sons. Don rises, smiling and affable.*)

DON: Ms. Todoravskia, it's really nice of you to come over on short notice.

KATE: No, I've been wanting to—

DON: Can I get you something?

KATE: Well—

DON: At this level in the executive suite, we could fly in crab's legs from Iceland. Just kidding. But in Iceland the crabs have pneumonia. Wouldn't affect their legs though. Just kidding. Tea, coffee, soft drink, bottled water, mixed drinks of all kinds, munchies, brownies my mother sends in . . . (*Does his Dracula imitation.*) Cigarette?!

KATE: No, I—

DON: You know, Kate . . . may I call you Kate? Nice dress, by the way. I deal with a lot of artists, and usually they look like they bought their clothes from the llama shop in Costa Rica.

KATE: Well, I—

DON: I can't tell you how impressed I was by that rehearsal of whatsit you let me see.

KATE: *Three Sisters.*

DON: Well, it just seemed like a metaphor for the lives we all lead, don't you think?

KATE: Well, I—

DON: Plus it confirmed my every doubt about corporate investment in Russia. In that way it was very personal for me.

KATE: I'm glad that you—

DON: So it's a real downer to have to pull the funding. Oh, I think we also have fruit juices.

KATE: The funding.

DON: The funding. In a way here, Ms. Todoravskia, I have to tell you I personally blew it. I've only been in Grants and Con-

tributions with Albert & Sons for a couple of months—
before that, they let me do real work—just kidding, and I
didn't realize when I gave you the okay that there had been
a policy change up top.

KATE: Do you mean—

DON: Let me just wrap this up and then we'll relate. We had sort
of turned our contribution policy on a dime based on the
fact that all this tobacco legislation, politically motivated law-
suits, advertising restrictions have made it clear to us that
our market focus in the future will be overseas where they
just plain old like a good smoke. Plus their life expectancy is
so low that we don't really constitute a health hazard. Hah!
Just kidding. Just kidding. And it's in those communities in
our target market we'll be looking to leverage our contributions. So the bad news is that I didn't have the authority to
give you the money. I hope this won't inconvenience you?

KATE: But you did authorize it.

DON (*smiling*): Poof.

KATE: But we're in the middle of the work.

DON: Poof.

KATE: We will have to default on the salaries and the board will
fire me.

DON: You know, I'm very interested in artists and how they
function, and a little research shows an overwhelming per-
centage of the best work didn't have grants. As far as I can
see, good art is almost invariably a product of good old-
fashioned adversity and rage. Anger is the engine of art, so
in an odd way this is a good situation for you. You don't
want to be the lap dog of big tobacco. We're the bad guys.
Great art is a personal passion, not a grant. Ms. Todoravskia,
Albert & Sons Tobacco is sorry to defund you, but that
doesn't mean we aren't proud to fuel your anger.

KATE: I cannot believe—

DON: I'm afraid that's all the time I have for you. I do however want to make a seventy-five-dollar personal contribution to your theatre. If you wonder about the cost basis, it's the same amount I give to public radio, which I actually use. (*She takes the envelope. He heads back for his desk.*) Oh, listen, I wonder if you have Holly Seabé's phone number?

(*Office is struck. The girls are talking—one seated. Kate enters with her suitcase.*)

KATE: Hi.

(*She puts down her suitcase.*)

LISABETTE: Hi.

CASEY: Hi.

HOLLY: Hi.

KATE: I, uh . . . are my eyes red? (*Furious*) I hate it when my eyes are red!! Sorry, I'm sorry. Look, I want to . . . uh . . . tell you how proud . . . proud I am of you . . . (*She pauses on the brink of something. It explodes.*) To hell with everybody!! Okay, that feels better . . . umm, it was very emotional to see this great play being so well done in our little theatre that has . . . struggled and . . . held on by its fingernails—*believe me*—for all these years. When I settled here, having attended Stanford, Harvard and Yale, I hoped—*I hoped!!*—well, those rehearsals were what I hoped for as an artist. They surpassed my hopes. It's one hell of a time to be fired, I'll tell you that.

LISABETTE: Oh my God . . .

KATE: Albert & Sons removed the funding.

CASEY: Oh God.

KATE: And when I told Joe Bob Mattingly, the Chairman of our Board of Directors, he said—

JOE BOB (*from somewhere out in the house*): Damn woman! You got no more sense than a hog on ice! I been pourin' my money an' the money of my friends down your double-talk rathole since Jesus was a pup, so my wife could drag me down here to see plays nobody can understand with a buncha people I would never invite to dinner, on the basis it creates some quality of life I'm supposed to have since I figgered out how to make some money. Half the time, that stuff doesn't have a story, and it's been five years since you done one takes place in a kitchen, which is the kind all of us like. The rest of the time it's about how rich people is bad and Democrats is good and white people is stupid and homosexuals have more fun an' we should get rid of the corporations an' eat grass an' then, by God, you wonder why you don't have a big audience! Now you just blew fifteen percent of your budget 'cause you riled up the tobacco interests, plus you got the colored rattlin' on my cage, an' as of this precise minute, you are out of luck, out of work an' outta San Antonio, Texas. See, I am closin' us down, lockin' the door, an' then, by God, we can go back to hittin' each other up to give to the United Way where it will, by God, do some poor handicap some actual, measurable good, an' I won't have to hear anybody say "aesthetic" from one year to the goddamned next! Now, *vaya con Dios,* darlin'.

JOE BOB AND KATE: You got three minutes to clean out your desk.

(*He disappears. Kate speaks to Casey.*)

KATE: So that's it. They said if I was out of the city before five o'clock I'd get six months' severance and my plane ticket. What, do you suppose, I thought I was doing here? Making theatre because . . . See I just can't remember. Well, I guess nobody told us everything has a purpose.

CASEY: Man cannot live by bread alone.

KATE: No, he needs salsa. (*Shakes Casey's hand.*) Actually, I think I hate theatre. It makes you think it was about something when it was actually only about yourself. It fascinates you. It seduces you. It leaves you penniless by the side of the road. Screw Thespis! (*She looks at the women.*) Run for your lives.

(*She exits. The women look at each other.*)

LISABETTE: Goodness gracious. (*Wipes tear.*)

CASEY: You okay?

LISABETTE: I guess.

JOBY (*from audience*): Don't let it get too sentimental.

CASEY (*without looking up*): Thanks for the tip. (*Turns to Holly*) So that this doesn't get too sentimental, why don't you pay for the production? You have the money.

HOLLY: Why would I do that?

CASEY: Self-interest?

HOLLY: Ah.

CASEY: You want the credit. You don't like to be pushed around. You're secretly thrilled you're good in the part. Based on proving you can act, you might get a film where you kept your clothes on. And I could use the distraction from the fact the biopsy was positive.

HOLLY: That's not too sentimental. Anything else?

CASEY: No, that's about it.

HOLLY (*seeing Ben enter*): Hi.

BEN: Stay.

HOLLY (*turns to Lisabette*): And you, little one?

LISABETTE: It might make you happy.

(*Holly chuckles.*)

HOLLY: Well, that aside, why not?

CASEY: You'll pay to get us open?

HOLLY: I'll get us open.

LISABETTE: No way?

HOLLY: They screwed with us, now they lose.

LISABETTE: You really mean it?

HOLLY: I don't want to talk about it, I want to do it.

(*At this point, Wikéwitch walks in with his suitcase.*)

WIKÉWITCH: So. Is not to be. Okay. I put life in small suitcase. You. You. You. On we go, yes? Is hard to tell what is good, what is bad. Everything is doorway to something else. (*Shaking hands*) Little Irina, okay, good-bye. Olga. Olga, she goes on. Vershinin. He finds another girl next town. (*To Holly*) Like cat you land on feet, yes?

CASEY: It's not over.

WIKÉWITCH: No?

CASEY: We have the money. We can open.

WIKÉWITCH: Where is money?

HOLLY: Here is money.

WIKÉWITCH: Ah. Is for what?

LISABETTE: So we can do your beautiful play.

WIKÉWITCH: Ah. Okay, okay. Honorable sisters and Lieutenant Colonel. Okay. I wake, wake, wake. No sleeping. Okay. I get up, pack suitcase, close suitcase. Knock, knock, knock. The-atre producer says no more money. Dead Chekhov. Okay. Bye-bye. Money, money, money. But, dear American actors, before knock-knock, I am pack. So why is this? Because work is finish. When do Chekhov, now, now, now, young, middle, old. So much you can do, only what you know. No more. Then wait for life to teach. You are sweet young people, but what I know (*points to head*) you cannot do. What for I do this? No sleep, no sleep. We must be a little realistic in this time. For you, Chekhov is fantasy. For me, life. You have nice, small talent. We can do together baby Chekhov. Okay, *but* I have . . . short time . . . short time now . . . no sleep . . . no time for baby Chekhov . . . I must take small suitcase, find big souls to do play, so I don't die with this Chekhov in my head. This you understand or not understand?

HOLLY: We're not good enough.

WIKÉWITCH: You do not understand. OK. Bye-bye. (*Goes to exit and turns back.*) You are good enough to do the Chekhov you are good enough to do. But is not good enough. (*He tips his hat and is gone.*)

LISABETTE: See, I've always been terrified that some guy dressed in black would show up and tell me I'm not good enough.

HOLLY: Yeah, but what he said was—

CASEY and HOLLY: You just have to do the Chekhov you're good enough to do.

LISABETTE: He did say that.

HOLLY: Okay. We'll do the Chekhov we can do.

LISABETTE: Really?

HOLLY: Really.

LISABETTE: Yes! Oh yes! (*To Casey*) Can you believe this? Can we please work on the last scene? (*She picks up the script.*) I want to work on the last scene.

HOLLY: Where from?

LISABETTE: The band. Ta-ra-ra boom-de-ay.

CASEY: We're over here.

HOLLY/MASHA: "Oh, but listen to the band! They're leaving us."

T-ANNE (*entering*): Sorry. Sorry to interrupt. Phone for you, Holly.

HOLLY: Take the message.

(*She turns back to the scene.*)

T-ANNE: Dreamworks.

(*A moment.*)

HOLLY (*to the others*): I'll be right back.

(*She goes.*)

LISABETTE: What's Dreamworks?

CASEY: Who are you? What planet do you live on? Spielberg.

LISABETTE: Oh, you mean—

T-ANNE (*as a stage manager, cutting to another place in the text*): Talk, talk, talk, talk, talk, talk, talk. Holly comes back.

(*She does.*)

HOLLY: I got a film.

CASEY: You are kidding?

(*Holly shakes her head. No, she's not kidding.*)

LISABETTE: That is great! That is so exciting! What is it! I never heard anybody say that, "I got a film." I was right here when you said it!

CASEY: When?

LISABETTE: What when?

CASEY (*directly to Holly*): When film?

HOLLY: Now. Yesterday. I'm replacing somebody who walked.

LISABETTE: Now?

HOLLY: They want me on a flight in ninety minutes. Jesus, I gotta pack. Rental car? How will I get rid of the rental car? Damn it, my dogs? How the hell am I going to do that? I'm supposed to film tonight.

CASEY: How long?

HOLLY: One month, LA; one month, Thailand. I mean, the part is dogmeat. Girlfriend stuff. Two scenes naked, three scenes I listen to the guy talk, one scene I get crushed by pythons. Two months I say a dozen sentences. Listen, I am . . . I am sorry, I am really sorry, but I am really happy . . . bad for you, good for me . . . me, me, me . . . and I can't even pretend I'm anything but euphoric! Kill me, I'm horrible! Gotta go, gotta go.

(*She starts to race out.*)

BEN: I'll come with.

HOLLY: Damn.

BEN: I don't have anything here. I got rid of everything here. You're it.

HOLLY: You just don't have a clue who you got mixed up with, do you?

BEN: I love you.

HOLLY: I got the call. We've just been fooling around while I waited for the call.

BEN: I'll just come out and hang.

HOLLY: Oh Ben. You just don't get it. This is the shot. You are a very sweet cowboy, but it makes you, don't you see, completely disposable, babe. Trust me, you don't want to hang around Malibu while I give head for billing. This is it. I will take no prisoners. You have to blow me off. You know what? (*She kisses his cheek.*) Go back to your wife. Sorry to be the meat grinder. It's just the way it plays out. (*Looks at him*.) I got a couple minutes, tell me to go screw myself. (*He shakes his head*.) Okay. (*She kisses him*.) Bye L. (*Hugs Lisabette. Appraises Casey*.) More I see of you, you could probably get it done for a hundred thousand. (*Casey chuckles; they hug*.) Anything I can do, you call me. We almost made it, huh?

CASEY: Almost.

HOLLY: I'm no surprise to you guys, I know that. Gotta go. Want to know the really worst part? I-am-so-happy!

(*She leaves*.)

CASEY: You okay, Ben?

(*He nods*.)

LISABETTE (*concerned*): What will you do?

(*He shakes his head—"I don't know."*)

CASEY: She was really beautiful, huh? (*He nods*.) Kind of like really sexy Russian roulette, right? Only you're alive.

BEN (*a pained smile*): Thanks.

(*He exits*.)

LISABETTE: What will we do?

CASEY: When the play's over, you pack.

LISABETTE: I live here.

CASEY: Then I will allow you to skip the packing.

LISABETTE: What will you do?

CASEY: What will I do? Oh, probably get my other breast lopped off, and then I think I will try to accept that you don't necessarily get to do what you want to do. I will try to be a grown-up about that. And after I'm a grown-up, I will try to like doing the things grown-ups like to do. Right now, I'm thinking hardware store. I am worried, however, that I will make a lousy grown-up and that I will cry a lot and be depressed.

LISABETTE: Oh God.

CASEY: Can I tell you something about theatre?

LISABETTE: Sure.

CASEY: Never ask an out-of-work actress what's next.

LISABETTE: Okay.

CASEY (*giving her a hug*): Pardon you, Jesus.

(*Chair is struck. An airplane gate table is rolled in, as well as three waiting room chairs that move as a unit. Holly enters with luggage.*)

AIRPORT ANNOUNCER: Because of weather, the following flights have been canceled or rescheduled: flight number one-seven-two-six to Los Angeles, flight number three-forty-three to Dallas/Fort Worth, flight number twenty-one-twenty-one to Seattle, flight number one-six-four-three to San Francisco . . .

(*Holly begins talking to a gate check-in person, overlapping the flight cancellations.*)

HOLLY: No, you don't understand, I have to be in LA by six P.M.

GATE MANAGER: Ma'am, we have weather cancellations or long delays on everything going west.

HOLLY: You said that. I am a famous television star who is shooting a movie at seven P.M. tonight.

GATE MANAGER: Wow, what movie?

HOLLY: Get me on a plane!

GATE MANAGER: Ma'am. Weather is weather, ma'am. There is nothing flying.

HOLLY (*overlapping his speech*): And if I'm not there for the shoot, I will lose the most important job of my career!

GATE MANAGER: I can get you on flight number one-oh-seven-seven arriving LA 7:30 A.M. tomorrow.

HOLLY: Too late.

GATE MANAGER: All I've got.

HOLLY: Look, is there a VIP lounge?

GATE MANAGER: Sure.

HOLLY: Is there a sofa in it?

GATE MANAGER: Absolutely.

HOLLY: I'll fuck you for a flight.

GATE MANAGER: You are one sad chick, and I don't have a plane.

HOLLY (*apoplectic*): I'll have your job, do you understand me?!

GATE MANAGER (*gently*): No, you won't, ma'am.

(*He exits.*)

HOLLY (*utter frustration*): Arrghrrrahhhhh! (*Smashes the bag down, kicks it, throws an enraged fit. She then sits with her head in her hands in a row of gate seating. Casey enters with her bag. Lisabette tags along.*)

CASEY: Holly? (*Holly rocks, keening.*) What's the deal?

LISABETTE: Are you okay?

HOLLY: Do I look like I'm okay?

LISABETTE: Oh no, what is it?

CASEY: Holly? (*Holly, crying, doesn't look up.*) What's the deal?

LISABETTE: What, what is it?

HOLLY: My flight's canceled, nobody's flying. I called my agent, he says they'll replace me.

LISABETTE: Oh no.

CASEY: You can't connect through another city?

HOLLY: You can't *land* on the West Coast. I'm cursed. It's my karma.

(*She leans on Casey, who now sits beside her.*)

LISABETTE: I drove Casey out for her New York flight. We thought we'd check to see if you left.

HOLLY: No, I haven't left! You can't see I haven't left? I can't take this, I can't, I'll kill myself. (*A band is heard in the distance.*) No planes! It's like some incredibly murderous cosmic joke. (*The band's sound intrudes.*) What the hell is that?

CASEY: There's some high school band playing in the terminal.

HOLLY: Does anybody have a goddamn Kleenex? That was my last Kleenex. My life is like a nightmare. I'm a nightmare. (*She blows her nose.*) What happened to Ben?

CASEY: He threw his stuff in his car and drove to Nashville. Said Texas was over, acting was over, his marriage was over, and you were over, the end.

HOLLY: Eat me!

(*She puts her head back in her hands. Silence, except for the band. Lisabette makes the connection with the last scene in* The Three Sisters *and sings softly.*)

LISABETTE: Ta-ra-ra boom-de-ay, ta-ra-ra boom-de-ay.

HOLLY: Oh please.

(*Casey wipes at her eyes with a Kleenex.*)

LISABETTE (*quoting*): "Let them have their little cry. Doesn't matter, does it?" (*They are in the familiar tableau. Holly and Lisabette sitting, Casey behind them. She looks at Holly.*) Your line.

HOLLY: So?

CASEY (*a pause*): It is, it's your line.

HOLLY: Do I give a damn?

CASEY: Yeah, you do.

HOLLY: "Listen. Hear how the band plays. They are leaving us. One has already gone, gone forever, and we are alone, left behind to start life again. We have to live; we must live."

LISABETTE: "A time will come when everyone knows what it was all for and why we suffer. There will be no secrets, but meantime we must live; we must work, only work! Tomorrow I set out alone. I'll teach in a school and give the whole of my own life to those who can make some use of it. Now it's autumn, but winter will come, covering everything with snow, and I will work; I will work."

CASEY: "The music plays so gaily, vigorously, as if it wants itself to live. Oh, my God. Time will pass, and then we shall be gone forever. They will forget us, our faces, voices, even how many of us there were. But our sufferings will become joy for those who live after us. A season of happiness and peace, and we who lived now will be blessed and thought of kindly. Oh, dear sisters, our life is still not finished. We will live. The music plays so bravely, so joyfully, as if in another moment we shall know why we live and why we suffer. If we could only know, if we could only know!"

(*A moment held in the traditional pose, and then Casey and Holly leave the stage. Everyone has gone except Lisabette. She look up in the audience and speaks to Joby.*)

LISABETTE: So how did we do?

JOBY: Oh fine. Not bad. Is it over?

LISABETTE: Sort of. I mean I'm the only one left. Their planes left.

JOBY: But not really.

LISABETTE: No, not really. I mean, in the play they left.

JOBY: They don't give me much space in the paper. I'm kind of between the car ads and the pet ads.

LISABETTE: I didn't have a lot of lines either. Not like a lead character or anything.

JOBY: You were good though, with what you had.

LISABETTE: Thanks. And?

JOBY: Oh. Well I . . . okay umm. So I would say . . . it played [*the time*], you know [*the date*], at [*the place*], and umm . . . a serio-comic, ummm, look at the creative drive and how the culture and, like, human frailty warp that, make it less pure . . . almost ludicrous, maybe break it . . . umm, call into question whether it's kind of over for the theatre . . . you know. Pretty good acting and everything . . . minimal set. I guess my question would be if plays, doing plays, doesn't speak to the culture, then examining why, or satirizing why, is kind of beating a dead horse . . . from the inside. So, uh, anyway, I only have about a hundred words to say that. You were good.

LISABETTE: Wow.

JOBY: Yeah. I could send you a copy.

LISABETTE: Thanks.

JOBY: I mean, I'm not a real critic . . . yet.

LISABETTE: Oh, you will be.

JOBY: Yeah. I don't know.

LISABETTE: Really.

JOBY: Yeah. Anyway. Bye.

LISABETTE: Bye.

JOBY: Bye.

(*Joby leaves. Airport is struck. T-Anne enters and sets a ghost light.*)

T-ANNE: 'Night, baby.

LISABETTE: 'Night. (*Lisabette remains in a single light. She looks around her.*) Wow. Crazy. It's so stupid, but I love to act. It always feels like anything could happen. That something wonderful could happen. It's just people, you know, just people doing it and watching it, but I think everybody hopes that it might turn out to be something more than that. Like people buy a ticket to the lottery, only this has more . . . heart to it. And most times, it doesn't turn out any better than the lottery, but sometimes . . . My dad runs a community center, and back in the day they did this play called *A Raisin in the Sun,* just about a black family or something, and it was just people doing it. He said there was a grocery guy and a car mechanic, a waitress, but the whole thing had like . . . I don't know . . . aura, and people wanted to be there . . . so much that when they would practice at night, 'cause everybody had jobs, they had to open the doors at the center and hundreds of black people would just show up, show up for the play practice. They brought kids, they brought dinner, old people in wheelchairs, and they would hang around the whole time, kids running up and down, until the actors went home, night after night at practice, and when they finished, these people would stick around and they would line up outside like a . . . reception line . . . like a wedding . . . and the actors would walk down that line . . . "How you doin'? How you doin'?" shaking hands, pattin' on the kids, and the people would give them pies and yard flowers, and then the audience and the actors would all walk out, in the pitch dark, to the parking lot together. Nobody knew exactly what it was or why it happened. Someday I'd like to be in a play like that. I would. So I guess I'll go on . . . keep trying . . . what do you think? Could happen. Maybe. Maybe not. (*She looks at the audience.*) Well, you came tonight anyway. (*Black out.*)

BREATH, BOOM

by Kia Corthron

Breath, Boom received its U.S. premiere at Playwrights Horizons (Tim Sanford, artistic director) in New York City, June 2001. Marion McClinton directed; the set and lighting design were by Michael Philippi; the costume design was by Katherine Roth; the sound design was by Ken Travis; the fight director was David Leong; the production stage manager was Jane Pole. The cast featured: Russell Andrews, Pascale Armand, Dena Atlantic, Kalimi A. Baxter, Caroline Stefanie Clay, Rosalyn Coleman, Donna Duplantier, Yvette Ganier, Abigail Lopez, and Heather Alicia Simms.

CHARACTERS

PRIX (PREE):	sixteen, seventeen, twenty-four, twenty-nine, thirty
ANGEL:	sixteen, thirty
MALIKA/SOCKS:	around seventeen, around thirty looking considerably older
COMET:	eighteen, twenty-six, thirty-two
JEROME:	thirties
PRIX'S MOTHER:	thirties, fifties
3 CORRECTIONS OFFICERS (C.O.s)	
CAT:	fifteen
OFFICER DRAY	
SHONDRA:	teens
FUEGO:	teens
DENISE:	thirties
PEPPER:	sixteen or seventeen
(ShIRL:	sixteen or seventeen
JUPITER:	fourteen
WOMAN:	coming out of the bathroom
JO:	around thirty
JO'S FRIEND:	around thirty

All female except Jerome.
Plenty of role doubling.

ACT ONE

Scene 1

Street corner. Prix, Angel, and Malika wait. Comet enters, pissed. She stares at them, particularly at Prix. They stare at her.

COMET: What.

(*She waits for them to answer. They don't.*)

COMET: Attitude? Don't even gimme that shit I *told*ju this is my birthday I'd appreciate the night off *please,* Toldju tonight my eighteenth big party *Ring!* Shit! Get the phone. I gotta leave my guests "Where ya goin'?" she says. "Stuff I gotta do" and you *know* she throwin' a fit, money she put out for that damn party "*I* know where you goin'! *I* know where you goin'! Huzzy!" Ain't that a sweet way talk to your daughter only daughter her eighteenth I think but say nothin', no time to bitch with her cuz I got the damn call, know my duty I come on down here and now yaw got nothin' to say? Hop my ass down to work cuz I'm called *my* birthday, *my* eighteenth birthday, leave my friends cuz *I* got a few, desert my *friends* to meet my *sisters* and now my sisters givin' me a look like why I got attitude.

(*She waits for them to answer. They don't.*)

COMET: *What?*

(*Prix gives Angel and Malika a look. Comet is suddenly terrified but before she can get away Angel and Malika pounce, beating the crap out of Comet: no mercy. Comet screaming. Eventually Prix herself throws in a few kicks or punches. BOOM. Prix looks up. Colored fireworks lights are reflected upon the girls. Prix stands, walks downstage, mesmerized by the lights. She says something, not loud enough to be heard over the pummeling and the fireworks.*)

When a few moments later, Malika realizes that Prix has spoken, she pauses in her violence and indicates for Angel also to halt.)

MALIKA: Whadju say?

PRIX (*focused on the fireworks, absently repeats*): "Don't kill her."

(*Malika and Angel are now aware of the fireworks and also stand, captivated, drawn toward Prix's area.*)

PRIX: What day's today?

ANGEL: I dunno. Memorial Day?

(*Prix, Angel, and Malika continue gazing. On the ground behind: a bleeding, near-unconscious Comet.*)

Scene 2

Prix's bedroom. On the wall are several colored-pencil drawings of fireworks. Angel and Malika are on the bed. Angel weaves long braids into Malika's hair. Before the phone finishes the first ring, Prix snatches the receiver.

PRIX: Yeah?

(*Prix grabs a pencil and pad and takes notes of the conversation.*)

MALIKA: I don't know why Prix don't get a cell, always gotta make sure she be by her phone the right time, or by the pay phone right time. She have a cell phone she take her business with her, convenient.

ANGEL: She got a beeper.

MALIKA: *So?* People prefer a cell phone—beeper—you got the delayed action, gotta call 'em, push your number in, then wait 'til *they* find a quarter, they find a pay phone, then probably they gotta stand on line for the pay phone you know what kinda time gap that makes? Beeper, 'less it life-and-death vital, people say forget it.

ANGEL: Just why she say she got a beeper, she say beeper encourage 'em thus: "'Less it life-and-death vital, don't bother me"

Girl! I hope you know these hairs is three shades lighter 'n your natural color.

MALIKA: They's highlights, J.W. likes it Ow!

ANGEL: J.W., J.W., you know how to have a conversation without havin' to plug your damn boyfriend's name every two seconds?

MALIKA: Last night he bought me roses off the street and stuck one in my hair. It was real sweet 'til that thorn stabbed my scalp Ow! I punched him and he punched me, then he goes ain't you just like Jesus, crown a thorns and we laughed and had sex and cookie dough ice cream OW!

ANGEL: Toldju I do it professional, professional hurts.

MALIKA: Wow. (*Looking around*) Somehow I imagined Prix's room be all black, no windows. You ever been here before?

ANGEL: She's my cousin.

MALIKA: You ever been here before?

ANGEL: Yeah I been here before. Too many times, one buildin' away, too far for my mother get off her butt and walk but close enough she send me errand-runnin' every five minutes, "Aunt Kerstine, Mom's done with this week's *Jet,* said you wanna read it." "Aunt Kerstine, my mother like to buy couple food stamps, you got some extra?"

MALIKA: Your mom's nice. Soft. Not hollerin' all the time I bet she never even whipped yaw.

ANGEL: Kiddin'? One time Darryl and me ate the cream out the Oreos, hid the hard dark part in the couch—

PRIX: Okay. (*Hangs up.*) Meet at McDonald's 10:35. Car'll come by 10:45, their party's hundred forty-first, they established a dumb routine habit a saunterin' in between 11:30 and midnight. Cruise St. Ann's, round the block. First sight a their car, hit and get out.

MALIKA: A'ight. Ow!

ANGEL: You got dandruff like nobody's business, what kinda shampoo you use?

MALIKA (*Refers to drawings*): I like your fireworks, Prix.

PRIX: Thanks.

MALIKA: My cousin rides planes sometimes. She does . . . I dunno, secretary, somethin', she wears a suit, she has business other cities, gotta take planes. She says they bring food to ya. Snack and a meal. She says them stewardesses get free flights, Spain. Africa. That's gonna be me, stewardess. High, high, winkin' down atcha from 37,000.

(*Phone rings. Prix snatches it.*)

PRIX: Yeah?

(*Prix realizes who it is, looks at Angel and Malika, irritated. They are puzzled.*)

PRIX: Yeah. (*Hangs up.*) Someone buzz her in. (*Goes to her desk.*)

MALIKA: Who is it?

(*Prix doesn't answer. From her desk she pulls multicolored pipe-cleaner figures shaped like fireworks. After a moment, Angel interprets the silence.*)

ANGEL: Comet.

MALIKA: *Comet?* I thought she was still in the hospital.

ANGEL (*shrugs*): Who else made her mad lately? ("*Her*" meaning Prix)

MALIKA: Who's mad at the people we're s'posed to hit tonight?

ANGEL: Not her she just followin' instructions. Nothin' personal anyway, just a drive-by, not like we shootin' anybody face-to-face. Get it.

(*Malika gets up but, before she gets to the buzzer, a knock is heard on Prix's door.*)

MALIKA: How she get in the buildin' without buzzin'?

(*Comet opens the door, stands in the doorway from the hallway: the sound of a man's and a woman's laughter. Prix, molding pipe cleaners into fireworks, looks up toward the door.*)

MALIKA: How you get in the buildin' without buzzin'?

COMET: Prix's moms and Jerome let me in.

PRIX (*turning back to her project, to herself*): Fuck.

MALIKA (*vague smirk*): I thought you were still in the hospital, Comet.

COMET (*enters, nervous*): Got out. Coupla days. Hi, Prix.

ANGEL: How's Jupiter?

COMET: Good! Missed me. Only two but she got a vocabulary, my mother say "Every day that brat cryin' 'I want my mommy!'"

ANGEL: You gettin' along better with your mother? (*Comet looks at her.*) Leavin' her to babysit while you's in the hospital.

COMET: Who else?

MALIKA: She give you that big birthday party ain't that a new thing? Generosity?

COMET: Mother a the year.

ANGEL: She was . . . Your mother . . . while you was in the hospital, all by herself she was babysittin'—

COMET: First bruise I'da found on my baby I'da killed that bitch. And she knew I was serious cuz when I come home first thing I inspect my daughter head to toe. Knew I meant it. Not even diaper rash. (*Pause*) Angel. Show me?

MALIKA: You ain't got it *yet*? (*Angel falls back on the bed laughing.*) Ain'tchu practiced?

COMET: Practice all the time! just . . . if I see her do it once more . . . Angel?

ANGEL (*enjoying it*): I dunno.

COMET: Come on.

MALIKA: Please Please Please Please!

COMET: I didn't say that! I just . . . (*Pulls a razor blade from her pocket.*) If I watch just one more time—

ANGEL: Okay.

(*Angel takes the blade from Comet. She puts it in her own mouth and twirls it around expertly, periodically flicking it on her tongue. Eventually she takes it out, hands it back to Comet.*)

COMET: God, I ain't never gonna be that good!

MALIKA: I can do it. Watch. (*Reaches for the razor.*)

COMET (*to Angel*): I lost so much blood tryin' it, I do it in fronta the bathroom mirror.

ANGEL: I lost blood too, at first. Your tongue gotta develop a crust.

MALIKA: You gotta keep practicin'. J.W. says I'm totally sexy when I do it, watch. (*Reaches for the razor.*)

COMET (*to Angel*): Practice any more I won't have a drop left. Watch.

PRIX (*still not looking up*): I find a spot a blood on my floor the owner's gonna lose six pints more.

(*Comet, who had started to put the blade into her mouth, doesn't. Off-stage voices:*)

JEROME: What did you say?!

MOTHER: I didn't say nothin'! I didn't say nothin'!

(*A bang, as if someone had been thrown against the wall. Prix doesn't respond. A beat after the bang, then she speaks:*)

PRIX: Yaw stayin' all night?

(*Angel and Malika get up.*)

PRIX: Don't be late, Malika.

MALIKA: Why you always sayin' me? I guess Angel ain't never been late, why you gotta—

PRIX: Don't be late, Malika.

(*Comet is looking at Malika and Angel.*)

ANGEL: Drive-by. McDonald's. 10:35.

MALIKA: You don't have to worry about me I'm starved. I'll bring J.W. for a bite 10 o'clock, by 10:35 I figure I be lip-smackin' Big Mac juice.

PRIX: Comet, stay.

(*Malika and Angel exit. Prix still hasn't looked up from her activity. Comet observes the room.*)

COMET (*looking around*): You sure like the fireworks.

PRIX: Everybody likes the fireworks.

(*Offstage: a few moments of laughter and sexual breathing, which irritates Prix. After it quiets, she turns to Comet:*)

PRIX: "I'm gonna be eighteen, they catch me doin' what I'm doin' when I'm eighteen they put me away for life I'm quittin'! I'm quittin' the gangs When my birthday comes I'm gone! Ain't a damn thing they can do about it!" I be eighteen myself two years and liar if I say it ain't crost my own mind, ain't a dumb idea. Mouthin' off about it was. Ways you coulda fucked up, got yourself thrown out. We'da kicked your ass and give ya the big punishment: you're gone. Now, stupid, gotcher ass kicked and here's the big punishment: you stay.

(*Prix goes back to her pipe-cleaner figures. Quiet a few moments. Comet mumbles something, then glances at Prix, waiting for Prix to ask her to repeat it. Prix doesn't.*)

COMET: I *said,* I thought we ain't s'posed to hit on our own, thought we only s'posed to spill blood a enemies. Or strangers.

PRIX (*dry*): Yeah, we ain't s'posed to. See how low you brung us. (*Beat*) Don'tchu know better than to walk into a deserted narrow place, your sisters jus' waitin' for ya?

(*Quiet again.*)

COMET: Whatchu wanna do? Shoot 'em off?

PRIX: Design 'em. (*Works quietly, then*) *And* shoot 'em off. Fireworks people ain't a architect, make the blueprint and give to someone else to build. Clothes designer never touch a sewin' machine. A fireworks artist, take your basic chrysanthemum, not to be confused with peonies, the latter comprised a dots but chrysanthemums with petal tails, the big flower, start with a pistil of orange then move out into blue, blue which comes from copper or chlorine, cool blue burstin' out from orange pistil, blue instantly change to strontium nitrate red to sodium yellow, cool to warm, warmer and the designer ain't the joyful bystander, she's right there pushin' the buttons and while the crowd's oohin' aahin' this'n she's already on to the next button. This quick chrysanthemum I'd start my show with and accompanying reports of course, bang bang and I'll throw in a few willows, slower timin' and a softer feelin', tension to relaxation keep the audience excited, anticipatin', then time for multiple-breakers, shell breakin' into a flower breakin' 'to another flower 'to another, then a few comets (*Points to drawing on the wall; refers to Comet*) Comets! Then, *then* if I had a bridge, a *Niagara,* fallin' from the edge and this wouldn't even be the finale, maybe . . . maybe . . . somethin' gooey, like "Happy Birthday Comet!" *Now* finale, which of course is the bombs and the bombs and the bombs and "chaos" can't possibly be the description cuz this be the most precisely planned chaos you ever saw! *Hanabi!* flowers of fire. My show people screamin' it, "*Hanabi! Hanabi!*"

(*Offstage*)

JEROME: Bitch, where is it? (*Slap*)

MOTHER: I ain't got it!

JEROME: You think I'm stupid?

MOTHER (*mocking*): "You think I'm stupid?"

(*A brief struggle with furniture banging. Comet is still admiring the fireworks art. Prix, vaguely embarrassed by her enthusiasm, turns back to her project.*)

COMET: Sounds like my parents.

PRIX: He ain't my father.

(*The offstage noise quiets.*)

PRIX (*not looking up*): This stuff gimme a sensa shape. But sometimes I need the fire.

(*Prix turns on her desk lamp, switches off the overhead lights. Pulls several pen lights out of her drawer, clicks them on. The bulbs are different colors. She begins moving them around, making different fireworks shapes and sounds. Comet smiles. Suddenly big offstage banging and arguing, screaming.*)

COMET: This fireworks finale I know too well. 'Bye.

(*Comet exits. Prix goes back to her work. The battle rages on. A huge crash, then silence. Prix continues working. Eventually:*)

MOTHER (*outside door*): Prix?

(*No answer. Mother opens the door, letting herself in, and shuts it behind her. She is bruised from the fight. Prix doesn't look up.*)

PRIX: Lock it.

(*Mother does.*)

PRIX (*dry*): Guess he didn't kill ya. (*Mother laughs nervously.*) You kill him?

MOTHER: No, no he's okay. That crash . . . I hardly hit him I think
he's mostly passed out. Wine. Lots and lots and lotsa . . .
(*Sudden defensiveness*) You think I wanted it? I got the
restrainin' order! I got it, fourteen years! Fourteen years
dumb! Fourteen years I been puttin' up with it, finally I wise
up, restrainin' order, six months it been effect, how many
times he been here that six months? Seven! And I called
the police first four times, him bangin' the door down. Slow
as they is and Jerome skilled with a paper clip, no problem he pick the lock 'fore they come, *if* they come why
bother?

PRIX (*still not looking up*): Didn't have to pick the lock tonight.

MOTHER: He was outside when I come home *okay?* I didn't
want him to come in. We was talkin' . . . Think I wanted it?
It gonna happen anyway, I know it, I know it while I'm
talkin' even though he ain't said it, I ain't said it, gonna happen and if I . . . if I let it happen, don't fight it, it don't
go over so rough. If I enjoy it a little, don't feel so much
like he made me. (*Beat*) I gotta get out. 'Fore he wakes,
you be okay, you ain't the one he's after. I'm gettin' out.
(*Beat*) You wanna come? (*Prix doesn't answer.*) I'm goin', you
be okay.

(*Mother's hand on doorknob*)

MOTHER: Keep the door locked.

(*Mother unlocks door and starts to open it. A toilet flush is heard.
Mother panics, shuts and locks the door.*)

MOTHER (*loud whisper*): Prix! (*Prix ignores her.*) Prix!

(*Prix, pissed and glaring, turns to Mother. Mother indicates the closet.*)

MOTHER: Can I—?

JEROME (*off*): Hey!

(*Mother rushes into closet, shuts door.*)

PRIX: Smart.

(*Prix sloppily kicks a large furniture piece in front of the door, then noisily throws open her window and slams it shut. She sits back down at her work.*)

JEROME (*outside the door, jiggling the doorknob*): I hear you! Don'tcha be hittin' the damn fire escape!

(*A clicking sound in the doorknob. Then Jerome forces the door open against the furniture and enters. He immediately rushes to the window, throws it open and steps out. A few moments later he returns, shutting the window behind him. He also looks roughed up from the fight with Mother. Prix continues her activity, not looking at him.*)

JEROME (*playing with his paper clip*): Whadju do, push her out?

(*Prix doesn't look up.*)

JEROME: Didn't notice her broken body writhin' on the ground so guess not.

(*Jerome moves toward Prix.*)

JEROME: Wonder what we do 'til your mama get back.

(*Jerome touches Prix sensually. At the first contact, Prix slams him against the closet door, surprising him, hurting him; takes a razor blade from her mouth and holds it against his throat.*)

PRIX: I ain't five no more.

(*Prix goes back to sit with her pipe cleaners, her back to Jerome. Stunned, he moves toward the door and exits. The outside door to the apartment opens and slams shut. A few seconds of quiet, then the closet door cracks open. A quiet weeping from inside. Eventually:*)

PRIX: If you weren't always playin' Helen Keller, bitch, you mighta knowed a long time ago.

(*The quiet weeping continues.*)

Scene 3

Institutional waiting room. Angel sits glue-sticking newspaper clippings into a scrapbook. Prix enters. She is startled to see Angel. Angel sees Prix.

ANGEL: Whatchu doin' here?

(*Prix stares at Angel. Angel chatters as she continues working on her scrapbook.*)

ANGEL: Oh that's right, you got a mother in, since no one but me and my mother ever visited her I forgot. Ain't seein' her today though, Ramey *and* Sonia in Fuckers! I come all the way out here LOCKDOWN! And Ramey's section's the lockdownest, by the time they let him go visitin' time's almost over. *And* all he wants to do five minutes we got is bitch bitch bitch, jail sucks, no shit? But how 'bout just one "Nice to see ya" to his girlfriend trekked all the way out here, hour and a half subway and bus, think he appreciate that. And I tell him too, then he wants to get pissed, *I* ain't understandin', shit. If the dumbass hadn't been hangin' with Carl I *told* him 'at greedy punk get him in trouble one day! Three outa four cash registers they cleared and the idiot waitin' around cuz Carl can't bear to leave the fourth untouched. While he's clearin' it, guess what? (*Makes a siren sound.*)

PRIX: This ain't the men's side.

ANGEL: Seein' my sister, toldja Sonia in too. (*Prix glances at Angel's book.*) Scrapbook. Thought Sonia like to see it. Was gonna show it to Ramey 'til he pissed me off. Wanna see it? (*Prix shakes her head no. Angel looks at her.*) Your P.O. make you come? (*Prix nods.*) Glad I ain't been caught yet, no Probation Officer slave-masterin' my life. Better go in, time's runnin' out. She know you here?

PRIX: P.O. told her. Probably just so P.O. can check on me after, see if I really come.

ANGEL: Better go. Time's runnin' out.

PRIX: What about you?

ANGEL: Forty-five minutes 'til they bring out the adolescents. But adult hour's now. She probably already there waitin' for ya. Go.

(*Beat.*)

PRIX: You doin' that job? tomorrow?

ANGEL: Nope, takin' the day off.

PRIX: Off?(*Angel looks at her.*) Maybe you ain't got that choice, Angel—

(*Angel indicates her watch. Prix reluctantly enters another space where Mother, who has been looking for Prix, sits at a table with a small partition that separates her from the other side. The partition comes about as high as the neck of a sitting adult. A Corrections Officer (C.O.) stands nearby. Prix enters. Mother sees her, smiles broad but nervous, not knowing what to say. Prix doesn't move. Then, a decision: she walks over and flops down in the chair opposite Mother. Prix turns her body to the side, away from Mother. She does not look at her.*)

MOTHER: Surprise! They told me you was here but I didn't believe 'em. You look . . . You been eatin' right? Aunt BiBi tole me you been eatin' okay, I ast her to check on you now and again, she been by, right? (*No answer. Singsong teasing a small child.*) I know what tomorrow is. (*No answer. Little more nervous.*) And your birthday next month, I ain't forgot nunna them holidays, I made somethin' for ya. (*Pulls out a pair of gloves. Prix doesn't look.*) Gloves! Hard to crochet 'em but . . . hope they fit.

(*Mother reaches for Prix's hand. C.O. makes a loud, surprised grunt and snatches the gloves.*)

MOTHER: Sorry! Sorry! You can check 'em before you give 'em to her. Her birthday comin' up, seventeen. (*To Prix*) Took me nine weeks to do it. Just learnin'.

(C.O. inspects the gloves and holds them out to Prix. Prix, who hasn't budged a muscle or shifted her gaze, does not look at C.O. C.O. shakes the gloves to get Prix's attention. Prix ignores C.O. C.O. lets gloves drop to the floor.)

MOTHER: When . . . When I get home I'm takin' you to Wave Hill. You never believed me, you think our neighborhood is all the Bronx is, uh uh. Bronx ain't just projects and bullets, there's parts got flowers, butterflies. Wave Hill, the Botanic Gardens. The Mansion in the Park! When I get home, first thing we do is go to the pretty things, no! No, 34th Street, twelve midnight. You never believed me 'bout that neither, toldja midnight, Empire State Building, lights out . . .

(Toward the end of Mother's speech Prix gets up and slips back to the other space—the waiting room. She sits in a seat near Angel who is still glue-sticking.)

ANGEL *(not looking up)*: How'd it go? *(No answer. Angel doesn't notice.)* Wanna see my scrapbook?

(Angel opens the scrapbook. The book is filled with newspaper clippings. Prix pays scant attention.)

ANGEL *(pointing to various clippings)*: You remember Jeff Pace? Seventh grade, he made that environmental poster with the seals, won the contest? We was pretty good friends, I went to his funeral. Jeanine, remember? Too flirty. I knew she'd end up gettin' it cuz her homeboys always settin' her up to whore-spy on the enemy. She specifically requested her sexy pink dress, I know cuz she borrowed a piece a my notebook paper in U.S. History for her will, and here her mother laid her out like Sunday School. Tony, my ex. You went to his funeral, right? *(Dancing a brief fast dance)* His had the best music. Oh! this whole spread, centerfold *and* next eight pages, all my big brother, all Vince. His football stuff, honor roll stuff. "Athlete honor student killed by stray bullet." That's Terri, Trish's little sister. She was eight, she got it in the head, hopscotchin' when a drive-by come flyin' through, remember? Here's Lenny—

PRIX: You comin' tomorrow?

ANGEL: Pick your ears, Prix, I said no. (*Prix gets up to leave.*) Who the hell workin' tomorrow? Everybody want the day off. (*Prix heading for the door*) You comin' to dinner?

(*Prix stops.*)

PRIX: Toldja I got a job to do. Somebody got to.

ANGEL (*shrugs*): My mother told me to ask you. (*Pause*) Wonder how come she up and did it. You moms. You know? (*Prix doesn't answer.*) Coulda done him in years ago. Why now? (*Beat*) First degree. Betcha: twenty-five to life. (*Beat*) You was two when she met him, right? And he with yaw all them years, you miss him?

PRIX: He wasn't my father.

ANGEL: My mom's gonna wonder why you ain't comin' to dinner, all alone tomorrow. Whatchu gonna eat?

PRIX: Egg rolls. Like every other night.

ANGEL: Okay, Prix. (*Back to her scrapbook*) Merry Christmas.

(*Prix exits. Angel turns the pages of her scrapbook, one by one, absorbed and content.*)

Scene 4

Jail cell. Bunk cots. By the lower bunk, a couple new fireworks drawings. A chair. Prix and Cat are in street clothes. Cat has a cloth band around her hair. Prix, in the chair, tears a page she has just written on from her notebook and stands to read. Cat listens.

PRIX (*serious*): Six months ago a sense of personal injustice would have had me reaching for the trigger. Today I find my greatest defense is in open dialogue. It is the accepting, nonjudgmental atmosphere of my counseling group that has allowed me to reevaluate the choices I've made. Your support has opened me to revisit my mistakes and has helped me to see my errors as attributable to social and economic circumstances of my upbringing as well as to personal choice. My home was violent, my teachers suspicious, potential employers uninterested. Sometimes I think if I had been shown one kindness in my life, perhaps things could have been different. While I am naturally apprehensive about the consequential changes our group will undergo, I celebrate the release of three of you over the next several days, and welcome those newcomers who will be filling your seats. On this last day that we are one, my sisters, I joyously thank you for replenishing my soul and touching my heart.

(*She silently looks at the page a few moments. Suddenly no longer able to contain it, she bursts into uncontrollable laughter. Cat follows suit.*)

CAT: "My sisters" "My sisters"!

(*Prix's laughter subsides. She sits, erases on the paper, edits.*)

CAT (*continuous*): That's funny, you're smart. They eat up that crap, how long it take 'em figure it's shit? I like to see the look on their faces I'm comin' to your group tomorrow.

PRIX (*not looking up*): You ain't in my group. (*At some point during Cat's next speech, Prix pulls out from under her cot a box of colored pencils and starts sketching. She doesn't look up.*)

CAT: I am now. I told Miss Collins I didn't feel comfortable in my group, she said Give it a try, you only been here a month, I said Some of them bitches threatenin' me, say they gonna take my teeth out. Randy. Scooter. She said I'll talk to 'em. I said I wish you wouldn't That really make life hell, I wish you just change my group please. The lie is, Randy and Scooter never said nothin' 'bout my teeth, I just hate their ugly faces wanted get away from 'em. The truth is, Miss Collins tell 'em what I said I *would* be in life-threatenin' trouble for lyin' 'bout 'em the first place. Luckily Miss Collins buy it I'm your group tomorrow. I like your group I like them people. (*Pause*) Lap a luxury. Three meals. Street clothes.

PRIX: You the only one around here ready to print up the welcome travelers' brochure for jail.

(*During Cat's next speech, Jerome enters the cell, eyes on Prix. Prix sees him; Cat doesn't. He exits. Prix goes back to her sketching.*)

CAT: I hear 'em! Cryin' on the phone, "My honey, my honey," "I miss my friends." Most of 'em's honeys was kickin' the shit out of 'em daily and their *friends?* Their best girlfriend's on the outside and so's their honey guess what one plus one is equalin'? (*Beat*) Could be worse. See them ugly green one-piece things they make the women wear? Least adolescents, we wear our own shit. (*Beat*) Easy time. Five months you be eighteen, outa here, eleven left for me, shit. Scotfree both us and I'm fifteen, three more years a minor, I get caught, easy time. Eleven months I *know* my roof? *know* my mealtimes? shit. Damn sure beats the fosters.

PRIX: Usually all I hear's you whinin' 'bout the clothes situation.

CAT: Lacka choices! I *love* my clothes, but wearin' the same five outfits gets limitin' after awhile. There's this cute thing I useta wear, black, kinda sheer, kinda spare, my belly button on the open-air market. They say No way, Stupid! Their Nazi dress code, what. They think wearin' it'll get me pregnant? in *here?* (*Beat*) Ain't my first time in. Fourth!

PRIX: Runaway.

CAT: Three more years I'm a fuckin' criminal for it! can't wait 'til eighteen! Runnin' away I be legal! (*Beat*) My broken arm was mindin' its own business wisht they'da minded theirs, dontcha never believe that crap about best to tell the counselor tell the teacher it'll makes things better. Cuz ya *will* get sent back home and just when ya thought things could get no worse, they do.

PRIX: *Sh!*

(*Prix moves toward the wall, leans against it. Someone is tapping against it, a code. Prix taps back in code. When the communication is complete, Prix sits back down to her sketching. Cat smiles.*)

CAT: What's the big one? Single most thing earned you all the gracious undivided esteem? I heard this: shot a enemy girl in the face. Then went to her funeral cuz yaw was best friends second grade, made all your sisters go, put the whole god-damn family on edge and every one of 'em knew and not a one of 'em said a word about it to you. (*Beat*) *And* one time jumpin' a girl in, she not too conscious, you jump your whole weight on her face ten times maybe? twelve? 'fore a sister pull you off. *And* when yaw stand around, eenie mee-nie minie pick some herb comin' down the subway steps to steal their wallet, you was the one everybody know could always knock 'em out first punch. *And* one time on a revenge spree, dress up like a man so no one identify you later, stick your hair under a cap and shoot dead some boy ten years old. *And*—

PRIX: Fifteen. (*Pause. Cat is confused.*) I don't kill no kids. Fifteen.

CAT: O.G.! you gonna earn it. Original Gangsta, people respect you long after you retire Take me in! (*No answer*) You get it. The high, right? This girl Aleea, she tell me all about it. The kickin' and smashin' and breakin' bones snap! Somebody lyin' still in a flood a their own blood, somebody dead it gets her all hyped up, thrill thing! And power, them dead you not, *you* made it happen! Them dead, *you* done it! You ever get that high?

PRIX: 'Course.

(*During Cat's next speech, Jerome appears to Prix in the cell. Cat doesn't see him. Prix takes Cat's hair band and effortlessly strangles Jerome to death.*)

CAT: Take me in! I tried once, not yours. Not the other neither I ain't enemy! Small little club I was interested in. Wore the right colors, I talked the shit. They wouldn't even jump me in, I said "I'll do it! Either way, all yaw stand in a line and rough me through it OR I'll take the toughest one on, two minutes!" They just laugh. (*Beat*) Maybe when we out . . . I know there's lots and lots a members, big network your group, maybe . . . I'd be good! Runnin' with my sisters, tappin' the codes—

PRIX (*strangling*): Wannabe.

(*Prix goes back to her sketching. Jerome exits.*)

CAT: They think I ain't tough I got it! I can fight! I was four, these two boys was six, tried to steal my bike I flattened 'em! And when my foster sisters steak-knife stabbed me and drowned me in the tub, somebody called a ambulance, he mouth-to-mouthed me back alive, said if I wasn't strong I'da stayed dead. (*Chuckles*) *She's* dead! Jessie, she the one screamin' "Hold her down! No air bubbles hold the bitch 'til she dead dead dead!" Look who's talkin', she with her homegirls and -boys thinkin' she a member in good standin', got drunk one night and said somethin' smart to a homey, he blew her head off. (*Laughs*)

PRIX: You ever wish you done it?

(*Beat.*)

CAT: *Huh?*

PRIX: You ever . . . You ever regret wasn't you pulled the trigger?

CAT (*confused*): She's dead.

PRIX: Yeah but like . . . that thought. Fantasy. It ever get stuck your mind? Wishin' the last thing she seen was you robbin' her last breath?

OFFICER DRAY (*off, yelling to someone else*): You heard me, I said Move on!

CAT: Bitch! You know that ol' crackhead Tizzy? Officer Dray told me I was mouthin' off, I wa'n't doin' nothin'! She goes

Move along and I do and she goes Don't roll your eyes at me! and I go I *moved* along and she goes Don't gimme nunna your lip! and I *go* (*What're-you-yelling-at-me-for? gesture*) and she goes Alright goddammit mop the floor with Tizzy! and I think Oh fuck but I do it, shit. And ol' Tizzy don't shut up, bitchin' all outa her head, and I go Oh shut up ya ol' crackhead bitch! And she goes, (*Suddenly struggling to contain laughter*) she goes, "Hey! One day you gonna be me!"

(*Prix stares out. Cat rolls on her bed, uncontrollable laughter.*)

Scene 5

Counseling room, represented by four or five folding chairs, indicating that this is half of a larger circle of perhaps ten people. Fuego and Shondra sit.

SHONDRA: What makes me mad? What makes me mad is the shit they call food. Allow us no chocolate but meanwhile what *is* that cold fried shit they slop on our plates? Tater tots? What the shit is tater tots? What makes me mad is goddamn body searches before visits, after visits. What makes me goddamn mad is havin' to sit here talkin' shit and listen to all yaw talkin' shit when I don't give a goddamn and yaw don't give a goddamn, that's what makes me mad. (*Cat enters.*)

FUEGO (*indicating the "counselor"*): I think she means what makes us mad on the outside.

CAT: Hi, Fuego. Hi, Shondra. (*Sits*)

SHONDRA (*eyes on "counselor"*): Hi. I *told*ju in individual counselin' why the shit I gotta be dredgin' up my business in fronta everybody.

FUEGO: So we can help each other. (*Breaks into laughter*)

CAT: Missin' classes when there's a lockdown, that's what makes me mad.

FUEGO: Fuck ain't nunna these bitches I look to for help 'less I need help gettin' my throat slashed, there I find lotsa helpful friends.

SHONDRA: I got no friends. I got sisters. And associates.

CAT: The clothes make me mad. How come only five outfits?

SHONDRA (*to Cat*): I catch you lookin' at my stuff in the shower again I'ma mess you up.

CAT: I wa'n't lookin' at you!

SHONDRA (*to "counselor"*): Don't tell *me* this ain't the place for that! I see some bitch lookin' between my legs I'ma—

CAT (*mumbles*): Like you two don't do it.

FUEGO: Whadju say?

SHONDRA (*to Cat*): Yeah, don'tchu worry about it.

FUEGO (*to Cat*): Whadju say?

SHONDRA: She said she was fuckin' lookin' where it was nunna her uglyass business to be lookin'.

CAT: I saw . . . I saw . . .

SHONDRA: Stupid obviously don't understand the difference, wants and needs. I *need* a man's touch but none around, I take what I can get. But if you *look*in', Tom-peepin', that's cuz you *wan*nit, you *want* a woman and you was probably doin' women out there—

CAT: I wasn't!

SHONDRA (*continuous*): and tell ya somethin' else . . .

CAT (*simultaneously with Shondra's next line*): I wasn't doin' it! (*Beat*) I WON'T DO IT NO MORE!

SHONDRA (*simultaneously with Cat's previous line*): . . . this be your one warnin'. I ever catch you—

(*Prix enters and sits. At first sight of her, Shondra and Fuego sit up straight, fall to silence. They don't look at her, or at each other. Cat continues speaking until she becomes aware of the sudden stillness. Cat is surprised by the fear-respect and takes it in. Suddenly Cat's head turns, as if called on by the "counselor."*)

CAT: Home? Mmmmm . . . I guess . . . the garbage. Makes me mad when the garbage gets piled high my street, the rats . . . It ain't even a strike! If it was a strike I'd understand but regular thing, that high garbage, these rats—

FUEGO: I don't understand the damn system, I don't see how I can get charged nine felonies when they only caught me doin' two. (*New thought, looks at the "counselor"*) They gotta prove it. (*Waits momentarily for an answer; when none comes*) They gotta prove it! right?

SHONDRA: Not respectin'. Cuz I been doin' it a long time, I got some experience. Then somebody, fourteen, fuck up the goddamn instructions, I get on her about it, she say, "I didn't forget the codes." I get on her about it, slam her head 'gainst the cement wall, "I didn't forget the codes." I slam it slam it slam it, "I didn't forget the codes." Last thing I hear some kinda mumble, "I didn't—" lyin' to the end out on the ground, out cold I kick her stupid stubborn face. All she had to do was admit it, shit. And if I'd killed the dumb bitch, guess *I*'d be the bad guy.

(*A silence.*)

FUEGO: My sister Enrica, she taught me backgammon, she's fifteen, I'm nine, we're still in Texas. Every time she roll double sixes, she go, "Boxcars! Boxcars! Lucky!" Then, one day Enrica suddenly all mean, screamin' all over the house, *loca!* And this bad mood don't pass. Hear me rollin' the backgammon dice, she come punchin' my face, Mami have to pull her off. Monday at school the girls giggle at me, "*Hermana* boxcar! *Hermana* boxcar!" Eventually tell me Enrica joined the gang, attached to a boy gang and new girls gotta roll in.

They hand Enrica two dice. Boxcars, but this game boxcars is bad luck. Twelve of 'em. Toughest boy was engine. Littlest boy caboose. (*Beat*) I like New York better. I like jumpin' in here, better 'n rollin' in, all I got from jumpin' in was a couple broken ribs they healed.

(*Silence.*)

CAT (*suddenly sobbing*): They took 'em away! They took 'em away!

SHONDRA: *What?*

CAT: Little boy!

FUEGO: What're you talkin' about?

CAT: Had a baby! Little boy, they make me they make me adopt him away!

FUEGO: Can't no one make ya ya musta said yes.

CAT: They said Do it! They said Do it!

SHONDRA: Where was ya gonna put him? Get a double cell, one be the nursery?

CAT: Before I was charged! I oughtn't be here no way, awaitin' trial, innocent 'til proven guilty, how come I gotta sit here for lacka five hundred?

FUEGO: *Five hundred?* (*Cat looks at her.*) Dollars? (*Cat nods, confused.*) Not five hundred thousand.

CAT: No!

FUEGO: Fuck I wish *my* bond was fuckin' five hundred dollars I'm here 'til I come up with the thousand here to eternity.

SHONDRA: Depends on whatchu in for. (*To Cat*) Whatchu in for?

(*Shondra knows. Caught, Cat is scared, refuses to answer.*)

SHONDRA: Well let's see what could possibly be judged that puny bail.

(*Shondra looking at Fuego. Fuego is confused a moment, then gets it.*)

FUEGO: *Prostitution?*

CAT: They ain't proved nothin' yet!

FUEGO: *Prostitution?*

CAT: FUCK YOU! like you any better!

FUEGO: *Hell*uva a lot better I ain't never taken no money for it I ain't never been *that.*

SHONDRA: If ya took it for money you be a (*To "counselor"*) No, I *won't* shut up! (*To Cat*) If ya took it for money maybe ya still have a little dignity. Funky filthy on the street, whore been tradin' it for a Big Mac. (*Fuego roars in laughter.*)

CAT: AIN'T TRUE!

SHONDRA: Is and you know it, I know somebody goddamn bought the burger. (*To "counselor"*) *What?*

CAT: You'da done it too! you was hungry! You was hungry like I was—

FUEGO: I don't get that hungry.

CAT: You don't know! (*Shondra and Fuego laughing hard*) FUCK YOU! YOU DON'T KNOW!

(*Shondra and Fuego doubled over laughing. Cat turns her back away from them. Freeze.*)

PRIX (*in her head*): What makes me mad is music. John Philip Sousa, trombone pansy crap. And I *tried* Handel, shit he *wrote* for 'em but most of it's too damn obvious. Still, I go for the *1812* cliché. And my head's designed about seven rap shows, comets for the basic beat, butterflies and palm trees the chorus. Chrysanthemums ain't on any regular rhythm but rather hit the hardcore politicals: "power" and "fight" and "black black black"! But it's all stupid, first of all the differential between speed a sound and speed a light means music and visuals ain't never be lined up perfect like some goddamn video, and who *needs* it? Fireworks got their own music: reports and hummers, whistles. Magic, each one born with that little sound. A gulp. A breath. And we holdin' *our* breaths, waitin' three . . . four . . . five . . . BOOM! And my *heart* boom boomin', the final moment of the finale bang! flash! (*Beat*) Then nothin' left but pastel smoke, pink, blue floatin' calm. Calm.

Scene 6

Cell. As Cat chatters she pulls the sheet off the upper bunk, then sits tying it. She is cheery. Prix reads a tattered paperback black romance novel, she does not look at Cat.

CAT (*admiration*): You the coldest fish I know! Ruthless! People know it too, you walk into a room, silence! (*New idea:*) Prix. Come to my geometry tomorrow. I like geometry but those dumb bitches just come in bitchin', bitchin' interrupt the class then I don't learn nothin' but you walk in, everybody shut up, everybody know who you are get quiet fast, come on, geometry! I like that math. Circles is three-sixty, a line goes on and on, rectangle versus the parallelogram, interestin'! Ain't fireworks geometry? Can't the study a angles and arcs be nothin' but helpful? Come on! Favor for me?

(*Prix chuckles to herself. Cat doesn't necessarily expect the refusal, but is delighted by it.*)

CAT: I know! You don't do favors! You the coldest fish I know! (*Beat*) You met Ms. Bramer? She's the new current events she's nice I hope she stick around awhile. She say the 6 o'clock news always hypin': "Tough on teens! Youth violence outa hand, try 'em like adults!" But she say news never say three times as many murders committed by late forties as by under-eighteens, Ms. Bramer say news never mention for every one violence committed by a under-eighteens, *three* violences committed by adults *to* under-eighteens. Ms.

Bramer say if we violent where we learn it? Sow what you reap.

PRIX: Reap what you sow.

CAT (*having just noticed Prix's reading material*): I know that book! passed to me months ago. She's a lawyer, pro bono, he's a big record producer. He's rich and she appreciates it but she don't know, loooves him but got that lawyer's degree and don't know she can lower herself to *that*. I didn't think you read that stuff, I love you and roses and wet eyes. (*Beat*) You ever plan your funeral?

PRIX: Fireworks.

CAT: Knew it! Nothin' somber for me neither, I got the tunes all picked out, went through my CD collection I know who my special guest stars be, I figure they come, like this poor unfortunate fifteen-year-old girl died, ain't the city violent and sad? We felt so depressed we come give a free funeral concert, her last request. Good publicity for them. Here's the processional tune: (*Begins humming a lively hip hop piece, interrupts herself*) processional, when the people first walks in with the casket. (*Resumes her humming, stops*) My coffin's gonna be open. Yours? (*Prix turns a page.*) I'm gonna look good, I got the dress picked and I want people to see it. You ever plan your suicide?

PRIX: Fifth grade.

CAT: Pills? Gun stuck up your mouth?

PRIX: Off the Brooklyn Bridge. (*Now puzzled*) Would that kill ya?

CAT: World Trade Center better bet, know how many freefall floors to concrete? Hundred ten!

PRIX: Knew this girl, Emmarine. Eighth grade social studies. Her thirteenth birthday tried, fucked it up. Now she got little cuts on her wrists and everyone at school smirkin' wherever she walks. On her locker, someone spray-paint EMMARINE,

SUICIDE QUEEN, like they ain't never thought of it themself, and someone else ex out QUEEN, write over it FLOP.

CAT: You noticed I ain't been around last twenty-four? Infirmary, doctor checkin' me out after this girl come up to me *pow!* She say, "What your name?" I'm tryin' to answer, "My name's Cat" but before I get the first word out *pow!* She punch me in my face I'm all knocked out!

PRIX: Not any damn home sets I'm gettin' professional stuff, Class B pyrotechnics, the flowers and 'falls and rain takin' up the whole sky, in my will the details of this spectacular will be specified, my careful plannin' will reap the benefits: the audience mesmerizement, the big boom!

CAT: Supper tonight, I seen her people, them girls follows her around, she weren't there guess they threw her in the bean. I come to her girls, say, "Your friend ask me what my name is. My name's Cat." But soon as I say "Your friend ask me what my name is" they start laughin' so hard I think they don't hear the second part, so I keep sayin' it louder but the louder I say it the louder they laugh. *"My name is Cat!"* (*Giggles*) "MY NAME IS CAT!" (*Giggles, stands on the upper bunk*)

(*While Prix speaks the following, Cat swings the sheet (which she has tied into a rope) around an overhead horizontal pipe and secures it. It is eventually clear that she has formed a noose. Standing on the edge of the bunk, she sticks her head through it: if she jumps off, she'll hang. Her cheeriness has vanished. Her eyes are closed, her breathing harsh and uneven. The most delicate push would be enough to knock her over.*)

PRIX: Most appropriate funeral finale cuz they wasn't just my life. My death. Tragic, someone gimme cotton socks, I *think,* Christmas present and I walk into the shop wearin' 'em. 'Cep' turns out they was silk. Static electricity, spark, boom! "God," they say, "how could this happen? To *her?* Always double-checkin' her clothing, she of all people." Scene a the unfortunate event, they note how I generously spaced apart each of my twenty-five fireworks houses so one accident is prevented from causin' a chain reaction and they'll wipe their wet cheeks, touched that I protected others, touched I died alone. So young, so young.

(*Now Prix turns to Cat, looking at her for the first time in the scene. Though Prix has not been aware of Cat's activity, she does not look surprised.*)

PRIX: Jump.

(*Blackout.*)

ACT TWO

Scene 1

Kitchen table. Prix and Jerome at opposite sides, he sipping coffee, she with a fast food milk shake. On the table are a clock radio, a gun and many vials of crack which Prix silently counts, moving her lips. She periodically glances at the time.

JEROME: Way I figure it, woulda made better sense I killed her. Statistically speaking, man kill his wife, whether from a argument whether he stalked her, crime a passion, three, four years tops. Woman kill her husband, response to him whoopin' the devil outa her decade or two, it's murder one, she get twenty-five to life. Seven years since she gimme the gun, she ain't yet served a third a the minimum time. Other way 'round, I'da been out, parta regular life four years now in the simple name a freedom, in the name a quality a human life, wouldn't me snuffin' her been the more logical choice, long run?

PRIX: You weren't her husband.

JEROME: Common law. Fourteen years we was together, common law husband—

PRIX: Shut up! you're mixin' me up.

JEROME: And common law father to you, man whose genes you got you never met. If your mama even know who that is so I'm the only father you ever . . . (*Prix looks at him.*) Okay! I wasn't the best daddy Who's perfect? Only said I was all the daddy you had. Maybe I wasn't around for *conception* maybe I didn't *breathe* life into ya not there glimpse your first breath, but I was around pretty much all the breaths thereafter I think I had a impact, your life. Sometimes . . . Sometimes your mama couldn't make the rent, I help her out a little. Once I remember her flat broke, I bought the shoes for ya.

PRIX (*flat*): I don't remember that.

JEROME: Seven years old tap-dancin' the shoe store, new white buckle sandals.

PRIX: You lied your whole life now guess you gonna lie your whole death.

JEROME: I gave yaw money! I remember . . . I remember helpin' with the groceries once—

PRIX: Shut up!

(*Beat. Jerome picks up the gun, studies it.*)

JEROME: Your mama always found it such a curiosity, fireworks fixation. All make sense to me, one way or another you love the bang bangs.

PRIX: Chinese invention, they find a purpose: beautiful. Spiritual. Not 'til a English monk put his two cents in do white people decide gunpowder for killin'. (*The noisy finish of the milk shake*)

JEROME: Ain't that a healthy breakfast, chocolate shake. Hey. Thought you had to go out, big appointment.

PRIX: Gotta do the inventory some point. Long as I'm waitin'— (*Eyes on clock radio*) When the fuck—?

JEROME: If you was smart you'da put your time inside to some kinda trainin', no need it have to be total waste but no. Your brain too much the street.

PRIX: Since they recently slashed the higher ed, I'm left with these options: specialize in shampoo, specialize in relaxers. I say I liketa specialize in Class B pyrotechnics. They say Ha ha, real likely they apprenticeship a felon with explosives.

JEROME: Boo hoo life so hard. Least you had counselin', school. I got nothin', dropped out and into the army, pulled in by the college promise, then they fine-print robbed me out of it. And the kinda job trainin' I got be real useful. Next time some country invade New York. Think I sit around woe-is-me? Always found somethin', *legal*. Street cleanin' janitor—

(*Phone rings.*)

JEROME: One time—

(*Prix makes a brief shush-noise gesture, glaring at him. Phone rings a second time, third. At the first sound of the fourth, she picks up. Lets the other person speak first.*)

PRIX: Oh, you.

JEROME: Maybe I wa'n't Daddy a the Year but I offered support, legal.

PRIX (*into receiver*): I was hopin' it was them, you're late. Come up, I gotta go.

JEROME: What, you think you be up for the complementary daughter award? You sure ain't the gran' prize! Your own mama, seven years and you ain't writ, ain't seen her, not since that probation officer enforce ya, sixteen.

PRIX (*into receiver*): I ain't got time, Comet.

JEROME: But then how couldja visit. Never bothered find out what prison she been moved to. Five years back.

(*Prix hangs up, obviously cutting off Comet. She puts on jacket, takes the gun back, then pulls from her jacket pocket a little notepad. She studies it.*)

JEROME: You ain't got that intercom fixed yet? All this time, still somebody gotta announce theyselves by the cross-the-street pay phone? Then you guess how long it take 'em get back across, buzz 'em in.

(*Prix, paying no attention to Jerome, pushes the buzzer and holds it a few seconds.*)

JEROME: Lucky. So far. You ain't been to jail since that year in juvie, and your auntie move into your apartment, bigger 'n hers, hold it for ya 'til ya get back. Be there when ya get out, family company. But, released, your damn attitude drive her out after four months, get caught your business this time you be put away *years,* and who you think hold on to your home this time? No one! Gone! (*Knock at the door*) Ain't twenty-four bit old still be playin' gang gal?

(*Prix glances through the door peephole, begins undoing the various door locks.*)

JEROME: You goin' back. Lucky, you been kickin' all six years since you got outa teen hall and your blind parole police ain't suspected a thing, but sometime you goin' down, I got a prediction for your life: jail—second home.

(*Prix, who's finished unlocking, relatches a lock.*)

COMET: PRIX! (*Pounding*)

JEROME: No, first.

PRIX: WAIT!

(*Pounding stops. Prix walks to the closet and opens it.*)

PRIX: Here's a present.

(*Prix takes out a cupcake with a candle, which is obviously a stick of dynamite.*)

JEROME (*pleased*): You remembered.

PRIX: I better let her in 'fore she breaks it down. You light the candle later.

(*Jerome smiles and exits. Prix opens the door. Comet enters. During her speech, the sudden reflection of various colored lights/fireworks comes from Jerome's direction. Prix notices without expression. Comet doesn't see this.*)

COMET (*drops into a kitchen chair*): Jesus givin' me all that shit for bein' late then take ten minutes to open the goddamn door! And I *told*ju in the first place I might be five minutes' delayed cuz my mother gotta come watch the baby I *do* have kids you know. And don't say Jupiter, ten years old, I ain't one a them damn mothers turn her oldest into babysitter. And the baby teethin', hollerin'—

PRIX: Needja to answer the phone.

COMET: You called me over here for that? When you gettin' a fuckin' cell phone, Prix? (*Prix, looking over her notes, ignores Comet.*) Why me?

PRIX: Cuz you on the payroll.

COMET: Call me all the way over here—

PRIX: They left a message on the machine, I better be here 11 to 11:30 cuz they be callin', they leave no number for me to call back. Meanwhile I have another appointment, pickup I gotta do now.

(*Prix pulls a backpack out of the closet, starts emptying it.*)

COMET: So fuckin' sicka this. Thought kids I'd give up the life. Welfare sure don't cut it. I gotta gangbang supplemental income for the luxuries: food. Diapers.

PRIX: Let it ring three times, *exactly three times.* The moment you hear the fourth ring start pick it up. Say nothin', they'll talk. Take notes. (*Tears relevant pages out, tosses rest of the pad to*

Comet) At the end they say "Got it?" you say "Got it." And you *have* it. (*Stares at Comet; no response*) *Okay?*

COMET: *Okay!*

PRIX: I'll be back fast they may not even call by then. Right on the corner. Five minutes.

(*Prix shuts the door behind her. Comet looks around, bored. Turns on the radio and searches 'til she finds a station she likes. Eventually the phone rings. Comet quickly turns off radio. Phone rings three times, then stops ringing. Comet is freaked, doesn't know what to do. Picks up receiver, then quickly puts it back. Eventually phone begins ringing again. She is confused, panicked. As the third ring commences she snatches the receiver, listens. Gives a little cry.*)

COMET: Shit! Shit! Shit! Shit! Shit!

(*She stares at the phone, crazy. Prix enters, sets her backpack down.*)

PRIX: They call?

(*Comet doesn't answer. Prix looks at Comet.*)

COMET: THREE! rang three times and I was waitin' for the fourth but it STOPPED! God it STOPPED and I was scared I miscounted or they miscounted or they toldju wrong then it started ringin' again GOD! God Oh Jesus I thought Oh Jesus Should I pick up? should I—I did! I—I guess I was afraid it would stop ringin' again so I guess I picked it up picked it up too soon JESUS! Oh JESUS they hung up! I picked it up JESUS I'm SORRY, Prix! Jesus they hung up I'm sorry, Prix.

(*Prix, seething, glares at Comet. Finally she begins to speak but before any words come out, the phone rings again. They both stare at it. At the top of the fourth ring Prix snatches the receiver and the pad. Comet's entire body relaxes. Prix jots down notes.*)

PRIX: Got it.

(*She hangs up. She sits in a chair, not looking at Comet. Thinking. Quiet.*)

COMET: Prix—

PRIX: 'Bye, Comet.

(*Comet goes to the door and opens it. Then suddenly she turns to Prix.*)

COMET: I ain't just nothin', Prix! Know that's whatchu think soft, Soft Comet, still cries at movies still cries at funerals, I don't want it! I never asked to be boss, Prix! You act like I'm failin' at ambition, Prix! I'M HERE! WHERE I WANNA BE I never asked for nothin' but a little stash to sell, just get me my kids by. I ain't got your leadership quality, Prix, don't name me worthless just cuz my personality don't got what yours does: the ice.

(*Comet exits. Prix stares thoughtfully after her for a while. Then she opens the bag and pulls out new vials. Silently she counts.*)

Scene 2

Prison cell. Prix and Denise in prison uniforms. Denise putting sponge rollers in her hair. Prix lying supine on her upper bunk staring at the ceiling. A personal letter out of its envelope lays flat on her belly.

DENISE: Four years we been together, I assumin' you got nary a friend in the world. Then ha ha, joke on me: here come a letter. That the first you had since you been in, right? (*No answer*) I seen the return. 'Nother prison. But can't be nothin' too excitin', no big deals bein' made cuz sure thing they tore 'at sucker open, read it, must be personal, I heard you's all alone in the world, who you got personal? (*No answer*) How come you got no kids? How ol' you, twenty-eight? By the time I was twenty-eight I had six and pregnant with number seven. I heard 'boutchu. I know 'boutchu but the rumors conflict. You been with it all, men, women, dogs. Flip side: never been touched. Which? (*No answer*) Come on! I got a cigarette bet on the former. Betchu lost your virginity early in the day, how ol'? thirteen? Twelve?

PRIX (*dry*): Five.

DENISE: *Yes!* Terror terror. You was one of 'em, right? I done a little damage my day but you was a biggie I hear. Pre-eighteen but you knew when to stop. Get the hardcore felonies erased, your permanent record. You be out soon, three years, right? Three be gone 'fore ya know it. I ain't even be parole eligible for at least next five.

PRIX: Two. (*Denise puzzled*) My sentence was six. Served four years I be out two.

DENISE: See! no time. My steady assignment was undercover, fool the white people, let the ATM people feel safe, thinkin' this white girl in with 'em. "Just don't open your mouth, Paley," what my girls call me, "don't open your mouth 'til you pull the knife cuz soon's you part them pink lips your cover be blown: projects all over!" (*Guffaws*)

PRIX (*as Denise laughs*): You *are* white.

DENISE: How I be white, onliest white people I ever see is TV. Teachers. Fifth-grade bus trip to the museum. Might be born white how I stay white no role models. (*Beat*) I don't mean to be in your business but I couldn't help but notice the return: same last name.

(*Long pause.*)

PRIX: Mother. Junkie. Started in jail I guess Never touched it when I knew her.

DENISE: When you knew her?

PRIX: Last time . . . sixteen.

DENISE: You was *sixteen?* Ain't seen her *twelve years?* (*No answer*) She wrote to tell you she's a junkie?

PRIX: Wrote to tell me AIDS. Early release. Pro bono.

(*Pause*)

DENISE: Not me. Not my kids, whatever happens . . . Every Tuesday I see 'em, once a month my mother, we stickin' it out, the family ties we—

(*Sudden teenage laughter, rowdiness, in the corridor. Denise rushes to the bars to see. After the young women pass, it is quiet again. Then:*)

DENISE: I like the Ladies' groups. You like 'em? The counselin', classes. I missed my 8:30 readin' class this mornin' and sat in on the adolescents' 10 o'clock to make up. Rowdy! Forgot how rowdy they get, way *we* was SO glad not to be around that no more, so glad not to *be* that no more. Least Ladies got *some* kinda respect, 'preciate we know how to be: polite to each other, quiet to each other. With them two new ones now we got nine, nine's a good group.

PRIX: Eight.

DENISE: Ain'tchu precise with the numbers today! Too bad you weren't so quick when ya screwed up the codes yesterday breakfast.

(*Pause.*)

PRIX: *What?*

DENISE: I heard that girl servin' the slop take your tray, tap it three times, plop the scrambled eggs your plate, tap the tray seven times. Three *seven*. Then I heardja pass by that other bitch and out the side a your mouth, "Thirty-*eight*."

(*Prix stares at her.*)

PRIX: She tapped eight times!

DENISE: I could see where you could make the mistake. She did somethin', took a little breath space between third and fourth taps and your mind accidentally filled in the extra.

(*Prix stunned, confused. Then looks at Denise, about to protest.*)

DENISE: Yeah. I'm sure.

PRIX (*incredulous*): She fucked me up. She fucked me up!

DENISE: Ain't the first time this month neither. Messin' up, tell ya, I useta be in it but when my babies startin' comin', *retire.*

And gettin' into a fuckup habit's one sure sign you bess do the same.

PRIX: Wait. That deal went down yesterday afternoon. I seen her yesterday evenin'. You're the one that's fucked up, if I'm screwed I'da sure knowed it by now.

DENISE: You're screwed. I overheard. She just waitin' for the moment.

PRIX: How do you know?

(*Denise doesn't answer. Prix yanks Denise's head back.*)

PRIX: *How do you know?*

DENISE: I just heard it! I ain't with nobody no more!

(*Prix still holds Denise's head back a few moments, then lets go.*)

DENISE: That's the point. On the outside lookin' in, comfy chair. Sit back, watch the sparks fly without bein' one of 'em. From my viewpoint, I can predict it all.

PRIX: She's gonna kill me, fuck.

DENISE: Predicted you'd mess up. When I was in it, thirty-seven meant shipment pickup in the laundry room, thirty-eight the gym. Guess things changed by now?

PRIX: She's gonna kill me! fuck!

DENISE: You been in it too long, in it too long ya lose it. O.G. everybody want it. O.G. Original Gangsta, shit. You earned that years ago, what you stick around for? Ain't twenty-eight bit old for the gangs? (*Grabs hair*) I'm gonna cut all this shit off. My hair get curlier when it's close, and them close cuts all sophistication. (*Pause*) When you said you was gonna make a fireworks show. You serious? (*No answer*) I sure as hell couldn't. Set a thing up, then see one a them hot sparks fly off, come fallin' down right on top a ya *no!*

(*Pause.*)

PRIX: Scariest is the opposite. Black shell. Send it up and somethin' go wrong: it don't explode. And in the blacka night,
you can't see where it's fallin'. You know that live explosive's
on the way back down, right down to ya. You just can't see
where it's comin' from.

Scene 3

*Denise sits on a bench smoking, watching Socks push a broom. Denise's
broom stands idle against the wall near her. Socks is bent and gray, her
face barely visible; she doesn't look into others' eyes. She has some teeth
missing, and gives the impression of a person who has aged too quickly,
who is really much younger than she appears. She speaks to no one in
particular.*

SOCKS: I useta have kids. I had three and the welfare took two, I
can't remember what happen to that other boy. His daddy!
that's what, motherfucker fought for him then wouldn't let
me come close. Yaw, shit! yaw should get a god-damn vacuum cleaner, how this thing s'posed to clean up all this shit?
Damn, how many straws left in this fuckin' thing, three?
Daddy, his goddamn motherfucker daddy took him. What
was that motherfucker's name?

C.O. (*off*): Get to work, Denise!

DENISE (*Mumbling to herself*): I ain't workin' with that ol' crackhead, you must be outa your damn—

C.O. (*off*): WORK!

(*Denise, pissed, lazily pushes the broom, no rhyme or reason.*)

DENISE (*simultaneously with Socks's next line*): My shift over five
minutes What's the goddamn point I start now? *hate* this
fuckin' job! hate workin' with fuckin' addicts and AIDS . . .

SOCKS (*Simultaneously with Denise's previous line*): Remember,
runnin' he ram that nail up his foot? You say "We take it out
It be fine" Bull-shit! I know what to do—emergency room:
tetanus. What planet you on?

DENISE (*continuous, louder*): *Shit,* Socks, you're sweepin' your goddamn dust on my toes!

(*Prix enters.*)

DENISE: Glad you're here, relieve me, nothin' 'round here but fuckin' addicts and AIDS. (*Prix takes Denise's broom, starts sweeping, ignores Denise.*) Ain'tchu lucky you got switched out the kitchen. This nuthouse crackhead, and guess who I was stuck with before her? *Socks! you sweep shit on my feet again I lay you out!* Some dumb ol' smack bitch, done the needle once too much now got the full-blown, this ain't a penal colony, it's a leper colony. (*Starts to leave*)

C.O. (*off*): Stay there, Denise.

DENISE: *What?*

C.O. (*off*): *Stay there.*

DENISE: Shit! what is it now. Guess I ain't worked hard enough for 'em guess they expect me to do some other goddamn job, I ain't no goddamn slave. (*Sits. Beat.*) You know two a the counselors quit. Just like the six others this year 'cept they ain't found a replacement yet, this means tomorrow's counselin' group got the goddamn adolescents mixed in, our nice quiet adult session have present the damn disruptin' brats.

C.O. (*off*): Toilet cleanin'.

DENISE (*To C.O., incredulous*): *Who?* (*Gets the answer*) Fuck! Fuck fuck fuck!

(*Denise exits. Socks and Prix push brooms in silence awhile. Eventually Prix absently sweeps near Socks.*)

SOCKS: Outa here! Outa here! that's your place here's mine, I ain't come close to you You don't come close to me! Space!

(*Socks goes back to work, sweeping more rapidly than before. Prix stares at her, stunned.*)

PRIX: Malika?

(*Malika [Socks] instantly stops pushing the broom, stares at Prix, terrified. Silence.*)

PRIX: Prix.

(*Malika continues to stare at Prix, confused as to what to do.*)

MALIKA: I gotta go to the bathroom. (*Pause*) I GOTTA GO TO THE BATHROOM! I GOTTA GO TO THE BATH-ROOM! I GOTTA GO TO THE BATHROOM! I GOTTA GO—

C.O. (*entering*): Okay, Socks, shut up!

(*C.O. snatches Malika's arm and starts to escort her off but Malika pulls back.*)

C.O.: Hey!

(*Malika hesitantly touches the C.O.'s metal name pin, sees her reflection in it. She glances in Prix's direction then exits with C.O.*)

Scene 4

The table with partition from Act One, Scene 3, this time Mother sits on the visitors' side. A C.O. nearby. Mother may appear a bit ill but has tried to look her best, perhaps over-doing the makeup a smidge. An uncomfortably long silence. Eventually Mother, tense, pulls out a compact mirror, checks her lipstick: The C.O. glances at her watch. Mother instantly jumps, snaps. Throughout Mother's speech the C.O. is unmoved.

MOTHER: Made up your mind, right? She's not comin' right who ast ya? Time, she got 'til five so shut it! Shut up all your comments, judgments, judge me *nerve!* Some nerve you got don'tchu *dare* label me, us you know nothin' you think Well how long she gonna sit? She been here since starta visitin' hours one P.M. don't she gotta go to the bathroom? I stay here 'til five I haveta, which is all I ast a you, tell me when

it's five (*C.O. looks at watch.*) no other reason you need to
open your mouth, snortin' like you got it all figured out,
our relationship, mother–daughter, nunna your biz—

C.O.: *Five.*

(*Mother is startled. She gathers her mirror, lipstick, purse. Exits.*)

Scene 5

*Prix is using the bathroom, her feet visible beneath the stall. Two
teenage girls enter, get in line for the bathroom. Prix is in prison garb, the
girls in street clothes.*

PEPPER: She's all snotty, like, "No one should be in here for
parole violation." I'm like "Mrs. Garcia, I couldn't help it."
She's like, "That's stupid, Pepper, all you had to do was show
up 4 o'clock like you s'posed ta." I'm like "Bitch, you *know*
where the goddamn juvenile office is *Told*ja I be crossin'
lines get myself killed," she's like, "Thought you weren't in
it no more." How stupid is she? Like just cuz I decide to quit
today the enemy conveniently get amnesia, don't remember
last week I was gang? Shit.

GIRL: She just ain't gettin' it regular. (*Both girls giggle.*)

PEPPER: Fuck, you always say that.

GIRL: The other day fiddlin' with her purse I saw her pull out a
condom. She put it back real fast hopin' no one noticed.

PEPPER: If she carryin' protection around I guess she gettin' it
regular.

GIRL: Women gettin' it regular has their men carryin' it around.
Woman gotta carry it herself just hopin' for a accidental
emergency. (*They're laughing bigger.*) She know I saw too, I
saw the look—

(*Jupiter enters. Pepper and the Girl immediately fall to silence, not looking at each other. The stall door opens: Prix sees Jupiter. Jupiter gives*

Pepper and the Girl a look. They push Prix back into the stall, slamming the door behind them. Sound: Pepper and the Girl punching and kicking the crap out of Prix. Jupiter keeps watch outside, then finally opens the door: the audience sees Prix being beaten severely.)

JUPITER: Okay.

(*The violence ceases.*)

JUPITER: Liked your speech. (*The girls giggle.*)

PRIX (*struggling to speak*): You didn't like it.

JUPITER: Pulled the heart, teared the eye. (*Long e in "teared"*)

(*Prix mumbles.*)

JUPITER: What?

PRIX (*still struggling against the pain*): Ancient. Years ago I wrote it, today remembered . . . few words, today . . . matters.

JUPITER: Matters to who? Pile a shit The Ladies liked it. The Ladies listen like you the prize poet Ladies The Ladies how the fuck old are ya ole ladies? Thirty?

PRIX: Twenty-eight.

JUPITER: Speak, Twenty-eight.

PRIX: You're fourteen. I came to your christenin'.

(*Jupiter violently raises Prix to her knees.*)

JUPITER: Speak!

PRIX: The accepting, nonjudgmental atmosphere of my group has allowed me to reevaluate my choices . . . helped me to see my errors attributable to . . . to upbringing as well as personal choice sometimes . . . Sometimes I think if I had been shown one kindness . . .

(*Prix stops. Pepper and the Girl, who have been rolling on the floor, gales of laughter, become quiet when they realize Prix has stopped.*)

GIRL: You didn't finish it.

PEPPER (*more eager than unkind*): Say the best part. Say it!

(*Prix gathers her strength.*)

PRIX: On this day . . . we are sisters—

(*The girls whoop it up.*)

PEPPER AND GIRL: "My sisters" "My sisters"!

(*Jupiter stares at Prix as the other girls roar.*)

JUPITER: You say that so fuckin' serious like you believe that crap.

(*Long pause.*)

PRIX: I don't.

JUPITER (*eyes still on Prix*): Get the fuck outa here.

(*Pepper and the Girl are confused. Jupiter glares at them. They exit quick.*)

PEPPER: Sorry, Jupiter.

JUPITER: Get up.

(*Prix does.*)

JUPITER: Usually I ain't s'hands off, don't order no one kick the
    shit outa someone without I'm right there in with 'em, but
    doctor said I gotta watch the physical stuff. First trimester.

PRIX: Sorry, Jupit—

(*Jupiter snaps open the toilet, puts Prix's head in and flushes several
times. She snaps Prix's head out and immediately pulls a razor from her
own mouth, puts it against Prix's throat.*)

PRIX (*choking*): Your mother . . . Your mother—

JUPITER: My mother fuck! Like I ever see the bitch between jail
    and the fosters *good!* And each time I'm took away she
    wanna bawl and bawl like she so Christ fuckin' sad fuck her!

Don'tcha be mentionin' her fuckin' stupid name to me
Don't be bringin' up no goddamn Comet!

PRIX: Your third birthday, she show me the shoppin' bag. Pooh
bear.

(*Jupiter glaring at Prix. Then suddenly slams Prix's head against the
back of the toilet.*)

JUPITER: Original Gangsta.

(*Jupiter exits laughing.*)

Scene 6

*Picnic table. Angel clears the remnants of dinner. A pattern that repeats
every few seconds: Prix looking into the sky, Angel looking at her watch,
Prix looking at her watch.*

ANGEL: Few broken ribs. There was this blod clot, scared us
awhile but then it cleared up. Told us they figure he be
released Tuesday. (*To kids in distance*) LET GO A HIM!
HEY, HE WOULDN'TA BEEN DOIN' IT TO YOU IF
YOU WEREN'T DOIN' IT TO HIM FIRST! And they
still chargin' him, resistin' arrest, how the fuck when they
ain't got a scratch and his body covered in blood? shit. I
don't know why he don't get ridda that damn car anyway,
he been stopped harrassed three times in four months ain't
he figured out yet cops don't like a black man drivin' that
make a car? GET DOWN! I TOLDJA STAY OUTA
THAT DAMN TREE! Guess your parole officer set you
up, some real excitin' job.

PRIX: Burger King.

ANGEL: He ain't like you and me, my brothers . . . Like Vince,
total innocent, football, *A*s and *B*s then walk into them
drive-by bullets. And Darryl. Darryl ain't done a wrong
thing his whole life, nothin' but take care a his girlfriend his

kids, which what sent him to jail first time. Illegal sale a food stamps ooh ain't they cheatin' on the taxpayers, ain't the taxpayers so mad he cheated thirty bucks this month feed his kids while business people writin' off two-hundred-dollar lunches every fuckin' day a the week but yeah, taxpayers pay that, that's fine, that's legal.

PRIX: Clear night.

ANGEL: Worst is sentenced him to lifetime a welfare, every time my baby brother try for employment, can't get past the application question: "You ever been convicted of a felony?" Why you keep lookin' at your watch?!

PRIX: Why you?

ANGEL: Somethin' up my sleeve *told*ja! Surprise!

(*A vague snicker from Prix, then:*)

PRIX: When?

ANGEL: Don'tchu worry about it I'll letcha know. When it's ready I'll letcha know. My question: what train you got to catch?

(*Beat.*)

PRIX: Daily check-in. She said she be in the neighborhood on the hour *don't be late.* If I get sent back sure ain't be cuza violation a parole.

ANGEL: My plans!

PRIX: Won't take more 'n a minute I ain't leavin'. (*Mutters slight chuckle*) Plans.

(*Beat.*)

ANGEL: Run into Comet the other day, supermarket. Big as a house. Invite me to her baby shower, Sunday. Wanna go?

(*For the first time Prix looks right at Angel.*)

PRIX: I ain't never in my life uttered a kind syllable to Comet now why you think she want me at her shower?

ANGEL: You useta go to that shit. "Free cake" you say.

PRIX: Only invited cuza office politics, me her boss. Then. (*Beat*) Why you invite me to this? Your oldest fourth grade and I ain't never bothered to meet none of 'em 'til today I ain't exactly close family.

ANGEL: Third grade. My mother thought it be nice to ask, havin' the picnic anyway why not make it a Welcome Home Prix. She called to work, your moms not feelin' well, all this food . . . (*Beat*) Didn't expect ya to accept. (*Chuckles*) First you don't. "Prix, you liketa come?" "No." Thirty seconds you call back, "Yes. I'll bring some chocolate chips." Why you change your mind?

PRIX: I dunno. Five weeks outa jail, somethin' to do 'sides work. TV.

ANGEL (*Beat*): Nice, delayin' things this year. Quiet. We in this spot every Fourth GIVE IT BACK! and the park wall to wall packed. Not all bad the kids chicken pox in bed over the holiday, here we are now, space and peace. (*Angel takes out a photograph, hands it to Prix.*) Happy Twenty-sixth a July.

(*Prix studies the photo.*)

PRIX: Where was *this?*

ANGEL: Our old old apartment. Don't remember it? (*Prix shakes her head no.*) We were six, first grade. Sonia was seven, Darryl three. And Vince! All us standin' fronta the tree like we told but big brother, Mr. Independent, gotta be on the bike.

PRIX: I remember those decorations. Yaw ever buy any new ones? Same ol' glitter bell, same ol' star. 'Cept . . . looks so new. (*Chuckles*) Darryl! That baby grin, people always tellin' babies to smile, only thing they know how to do is show their teeth and grit 'em.

ANGEL: Like your smile was any realer. Prix the Sad Sack, even if
we Freeze Tag even if we double-dutch you one a them kids
always got somethin' unhappy behind all the giggle-play.

(*Prix studies the picture more closely.*)

PRIX: I'm smilin'.

ANGEL: Look at it.

(*Prix studies the picture again. Now she sees it and, as best she can,
suppresses the sudden, painful memory. Then looks at her watch.*)

PRIX: Time.

(*Prix snatches her empty backpack, looping it on one shoulder, and
quickly gets up to leave.*)

ANGEL: I *knew* it! I *knew* it!

PRIX: What?

ANGEL (*clutching part of the backpack*): You makin' a connection!
Month out and already you back. Not around my kids! I left
it years ago, Prix, I grew up!

PRIX (*mutters as she exits*): You don't know what you're talkin'
about.

ANGEL (*calling to Prix*): Don't I? *I* learned somethin'! *I* learned
somethin'!

(*Angel starts clearing table again, slamming stuff.*)

ANGEL (*to kids*): COME ON, YAW, WE LEAVIN'!

(*Angel continues clearing. Then, aware that the kids have ignored her:*)

ANGEL: COME ON!

(*Prix returns with a stuffed backpack. Angel sees.*)

ANGEL: Fuck you, Prix! I don't *know* you Ain't settin' *me* up
guilt by association GO! Bring that shit around my kids (*To
kids*) COME ON! (*To Prix*) Fuck you! Fuck you! Fuck—

(*Prix has unzipped the bag for Angel to peer in. Angel does, and is surprised. Prix pull out a rocket, touching it tenderly.*)

PRIX: I got it planned. This ain't the big show I always wanted, Class B, but I do okay with these home 'works, aerials and fountains and Roman Candles, rockets, still meticulous with the color effects, style. Whole show won't be five minutes, I could drag it out make it last and everyone waitin', waitin' anticipatin' the next shell but the excitement, the euphoria is in the momentum don't drop it. I paint the emotional rhythms, some calmer than others these peaks and dips important to prevent monotony, just never let drop the thrill to nil.

(*Angel, fascinated, pulls out a few of the fireworks and looks them over.*)

ANGEL: My kids regret I call they pay me no mine when I tell 'em what they missed. (*Still fascinated, then*) Hey! These can't explode by touch can they? My hands kinda hot and sweaty ain't gonna light no fuse, right? Mushroom cloud?

PRIX: When it's over . . . You ever see what it's like, enda the big Fourth show, East River? Two types a people. First is the two million who seen it, walkin' in a daze a beauty high. Harmony. Second is the people in the cars waitin' for the harmony heads–in–the–clouds people to cross the damn street, beepin' and all fury, impatient anyway but now hoppin' mad cuz they confused: How come pedestrians ain't gettin' mad right back? Cuz just when we thought couldn't get no more radiant no more splenderous than it already has it does, sometimes so high I wish it *would* stop, I think can't nobody stand this much . . . beauty? No. Ecstasy.

(*Prix studies the sky. Then looks at Angel.*)

PRIX: Stand back.

(*Angel exits. Prix walks around a bit, anxious, preparing herself. Then stoops. Lights a match. The fireworks. Prix stares. Elation. Sound: slow* squeaky wheels. Prix looks to the approaching sound. Jo enters in a squeaky wheelchair. Slowly turning, Prix stares at her.)

JO: You done it.

(Prix smiles. Then she sees Jo's eyes, she looks at the wheelchair: it dawns on her. Prix begins shaking her head.)

PRIX: No . . .

JO: YOU DONE IT!

PRIX: NO! Done what? I don't know you!

JO: You know me.

PRIX: Don't!

JO: YES!

JO'S FRIEND (entering): C'mon, Jo.

JO: She says she don't know me!

FRIEND: She knows you.

PRIX: I don't!

FRIEND: Bitch! she knows! (Prix vehemently shaking her head.)

JO: You sixteen, me seventeen, the zoo. (Prix blank) BRONX ZOO! REPTILES!

PRIX: I DON'T REMEMBER!

JO: She says she don't remember!

(Angel enters.)

FRIEND: Fucker!

PRIX: I don't know, I don't—

JO: She don't remember!

FRIEND: BITCH!

PRIX: It mighta happened! I ain't sayin' it didn't happen, a lotta
       stuff . . . Long time ago, lotta stuff blur I don't remember it
       all! Lotta stuff I did Don't remember it all! (*Friend wheels Jo
       off.*) DON'T REMEMBER IT ALL!

(*Just before Friend gets Jo off, Jo pushes Friend's hands away and, with
great effort, turns 180 degrees around to face Prix. She stares at Prix a
long time, and Prix stares back until she can't stand it. She looks away.*)

JO: This ain't the half of it.

(*Jo turns back around, wheels herself off, accompanied by Friend. Prix
stares where they exited, then swings around to Angel.*)

PRIX: I don't remember her! (*Angel says nothing.*) You know her?
       I don't! I don't remember her! (*Angel says nothing.*) It ain't
       s'posed to be like this! It ain't . . . if we had differences,
       gone! Gone, You ever see the Fourth, East River? *Every-*
       body's happy, everybody, no anger! No anger! (*Beat*) I didn't
       do 'em right. Maybe I done 'em wrong musta put the
       wrong colors together, clashed some colors dampered the
       emotional scheme WHAT'D I DO?

(*Pause.*)

ANGEL: It's time. Come on.

PRIX: You remember her? (*Angel shakes her head no.*) I know! I
       had two greens together, too much repetition too much
       cool. I fucked it up.

ANGEL: Maybe she just crazy.

(*Prix turns to Angel quickly. This suggestion gives her great hope. Just
as quickly she is disappointed when she sees that Angel doesn't believe
what she just said. She turns back to stare in Jo's direction.*)

PRIX: I ain't callin' her a liar just . . .

(*Pause.*)

ANGEL (*exiting*): It's time. Come on.

(*Prix continues to stare after Jo. Finally she turns around. Angel is gone. Confused, she looks for Angel in the dark. In a narrow space, Prix is startled to find Angel and a hugely pregnant Comet.*)

PRIX: Comet . . .

(*Comet gives Angel a look. Prix, suddenly feeling surrounded and terrified, gives an unconscious cry, backing up. Comet and Angel pull out from behind their backs several of Prix's colored pen lights and form fireworks for Prix. Prix suppresses her sobs.*)

Scene 7

34th Street and 5th Avenue. Prix's Mother, tired, weak, on the corner. The lights of the city reflect upon her, particularly the blue and yellow of the Empire State Building, as she stands right in front of it. Prix enters. Her voice is flat, expressionless, if she has worried at all about her Mother, she conceals it well.

PRIX: What.

MOTHER (*pleased*): Found me! (*The effort to speak sends her into a coughing fit.*)

PRIX: Your goddamn note was pretty specific, 34th and 5th. Half expected to see your guts splattered where you're standin' why the hell else you be at the Empire State Buildin' midnight.

MOTHER: *Almost* midnight. Remember? (*Prix stares at her, still expressionless.*) Lights out! Midnight, they turn off the Empire State.

PRIX: You come all the way down here for that. (*Mother grins.*) Let's go. (*Turns to leave*)

MOTHER: *NO!* Wantchu to see.

PRIX: I believe you, come on.

MOTHER: You don't believe me.

PRIX: If ya gone to all the trouble a comin' down here to prove
it must be true. Come on, we'll watch it on the way to the
subway, you know they space the trains half-hour apart after
twelve. (*Mother won't budge.*) They got me on the goddamn
breakfast shift I gotta be there goddamn five A.M. prepare
the goddamn powdered eggs and biscuits. We leave now and
if the odds with us, no wait for the train, maybe we make it
home by one, maybe I get a luxury three hours' sleep.

MOTHER: I hate they give you that job! That's parole board's idea
a keepin' you outa jail, can't support yourself plus they know
you got me, how they speck you to survive?

PRIX (*more to herself*): I found a little supplemental income.
(*Mother scared*) Don't flip I ain't in it no more just here and
there: sell a few food stamps, bitta herb. Don't freak.
Retired. Thirty pretty old to still bang in the gangs. (*Beat*)
How much longer?

MOTHER: Seconds.

(*Prix, hands in jacket pockets, leans against a pole.*)

MOTHER: What day's today? I mean, what's blue and yellow?

PRIX: Nothin'.

MOTHER: Somethin'.

PRIX: Nothin'. Red Valentine's, red and green Christmas, red
white and blue Fourth, people start assumin' every Empire
State color combo means somethin'. 'S arbitrary, every day
ain't a holiday but Empire still gotta be lit.

MOTHER: 'Til midnight.

(*Pause.*)

MOTHER: You ever thinka him?

PRIX: Who?

(*Mother looks at Prix. Now Prix understands who Mother means. She is
startled to realize she hasn't thought of him.*)

PRIX: No. No, useta. Useta think about him all the time. Not lately. Not in years.

(*Pause.*)

MOTHER: Different. Was a time you'da seen that note from me, tossed it in the trash, gone 'boutcher business. Seems you different all growed up, seems you ain't s' mad no more. (*Prix says nothing.*) These colors. They nice together?

(*Prix studies them.*)

PRIX: Blue and yellow, cool and warm. Sweet. Fireworks, blue's hardest color to mix.

MOTHER: Shoot. Nursin' a little bitta flu, 'f I'da known 'boutcher fireworks show . . .

(*Beat.*)

PRIX: Didn't work out. Think I keep it a spectator sport from now on.

MOTHER: We go to the fireworks, I can't hardly look at 'em. Busy starin' at your face. The wonder, happy happy. And best is when it's over, after the last big boom the moment the lights all out, I see in your eyes a . . . sweetness. Calm after the joy storm.

(*The sixteen-note church bell's hour tune begins, followed by the twelve tolls. Soon after the tune starts, Prix speaks:*)

PRIX: Midnight.

MOTHER: Wait.

(*They watch in silence a few moments.*)

MOTHER: Prix. What happen to all your artwork? Fireworks things.

PRIX: Angel saved the pen lights. Rest got lost or thrown out while I was in jail.

MOTHER: Them figures? Pipe cleaners?

PRIX: Gone.

MOTHER: Useta always be new ones, you constant re-creatin'.
How come you ain't replaced 'em? I don't ever see ya doin'
your sketches no more, that was your one thing, one thing
hope you ain't lost interest. (*Prix says nothing.*) I wisht I'da
kept one. Wisht you still made 'em pipe cleaner figures I
wisht I had one for me. (*Pause*) Prix. I know . . . I know you
ain't much into grantin' favors but . . . (*Pulls much change
from her pocket*) I found some money today, I thought—

PRIX: I toldju not to do that! Panhandlin', Jesus! we ain't fuckin'
beggars!

MOTHER: I just thought, maybe you can't afford the pipe cleaners, maybe that why you don't do it no more.

PRIX: Do I look like I got time to fool around, arts and crafts?
Grown woman.

(*Beat. Then Mother holds out coins to Prix.*)

MOTHER: Prix. You make one? For me?

(*Prix, pointedly looking at the building, away from her Mother. She
shakes her head no. Mother stares. Then, sudden and desperate:*)

MOTHER: PRIX! YOU MAKE ONE? FOR ME?

(*The force of her emotion causes Mother to drop her coins. She falls to her
knees to pick them up. Prix starts to help but Mother violently waves her
away. Prix gazes at her Mother, for the first time in the play really seeing
her. Mother gathers most of the money, then stops. Just after the twelfth
and final bell toll, Mother lifts her face to look at Prix.*)

PRIX: Yes.

(*The lights of the Empire State Building go out.*)

COLLECTED STORIES

by Donald Margulies

Influence is simply a transference of personality,
a mode of giving away what is most precious to one's self,
and its exercise produces a sense and, it may be,
a reality of loss.
Every disciple takes away something from his master.
Oscar Wilde, *The Portrait of Mr. W. H.*

Time is the school in which we learn,
Time is the fire in which we burn.
Delmore Schwartz,
"Calmly We Walk Through
This April's Day"

Collected Stories was produced by Manhattan Theatre Club (Lynne Meadow, artistic director; Barry Grove, executive producer) in New York City, on April 30, 1997. It was directed by Lisa Peterson; the set designer was Thomas Lynch; the costume design was by Jess Goldstein; the lighting design was by Kenneth Posner; the sound design was by Mark Bennett; the dramaturg was Paige Evans; and the production stage manager was Jane E. Neufeld. The cast was as follows:

RUTH . . . . Maria Tucci
LISA . . . . Debra Messing

Collected Stories received its world premiere at South Coast Repertory (David Emmes, producing artistic director; Martin Benson, artistic director) in Costa Mesa, California, on October 29, 1996. It was directed by Lisa Peterson; the set designer was Neil Patel; the costume design was by Candice Cain; the lighting design was by Tom Ruzika; the sound design was by Mitchell Greenhill; the dramaturg was Jerry Patch; and the stage manager was Cari Norton. The cast was as follows:

RUTH . . . . Kandis Chappell
LISA . . . . Suzanne Cryer

Collected Stories was commissioned by South Coast Repertory and was developed there as well as at the Sundance Institute Playwrights' Lab in 1995. The author is grateful to all the folks at those places, particularly Jerry Patch and Lisa Peterson, both of whom were there at the beginning and helped him find a play amid a motley handful of pages.

CHARACTERS

RUTH STEINER   55–61
LISA MORRISON   26–32

SETTING

Ruth's apartment in Greenwich Village,
1990 to 1996

SCENES

ACT ONE
SCENE 1:   September 1990
SCENE 2:   May 1991
SCENE 3:   August 1992

ACT TWO
SCENE 1:   December 1994
SCENE 2:   October 1996
SCENE 3:   Later that night

ACT ONE

Scene 1

Late afternoon. September 1990. The Greenwich Village apartment of Ruth Steiner, a writer, who looks every bit her fifty-five years. She is reading a short, typed manuscript while dipping mondel bread in tea. A jazz station is on. She makes notes in the margins. The downstairs buzzer sounds. She finishes making her notation. The buzzer sounds again. With no urgency, she gets up, opens the window—with difficulty; it sticks—and calls to the street below.

RUTH: Hello-o-o. Hello? Up here.

LISA (*three stories below, barely audible*): (Oh, hi! Lisa. Remember?)

RUTH: I'm throwing down my key.

LISA: (What?)

RUTH: The buzzer doesn't work, I'm throwing down my key.

LISA: (What? I can't—)

RUTH (*waving a key ring*): My key, my key! I'm throwing down my key!

LISA: (Oh! You want me to let myself in?)

RUTH: Yes! (*Mostly to herself*) That's *just* what I want you to do. (*Calls*) I'm throwing it down. Back up, I don't want to hit you!

LISA: (What?)

RUTH: I don't want to *hit* you, back *up!* (*To herself*) Jesus . . . (*She tosses the key ring out the window.*) By the tree. The *tree.* No no no. Yes yes!

LISA (*overlap*): (Got it!)

RUTH: Good! Three-F.

LISA: (What?)

RUTH: Apartment Three-F! F! (*To herself*) As in fucking-can't-believe-this.

LISA: (What?)

RUTH: F! F! F as in Frank! Three-F! (*She ducks her head back in; to herself*) Is it me or is she deaf? (*She tries to shut the window, but it's stuck.*) Oh, for God's sake. . . . (*Ruth continues to struggle in vain to shut the window. Soon, Lisa Morrison, twenty-six, breathless from her trek upstairs, appears at the front door, which had been ajar all along.*)

LISA: Professor?

RUTH (*her back to Lisa; working on the window*): Yes yes! Come in!

LISA (*pushes open the creaky door, sees Ruth*): Hello! I'm sorry I'm late.

RUTH: That's all right.

LISA: I hadn't checked my mailbox? So I just got your note we were meeting *here* and not in your office like fifteen minutes ago?, and practically *ran* all the way? And then on top of that I got lost . . . ?

RUTH (*still struggling with the window; preoccupied*): Mm. Yes. Well.

LISA: You need help with that?

RUTH: Why, yes! As a matter of fact I do. See if you have any better luck with this, will you, dear?

LISA: Sure.

RUTH: The damn thing's warped and I'm freezing. (*Lisa puts her bookbag down on a chair and crosses to the window. Ruth wraps a throw blanket around herself and watches Lisa work on the window.*)

LISA: It's stuck.

RUTH: I know it's stuck; it sticks. These goddamn old windows. . . .

LISA: Have you got a screwdriver or something?

RUTH: A screwdriver?

LISA: Yeah, *you* know, to like. . . . (*Lisa continues to try to maneuver the window while Ruth exits to the kitchen and rummages through drawers.*)

RUTH (*off*): There's a particular angle, I've found it before. . . . You have to . . . If you jiggle it just right. . . . My arthritis. . . . (*Ruth returns with a metal spatula.*) I couldn't find a screwdriver; try this.

LISA: A spatula?

RUTH: Yeah, see if you can. . . . (*Lisa wedges the spatula between the window and the frame.*) There you go. . . . (*Lisa manages to get it closed.*) Excellent! Thank you, thank you.

LISA: Hey, no problem; I do windows. (*A small laugh, then*) So. Hi.

RUTH: Hi. (*Picks up Lisa's assignment.*)

LISA: It's nice to *be* here. I mean, I was beginning to think I was never gonna find this place.

RUTH: Oh, really? Why? It's not that difficult.

LISA: I know, but you know how you're walking along and all of a sudden West Twelfth and like West *Some*thing Streets intersect?

RUTH: Oh, yes.

LISA: And it's like, "*Wait* a minute?, what is going *on* here?" Like *Alice Through the Looking-Glass* or something.

RUTH: Mm. Yes.

LISA: Anyway, this is such a neat place. It's so nice of you to have me over.

RUTH: Have you over?

LISA: *You* know what I mean.

RUTH (*continuous*): I hardly think of this as "having you over."

LISA: I know. I meant . . .

RUTH (*continuous*): This isn't exactly a social call.

LISA: I know.

RUTH (*continuous*): I *do* this from time to time: meet with my students *here*.

LISA: Uh-huh.

RUTH (*continuous*): Mainly because I'm a terrible slug. And if *one* of us has to schlep, it may as well be you; you're younger.

LISA: No, what I meant was, it's so nice to be in a real *home* for a change, where a real person actually *lives,* with real furniture and books and art and stuff? I mean, graduate students? They just don't live in *real* places with *real* histories. My apartment? I mean, it's so makeshift and sad. Milk-crate bookcases and ratty old furniture. Completely lacking in *dignity.* And the surfaces are always sticky?, because nobody really cleans up after themselves. (*Ruth is looking at her intently.*) What.

RUTH: *You're* Lisa?

LISA: Yes . . . ?

RUTH: Lisa Morrison?

LISA: Uh-huh?

RUTH: *You* wrote "Eating Between Meals"?

LISA: Uh-huh. Why?

RUTH (*shows her typescript*): You wrote *this?*

LISA: This is my tutorial—remember we had a tutorial?

RUTH (*over ". . . we had a tutorial?"*): Yes yes, I know, but isn't that funny, I thought you were someone else.

LISA: What do you mean?

RUTH: You're not who I thought you were; I confused you with another student.

LISA: Oh.

RUTH: I really should start paying attention to those goddamn seating charts; my memory is shot to hell. I had someone *dark*er in mind. In *all* respects. I decided that Lisa Morrison had to be that *serious* young woman.

LISA: Oh.

RUTH: That mousey Anita Brookner type, the one who never makes eye contact.

LISA (*thinks, then*): Janet?

RUTH: That dreary *dark* girl with long bangs that look like she trims them herself by chewing on the ends, who wears those terribly long tartan skirts.

LISA: Janet Spiegel, yeah.

RUTH: *That's* right, *that's* Janet *Spieg*el. Now why did I think she was you? (*Lisa shrugs; a beat.*) Hm.

LISA (*jocularly*): Are you disappointed?

RUTH: What?

LISA: I mean, that I showed up looking like *me* and not like Janet?

RUTH: No no, it's just that you don't particularly look like your story. Very often, almost without exception, my students tend to *look* like their stories.

LISA: Hm. Isn't that interesting.

RUTH (*continuous*): I've prided myself for years for being able to match the student with the story. It's a game I play with myself. I'm so rarely wrong.

LISA (*self-effacing*): So you're saying I don't look very serious?

RUTH: What?

LISA: No, that's okay. I'm just curious. You said you thought the person who wrote the story was a *serious*-looking person, that's what you said. So am I *not* a serious-looking person?

RUTH: Young lady. . . .

LISA: No, I'm curious. Am I?

RUTH (*a beat*): No; you're not.

LISA (*wilts slightly*): Oh. (*A beat.*) But, wait: If you thought the story *I* wrote was written by a serious person. . . . Does that mean you thought it was a serious story?

RUTH (*a beat*): Perhaps. (*A beat*) Can I offer you anything?

LISA: Um, yeah, sure. Thanks.

RUTH: Tea, or . . . ?

LISA: Actually, I would *love* a cup of coffee.

RUTH: Well, actually, I don't *have* coffee.

LISA: Oh.

RUTH: I don't drink coffee. I have *tea*. . . .

LISA: Oh, okay, I'll have tea.

RUTH: English Breakfast?

LISA: Do you have any herbal?

RUTH: No, I have English Breakfast.

LISA: English Breakfast'll be fine.

RUTH: Good. English Breakfast it is, then. (*She smiles, goes to kitchen.*)

LISA (*calls*): Thank you. (*She winces to herself at her faux pas; silence; she looks at the bookshelves, picks up an old leather-bound volume.*) Oo, what a beautiful edition of *Middlemarch*. . . . My copy is falling apart, I've read it so many times. . . . (*She briefly looks at it, returns it to the shelf, continues browsing. She finds a story collection by Delmore Schwartz.*) Wow, *In Dreams Begin Responsibilities; I love In Dreams Begin Responsibilities.* (*She flips through the book.*) I love where he's dreaming he's in the movie theater watching his parents' courtship on the screen? And just as his father proposes to his mother he shouts out . . . ? (*Finds the passage.*) Here it is: (*Reads quickly*) "Don't do it. It's not too late to change your minds, both of you. Nothing good will come of it, only remorse, hatred, scandal, and two children whose characters are monstrous." I *love* that. (*Finds an envelope stuck in the book.*) Oh my God! Is this letter really from Delmore Schwartz himself?!

RUTH (*off*): Put that back, please.

LISA (*over ". . . please"*): Oh, I'm sorry. . . .(*Flustered, she puts it back.*)

RUTH (*off*): That's all right, just put it back.

LISA (*calls*): Sorry. (*Pause. She sees a book splayed open by Ruth's chair.*) Oh, Jane Smiley. Supposed to be really really good. These are novellas, right?

RUTH (*off*): Yes. (*Lisa steals a look at Ruth's comments on her typescript. The phone rings. It rings again. She isn't sure what to do.*)

LISA: Phone! Hello? Professor? Ms. Steiner? Do you want me to get it?

RUTH (*off; unperturbed*): No no. (*The ringing continues. Ruth enters with a cup of tea and snack food on a tray.*)

LISA: Oh, thank you! (*The ringing continues.*) Is your machine working?

RUTH: My machine?

LISA: 'Cause it's ringing a *lot*. Shouldn't it pick up after like four or five rings?

RUTH: I have no machine.

LISA: Oh. You have no machine? Really? Wow.

RUTH: Why? What do I need a machine for?

LISA: I don't know. . . . I mean, I would think, someone as important as you . . . ? God, how do you live without an answering machine?

RUTH: If it's work-related, they'll call my agent. If it's my agent, she'll know to call back later; my friends would know the same.

LISA: What if it's an emergency?

RUTH: I have no children, my parents are dead. What could possibly be so urgent? (*The ringing continues.*)

LISA: Look, why don't you just answer it and tell them you'll call them back?

RUTH: I don't want to answer it; why should I answer it? I have company.

LISA: Oh. Who?

RUTH: You.

LISA: Oh. Right. (*The ringing stops.*)

RUTH: See that? Couldn't've been *that* important. (*Lisa smiles, samples a piece of mondel bread.*)

LISA: Mm. This is good. What is it?

RUTH: Mondel bread.

LISA: Mondel—?

RUTH: Jewish biscotti. (*She demonstrates by dipping the cookie.*)

LISA (*smiles*): Oh. (*She dips one and spills some tea.*) Oo, shit. I'm sorry.

RUTH (*hands her a napkin*): That's quite all right.

LISA: You know, I'm really much more together than this—

RUTH: *Are* you—

LISA (*continuous*): —But I'm like really really nervous?

RUTH: Are you really? Why is that?

LISA: Why?! Because I can't believe I'm *here,* okay? I can't believe I'm sitting in Ruth Steiner's apartment, on Ruth Steiner's sofa?, sipping tea with Ruth Steiner?, out of Ruth Steiner's china teacups?

RUTH: Oh, come now. . . .

LISA: No, I mean, this is where you wrote *The Business of Love,* isn't it?

RUTH: Well, here, and on the Vineyard. A lot of places. On buses, in restaurants, on the Broadway local. But, yes.

LISA (*refers to a framed print*): This is the Matisse that hangs over Lydia's bed in "All the Wrong Places."

RUTH (*impressed*): Yes.

LISA: I remembered the dancers; she imagines herself dancing with the dancers at the end.

RUTH: That's right.

LISA (*at the window*): And that's the playground where Joanna's little boy in "The Silent Child" falls and gets a concussion, isn't it?

RUTH (*a beat*): Well, yes, it is.

LISA (*a beat*): Eric.

RUTH: Eric?

LISA: The little boy's name: Eric.

RUTH: I'll take your word for it.

LISA: How long have you lived here?

RUTH: You don't want to know.

LISA: Yes I do.

RUTH: A very long time.

LISA: Like ten years?

RUTH: No, more like thirty-one.

LISA: Wow. Thirty-one. So, you wrote every story you practically ever *wrote* here, didn't you?, under this roof, in these little rooms. These are the books you read. . . .

RUTH (*amused by her reverential tone*): Oh, please. . . .

LISA (*continuous*): This is the floor you paced. This is the view you saw from your window.

RUTH (*flattered*): Oh, knock it off. I think you're going a little overboard, dear, honestly.

LISA (*over ". . . dear, honestly"*): Why, you think I'm sucking up to you?

RUTH: Well, it *has* occurred to me, yes. . . .

LISA: I don't mean to. What I'm trying to tell you, Ms. Steiner, in my very clumsy stupid way. . . . Being here?, studying with you . . . ? It's like a religious experience for me. (*Ruth laughs.*) No, really, it *is*. I mean, your voice has been inside my head for so *long,* living in this secret place?, having this secret dialogue with me for like years? I mean, ever since high school when I had to read *The Business of Love* . . . ? I mean, from the opening lines of "Jerry, Darling," that was it for me, I was hooked, you had me. I knew what I wanted to do, I knew what I wanted to be.

RUTH: Oh, dear, I did all that?

LISA: Yes! I read all your stories, all of them, like five or six times? I devoured them. I couldn't get enough, I kept wanting more. I even went to the library?, to look up your uncollected stories?

RUTH: Oh, my, that *is* devotion.

LISA: I sat there one day and read whatever I could find.

RUTH: There's a very good reason why they remain uncollected.

LISA (*disputing Ruth*): Oh, no. They all have wonderful things in them. All of them. The three in *The New Yorker?*, the ones in *Ms.* like from the early eighties?, that amazing one in that *Esquire* summer reading issue?, *you* know: the Coney Island lifeguard one? *The Kenyon Review?*

RUTH: Yes yes yes.

LISA: So if I seem like a sycophant or an idiot or something it's only 'cause I'm trying to tell you what a privilege it is to be breathing the same airspace as you, that's all. I write much better than I talk so I probably should just shut up.

RUTH: Yes. I mean, yes, you *do* write better than you talk. (*A beat.*) Where'd you do your undergraduate work, Lisa?

LISA: In New Jersey?

RUTH: Uh huh. Where in New Jersey?

LISA: Princeton?

RUTH: Yes, I think I've heard of it. (*Glances at her watch.*) Jesus. . . . We'd better. . . . (*meaning, deal with the story*)

LISA: Of course.

RUTH: Otherwise I could so easily see myself pissing away my entire afternoon. . . .

LISA (*disarmed, embarrassed*): I'm sorry. (*Gets out a notebook and pen.*)

RUTH: Just listen first.

LISA: Hm?

RUTH: Why don't you try listening?

LISA: Oh. Okay.

RUTH: Don't immediately start writing down everything I say. Listen. Digest.

LISA: Okay. But what if I forget? I mean, I might forget something you say that's really important.

RUTH (*over ". . . really important"*): If you forget, it probably wasn't worth remembering in the first place. Not everything I say is going to be clever or wise, you know.

LISA: Uh huh.

RUTH: You may think I'm full of it and that's okay, too. *You're* going to have decide for your*self* what is useful criticism and what is not. I'm not a *doc*tor, you know, I don't dispense prescriptions: If you do such-and-such and such-and-such, your story will be perfect. It doesn't work that way.

LISA: If only it were that easy, huh?

RUTH: I'm not going to tell you *how* to write because I *can't,* I don't pretend to know myself. Writing can't be taught.

LISA: Do you really believe that?

RUTH: As far as I'm concerned, the university is taking your money under false pretenses. (*Lisa laughs.*) *Tal*ent can't be learned; it's innate. People who tell you otherwise are not to be trusted; they're snake oil salesmen, all of them.

LISA: John Gardner said— Did you know him?

RUTH: A little; he wasn't my type.

LISA: Well, he said something like, "Genius is as common as old shoes." Do you think that's true?

RUTH: Oh, that is sheer and utter bullshit. Everybody and his idiot cousin's a goddamn genius: Please. Never pay attention to what writers have to say. Particularly writers who teach. *They* don't have the answers, *none* of us do. The good ones ask the right *questions*, that's the key. The ones who aren't so good, well, they have their own agendas, something that usually has to do with ego gratification. All I can do as an artist who teaches, is Tell You What I See, feed back to you what I see as a kind of reality test and ask the right questions.

LISA: Do you really resent it?, I mean, having to teach?

RUTH: No! I en*joy* it.

LISA: But don't you hate that it takes you away from your work?

RUTH: I don't mind. I rather like the distraction. For one thing, it gets me out of the house. Which is not a small thing. It gets me talking about what I do—hell, it gets me *talk*ing, period. Otherwise I'd be alone far too much, and remain *si*lent far too much, and I'm alone enough as it is. You develop bad habits when you spend too much time alone.

LISA: Really?

RUTH: You're the absolute monarch in your own little kingdom. You have to answer to no one. That's a very dangerous thing for a creative person. Teaching keeps me honest. It keeps my brain active. I'm forced to be critical, to put on my thinking cap. I have to say *some*thing, so I find something to say.

LISA: Is it true you need a new assistant?

RUTH: What?

LISA: I heard you need a new assistant.

RUTH: Yes.

LISA: I heard she graduated and you haven't picked a new one yet.

RUTH: That's correct.

LISA: Can I apply? I mean, are you taking applications or do you already have somebody in mind?

RUTH: No, I don't have anybody in mind.

LISA: Well, then, can I apply?

RUTH: You can do whatever you like. It's not exactly a glamour job. I can be a totally despotic employer.

LISA: I don't care.

RUTH: You don't, huh. Well, look, we've gotten off the track here. We're here to talk about *this* (*meaning the manuscript*). All right? Let's talk about "Eating Between Meals." (*Lisa takes a deep breath.*) I like your title, by the way.

LISA: Oh, yeah? Thanks.

RUTH: It's a good title. I wish I'd thought of it.

LISA: Really? You don't think it's too on the nose? I mean, for a story about bulimia?

RUTH: No, I like it. I think it's got a nice healthy sense of irony.

LISA: Thanks. Yeah, I kind of liked it, too.

RUTH: Do you have a new story in the works?

LISA: Um, yeah, I think I do.

RUTH: Good.

LISA: It's about a divorced dad? Who takes his twelve-year-old daughter to Disneyland with his new girlfriend? And the three of them share a hotel room?

RUTH (*over ". . . share a hotel room?"*): Wait wait wait. Don't *tell* me.

LISA: What?

RUTH: Don't tell me about it, write it, I don't want to hear it.

LISA: Oh. Okay.

RUTH: (*continuous*): Telling takes away the need to write it. It relieves the pressure. And once that tension dissipates, so does the need to relieve it. First write it, then we'll talk about it.

LISA: Okay.

RUTH (*proceeding*): Okay, let's see what we've got here. . . .

LISA: Um, the story's kind of autobiographical?

RUTH (*feigning surprise*): No!

LISA: I guess that was a stupid thing to say, huh? It's obvious, right?

RUTH: It's not that it's obvious, it's inconsequential. I don't care what the basis of a story is as long as it's a good story. Now: Let's look at your opening paragraph.

LISA: Uh huh.

RUTH: Where your protagonist . . .

LISA: Jessica?

RUTH: Yes, where Jessica goes into the supermarket.

LISA: Uh huh.

RUTH: Who *is* Jessica?

LISA: Who *is* she?

RUTH: I don't really have a sense yet of who she is. Tell me about her.

LISA: You mean you really want me to . . . ?

RUTH: Yes.

LISA: Oh. Well. . . . (*A beat.*) Um . . . She was like the baby of her family? Had two older brothers she adored who were like ten and twelve years older?, who babied her to the point of domination and then went away to school and as far as she was concerned abandoned her?, left her all alone to deal with her infantile, incompetent parents just as their marriage was turning into an ugly suburban nightmare? Who was pampered and pretty and all that but felt worthless and undeserving anyway?, and would do anything for attention, even if it meant hurting herself? (*A beat.*) Like that. Does that help?

RUTH (*impressed by what was revealed*): Yes. (*Reads*) "The automatic door sprang open. I entered into a world of plenty—"

LISA (*over "... of plenty"*): Wait a second, you're gonna *read* it?

RUTH: Yes.

LISA: Out loud?

RUTH: Yes. Why?

LISA: Oh, it's just, I don't know, I didn't know you were gonna read it *out loud.*

RUTH (*over "out loud"*): Lisa, you're going to have to get used to hearing your own words. We're going to begin reading aloud in class next week.

LISA: You mean we're gonna be reading our own stuff?!

RUTH: Yes.

LISA: Oh, God, you're kidding.

RUTH: If *you* can't bear to hear your own words, how can you expect anybody else to?

LISA (*a groan*): Ugh. I'm a terrible reader. I have a terrible voice.

RUTH: It's not about performance, it's about responsibility, about claiming ownership. That's very very important.

LISA (*sighs*): Okay.

RUTH: All right? Are you going to survive this tutorial, or are you going to require oxygen?

LISA: No, I'm okay. (*She closes her eyes.*)

RUTH (*reads*): "The automatic doors sprang open. I entered into a world of plenty, a cornucopia of temptation, of sustenance and sin, where the music of love was Muzak and anything was possible." (*A beat.*) Hm.

LISA: What.

RUTH: Let's think about that phrase for a minute: "anything was possible."

LISA: Yeah . . . ?

RUTH: I don't know, there's something terribly *weak* about that phrase.

LISA: Really? Weak? I'm sorry.

RUTH: "Anything was possible." It feels too general, I think, it's unsatisfying.

LISA: Huh.

RUTH: I like "the music of love was Muzak," I like that, I like "the world of plenty," "cornucopia of temptation," that's all very nice. Just think about that one phrase; give it a little more thought. Good.

LISA: Can I write this down?

RUTH: All right, if you must. Okay. (*Reads*) "I took a red plastic basket from a 'help-yourself' stack and made my way through the crush of harried women pushing shopping carts loaded with unruly toddlers, past precarious towers of brightly packaged foods."

LISA (*a beat*): What.

RUTH: That sentence. Maybe it's all those bloody adjectives. Look at that: You've got a *shit*load of them: "harried . . . unruly . . . precarious . . ." *Lose* some of them. You don't *need* all that. Less *is* more, for Christ's sake. (*Reads*) "Food was everywhere." Thank God.

LISA: What.

RUTH: A blessed three-word sentence. (*Reads*) "The endless walls of cereal boxes in primary colors made me think of Christmas." Good. Nice. Clean, clear, specific, evocative. (*Increasingly impressed as she reads*) "In the condiment aisle I encountered an overweight little girl, her mouth and pink jogging suit smudged with chocolate, spinning herself around like a sugar-crazed dervish, her mad dance ending only when she dizzily collided with a wall of gerkins. Three glass jars toppled in rapid succession, exploding onto the linoleum like fabulous green water balloons. Shards of glass glistened among the garlic pickles. The girl looked up, saw me, and grinned, delightedly, before taking off down the aisle, leaving her mortified mother and the briney mess behind her." (*Pause. Lisa is smiling, pleased with what she hears. Ruth, impressed, looks at her differently; rereads it to herself; with admiration.*) ". . . *fabulous* green water balloons." Hm. I love that girl. Where did that little girl come from?

LISA: Oh, her? That's me. It's a true story. Only it wasn't pickles, it was ketchup. I thought ketchup might be too, *you* know.

RUTH: Yes. Do you know what you did here? (*Lisa shrugs.*) You really don't, do you?

LISA: I don't know, I guess I was struck by this idea of encountering myself as a child? You know? Like this spectre in the supermarket? This fat girl with chocolate on her face spinning wildly and making a mess of things and pissing her mother off and not *caring* she was pissing her mother off, but rather en*joy*ing it?

RUTH: Yes. That's right. (*A beat.*) Did you have any sense at all as you were writing it: "this is good, this is going well"?

LISA: Oh, I don't know, maybe.

RUTH: Sure you did. You must have. We all experience that. It's part of the thrill. It's when the muse takes over and one is channelling for the muse. (*A beat. Back to the story.*) "The ice cream was displayed in a long corridor of frosty glass cases, like precious Etruscan vases in a museum." Now, here I have a question for you. Are you familiar with Etruscan vases?

LISA: Not overly, no. I mean, I've *seen* them?

RUTH: Uh huh. I would think about that image. Why *Etruscan* vases?

LISA: Why Etruscan?

RUTH: Yes, why not just *ancient* vases or *Greek* vases or whatever? What is it about *Etruscan* vases?

LISA: I don't know, I like the word?

RUTH: Uh huh. It's a very nice word, isn't it, but why don't you go to the Met and sit with the Etruscan vases for a while and get acquainted with them? See if that's what you really mean to say.

LISA: You mean it?

RUTH: Absolutely. We must never be arbitrary. There is so much goddamn arbitrariness in the world, we mustn't let it seep into our stories. God, not our stories. They're just too damn important. We mustn't devalue our stories with flippancy. That would be the death of us all.

LISA: God, that makes like so much sense? (*Writes in her note-book*.)

RUTH: Hm. (*A beat, a breath, a shift*) Um, Lisa?

LISA: Did you not want me to write?

RUTH: No no, that's not it. (*A beat.*) Do you mind if I ask you something?

LISA (*equivocally*): Uh, okay. Sure. (*Pause.*)

RUTH: Why do you talk like that?

LISA: Excuse me?

RUTH: You have a tendency to add question marks to the ends of declarative sentences. Do you know that?

LISA: Oh, God. . . .

RUTH: When a simple, declarative sentence will do, you inflect it in such a way. . . . When I asked you where you got your bachelor's, you didn't simply say, "Princeton," a statement of fact, you said, "Princeton?" You hear how my voice went up?

LISA: I can't believe I'm still *do*ing that; I *used* to talk like that, when I was younger.

RUTH (*over "... when I was younger"*): I didn't mean to embarrass you, I thought you could shed some light. I'm not saying you do it all the time but you do it often enough for me to notice. And it's very striking because you're obviously an intelligent, gifted young woman but it's really kind of *dopey,* if you ask me.

LISA: It is, it really is; it's awful.

RUTH: You're not alone. Most of my students speak this way. I'm not absolutely certain but I think more young *women* speak this way than young men. And there's something almost *poignant* about it, all these capable young women somehow begging to be heard, begging to be understood. "Can you hear me?" "Are you with me?" "Am I being heard?"

LISA: I know.

RUTH: You've all cultivated this common dialect of American youth. A nonregional, national dialect.

LISA: Uh huh.

RUTH: Students from the backwoods of Georgia sound the same as students from Chicago, or Great Neck.

LISA: Is it television do you think? (*A beat.*) That was a question. I mean, I think it *is* television.

RUTH: Probably. Why not? We blame television for everything *else* that's going to hell in our society, why not this, too?

LISA: It's a vicious circle, I think: television portrays young people in a certain way, young people watch a lot of television. . . . And it's really insidious. Like a media conspiracy to undermine youth or something.

RUTH: But you kids are complicit in this! Role models are *chosen!* You're selling yourselves short!

LISA: By sounding like a bunch of airheads?

RUTH: Yes! Listen to yourselves! Nobody's going to take you *seriously* in the real world! Who's going to take you seriously if you talk like that? No one! Why should they? If I were you, I'd do everything I could to erase it from my memory; expunge it from my speech center. The moment you hear yourself doing it, stop and correct yourself. Pretend I'm your mother telling you to stand up straight: Tell me to drop dead but do it. You'll thank me for it one day, believe me. All right, let's get on with this, we haven't even gotten through the first page.

LISA (*over ". . . the first page." Blurts, mustering all her courage*): So do you think I'm any good?

RUTH: What?

LISA: Never mind.

RUTH: Do I think you're any good? (*Lisa nods. A beat.*) Well, it's a bit early to say, don't you think?

LISA (*over "don't you think?"*): Yeah, but, still, you must have formed *some* opinion by now. I mean, you've been doing this a long time, right?

RUTH: Twenty-odd years.

LISA: Right, so I'll bet your antennae are pretty well tuned. You know it when you see it, right?

RUTH (*amused*): This is your first tutorial!

LISA: I know.

RUTH (*continuous*): Ask me again six months from now.

LISA: My parents, of course, think this is the most ridiculous thing I've ever done and I've done plenty of things in the realm of the ridiculous. I'd hate to give them the satisfaction. Please, I just need to know if you think I'm wasting my time. Am I? That's all I need to know. (*Pause.*)

RUTH: No, I don't think you are. (*Lisa sighs audibly.*) I wouldn't re*tire* just yet if I were you. You have a lot of work to do. An awful lot. But the *stuff,* I think, is there.

LISA: The stuff? Really? You think I have the stuff?

RUTH: It's very raw, mind you. But yes.

LISA: Oh, God. You're not just saying that?

RUTH: Why would I say something like that if I didn't mean it?

LISA: I don't know, because I'm paying like all this tuition?

RUTH (*charmed, laughs*): No, rest assured: I'm a terrible liar. (*Back to the story. Reads.*) "My eyes grew wide in the dazzling fluorescence. As I—"

LISA: Is there an actual application form I need to fill out? Or can you just put my name on a list?

RUTH: Again with the job? Young lady, I don't know what you think this job *is; I* wouldn't want this job.

LISA: Why not?

RUTH: *Noodg*ing me about this and that, *doc*tor appointments, *con*ferences.

LISA: I can noodge.

RUTH: Listen, it's no great honor, believe me: keeping track of my mail, my schedule; keeping my office from teetering on the brink of chaos, which is where it already is.

LISA: Okay.

RUTH: I assure you, there are a lot better things to do with your time than baby-sit an old fart like me.

LISA: I don't care.

RUTH (*a beat*): Well, if you really want to apply. . . .

LISA: Yes?

RUTH: Apply through the office. Talk to Mrs. Gonzalez.

LISA: Mrs. Gonzalez?

RUTH: She has the applications.

LISA: Okay. (*Ruth shrugs, sips her tea. Pause. She continues reading.*)

RUTH: "My eyes grew wide in the dazzling fluorescence. As I reached inside the icy freezer for the Macadamia Brittle, my heart beat quickly in feverish anticipation, as if I were preparing for a tryst with a lover and not for an after-school binge." (*A beat.*) Nice.

Scene 2

May 1991. Night. Lisa is puttering in the apartment, sorting through piles of books and papers, making them more orderly. We hear keys jingling at the front door. She excitedly goes to it.

LISA: Oh, hi! Wait! Hold on a sec. . . . (*She unlocks the door. Ruth enters carrying overnight bags.*)

RUTH: What are you doing here so late?

LISA: I got your mail and watered your plants and stuff and decided to stick around and wait for you. Welcome home! (*Lisa takes her bags.*)

RUTH: Thank you.

LISA (*continuous*): If you had told me what train you were catching, I would have met you at the station. You wouldn't have had to schlep so much.

RUTH: That's all right. I took a cab. (*She takes off her shoes, walks around in her stocking feet.*)

LISA: So! How was Washington? I mean, I *know* how Washington was: You were so fabulous.

RUTH: How do *you* know?

LISA: I saw you on C-SPAN.

RUTH: Oh, God, you're kidding.

LISA: Oh, no, you were so great.

RUTH: Really? How did I look?

LISA: You looked wonderful! You were so poised, and funny. They loved you.

RUTH: Who?

LISA: The committee.

RUTH: How could you tell? It was like talking to a convention of undertakers.

LISA: That was so funny when you said, "*You're* politicians. *I'm* a writer; we all have crosses to bear"? That was so great. You didn't seem nervous at all.

RUTH: I wasn't.

LISA: I would've been a wreck.

RUTH: It's all a show. All of it. I was just playing a part: the feisty older woman who cracks wise and gets away with saying just about anything. If she were alive today, Thelma Ritter would play me in the movies.

LISA: And what you said about "a few inches of immortality on the library shelf"? That was beautiful. God, when you talked about how you nearly gave up writing to work for that plumbing company?! I didn't know that happened.

RUTH: It didn't.

LISA (*a beat*): What do you mean?

RUTH: It didn't happen.

LISA: But you said. . . .

RUTH: Yeah, I know.

LISA: You mean it isn't true?

RUTH: There are *elements* of truth in it—I *did* do office temp work and I *was* offered a full-time job at a plumbing supplies company and I *did* get an NEA grant—but never for a moment did I seriously contemplate giving up writing.

LISA: Well, then, why . . . ?

RUTH: Why did I say that?

LISA: Why did you lie?

RUTH: I didn't lie. I exaggerated.

LISA: Isn't that the same thing?

RUTH: Tell me: Would I have made a compelling case for the National Endowment—before the House of Representatives—if I had simply recounted the facts of my career? Absolutely not. Where's the drama if there's nothing at stake? (*While looking at her mail*) So, using the elements of truth, I spun a tale. I threw a crisis into the mix and allowed myself to be rescued at the eleventh hour by the U.S. Cavalry. I exaggerated. What is art if not an exaggeration of the truth? Made a good story didn't it?

LISA: Oh, yeah, God. (*A beat. Re: the mail*.) I sorted everything. Mail that looked important out here, and everything else. . . . Boy, you sure do get a lot of catalogues and junk. More than I do, even. (*Ruth dumps a pile in a wastebasket*.) I would've thrown all that out but I wasn't sure if you liked looking at catalogues. I mean, some people do.

RUTH: How long have you been here?

LISA: A few hours. No, more than that. I came over to water the plants and stuff.

RUTH: So you said.

LISA: I stayed and read here a while. I confess. It's a good thing I was here: You got so many calls! So many people were expecting to leave a message on your machine, but then of course I'd have to explain you don't *have* a machine, so then we talked about *that*. . . .

RUTH: Who called?

LISA (*gets messages*): I couldn't believe it! Norman *Mailer* called, Susan Sontag. . . .

RUTH: Oh, yes? How is Susan? I haven't spoken to her in quite a while.

LISA: She seemed fine. I couldn't believe I was *talk*ing to these people! Ed Doctorow. See? (*Shows her that message*.) I couldn't believe it, he said, "Tell her *Ed* Doctorow called to send his love and appreciation." "Ed." I was talking to "Ed." It was surreal. All these literary giants on the other end of the telephone! Don't worry, Professor, I tried not to embarrass you. I didn't gush too much—or, at least, I don't *think* I did; I didn't want them to think you'd hired an idiot for an assistant or anything. But they were all really so nice.

RUTH: Are you surprised?

LISA: No. They just seemed so . . . *normal.*

RUTH: I wouldn't go *that* far. (*She begins to stash some letters on her desk but, disoriented by its lack of clutter, stops.*) What happened to the pile that was here?

LISA: Oh, I straightened up.

RUTH: Oh, no! Why the hell did you do *that?!*

LISA (*becoming rattled*): Remember?, Before you left?, I asked if you'd like me to straighten up a little bit?

RUTH (*over ". . . a little bit?"*): Straighten up, yes. Reorganize my life, no; I did not authorize you to reorganize my life.

LISA (*over ". . . reorganize my life"*): I'm sorry . . . I really didn't do anything other than . . .

RUTH (*over ". . . other than"*): I thought "straighten up" meant you were gonna take a *schmatah* and dust! Dusting is something this place could use! How am I supposed to *find* anything now?!

LISA: Just ask me. What are you looking for?

RUTH (*Over "What are you . . ."*): *Ask* you?! I don't want to *ask* you. . . .

LISA: I'll tell you exactly where it is. I didn't throw anything out or anything, I just made neater piles.

RUTH: I didn't *want* neater piles, I liked my piles the way I had them.

LISA (*fighting back tears*): I'm sorry, I didn't mean to. . . .

RUTH (*continuous*): There *was* a method to my madness, young lady, which served me well most of my life, thank you very much.

LISA (*over ". . . thank you very much"; embarrassed, losing it*): I'm really, really sorry. I was only trying to . . . (*shuffling papers around*) I'll put everything back the way it was. . . .

RUTH (*takes papers out of her hands*): Just leave it alone! (*A beat. Lisa crumbles. Afraid that tears might flow, she gets her coat.*)

LISA (*softly*): Sorry. . . .

RUTH: Oh, shit, you're not gonna *cry*, are you. . . .

LISA (*tearfully; heading for the door*): No. . . . Well . . . Good night, Professor. Sorry for any inconvenience. . . .

RUTH: Oh, for God's sake . . . (*Calls*) Lisa. Hey. Get over here.

LISA: What. (*Ruth cocks her head; she wants Lisa to come back into the room. Lisa hesitates before she does. Pause.*)

RUTH: Thank you for checking my mail and watering my plants.

LISA: You're welcome.

RUTH (*going to her handbag*): Let me give you a check. . . .

LISA (*hurt, insulted*): No! I don't want a check!

RUTH (*getting out her checkbook*): No, let me. It was above and beyond the call of duty.

LISA: You don't get it, do you? Put it away (*the checkbook*). Please. (*Ruth does. A beat. Avoids eye contact.*) You know? All I want . . . (*Takes a deep breath.*) I want so much to please you. You know? And no matter what I do, it's wrong. I always seem to get your disapproval when it's the opposite I want so badly. All these months, ever since school started, it's been both wonderful and excruciating working for you. I mean, to be so close to you, when I admire you *so* much. . . . But every day I see you it's like a test: What faux pas will I make? What will I do that'll annoy her *today?*

RUTH (*compassionately*): No. . . .

LISA: Yes! It's true. There's always something. Some invisible line I've crossed. Or, or something I've bungled out of sheer panic.

RUTH: Panic?

LISA: Yes. You intimidate me so much. When I show you something I've written, or even when I *talk* to you I think, What value could *my* words possibly have to *her?*

RUTH: Oh, dear.

LISA: You're so . . . I mean, I *knew* you were difficult—you *told* me as much. But you really seem to take *pride* in being difficult, though, and that I don't understand. (*Stopping herself*) I've said too much. Look, maybe I'm just not cut out for this, you know? Maybe I'm not. My skin's not thick enough. Oh, well . . . (*She struggles to remove Ruth's key from her key chain, and then sets it down.*) I'm sorry I touched your things. I thought you would appreciate it; I'm sorry. (*Still not looking at her, she starts to head for the door.*) If you're hungry, there's dinner in the fridge.

RUTH: Oh?

LISA: It's nothing. I made a little tuna niçoise, that's all. If you don't like it, that's all right, just throw it out.

RUTH: I'd love a salad.

LISA: Good.

RUTH: Thank you.

LISA (*nods, then*): It's in the fridge. So whenever you . . .

RUTH: That was awfully thoughtful of you.

LISA: I figured you'd come home late and everything. . . . Well, enjoy it. (*Starts to go.*) Good night, Professor. See you in class. . . .

RUTH (*suddenly; stopping her*): Why don't you join me?

LISA: Oh. No. I couldn't do that. . . .

RUTH: Why, do you have other plans?

LISA (*shakes her head, then*): Not really.

RUTH: Is there enough for two?

LISA: I suppose.

RUTH: Then why don't you join me?

LISA: Um. . . .

RUTH: You wouldn't leave me all alone. Would you? Not on the night of my Washington triumph. Sit down. (*Lisa hesitates, then approaches the table. Ruth picks up the key, hands it back to her, and starts for the kitchen.*)

LISA: I can do that. . . .

RUTH (*over ". . . do that. . . ."*): No, no. Sit. (*Ruth exits. Lisa puts the key back on her chain and sits at the table. Ruth returns with food and plates on a tray. Lisa takes it from her. Ruth turns on the radio then joins her.*) Oh, this looks perfect! (*They set the table together in silence. Ruth helps herself, then passes the bowl to Lisa.*) Help yourself. (*Lisa takes the bowl and serves herself. Lights fade as they begin to enjoy their first meal together.*)

Scene 3

About a year later. August 1992. Sunday brunch. An electric fan is blowing. Ruth is seated; Lisa enters from the kitchen with a tray of iced tea, in the middle of a heated discussion.

LISA: Not only is it appalling that he seduces this . . . girl. . . .

RUTH: How do you know he seduced her?

LISA: Ruth! Of course he seduced her; he must've seduced her, it wouldn't've taken much; those photographs?! I'm sure she was in awe of him, this famous older man?; he took advantage of her youth and inexperience.

RUTH: Well, that's not very fair to her, is it. She's a thinking, feeling young woman. Isn't it possible they both fell in love?

LISA: Oh, please, Woody's not in love with that girl.

RUTH: How do *you* know?

LISA: How *could* he be? It's all about his narcissistic need for control, that's what it is. (*Ruth laughs.*) You know how he finds these women and remakes them in his image? They even start *talk*ing like him. Did you read her interview in *Time?* It's like all her answers were scripted. He put the words into her mouth, I'm sure of it.

RUTH (*amused*): *Lis*ten to you.

LISA: Anyway, not only is it appalling that he did it, but that he doesn't seem to think that there's anything *wrong* with it?! That's what's so galling. "No moral dilemmas whatsoever"! Did you see that in here? (*Meaning* Time) How could he find no moral dilemmas whatsoever?

RUTH: He wasn't looking, so he didn't find any.

LISA: His girlfriend's daughter?!

RUTH: Ex-girlfriend's daughter, a*dopt*ed daughter.

LISA: So what? He was still practically a father to her!

RUTH: Not her father, it's not the same.

LISA: Why isn't it? They were together twelve years! Most of this girl's life! If he wasn't her father, her father *fig*ure, then. And what about the twenty-five *other* kids she's got? How do you do that to them? He's fucked up a whole family!

RUTH: Now, now. He says he never looked twice at the girl.

LISA: If you believe that shit.

RUTH: Well, maybe it's true. Maybe she was there all along and he suddenly awakened one day to her irresistible charm.

LISA: What, like *Gigi?* (*Ruth laughs.*) Ruth, come on, this is aberrant behavior, don't you think? Hitting on your ex-girlfriend's daughter?

RUTH: When something like this happens, it's hypnotic, it's magnetic, it's irresistible. There is no reason. Reason and morality have nothing to do with it. Particularly when the girl is as naive and impressionable as . . . "My Lai" or whatever her name is. (*Lisa laughs.*) The allure of a famous older man is an incredibly powerful thing.

LISA: Well, *that's* provocative, Ruth.

RUTH: Yeah? Well, never mind, you. (*A beat.*) Why is gossip so delectable, anyway?

LISA: Gossip's gotten a bum rap. It's a neglected art form. Our new literature. It's got everything: mythology, spectacle, Oedipal drama, morality play. . . .

RUTH (*over ". . . morality play. . . ."*): Oh, I don't know, I think it's that we've all got this whopping case of *schadenfreude.* Gossip is fun. It's fun to watch the mighty stumble and fall. Let's face it. We gawk and gasp and click our tongues but deep down inside we're gloating our asses off.

LISA: I'm not gloating, I'm hurt.

RUTH: Why are you hurt? Why are you so personally affronted?

LISA: Woody was supposed to be the great moralist. The conscience of our age.

RUTH: Bullshit. Who said? A couple of critics? The guy makes some clever movies and already he's the conscience of our age?! Honey, nobody asks to be the conscience of an age. That's a hell of a thing to have to live up to.

LISA: I mean, at the end of *Hannah and Her Sisters,* what did he show us? That domestic happiness was finally possible, even for a loser like him. There was hope for all of us. And *now* look: It all turns out to have been a sham. I feel so betrayed.

RUTH: How were you betrayed? Lisa! I don't see it. The lines got *blurred,* that's all. You've mixed up the persona with the man. He's entitled to a private life, for God's sake. I don't give a shit what he does in private, I don't want to *know* about it.

LISA: Why are you defending him?

RUTH: I'm not defending him. . . .

LISA (*good-humoredly*): Yes you are. And I'm finding it very irritating, Ruth, I really am.

RUTH (*over ". . . I really am"*): I want to know why you're so worked up about this. It's more than a movie star misbehaving, obviously. You've forgotten he's a movie star. Movie stars misbehave all the time. Always have. That's what they do. That's why we invented them: So they could act out for all of us. It's not the misbehavior. It's what it represents.

LISA: Oh, thank you, Dr. Freud. So what are you saying? I'm still pissed at my father for leaving my mother?

RUTH: Uh, well. . . . Now that you mention it, darling. . . . (*Bingo.*)

LISA: All right, so? (*A beat.*) I went over all this with my shrink yesterday. A whole session on Woody, Mia and Daddy Dearest.

RUTH: Can you imagine the therapeutic impact Woody's little indiscretion is going to have?: *Thousands* of people, lying on couches, all over Manhattan, moaning to their analysts about it?

LISA: I couldn't be*lieve* the shit that poured out. Feelings of rage, betrayal, abandonment. Like I was twelve years old all over again. My father isn't talking to me, by the way.

RUTH: Oh, really, why?

LISA: I don't know. (*A beat.*) I gave him the Disneyland story to read.

RUTH: Oh, dear.

LISA: Yeah, and he hated it.

RUTH: Well, that's no surprise.

LISA: He was furious. "Katherine was so upset, she cried. How could you do that to her?" I didn't give the story to *Kather*-ine to read, I gave it to *him*. "Why would you want to hurt us like this? She's only gone out of her way to be nice to you, blah blah blah." Oh, God, it was horrible. I never should've written it.

RUTH: Well, that just wasn't an option; you *had* to write it.

LISA: Didn't I?

RUTH: Absolutely. The question is: Why'd you give it to him to *read?* Hm? It's not a very flattering portrait.

LISA: I know.

RUTH (*pokes at her affectionately*): So why'd you give it to him?

LISA: I don't know, I wanted him to read it.

RUTH: Why?

LISA: So he'd have *some* idea of what I'm doing. He has no idea. He hasn't read my stuff since high school.

RUTH: Well, the Disneyland story was a pretty tough introduction to your work, don't you think?

LISA (*over ". . . don't you think?"*): Yeah yeah, I suppose so. But I didn't want to be *secre*tive about it, that didn't feel right, either. I thought I was doing the right thing.

RUTH: What did you hope to accomplish? (*Lisa shrugs.*) To gain his respect?

LISA (*mostly to herself*): I don't know. . . .

RUTH: His approval? To show him what a good little writer you are?

LISA: I guess. Yeah; that's *exac*tly what I wanted: I wanted his approval. Pretty infantile, huh?

RUTH: Well, then why'd you give him this particular story? I mean, you could've given him one of the more *benign* stories to read if you were interested in having him read something, couldn't you?

LISA: Yes. . . .

RUTH (*continuous*): But you chose to go right for the jugular and I think that's very interesting.

LISA: If I'm gonna write what I know, it's inevitably gonna hurt some people's feelings, right?, somebody's feelings are gonna get hurt.

RUTH: True, that's a risk you're just gonna have to take. You can't censor your creative impulses because of the danger of hurting someone's feelings.

LISA: Even if it's my father's?

RUTH: Even if it is. If you have a story to tell, tell it. Zero in on it and don't flinch, just do it. You know the photographer Robert Capa? He took that famous picture of the falling soldier during the Spanish Civil War?

LISA: Oh, yeah. (*They both briefly mime falling backward.*)

RUTH: Right. He said about his work, "If it isn't good enough, I didn't get close enough." And the same could be said for fiction. You've got to get in there and shoot. I guess what *I* want to know is: (*A beat.*) Why'd you show him a story he never had to see?

LISA: Well, actually, he *would* see it; this was sort of a preemptive strike.

RUTH: Oh?

LISA (*a beat*): It's being published.

RUTH: It is? (*Lisa nods.*) How did *that* happen? I mean, I thought we'd already heard from everyone we'd sent it out to.

LISA: We did. (*A beat.*) I also sent it to *Grand Street*.

RUTH: *Grand Street*. Really. But I thought we'd decided *not* to send it to *Grand Street*.

LISA: We did.

RUTH: I thought we'd decided that wasn't exactly the right journal for it. And I didn't know anybody there.

LISA: Right. But I decided to send it in anyway, just for the hell of it, and see what happened.

RUTH: Oh. (*A beat.*) But what about a letter? You didn't ask me to write them a letter, did you?, because I don't remember. . . .

LISA (*over ". . . because I don't remember"*): No, I just sent it. With a cover letter of my own, *you* know, the basic.

RUTH: Well! And they're publishing it?

LISA: Uh huh. That's what they said.

RUTH: Well, how do you like *that?!*

LISA: Yeah.

RUTH: I never would have guessed they'd go for it; it didn't seem like their cup of tea at all.

LISA: I know; that's what we thought.

RUTH: Well, congratulations!

LISA: Thanks. It'll be in the winter issue. Not the fall, but the winter. Out in December.

RUTH: Well, isn't that nice! You'll be a published writer.

LISA: I know.

RUTH: Congratulations.

LISA: Thank you.

RUTH: Your first published story. Isn't that wonderful!

LISA (*over "Isn't that . . ."*): Yeah, I can't believe it.

RUTH: Well, we'll have to celebrate.

LISA: Yes. Let's.

RUTH (*a beat*): What did they do? Call you?, write you?

LISA: They wrote me.

RUTH: Uh huh. When?

LISA (*shrugs it off*): The other day.

RUTH (*nods; a beat*): I've spoken to you every single day this week and I didn't hear a word about a letter from *Grand Street*.

LISA: I just found out.

RUTH: The other day, you said.

LISA: I don't remember *when* exactly; what difference does it make?

RUTH: Well, it *is* sort of curious. I mean, why didn't you call me immediately?

LISA: What?

RUTH: Why wasn't I the first person you called?

LISA: Oh, Ruth. . . . Maybe you *were.* You'd never know: If you'd bother to get a machine . . .

RUTH: Oh, so you're saying you *did* call me?, or you *might* have called me?

LISA: Ruth, I don't understand this.

RUTH: I just think it's very curious, dear: The person most invested in your progress and you wait till *now* to tell me? In a most roundabout way, I might add.

LISA: Ruth, you're reading way too much significance into all this.

RUTH: Am I?

LISA: I'm telling you *now;* I told you *today.* I wanted to tell you face-to-face.

RUTH: I thought you said you tried calling me.

LISA: You're impossible, you know that?

RUTH: *Did* you? *Did* you try calling me? Or was that a convenient lie?

LISA: Why would I lie?

RUTH (*picks up the* Times Book Review *to read*): Well, I don't think you're being totally up-front with me.

LISA (*confused; takes away the paper to continue the discussion*): Ruth . . . ?

RUTH: What's the matter?, you didn't think I could take it?

LISA: What?!

RUTH: You were cushioning the blow?

LISA: What blow?

RUTH: You thought I'd be threatened by your success?

LISA: No! (*a beat.*) I didn't tell you . . . I felt a little funny, I guess, because I submitted it on my own.

RUTH: But you'd hoped, of course, they'd accept it. (*They are looking at one another. Ruth is enraged; Lisa is incredulous.*)

LISA: What?!

RUTH: Admit it! (*Ruth snatches back the* Book Review *and resumes reading it. Silence.*)

LISA: It's just a little journal; nobody really reads it anyway. (*Lisa waits for Ruth to respond, but she doesn't say anything. The phone rings four times; neither answers it. An extended silent sequence follows in which Ruth reads, sips iced tea; Lisa stretches out on the sofa with her back to Ruth, flips through the Sunday magazine, works on the puzzle, nibbles on a bagel, etc. Ruth, feeling a bit remorseful, glances at Lisa but continues reading. Lisa sits up. After a pause*) Ruth? (*A beat.*) Tell me about Delmore Schwartz?

RUTH (*a beat*): What!

LISA: I want to hear about you and Delmore Schwartz.

RUTH: What are you talking about?

LISA: Tell me.

RUTH: I don't know what you're talking about.

LISA: He was your famous older man, wasn't he?

RUTH: Oh, for God's sake. . . .

LISA: Wasn't he, Ruth?

RUTH: I never said any such thing.

LISA: I know, but he was, wasn't he?

RUTH: How did you get *that?*

LISA: It didn't click, till just now. When we were talking about Woody. . . .

RUTH: Oh, that's ridiculous.

LISA: I'm right, aren't I? (*Ruth scoffs.*) Ah ha. I am. I can tell. (*Teasing*) Come on, Ruth. . . .

RUTH: What do you *want* from me?

LISA: I want you to tell me.

RUTH: There's nothing to tell.

LISA: Ruth. . . .

RUTH: It's really none of your business.

LISA (*laying off*): All right. (*A beat.*) Look, if you don't want to tell me, that's okay, I understand. I was only trying to get you to talk to me. But if you don't want to tell me . . . I understand. No, really. (*Pause. Lisa returns to the puzzle. After a moment, Ruth, distracted, takes off her glasses.*)

RUTH: Ach, it was a million and one years ago. (*A beat. Lisa puts down the magazine.*) Another lifetime. (*Pause.*) I . . . I was quite young.

LISA: How young?

RUTH (*sighs, then*): Twenty-two. (*Pause.*) But a young twenty-two. (*A beat.*) An innocent in many ways. A virgin. I was a *good* girl, a nice Jewish girl, a *passion*ate girl, one of those passionate, virginal girls who'd read Dickinson and Hopkins and sob her eyes out. Poetry was my love, my romance, my religion. What a time. (*Pause.*)

LISA: When was this?

RUTH: '57, '58. The city was teeming with beatnik poets and old lefties. Smoky bars and late-night sessions. Every once in a while you'd glimpse a Ginsburg, or a Berryman, on the street, in a bookstore—the Eighth Street, the Gotham, or the Strand—and the rush of possibility would intoxicate you and keep you plodding along for days and weeks—until your *next* close encounter. (*A beat.*) I'd just come to the city from Detroit, to be a poet, of course, and took an apartment, a tiny walk-up, on Grove Street, above an Italian restaurant. The place smelled of garlic. Always. It was wonderful. My pillow smelled of garlic, my clothes. I had a roommate named Elaine, who was also from Detroit, the daughter of a friend of a family friend and an aspiring actress who would soon marry a rich man and give up her dream forever and die of breast cancer at thirty-nine, and the only soul I knew in all of New York City. (*A beat.*) One sleeting night, Elaine schlepped me into a bar on Hudson Street—the White Horse Tavern—and there, sitting in a booth, his wide handsome moon face shining, his big voice booming for all to hear whether they liked it or not. . . . There, performing for the two adoring pretty coeds who sat at his table. . . . There was the great poet Delmore Schwartz, mad prophet, squandered genius, son of "Europe, America and Israel."

LISA: Oh, Ruth, this is incredible.

RUTH: We sat across the aisle, Elaine and I, and he included us in his rant, I don't know, about DiMaggio one minute, Kierkegaard the next. After midnight, the first team of cheerleaders grew tired and left, and Elaine and I moved our drinks into his booth. Seeing his shining face across the table now, his eyes darting about, gleaming with brilliance. . . . There was so much going *on* in there. And he was already way past his prime at this point. He was gray and bloated and going to seed. His overcoat reeked of stale smoke and his teeth were baked yellow from tobacco. That enormous head with those widely-spaced eyes. There was still something magnificent about him. He had been quite beautiful, once.

LISA: I know, I've seen pictures.

RUTH: So, yes, the power was undeniable. (*A beat.*) He was only forty-four but there was something ancient about him, something terribly mortal and immortal at the same time, if that makes any sense. He seemed to possess so much wisdom and yet, even then, even that first sleeting night, he seemed doomed. (*A beat.*) What sheltered Jewish girl from Detroit, what self-styled poet, what virgin, would *not* have succumbed? (*Lisa shakes her head.*) And I was pretty then, too.

LISA: I'm sure; I know.

RUTH: You've seen pictures.

LISA: Yes!

RUTH: Well, pretty enough. Shapely, anyhow. I looked damn good in those tight, co-ed, Lana Turner sweaters. I was good company for a man like Delmore. Being my father's daughter had provided me with years of practice. I was a good listener but I also had a real mouth on me, which he'd point out frequently, with pleasure. I would tease him, provoke him, take outrageous positions just to get a rise out of him, which I always did. (*Pause.*) I stuck by him for over a year but he was descending rapidly by then. He was quite mad, you know. Oh, he had his moments, lucid, marvelous moments but, when they came, the rampages were fiercer and fiercer. He could be cruel, inconstant. His *aura* sustained me. (*A beat.*) I'd go to his awful rented rooms while he was out, *you* know: sordid furnished rooms with a sink and a hot plate, and I'd wash the dishes that piled up for days and clean up his mess and mend his clothes and he'd come in . . . and never say a word of thanks. One day I let myself in and found *another* bright-eyed girl lovingly washing his socks in the sink. "Oh," she said, surprised to see me. I turned around and left and never came back. (*A beat.*) You probably know the rest of the tale: how he was staying in one of those hotels when he died in '66; how his body lay unclaimed in the morgue for days. (*Pause.*)

> *"The years pass and the years pass*
> *& still I see only as in a glass*
> *darkly and vaguely—*
> *waiting, in 'grinding misery'*
> *for the fountain of poetry*
> *to flow and overflow once again."*

(*Pause.*)

LISA (*a sigh*): Wow.

RUTH: Poor schmuck. (*Pause; suddenly saddened*) I don't talk about this; why'd you make me talk about this?

LISA (*over ". . . talk about this?" Gently*): I'm sorry.

RUTH: It's too painful conjuring up that girl, that affair. I sewed that man's trousers. I held him when he woke up in a cold sweat. I took lots of shit from him in the name of poetry. I'm not particularly proud of all that happened and yet . . . it *was* my shining moment.

LISA: No; it wasn't.

RUTH (*looking right at her*): It *was*. It *was*. (*Pause.*)

LISA: And you've never written about it. (*Ruth shakes her head.*) Really. (*Ruth nods.*) How come?

RUTH: Some things you don't touch. (*Long pause.*) Listen, I don't mean to be a big old baby. (*Ruth, in a conciliatory gesture, goes to Lisa.*)

LISA (*approaching her*): Oh, Ruth. . . .

RUTH: You know I'm happy for you, don't you?

LISA: Of course I know that.

RUTH: I'm very very proud.

LISA: I know. I know. (*Ruth envelopes Lisa with her arms and holds her very tightly. She is distracted; her smile fades. Silence.*)

ACT TWO

Scene 1

Nearly two and a half years later. Early morning. December 1994. Ruth is seated, reading the book page of the daily New York Times; *Lisa, still wearing her coat, restlessly monitors Ruth's reaction. Long silence.*

RUTH (*barely audible*): Mm.

LISA: What.

RUTH: I was clearing my throat. (*Silence. Ruth puts down the paper and looks at Lisa. A beat.*)

LISA: Well . . . ?

RUTH (*a beat*): It's good.

LISA (*with trepidation*): Yeah?

RUTH: It's very good.

LISA: Oh, God.

RUTH: Do you want me to read it to you or not?

LISA (*over ". . . or not?"*): No no no. Just the highlights.

RUTH: The highlights, huh? (*Looks over the review.*) Well, the closing paragraph is to die for.

LISA: It is?

RUTH (*offering the paper*): You're sure you don't want to—?

LISA: No no no. I want *you* to.

RUTH (*reads from the review*): "Despite the occasional misstep—"

LISA: Oh, shit, wait, there are missteps?

RUTH: Minor, minor, not to worry. (*Continues*) "Despite the occasional misstep, Ms. Morrison's is a distinct, albeit youthful, voice that must be reckoned with."

LISA: Oh, God. . . .

RUTH (*continuous*): "In the dozen compact, well-observed stories that comprise *Eating Between Meals,* she proves herself a keen and clever chronicler of the new lost generation." (*A beat.*) Well! (*Silence.*)

LISA: What was that?, "keen and clever . . . "?

RUTH: "Keen and clever chronicler." (*Lisa takes the paper, looks it over.*) Our Michiko seems to have been bit by the alliteration bug.

LISA (*a beat; reads*): "As in Tolstoy,"—whoa!—"the unhappy families in Ms. Morrison's universe are uniquely compelling."

RUTH: All right all right, maybe you *shouldn't* read it; you'll start believing that shit.

LISA (*pause; still looking over the review*): Okay, so she doesn't like "Family Reunion."

RUTH: Mm. Neither did I.

LISA: She says I try too hard.

RUTH: Yes.

LISA: It's "stylistically self-conscious."

RUTH: I wasn't gonna say I told you so, but . . .

LISA (*still on the review*): Oh, good, she likes "Disneyland." (*Rushes through*) "A harrowing story in which a pubescent girl is forced to confront her father's sexuality." That's good. (*Pause. Lisa reads silently.*)

RUTH: You know what the problem with that story was?

LISA (*still reading*): Hm?

RUTH: That *story*.

LISA: What story?

RUTH: "Family Reunion." It was too fancy. All those interior monologues for all the members of the family: you didn't need all that. Remember I told you?

LISA: I thought you weren't gonna say I told you so.

RUTH: It *is* stylistically self-conscious; she's right.

LISA (*tuning her out, still reading to herself*): Uh huh.

RUTH (*a beat*): You know how it came off? It came off as a young writer showing off some pyrotechnics just to prove how versatile she is.

LISA (*somewhat annoyed*): Okay! (*Silence while Lisa finishes reading. She puts down the paper. She seems depressed. Softly*) Wow.

RUTH: How do you feel?

LISA: I don't know yet.

RUTH: That's a splendid review, you know; it doesn't *get* much better than that.

LISA: I know.

RUTH: Your life will never be the same, you know, from this morning on.

LISA: Thank you very much.

RUTH: Now when they print their lists of promising young writers, *you'll* be on them.

LISA: Oh, God.

RUTH: You're on the map. Yesterday you were undiscovered country, today you're on the map. (*She takes Lisa's hand. Genuinely*) Good for you, sweetie.

LISA: Why do I feel so awful?

RUTH: That's understandable. There's nothing worse than getting what you wanted. (*Getting up*) Now: What do I have that we can toast with . . . ?

LISA: It's not even nine in the morning!

RUTH (*exiting to kitchen*): So what? We have to celebrate. (*Off*) After *The Business of Love* came out, you know, I was a total mess.

LISA (*calls*): You were?

RUTH (*off*): Oh, God, yes. I sank into a terrible depression.

LISA: Really?

RUTH (*comes back in*): I thought I had a bottle of champagne but it's one of those sparkling ciders somebody brought to Thanksgiving years ago that nobody ever drinks. Do you mind? (*Lisa shakes her head; Ruth returns to the kitchen.*)

LISA (*calls*): You really got depressed?

RUTH (*off*): Oh, yeah. It took me months, maybe *years* to get over it—that is, if I ever truly did. It was a terrible shock: recognition. I was so inured to living in obscurity, writing my little stories and shipping them off to these tiny esoteric journals. I thought I was looking at the rest of my life. (*Returns with glasses and opens the bottle.*) I'd given up hope. *No* hope was the code by which I lived. It was strangely comforting; it left little room for disappointment. I was a bit older than you, you know, a rather late bloomer compared to you. The *Times* played me up quite a bit. I was hailed as "a brave new voice," "an urban balladeer." I had my "finger on the pulse of the city," they said, or some such nonsense.

LISA: Uh huh.

RUTH: They put me on the cover of the *Book Review* with a picture of me wearing these terrible—I can't believe I ever wore them—harlequin-like glasses. There I was, the new lady writer of the moment, smiling painfully, at my desk, not knowing *what* to do with my hands. (*A beat. In conclusion, as she pours*) You've got to view this purely as an economic development. Maybe some grants will start to come your way, some neat opportunities. And that's very nice. But the fact remains you still have to do the work and you still have to put up with assholes. Only *now* doing the work will be harder, and the assholes you'll have to put up with'll be of a slightly higher-echelon of assholes. And, that, as far as I can tell, is the definition of success. (*She raises her glass. A beat.*) To perseverance, hard work—and Michiko Kakutani.

LISA: Amen. (*They drink. Pause.*) I couldn't've done it without you, Ruth.

RUTH: I know, I know.

LISA: I mean it.

RUTH: I know, dear, so do I. (*Lisa smiles. Pause.*)

LISA: So, what do I do now?

RUTH: You'll do what you need to do.

LISA: I don't know what that is.

RUTH: It'll come. You'll figure it out.

LISA: How long should I give it?

RUTH: How ever long it takes.

LISA: What if it never comes?

RUTH: Lisa. . . .

LISA: What if this is it?

RUTH: Come on. . . .

LISA: No, seriously. What if I'm a one-book wonder?

RUTH: Oh, please. . . . You're *not*. . . .

LISA: How do you *know?* What if I'm not really a writer after all?

RUTH (*over ". . . after all?"*): Lisa! Jesus! Stop doing this to yourself!

LISA: Everything I've tried to write, all these weeks, waiting for the book to come out . . . I don't know, I've got to come up with something *big*ger than myself, you know? Out*side* of myself. I've got to get out of the suburbs. I need to get away from people my own age. It's hell being "the voice of a generation."

RUTH: That title is, what?, five minutes old?

LISA: I've blown the lid off bulimia in the suburbs. Whoopee. Big news, right? What do I do for an encore? It all seems so small now, so puny.

RUTH: What does?

LISA: My whole world. *You* know: disaffected youth, disaffected parents. Sex and drugs in the family room. Uh . . . Mother drinks, father cheats. What else? Oh, yes: Sorority sister makes a pass at a party: Too much to drink and a kiss in the pool. You name it, I've told it all. Crammed everything I know into a mere hundred and eighty-six pages. And that's with title pages and like a large-print-edition typeface that I find really embarrassing. (*A beat.*) It's pathetic. I looted my diaries for tasty morsels. My frenzied, angst-ridden, adolescent jottings: I stole whole chunks.

RUTH: We're all rummagers. All writers are. Rummagers at a tag sale. Picking through the neighbors' discards for material, whatever we can get our hands on. Shamelessly. Why stop at our own journals?

LISA: Well, the truth is, I'm not so angry anymore—I mean I'm in "treatment," okay?, and moved to *Chels*ea, so *now* what do

I do? I've *done* my parents. I've *done* my family. I'm not *an*gry with them anymore. *Fuck* them. I write all *day,* allegedly. I don't *see* anybody, I don't *go* anywhere because I'm allegedly writing all the time. My boyfriend's a *lawyer;* need I say more? My *friends* are all boring because they're all in exactly the same place I am. My life? I have no life. Every little quasi-idea that pops into my brain seems so banal, so *television.* (*A beat.*) So, I spend my days writing alleged stories about creatively-paralyzed women in their twenties who live in cramped but cozy Chelsea apartments. (*A beat.*) You were lucky.

RUTH: Why was I lucky?

LISA: You had all that rich, wonderful, *Jewish* stuff to draw on.

RUTH: Why was that luck? That was what I knew; I started out writing what I knew, just like you and everybody else who writes.

LISA: Yeah, but that culture!, that history! The first-generation American experience and all that. Nothing in my experience could possibly approach that. What do *I* have? *WASP* culture. Which is no culture at all.

RUTH: Oh, really? Tell that to Cheever and Updike.

LISA: Oh, God, I've got to write a novel, don't you think? Isn't that what they want?

RUTH: Who?

LISA: Isn't that what they expect? The literary establishment. I mean, in order for me to be taken seriously?

RUTH: Why? *I* never did.

LISA: Yeah, I know, but don't you think that hurt you?

RUTH (*bristles slightly; a beat*): Hurt me?

LISA (*backpedaling*): I mean, not *hurt* you, but don't you think it affected you?, affected your reputation?

RUTH: No.

LISA: Oh. Okay. (*Pause.*)

RUTH: Why? Do *you* think it did?

LISA: No, I just thought that maybe *you* felt that way.

RUTH: No. I don't. Why? Have I ever *said* as much?

LISA: No, it's just, as I see it, and maybe I've got it all wrong, but as *I* understood the game, the well-received first *collection* is like a rite of passage; the well-received first *novel* is coming-of-age. It's arrival, acceptance. Proof that you weren't a fluke.

RUTH: I don't know who came up with those rules. But *I* certainly never played by them. As far as I'm concerned, a writer is a writer, no matter *what* form that writing takes.

LISA: I don't know, I think this is the playing-with-the-big-boys thing of mine. *You* know, that I can't possibly play with the big boys? Probably has something to do with my father always telling me how I couldn't *do* things. This subtle form of sexism. Not so subtle, really, sub*ver*sive. (*A beat.*) I mean, I feel as if I've *said* it all already, everything I could possibly have to say, I've already said it, in twelve, what did she call them?, "compact, well-observed stories."

RUTH: Uh-oh, memorizing your reviews. I knew it. (*Pause.*)

LISA: What if the *Sunday Book Review* hates it?

RUTH: Honey, relax, they might not even review it. Or if they do, it might be one of those perfunctory little blurby things that nobody pays attention to anyway. (*Pause.*)

LISA: The advance word must be pretty good. *Publishers Weekly* and *Kirkus? They* liked it.

RUTH: Uh huh. (*Pause.*)

LISA: And *Mirabella*'s doing a piece on me, did I tell you?

RUTH: No. See?

LISA: They want to take my picture. Should I let them?

RUTH: Why not?

LISA: I don't know, it doesn't seem right. I should be writing, I shouldn't be doing photo shoots.

RUTH: What the hell? It's only a picture. It might be a damned good picture. Enjoy yourself. As long as you don't wear harlequin glasses. (*Pause.*)

LISA: I wonder if they'll let me keep the clothes.

RUTH: Lisa!

LISA: You know how you hear how men can't handle success? Men get famous and it's all about sex? I get *my* first little taste of fame and all I can think about is shopping. (*Pause.*)

RUTH: Tell me—I've got to ask you something.

LISA: What.

RUTH: Maybe this isn't the right time. . . . It's your day. . . .

LISA: No, tell me, what.

RUTH (*a beat*): Do you realize it's been over a week since I gave you my new story and you haven't said a *word?*

LISA (*over ". . . and you haven't . . ."*): Oh, shit, I know I know, I'm sorry I'm sorry. . . .

RUTH: I *gave* it to you because I was anxious to hear what you thought.

LISA: I know, and I was incredibly honored that you did.

RUTH: Ah, well, but you've probably been too busy and distracted and haven't had the time to. . . .

LISA: Well, actually, I *did* read it.

RUTH: You did? (*Lisa nods.*) Oh.

LISA: I read it the night you gave it to me. I liked it very much.

RUTH: Then why the hell didn't you *tell* me, you little shit?! Instead of making me twist slowly?!

LISA: I don't know, I didn't *mean* to. I didn't know what to say.

RUTH: How about "I liked it"? That would've been great for starters.

LISA: I mean, I wasn't sure of the protocol.

RUTH: Protocol?! With *me?!*

LISA: I felt shy. You'd never given me a new story of yours to read and asked me what I thought before.

RUTH: We're colleagues now. The morning paper confirms it, doesn't it? So, tell me: What did you think?

LISA: I told you.

RUTH: All right, so you liked it. What did you like about it?

LISA: Ruth. . . .

RUTH: Come on, kiddo, "voice of a generation," speak.

LISA: I liked the characters. The mother and daughter.

RUTH: Did you find them believable?

LISA: Totally.

RUTH: Why?

LISA: It's what you do, Ruth, like nobody else: the way you capture the essence of relationships. I mean, the structure is so brilliant: these two women squabbling in the kitchen over the years, while baking birthday cakes? You're amazing.

RUTH: Cut the flattery. I wasn't fishing, I want to know what you thought.

LISA: You really do.

RUTH: Yes.

LISA: Okay. (*A beat.*) I had problems with it.

RUTH: Ah. Well. Now we're getting somewhere. What kind of problems?

LISA: Well. You do such a beautiful job of creating these quirky, utterly recognizable women—I saw a lot of myself in Emily, actually.

RUTH: Huh!

LISA: And then, I've got to say, I felt really manipulated and disappointed by the ending.

RUTH: Oh? Disappointed? How?

LISA: I mean, sentimentality is not your thing; it never has been. It's such a wonderful story but giving the mother a terminal illness. . . . You didn't have to do *that*.

RUTH: Really.

LISA: You begin to fall in love with Martha, even when she's being hypercritical of everything Emily tries to do; I mean, she even has something to say about the way Emily pours the *vanilla,* for God's sake. But she's funny and honest, and Emily seems to know how to hold her own with her, and they're fun to eavesdrop on as Emily grows up and Martha grows old. So when you don't *take* them anywhere, and don't *resolve* the relationship between them . . . I don't know, I felt really cheated.

RUTH: But that's life, isn't it? What relationship is ever truly resolved? People, perfectly likable people, inexplicably, inconveniently, behave badly, or take a wrong turn, or get sick and die. It happens. Besides, the final struggle in the story is an internal one—Martha's—and it's not *about* her illness, it's about her *inability* to tell her darling girl that she's very very sick. Those are two different things.

LISA: True.

RUTH (*continuous*): She can't bring herself to do it. She continually decides she's going to, in that last section, but she always loses heart. It's as if saying it out loud would make it too real. It would let death into the room, and she can't *do* that.

LISA: No, you're right. I see it now. You're absolutely right. In the end, what makes it so moving is that you sense that this might be the very last cake the two women will get to bake together. That this prosaic little ritual is about to be wrenched apart. And it's very very sad.

RUTH: So you *were* moved by it.

LISA: Oh, God, yes. I was just mad at you for killing her off.

RUTH (*a beat; nods, her mood has become more solemn*): Well, good. I'm glad you liked it. Thank you. Thanks for reading it.

LISA: You're very welcome. It was my pleasure. It was a real treat to read Ruth Steiner's latest, before anybody else.

RUTH: What you have to say means a great deal to me, you know.

LISA: No, I *didn't* know that.

RUTH: No? (*Lisa shakes her head.*) How could you not know that? It works both ways, you know. Am I supposed to just give and give and expect nothing in return?

LISA: No, of course not.

RUTH (*continuous*): I can't just applaud you and pat you on your back and offer unconditional love and support. *I* could use a little reassuring, too. (*Ruth is suddenly tearful.*)

LISA: Ruth. What is it?

RUTH (*shakes her head dismissively, then*): This is complicated for me, you know.

LISA: What is?

RUTH: What's happening for you. It's very complicated.

LISA: Ruth? Are you jealous?

RUTH: Don't condescend.

LISA: I'm not; I'm sorry; I didn't mean to. . . .

RUTH (*over ". . . mean to"*): It's not about envy—well, maybe it *is* about envy. But it's not pro*fessio*nal jealousy, it's . . . You know what it is? I'm jealous that you have all of life ahead of you. I can't sit back and watch you do the dance that I danced long ago and not think about time. I can't. (*A beat.*) *That's* what it's about. Don't you see? Time. (*Pause. She turns to Lisa and looks like she is about to say something. Lisa leans forward in her chair. Pause. Ruth changes her mind.*) Cheers. (*She downs her drink. The meaning of Ruth's behavior begins to dawn on Lisa as the lights fade.*)

Scene 2

The auditorium of the 92nd Street Y. October 1996. Sound of applause. Lisa, wearing a flattering dress, nervously stands at a lectern and speaks into a microphone to the assembly.

LISA: Hello. (*She clears her throat, sips water.*) Hi. Thank you so *much* for that. It's so nice to be here at the 92nd Street Y, and be a part of this long literary tradition. I'm really honored. Thank you. I never expected such a turnout. Wow. I'm Lisa Morrison, by the way—just in case you're in the wrong room. (*A beat.*) Um . . . (*Takes a deep breath.*) I'm a little nervous. Forgive me. I'm new at this. I've never spoken in front of so many people before. I guess as long as I speak clearly, and with conviction, this should go reasonably well. It's important that you're able to *hear* me. At least that's what I was taught, and I was taught by a master. (*She scans the audi-*

ence looking for Ruth but doesn't see her. She takes a sip of water, then a deep breath.) What I'd like to do, for starters, I'd like to begin with an extract from my new novel—what am I talking about? My *first* novel, my *only* novel—*Miriam's Book,* which is being published next month by Viking? (*Corrects herself.*) By Viking. And then, if my voice holds up—(*Clears her throat for effect.*)—I thought I'd read one or two stories from my debut collection from a couple of years ago, *Eating Between Meals.* (*There is scattered applause, which surprises and amuses her.*) Gee. Well! I feel like Joni Mitchell in *co*ncert all of a sudden. (*Imitating a fan*) "Do 'Circle Game'!" (*A beat.*) Anyway, rather than describing too much about the book, I thought I would just start at the beginning. How's that? (*A beat.*) *Miriam's Book* (*A beat.*) The prologue is titled "Night Falls Fast," which is taken from a poem called "Not So Far as the Forest" by Edna St. Vincent Millay that appears in the beginning. Do you know that poem?, are you familiar with it? (*A beat.*) Shall I read it? Okay, why don't I. (*A beat. Deep breath.*) "Not So Far as the Forest."

(*A beat. She reads; once she overcomes her nervousness, she reads quite well.*)

> *That chill is in the air*
> *Which the wise know well,*
> *and even have learned to bear.*
> *This joy, I know,*
> *Will soon be under snow.*

> *The sun sets in a cloud*
> *And is not seen.*
> *Beauty, that spoke aloud,*
> *Addresses now only the remembering ear.*
> *The heart begins here*
> *To feed on what has been.*
> *Night falls fast.*
> *Today is in the past.*

> *Blown from the dark hill hither to my door*
> *Three flakes, then four*
> *Arrive, then many more.*

(*Pause. She sips water, then reads, with growing confidence.*)

From the window of my apartment in Washington Heights, I can see a sliver of Hudson between two grey-brown buildings and, beyond it, the high-rise towers of northern New Jersey. It is a still and sticky September night and my window is open to the sounds and smells of West 174th Street. Across the way, down below, a souped-up car stereo blares salsa through a busted woofer while an overweight middle-aged couple dances on the sidewalk, spectacularly, in their bare feet.

The constant cries of ambulances, like loons in the city night, mingle with the radiant blast of music and the particular, gleeful noises of children at evening play. Somewhere out there, on this Indian summer night, in a narrow anonymous galley kitchen, someone is cooking with garlic.

I found my mind drifting tonight while reading or, rather, attempting to read a poem by one of my first-year Columbia graduate students, a dreary earnest girl, who tries drawing a parallel between the sexual abuse she suffered as a child and the situation in Bosnia. The poem is unwieldy, pretentious, and self-indulgent but tomorrow, in tutorial, over mondel bread and tea, I will tell her it is *ambitious.*

I had gotten to the bottom of the third page and realized that I had absorbed not one word for some time. It was then that the timeless scent of garlic shocked my smelling sense and swept me, instantly, nine miles south and four decades back, to a crumbling but quaint railroad flat on Mulberry Street in the year nineteen hundred and fifty-seven.

I was young, very young, twenty-two in '57, a young twenty-two, not only a virgin but an innocent, a poet manqué from faraway Missouri, a Jewess from a place called St.

Louis. New York had beckoned, like a beautiful dark lover with smoky breath and bloodshot eyes; I swooned and flew into his vampire arms with abandon, and left the stultifying beige safety of my parents' house forever.

The echoing sounds of collicky babies, wronged wounded lovers, and Caruso on a crackling 78 greeted me as I first made my way up dim uncertain stairs to the unlikely garden of my new freedom. Giordano's Restaurant was on the ground floor. Angelo, the chef, got his marinara started at six every morning by throwing crushed garlic into a huge sauce pot of scalding oil. I could hear the sizzling meeting of garlic and olive oil upstairs, and imagine magnificent bursts of fireworks and symphonic crescendoes greeting each fistful. The aroma travelled through the screen door at the back, up the rusted fire escape, into my open window and caressed me as I lay in my bed.

So, when I am struck by the smell of garlic, as I was tonight, mixed with the dusty nighttime city air, I think of the intoxicating perfume of my youth, of that first summer on Mulberry Street, of long walks at all hours, of mildewy book stores, smoky coffee houses, of poetry and promise.

And I think of Emmett Levy.

Emmett Levy. Poet, madman, raconteur. The notorious and the legendary Levy. Great thinker, good poet, drunkard extraordinaire.

At forty-four, he had lived too long but would not die soon enough. His death would be ungentle, attenuated over nine desperate years, and I, a girl half his age, would see him through seven of his final seasons in a variety of roles: lover, nurse, mother-confessor, muse. I would love him and despise him, worship him and wish him dead. (*A beat.*)

This is the story of those seven seasons in heaven and hell, so many years ago, when I was a girl of twenty-two, and lost my heart to a beautiful dark angel, a poet, named Emmett Levy. (*Pause.*)

And that's the prologue. Shall I go on?

Scene 3

Ruth's apartment. Later that night. Ruth, wearing a cardigan over pajamas, stands at the window. Lisa opens the door but the chain is on.

LISA: Damn. (*Calls*) Ruth? Ruth, are you all right? (*Waits.*) Ruth?

RUTH: Yes?

LISA: Ruth. Thank God. Open the door; the chain is on.

RUTH: What?

LISA: The chain, the chain is on the door.

RUTH: Oh. So it is.

LISA: Are you all right?

RUTH: Yes. I think so. As good as can be expected.

LISA: Are you going to let me in?

RUTH: Oh, I suppose so. . . . (*She undoes the chain.*)

LISA: Thank you. (*She's carrying a grocery bag.*) Your door is usually open; since when do you use the chain?

RUTH: Only when I'm expecting burglars.

LISA (*gives her a look; a beat*): What happened tonight?

RUTH: What happened?

LISA: I was worried about you.

RUTH: *Were* you. I didn't say I'd make it for sure, I said I would try.

LISA: I know, but still, I was hoping. I guess you weren't feeling up to it.

RUTH: You could say that.

LISA: That's what I thought. (*An uncomfortable beat.*) I brought you something.

RUTH: Oh?

LISA: I wanted to bring you something, I didn't know what to bring.

RUTH: What is it? (*Lisa removes a container from the bag.*)

LISA: Cottage cheese. You said you had a craving for cottage cheese.

RUTH (*over ". . . cottage cheese*): What size curd?

LISA: What?

RUTH: The curd, the curd. What size curd did you get?

LISA (*looks at the label*): Large.

RUTH: I prefer small.

LISA: Oh, of course. I forgot.

RUTH: How could you forget?

LISA: I wasn't thinking. I'm sorry.

RUTH: The hell with it.

LISA: I'll return it.

RUTH: Nah. . . . Don't bother. (*Silence. Lisa senses the chill in the air.*)

LISA: What would you like me to do? Would you like me to go down and see if I . . . ?

RUTH (*over ". . . if I"*): No no.

LISA: The Korean market is still open.

RUTH: Never mind.

LISA: Are you sure?

RUTH: I'm sick to my stomach anyway. Can't keep a goddamn thing down. I must have a calcium deficiency; I dream of dairy products. Forget it. If I don't eat it, Monica will. (*Lisa goes to put it in the fridge, returns.*)

LISA: Monica?

RUTH: My visiting nurse.

LISA: I thought her name was Beverly. (*She is picking up around the room: journals, periodicals, mail.*)

RUTH: Beverly?! That was ages ago!

LISA: Sorry. I lost track. What happened to Beverly?

RUTH: Irreconcilable differences. Now I've got Monica. Who doesn't do housework. A big, beautiful, mocha-colored woman from St. Kitt's. With a bubbly, melodic voice. She calls me Mommy. "Are you hungry, Mommy?" "Are you cold, Mommy?" I hated it in the beginning: How dare this stranger patronize me like that? Then I started to like it. I *liked* being called Mommy. No one's ever called me Mommy before. (*A beat.*) I don't see you anymore.

LISA: I was here last week.

RUTH: Not last week, couldn't've been last week.

LISA (*over ". . . last week"*): So maybe it was ten days ago.

RUTH: I'm telling you it's been *weeks;* Monica's been coming for weeks.

LISA: Has it really been that long?

RUTH: Yes!

LISA: I'm sorry; I've been busy. The book.

RUTH: Yes. Of course. The book. (*Pause; re: Lisa's tidying.*) Leave it.

LISA: You have junk mail here from Christmas.

RUTH: You don't have to pick up after me, I can still pick up after myself.

LISA: I'm just straightening up.

RUTH: Whenever *you* straighten up, things disappear.

LISA (*flips through a* New Yorker): Did you read the Janet Malcolm piece in here?

RUTH: Life's too short for *The New Yorker.*

LISA: It's good; you should read it. (*She puts it beside Ruth's chair.*)

RUTH: I don't have time to read. I have all the time in the world and no time at all. My life is a paradox. That's quite a lovely dress you have on.

LISA: Oh, thank you.

RUTH: Looks expensive.

LISA: It was.

RUTH: That's what you wore tonight?

LISA: Uh huh. I wanted to look *serious*—but sexy. Too much?

RUTH: For the 92nd Street Y? Perhaps. How'd it go?

LISA: Actually, it went fine. It was fun.

RUTH: Good.

LISA: There were a couple of candy-wrapper crinklers I wanted to kill, but aside from that. . . .

RUTH: I used to love readings. I always found them exhilarating. I loved playing all the parts. And getting laughs. I loved the laughter. I'm just an old ham, you know that.

LISA: Yes; I do.

RUTH: And it isn't just any old laughter; it's the self-congratulatory laughter of people who want you to know that they get *every*thing.

LISA (*smiles, then*): This Barnard undergrad cornered me afterwards, saying she couldn't *wait* to meet me? It was really weird finding myself in a position of being pursued, when all my life I've been the pursuer—but she really wasn't interested in what I had to say; all she wanted was to talk about herself! (*Lisa observes Ruth lost in thought, not really listening. Pause.*) Ruth? Would you like some tea?

RUTH: Hm? Thank you, I would. (*Lisa goes to the kitchen to put water on, etc. Pause.*) You know? (*A beat.*) I . . . I should have had children of my own. It's my own damn fault. Too picky. I never met a man I could see myself having a child with. (*A beat.*) Nowadays the choice of partner would be totally irrelevant, I know, but it was a more conservative time then; things were different when I was ovulating. I should have just gone ahead and gotten pregnant with the next unsuspecting man that came into my life, snared him for his sperm, and raised that child on my own. But I was never really the sort of woman who could do something like that. That would have required a brand of courage I sorely lacked. I was never truly Bohemian, never, that was all an act. A reaction to the fear, no doubt, of being hopelessly conventional. (*Lisa returns holding a saucer and cup of tea.*) It would have been good for me, I think, having a child.

LISA: Yes?

RUTH: I might have become a different person. A better writer, maybe; a better human being, possibly. My life surely would have been *different*. Instead, I spent many many years, too many years, nurturing other people's gifted children. (*A beat.*) The first day of every class I ever taught—thirty-two years, thirty-two first days—I'd scan the faces and try to predict who out there would one day dazzle me. Who would thrill and astonish me with their promise? Who will it be this year? I'd want them, like a vampire wants fresh blood. I'd want to fill them up with what I know, these beautiful hungry empty vessels, and watch them grow. I've had a succession of chosen daughters through the years, mostly daughters. A few sons. Unformed, talented, as susceptible to my wisdom as I was to their youth. But none I loved as much as you.

LISA: Ruth. (*Pause.*)

RUTH: I read your book.

LISA: Yes. I figured.

RUTH: Well, most of it, anyway. As much as I could possibly read right now. My eyes are stinging. There are tons of typos in the copy you gave me, tons.

LISA (*over ". . . tons"*): I know, it's an advance copy.

RUTH: I hope they're planning on correcting them.

LISA: Of course they are.

RUTH: I marked the margins anyway. Force of habit. There are some truly egregious errors in there.

LISA: I know.

RUTH: One whole section is suddenly repeated. I thought I was losing whatever mind I have left. Either that or you'd gone Joycean on me. And experimental fiction, as we both know, is not your style. (*Silence.*) Lisa Lisa. If you had only asked me what I thought. If you had only asked me.

LISA: Ruth.

RUTH: I would have told you you were making a mistake.

LISA: I didn't know what to do, I didn't know how to handle it.

RUTH: Stay away from Schwartz; leave him out of it. He's mine, not yours. Besides, he's been done to death, picked over by so many vultures in the name of literature, and Bellow finished him off for everyone. If you had *asked* me. If you had only *asked* me.

LISA: Ruth.

RUTH: If you had only asked my advice. Forget my permission.
If you had asked my advice. I'd have told you to look else-
where, leave him alone, leave him out of it. They'll compare
you to Bellow and your work simply can't support it, darling. It can't. You're not good enough. You may never be
good enough. Why call attention to it? If you had asked me
what I thought, I would have told you. But you didn't ask.
Instead you skulked like a thief. Avoided me for two and a
half years—

LISA: No, I didn't. . . .

RUTH *(continuous)*: —evaded my questions, failed to look me in
the eye.

LISA: Ruth. . . .

RUTH: You did, you did, my darling, I knew something was up:
When you *did* come to see me, you couldn't *look* at me. I
thought it was my appearance, that I was looking so awful
you couldn't look me in the eye.

LISA: No!

RUTH: I could have used your friendship but you were too busy
going through my panty drawer, scavenging through my
personal effects.

LISA: That's not what I did!

RUTH: Then why did you skulk? Why couldn't you look at me?

LISA: I don't know, I . . . I needed some distance.

RUTH: "Distance"!

LISA: I needed to separate from you.

RUTH *(amused)*: That you did, my darling, that you did.

LISA *(over ". . . that you did")*: You wouldn't know what it's like,
to have to get out from under you, from under your influence, you couldn't possibly know what that's like!

RUTH (*over "... what that's like!"*): Everything I told you. Everything I shared.

LISA: Ruth.

RUTH: What a fool I was.

LISA: No.

RUTH: It was all *material* to you! That's all it was.

LISA: That's not true.

RUTH: Here I was, regaling you with stories from my life like the
pitiful old woman you've made me out to be ...

LISA (*over "... you've made me out to be"*): "Pitiful"?! No no ...

RUTH (*continuous*): ... and all the while you were taking notes!

LISA: That isn't true! I was listening! I was cherishing every
minute!

RUTH: I'm sure.

LISA: If I had told you and you'd disapproved—(*Ruth turns away,
busies herself.*) *Listen* to me: If you had disapproved, I don't
know what I would've done.

RUTH: Uh huh.

LISA: I never could've written it. How could I have written it? I
might have lost *you* and I would have lost my novel, too. I
was scared.

RUTH: Poor thing.

LISA: I didn't know what to do! You were the one person who
could advise me but I couldn't discuss it with you.

RUTH: Clearly you listened. You listened all right. You took it all
in. And set it all out for the world to see.

LISA: What, what did I do that any good writer wouldn't have
done? that you wouldn't have done yourself? A story grabbed
me and wouldn't let go.

RUTH (*over ". . . wouldn't let go"*): No, no, dear, that's where you're wrong: it didn't grab *you;* you *seized it,* it didn't seize *you.* Have you no conscience?! Have you no moral conscience?!

LISA: I have a conscience.

RUTH: *Do* you? *Do* you? You went ahead and did it anyway! That's what's so remarkable. You did it anyway.

LISA: What did you teach me: You taught me to be ruthless.

RUTH (*struck by the unintentional pun*): So to speak.

LISA: If something captures your eye, you told me, grab it. Remember? Like a good photojournalist: Go in and shoot. (*Ruth is evading her, Lisa follows her around the room.*) Remember, Ruth?—Don't walk away!—That's what you taught me! Don't worry about feelings, you taught me that, worrying about feelings is sentimental and God knows we mustn't be sentimental.

RUTH: You've crossed the line, though, sweetie. You've crossed the line.

LISA: Why, because it involves you?

RUTH: I would think that would enter into it, yes! I was a fellow *writer* telling you these stories, not a longshoreman or a, a *waitress,* for God's sake! A fellow writer! It's a matter of professional courtesy, I would think. What did I need to do? proclaim them off-limits? Plant a flag? Make you *sign* something? You were my friend, goddammit!

LISA: I wish you wouldn't use the past tense.

RUTH: Once upon a time writers made things up, you know. Can you imagine?

LISA (*over "Can you imagine?"*): Oh, come on. You used people all the time! Don't give me that shit. Whatever you could get your hands on, you took.

RUTH (*over ". . .you took"*): If I used people for my stories, my dear, they were people who had no voice, no outlet for expression.

LISA (*over ". . . for expression"*): Oh! Well! Is that so! That's awfully condescending of you, Ruth, really. How do you know? How do you know that?

RUTH: It's the truth!

LISA (*continuous*): You're always making these pro*nounce*ments! When did the Little People you built your *career* on choose *you* as their advocate?!

RUTH: I gave them a voice where they had none.

LISA: Well, there you go: We all play God. Don't we? We all put words into people's mouths. You taught me that, Ruth.

RUTH (*over "You taught me that, Ruth"*): No no no, what you've done is something else, it's something else. I *have* a voice. I *have* the tools.

LISA: Ruth. . . .

RUTH: Use your own goddamn life! If yours isn't rich enough, too bad; that's not my problem. Don't thumb a ride and hop aboard mine. Hitchhiker!

LISA: Ruth! What do you make me out to be? You make me sound like the most mercenary person imaginable. The last thing I wanted was to hurt you.

RUTH: *Was* it? Oh, I don't know, I think you might be deceiving yourself, dear.

LISA: How?

RUTH (*continuous*): I think there's something terribly Freudian going on here, don't you? The Oedipal struggle to the finish. You destroy me and claim my lover for yourself, take him to bed with you. I think you *want*ed to destroy me.

LISA: That's ridiculous.

RUTH: You wanted to obliterate me.

LISA: No, no, I wanted to *honor* you!

RUTH: *Honor* me?!

LISA: It was my gift to you.

RUTH: Your *gift?!*

LISA: Yes! I was honoring you. For all you've given *me*.

RUTH: Well, I don't want your gift. How do you like that? I'm very sorry, that isn't very gracious, I know, but your gift doesn't honor me. I want the receipt so I can exchange it for something else but you're telling me there *is* no receipt. It's take it or leave it!

LISA (*genuinely*): What exactly is so offensive to you? I don't understand it.

RUTH: You don't?!

LISA: No.

RUTH: You've stolen my *stories*, Lisa. My stories! What am I without my stories? I'm nothing. I'm a cipher. I'm as good as dead.

LISA: But they *aren't* your stories, Ruth. Not anymore. They stopped being your stories when you told them to *me*. They changed my life so how can they be solely your stories anymore? You don't *own* them.

RUTH: Oh, no?

LISA: No! You are a part of my life now, Ruth. Our lives intersect. My experience includes your experience. I am the sum of your experience and my experience and everybody else's experience I've ever come in contact with.

RUTH (*over ". . . come in contact with"*): Yeah yeah yeah.

LISA: I couldn't tell your stories, not the way *you* would, I couldn't *possibly* do that. But I *can* take your experiences, what I *know* of them, what I *make* of them, and extrapolate, *that* I can do, but my book doesn't pretend to be the *truth*. Miriam isn't *you*. (*Ruth scoffs.*) She *isn't*.

RUTH: I know that line, *bubeleh;* believe me, I've used it.

LISA: All right, she's as much me as she is you.

RUTH: That lonely, pitiful woman, pining for Delmore Schwartz?

LISA: No, no, the young, impressionable disciple who wants nothing more than the high regard of her mentor.

RUTH: Is *that* what you were going for?

LISA: Yes!

RUTH: Then you've failed miserably; I don't see that at all.

LISA: That's 'cause you don't *want* to see it! You've totally, willfully, misread her! Miriam isn't pitiful. She's vital, funny, self-ironical. She sees the affair for what it truly was, in ways you obviously cannot!

RUTH: What is that supposed to mean?!

LISA: You're the one who calls it the "shining moment" of your life, for Christ's sake, Ruth!, that's what you told me! You wear it like some kind of masochistic badge of honor.

RUTH: Who the hell asked *you?*

LISA (*over ". . . asked you?*"): You've let that one brief affair define your entire life!

RUTH: I have not! That is absurd!

LISA (*continuous*): You're like a professional war widow or, or Miss Havisham in her wedding dress or something!

RUTH: That is not who I am! That's insulting!

LISA: I'm sorry.

RUTH: You gonna lay some postfeminist crap on me now? Huh, Lisa?

LISA (*wearily*): No.

RUTH (*continuous*): How only *you,* with the benefit of a modern, feminist perspective, can put *my* affairs in their proper place? Is that it?

LISA (*over "Is that it?"*): I wanted to reclaim for you a part of your life, okay? I wanted to give something precious back to you.

RUTH: Really! And who the hell asked you?! Who *asked* for your revisionism of *my* life?

LISA: Oh, boy. . . .

RUTH (*continuous*): Not I. Not I. I've got news for you, kiddo, you wouldn't *be* where you so smugly sit if it weren't for women like me.

LISA: Yes, Ruth.

RUTH (*continuous*): It's our own damn fault: Our dirty work made your arrogance possible.

LISA (*over ". . . possible"*): Oh, please. Spare me the you-girls-have-it-so-easy shit.

RUTH (*over ". . . so-easy shit"*): The way you take and take with this astonishing sense of entitlement! And not only have you usurped my love affair, oh no, but you've taken my entire milieu and passed it off as your own!

LISA: How? I don't know what you mean.

RUTH: You don't? Jewish intellectual life? New York in the fifties? Delmore is one thing, but to take on territory that is so identifiably mine?!

LISA: How is it yours? Do you have dibs on the entire spectrum of Jewish experience, too, Ruth? Exclusive rights?

RUTH: Look at my body of work! Look at it! You know it backwards and forwards, for Christ's sake!

LISA: You were a point of departure, like any inspiration.

RUTH: It's my *voice,* dammit! What you've done is mimickry, it's not art, it's not homage. It's parody. You had no right!

LISA: No right?! What about my right as an artist?!

RUTH: You have to *earn* that right! Who gave *you* the right to write about Jews?

LISA: What, because I haven't lived it I can't write it? Is that what you're saying? I can't write about Jews because I'm not Jewish? Do you really mean that?

RUTH (*over "Do you really mean that?"*): I'm saying it's bogus coming from you. Inauthentic. Irresponsible.

LISA: And when *you* got into the heads of welfare mothers that was, what, social realism? Ruth, come on, you're not being fair. You're contradicting everything you ever taught me about writing!

RUTH: And what do *you* know about "fair"? The things you've got me doing, saying, thinking. . . .

LISA: Not you, *Miriam.*

RUTH: Either you're being disingenuous or very naive. Of course it's me. There is no fact, there is no fiction. The line is blurred. As far as everybody is concerned, it *is* me, so it might as well *be* me.

LISA: Ruth. . . .

RUTH: Everybody knows you were my protégée.

LISA: So?

RUTH: So, you're pandering to the public. Like some tell-all rag.

LISA: No. . . .

RUTH: *You* know how that is: You read a book and all the time you're guessing. You're smacking your lips and you're guessing.

LISA: So what? So what if they do?

RUTH: This is *my life,* dammit! You've appropriated *my life!* Maybe you thought it was up for grabs.

LISA: Ruth. . . .

RUTH: Maybe you thought I was fair game.

LISA: No. . . .

RUTH: Maybe you thought I'd be dead by now!

LISA (*a beat*): That's a horrible thing to say! How can you say that to me?!

RUTH (*over ". . . say that to me?!"*): Don't act so shocked, my darling. I'm sure it occurred to you, it would have occurred to me. . . . (*A beat.*) You've taken my life and turned it into pulp!

LISA: How can you call it pulp?!

RUTH: Forgive me, dear, but that's really what it is. Gossip. More grist for the mill.

LISA: Can't you tell it was written with love?

RUTH: Those sex scenes. Lisa! Oh dear God. Didn't I teach you *any*thing? What did I tell you about sex scenes? They always read like automotive mechanics, darling: Bodies and parts. (*Flipping through the book, paraphrasing*) That scene in the stairwell of her walk-up! (*Gasps.*) The huffing and puffing! The creaking of the stairs! *Oy gevalt!*

LISA (*making motions toward leaving*): Forget it.

RUTH (*continuous*): His wet wool coat smothering her! His bear-like *hugeness* pressing pressing into her! Deeper and deeper and deeper! (*Ruth is laughing, almost maniacally, Lisa can't stand this but cannot bring herself to walk out. Pause.*) He was impotent, darling. The great love of my life, your romantic hero. He was so destroyed by drink and Dexedrine by then, there *was* no sex, not sex as you so grotesquely imagined it, anyway.

LISA: So what? My book is fiction.

RUTH: Your "book" is shit. (*She tosses the copy to the floor. Pause. Lisa goes to it and picks it up. Silence.*) You know what I would do if I were you, darling? Not that you asked me. If I were you, I'd buy back all the copies, every single one, and set a nice big bonfire in Tompkins Square Park. It shouldn't be a total loss: At least the homeless could warm their hands on it.

LISA: If I were in your place, if *my* life inspired a disciple of *mine* to write about it, I would be gratified.

RUTH: *Would* you?

LISA (*continuous*): I would be honored. I wouldn't be doing this.

RUTH: But the book isn't any good, Lisa. It's not gonna do you any good at all.

LISA: A lot of people would disagree.

RUTH: Pulp it. Shred it.

LISA: You know I can't do that; that's not an option.

RUTH: Work out a deal with your publisher. They're gonna take a bath on it anyway. Give back your advance. I'm sure they'd be delighted. They'll be getting off easy.

LISA: I can't believe you're doing this to me. You know how vulnerable I am . . . my first novel being published. . . .

RUTH: I'm only telling you what I think would be the mature and honorable thing to do. Admit your failure, take the loss and chalk it up to experience. Admit your moral and artistic failure. Because if you don't, I'll do everything I can to stop it.

LISA: Stop it? What do you mean, stop it?

RUTH: *Stop* it! *Stop* it! I've spoken to my lawyer.

LISA: You what?

RUTH: Doesn't that sound corny? But I have; I called him today.

LISA: Oh, Ruth, this is foolishness.

RUTH: Is it?

LISA: I've done nothing wrong, nothing illegal. You have no legal grounds.

RUTH: I don't know, but I do have moral grounds. I still have sense and I still have friends and I'm gonna make a really big stink.

LISA: You don't want to do that. . . .

RUTH: Oh, I do, I've got to. You've given me no choice.

LISA: You'll only get the opposite result. People will want to read the book. And *then* what would you have accomplished?

RUTH: I'm not gonna let you get away with this. People have got to know I was robbed.

LISA: You don't need that kind of publicity, Ruth. It'll be humiliating. A great teacher suppressing her student? The champion of free speech? You don't want to be remembered as a crank. I'd hate to think of you degrading yourself like that.

RUTH: And what have *you* done to me? Hm? What have *you* done?

LISA: You *wanted* me to write about him, didn't you.

RUTH: I what?!

LISA: "Don't talk about it, write it." Remember that, Ruth? That was one of the first lessons you ever taught me.

RUTH (*over ". . . ever taught me"*): Oh, please, you're gonna throw *that* in my face?

LISA (*continuous*): Telling a story takes away the need to *write* it, it relieves the pressure.

RUTH: You actually believe that shit?

LISA: Yes. Of course I believe that, Ruth. You taught it to me. (*A beat.*) The day you told me about him I knew, by the *way* you told me, by the *language* you used. It had been written in your head long ago. When you said it out loud that day, when you released it, I knew, I could sense, that you were giving it to me.

RUTH: *Giving* it to you?!

LISA (*continuous*): You *wanted* me to use it.

RUTH: Bullshit! That has got to be the worst argument for theft I've ever heard! What are you saying, I left the window open?

LISA: I'm not saying it was conscious. . . .

RUTH: Look, I'm perfectly capable of writing my own stories, thank you.

LISA: But, face it, Ruth, you were never gonna write this one.

RUTH: What?! Excuse me? How do you know that?!

LISA (*over "How do you know that?!"*): I'm sorry, but it's true.

RUTH: What, do you think you know *every*thing about me? Do you think I was stupid enough to reveal *every*thing to you? How do you know I haven't already written it?

LISA: Ruth. . . .

RUTH: How do you know I *haven't*? Maybe it's *here*. . . . (*She pulls open a file drawer and tosses files to the floor.*) Maybe it's right here. . . .

LISA: Ruth, please. . . .

RUTH (*continuous*): Maybe I *have* written it. Just because I didn't run to a publisher with it . . . !

LISA: Don't do this. (*Lisa touches Ruth's arm to calm her, but Ruth violently pulls away. Silence.*) This isn't about you and me, Ruth, and you know it.

RUTH: Oh, no? What's it about? (*A beat.*)

LISA: It's about death.

RUTH: Death. Is it? I see.

LISA: Death is the third party here. You're angry at death.

RUTH: I'm angry at death. Thank you very much.

LISA: And I don't blame you, Ruth.

RUTH: You don't. How kind.

LISA: Please don't be angry with me. The last thing I wanted was for you to be angry at me. (*Pause.*) I know the past few years have been a terribly rough time for you. I know that. And it pains me. It does. I'm so sorry you haven't been feeling well.

RUTH: I feel fine. (*Pause.*)

LISA: What I mean is, I think it's the disease talking, Ruth, it's not you.

RUTH: I see.

LISA: It's clouded your thinking. You've displaced your anger onto me. And if that's what you need to do, fine, I'll take the beating. But I'm not your enemy, Ruth. I love you.

RUTH: You love me.

LISA: Yes. (*Pause.*)

RUTH: Tell me: What did you think my reaction would be? Silence? Approval? What?

LISA: I don't know, I thought you'd feel. . . . Pride. Satisfaction.

RUTH (*incredulous*): Satisfaction?

LISA: For having been a good teacher. (*Long pause. Lisa moves close to Ruth, put her arm around her and holds her for a moment; Ruth doesn't respond.*) Ruth. (*Silence.*)

RUTH (*exhausted*): Go home.

LISA: What?

RUTH (*breaking Lisa's embrace*): I can't talk to you anymore.

LISA: Don't say that.

RUTH: Our trust is broken. I feel like I've been bugged. My dear young friend turned out to be a spy. A spy who sold my secrets.

LISA: Ruth, please. We can talk about this.

RUTH: Look, do me a favor, take out the trash with you, I've got a leaky bag. (*Silence. Lisa goes to the kitchen, returns with the trash bag, and looks at Ruth for a long beat; Ruth's back is to her. Silence.*)

LISA: Ruth . . . ?

RUTH: (*still facing away*): Go home. (*Lisa takes her in for one last moment before leaving shutting the door behind her. Ruth is alone. Silence. The phone begins to ring; it rings many times. We think she may finally answer it but she doesn't. Lights fade slowly.*)

FIVE WOMEN WEARING THE SAME DRESS

by Alan Ball

Five Women Wearing the Same Dress was first produced by Manhattan Class Company (Robert LuPone and Bernard Telsey, executive directors, W. D. Cantler, associate director), in New York City, on February 13, 1993. It was directed by Melia Bensussen; the set design was by Rob Odorisos; the lighting design was by Howard Werner; the costume design was by Karen Perry; the sound design was by Bruce Ellman; the production managers were Laura Kravets Gautier and Ira Mont; and the stage managers were Hazel Youngs and Katherine Lumb. The cast was as follows:

FRANCES:	Dina Spybey
MEREDITH:	Amelia Campbell
TRISHA:	Ally Walker
GEORGEANNE:	Betsy Aidem
MINDY:	Allison Janney
TRIPP:	Thomas Gibson

Understudies: Orlagh Cassidy, Jack Gwaltney, and Linda Marie Larson

CHARACTERS

FRANCES:	a bridesmaid
MEREDITH:	a bridesmaid
TRISHA:	a bridesmaid
GEORGEANNE:	a bridesmaid
MINDY:	a bridesmaid
TRIPP:	an usher

ACT ONE

The play takes place in Meredith's bedroom, a large, comfortable room on the second floor of a renovated turn-of-the-century mansion in a stylish, old-money suburb of Knoxville, Tennessee. There is a big brass bed, two large dressers, a vanity with a mirror. A compact shelf stereo system with CD player. A portable stair-climbing exercise machine. A large walk-in closet. A door leads to a bathroom; another to the hall. A large window with a window seat is suggested downstage.

The room has been decorated by Meredith's mother in a cluttered, eclectic combination of light Victorian and contemporary, mixing antiques and rich, deeply hued linens and wallpaper with stark white custom shelving and high-tech lighting. A plush Persian rug covers the hardwood floor. Pillows abound. The effect is tasteful and inviting, not quite luxurious but definitely comfortable—it is clear this home is inhabited by the wealthy. The air of traditional privilege is disrupted, however, by a prominent poster of Malcolm X on the wall.

Underscoring the entire scene is an atmosphere of age and durability, conveyed by the original architectural details that remain: huge, multipaned windows, exquisite molding, the sheer height of the ceiling. There is history in this room.

It is shortly after noon on a day in summer.

A few moments of silence, then someone knocks softly at the door.

FRANCES (*off*): Yoo-hoo. (*After a moment the knock is repeated, slightly louder.*) Anybody home? (*A long pause, then the door opens slowly and Frances peers around it.*) Meredith? (*Frances is a sweet-faced woman, twenty-one years old. She wears an expensive, off-the-shoulder bridesmaid's gown with a voluminous skirt, in peach or lilac or one of those horrible wedding pastels. She also wears an elaborate hat that matches her dress and she carries a bouquet. She enters the room tentatively and shuts the door behind her, moving stiffly in her dress, as if it intimidates her, which it does. She spots a jewelry box on top of the vanity, crosses to it, opens it, and inspects its contents.*) Oh, my. (*She pulls out a glittering rhinestone bracelet. Handling it carefully, almost reverently, she puts it on her wrist and fastens it. Holding out her arm, she admires the bracelet in the mirror, assuming a series of poses she considers to be glamorous.*)

MEREDITH (*off*): Mother, I am just going upstairs— (*A telephone somewhere in the room begins to ring. Off*) I am not answering that. (*Alarmed, Frances struggles with the bracelet, vainly attempting to unfasten it. Meredith can be heard stomping up the stairs. Off*) No, ma'am, I am not answering that. You will not get to me this way. (*As Meredith gets closer, Frances panics. Unable to unfasten the rhinestone bracelet, she looks around the room for a place to hide. She scurries under the bed just as Meredith throws open the door and enters. Meredith is twenty-two years old. Athletic. Under a black leather motorcycle jacket she wears a dress identical to the one Frances wears; she seems resentful of it. She is also wearing a similar hat and carrying a bouquet. She has a beat-up backpack slung over one shoulder and sports a pair of sinister-looking sunglasses. She slams the door behind her and locks it, stares at the still-ringing telephone, frowns, and picks up the receiver.*) Mother, what? I am just dropping off my stuff. No ma'am, this room is off limits to you today. Mother. Bye-bye. Bye-*bye.* (*She hangs up the receiver, then kicks off a pair of pumps dyed to match her dress, throws the bouquet and the backpack on the bed, and crosses directly to the vanity. She grabs the jewelry box and digs through it.*) Shit! (*She checks the surface of the vanity frantically.*) I can't *believe* this! (*She crosses to the bed, pulls up the bedspread, and then gets down on her hands and knees and reaches under the bed. Crying out*) Who is that?

FRANCES (*from under bed*): Oh, it's just me. (*Frances emerges sheepishly from under the bed, keeping the bracelet on her wrist hidden behind her back. Sweetly*) Hi, there.

MEREDITH: Frances, what the hell are you doing?

FRANCES: Oh, well, there aren't too many people downstairs, and nobody I really know too well, aside from Mama and

Daddy and Uncle Reece and Aunt Kitty, so . . . I guess I'm just looking for a friendly face (*a nervous laugh*).

MEREDITH: Under my bed?

FRANCES: No, I—well, when I heard you coming in, I got scared, I realized I really shouldn't be here. I tried to hide from you, Meredith. I hope you can forgive me.

MEREDITH (*staring at her*): Well, sure. (*She pulls a milk crate from underneath the bed and digs through it.*)

FRANCES (*struggles with the bracelet behind her back*): It's just that this room is so beautiful. I remember whenever we came to visit when I was little, and Tracy still lived in here? You and her and all the other cousins would be having tea parties in her playhouse out back, but I would sneak up here and sit in the middle of this room and pretend it was mine. Of course, I just worshiped her. Tracy.

MEREDITH: You and everybody else. Herself included.

FRANCES: That's why I was so thrilled to be in her wedding. (*Meredith, unable to find what she was looking for in the milk crate, shoves it back under the bed and groans in frustration.*)

MEREDITH: Where the hell *is* it?

FRANCES (*nervously*): What are you looking for?

MEREDITH: I am trying to find a joint that I was saving for this reception—

FRANCES: A joint?

MEREDITH: I know I had one in my jewelry box, and if Tracy took it, that would be just like her.

FRANCES: Oh, surely she wouldn't!

MEREDITH: Oh, surely she *would*.

FRANCES (*shocked*): Take drugs? On her wedding day?

MEREDITH: Have you noticed how calm she is today? How *serene?* She has been a nervous wreck for weeks. She had to be high. (*Catches sight of herself in the mirror.*) Oh, lord. (*Takes off her hat.*) And then she has the gall to make us wear these horri-ble—*things* on our heads, so we all look like the flying *nun*—

FRANCES: I like this hat.

MEREDITH: Are you serious? Look at yourself in the mirror, Frances, you look ridiculous.

FRANCES: Well—

MEREDITH: You look like a lamp. At least you can wear this dress, though. Makes me look like a linebacker. (*Meredith observes herself critically in the mirror, frowns, and gets a pack of cigarettes out of her backpack.*) You want one?

FRANCES: No thanks. I don't smoke. I'm a Christian.

MEREDITH (*digging through her backpack*): Of course, wouldn't you know it? Now I can't find any matches. (*She goes into the bathroom, where she can be heard continuing her search. Frances works frantically to get the bracelet off her wrist.*) I mean, okay. I can certainly understand why Tracy would want to be stoned today, just to get through this ordeal. But she could have at least asked. I mean, she just *took* it! Typical. (*Frances finally gets the bracelet unclasped and slips it back into the jewelry box, greatly relieved.*)

FRANCES (*has learned her lesson*): Thou shalt not covet.

MEREDITH (*in bathroom*): And then all that stuff about obedience, everybody was acting so serious, I was like, Tracy? Obey Scott? She already runs that poor boy's life. I mean, what a joke! Tracy, the blushing bride. Excuse me while I barf. (*Cries out*) Oh, my God!!

FRANCES (*startled*): What? (*Meredith enters from the bathroom hold-ing a joint in front of her, reverently.*)

MEREDITH: Look. It was in the medicine chest! We are in business now! (*She grabs an ashtray and sits on the bed. Whining*) Shit, we still don't have any matches! (*There is a knock at the door. Irritated*) Mother, I told you my room is off limits!

TRISHA (*off*): Meredith?

MEREDITH: Trisha! (*She leaves the joint and ashtray on the bed, crosses to the door, unlocks, and opens it. Standing outside is Trisha, a striking, glamorous woman in her early thirties. She is dressed exactly like Meredith and Frances, but unlike them, she wears her dress well and moves gracefully in it. She carries a stylish, oversized shoulder bag.*)

TRISHA (*cheerfully*): Hey, babe!

MEREDITH: Do you have any matches?

TRISHA: Uhm, I think I might have a lighter.

MEREDITH: Thank God! You just saved my life. (*Meredith motions her in and rushes back to the bed. Trisha enters and shuts the door behind her.*)

TRISHA (*friendly*): I would have gotten here sooner but some creep with whom I apparently share some sort of history cornered me in the parking lot and chewed my ear to a bloody stump about how great it was to see me again, and could we get together soon, and so I said sure, did he have three hundred dollars, just to shut him up.

MEREDITH: Trisha! You didn't! What did he say?

TRISHA: He asked if I could wait for him to run to a cash machine, can you believe it? (*Friendly*) Hey, Frances!

FRANCES: Hi there.

TRISHA: How are you doing?

FRANCES: I'm fine. Thank you so much for asking. (*Trisha crosses to the vanity.*)

TRISHA: Oh, Meredith, your mother said she wants you downstairs to greet the guests while she freshens up.

MEREDITH: Please. That woman hasn't been fresh in thirty years. While she pops a couple of Xanax is more like it.

TRISHA: I could use a couple of those myself.

MEREDITH: Well, as soon as you get that lighter out, we're going to get stoned.

TRISHA: Oh, boy. I haven't been stoned in ages. Promise you won't let me do anything stupid, okay?

MEREDITH: You would never do anything stupid.

TRISHA (*a laugh*): Are you kidding? I looked out at the congregation during the ceremony, it was like half the men I saw, I think I may have slept with. God, I dread this reception. Do you think anyone would notice if I left?

MEREDITH: Yes, don't you dare leave me here alone.

TRISHA (*looking at her reflection in the vanity mirror*): God, would you look at me? I look terrible.

MEREDITH: You look like a million bucks, as usual.

TRISHA: I had to put about a gallon of white-out underneath my eyes this morning. (*She pulls a cosmetics bag from her purse and begins to skillfully retouch her makeup. The other women watch her, slightly cowed by her natural authority; this is a woman who knows how to be beautiful.*) So Frances, did you enjoy the wedding?

FRANCES: Yes, it was so beautiful.

MEREDITH: It was ridiculous.

FRANCES: Tracy's dress sure was something.

MEREDITH: Yeah, it was a float.

TRISHA: You've got to hand it her, though, she carried it off. I could never wear anything like that with a straight face.

MEREDITH: She didn't wear it. It wore *her*. If she has any sense at all, she'll put it on a mannequin and just roll it around the reception and leave herself free to mingle.

TRISHA: I shudder to think how much that thing cost.

MEREDITH: Six.

TRISHA (*turns to her*): That's obscene.

FRANCES: Six hundred dollars?

MEREDITH: Six *thousand*.

TRISHA: She talked me into designing her invitations for free, and then she made me go through *eight* revisions, and she spent six thousand dollars on her *dress?* That is totally obscene. Your poor father must be paying a *fortune* for this wedding.

MEREDITH: Don't you know it. But Daddy put his foot down— for a *change*—and said no way was he spending six thousand bucks on something she was only going to wear once, so she had to buy it herself.

TRISHA: Wow. I guess she makes pretty good money working for Pepsi.

MEREDITH: I guess. She offered to get me an interview over there. I told her I would rather work at McDonald's. I have spent my entire life being Tracy Marlowe's little sister, the last thing I want to do is go work at the same place she does. Trisha! Where is that lighter?

TRISHA (*handing her purse to Meredith*): It's in there somewhere.

MEREDITH: Good lord, what the hell do you keep in this thing?

TRISHA: Only my entire life. (*Meredith starts to dig through the purse.*)

MEREDITH: I about died when they knelt down and somebody had painted "Help Me" on the soles of Scott's shoes—

FRANCES: Oh, I *hated* that. How could somebody do something so nasty? A wedding is a sacred occasion.

MEREDITH: Well, *I* thought it was priceless.

TRISHA: Yeah, I figured you thought that was pretty funny.

MEREDITH: I wasn't the one who did it, if that's what you're implying. I wish I had been. Trisha! Do you know who did? Who? Tell me.

TRISHA: I don't know.

MEREDITH: You lie.

TRISHA: Meredith, I have no idea. It could be any one of those overgrown frat boys.

MEREDITH: I wish I knew which one. I would give him a blow job. (*She pulls an accordion pack of condoms from Trisha's purse.*) God, do you think you have enough condoms here?

TRISHA: Hey, the Scout motto is Be Prepared.

MEREDITH: That's the Boy Scout motto.

TRISHA: Well, then, the Girl Scout motto is Be Extra Prepared, because chances are the Boy Scout is an irresponsible jerk. (*Meredith finds the lighter and lights the joint. She inhales deeply.*)

MEREDITH (*exhales, laughs*): "Help me."

FRANCES: Pew! That stuff stinks.

TRISHA: Poor Scott. He turned about three shades of red, didn't he? I think he thought he had done something wrong.

MEREDITH: He did. He married my sister, that's about as wrong as you can get. God, I'm glad I found this joint.

TRISHA: I think Scott and Tracy are a perfect match.

FRANCES: Oh, I do too.

TRISHA: They're both smart, good-looking, rich—

MEREDITH: *Really* white.

FRANCES: And you can tell he really loves her.

MEREDITH: Yeah, well, any dog loves its master.

TRISHA: Now, Meredith, be nice.

MEREDITH: Oh, Trisha, don't be such a cheerleader. I want to have fun today. Fat chance. Everybody here is so aggressively *normal,* it's like the bland leading the bland. I was hoping Scott's lesbian sister would perk things up, but she's about as much fun as having your teeth cleaned.

FRANCES (*shocked*): Scott's sister is a—a—and everybody just *knows* about it?

TRISHA: I guess. (*To Meredith*) She's pretty much out, isn't she?

MEREDITH: God, yes. She rubs it in everybody's face.

FRANCES: My goodness. I don't think I've ever seen one before.

MEREDITH: Well, now you've seen three.

FRANCES: Who else?

MEREDITH: Those two flute players that played during the ceremony.

FRANCES: You're kidding.

MEREDITH: Nope.

FRANCES: But—they looked just like *real* women. And them playing in church like that, isn't that kind of sacrilegious?

TRISHA: I don't think you need to worry about it, Frances.

MEREDITH: Really. So far, this has been the most candy-ass wedding I've ever been to in my life. Things better pick up at the reception. I want something really sick and fucked up to happen. (*Trisha, having finished touching up her makeup, crosses to Meredith and takes the joint from her.*)

TRISHA (*laughs*): To you or to someone else?

MEREDITH: Either way, I don't give a shit.

TRISHA: Well, I bet you won't be disappointed.

MEREDITH (*senses dirt*): Why? What's going on?

TRISHA: Nothing.

MEREDITH: Tell me.

TRISHA (*offering joint to Frances*): Frances, you want some of this?

FRANCES: No ma'am. I do not take drugs. I'm a Christian.

TRISHA: I'm so sorry.

MEREDITH: It's Georgeanne, isn't it?

TRISHA: What?

MEREDITH: I saw her crying during the ceremony.

TRISHA: So? Lots of people cry at weddings.

MEREDITH: No, this had nothing to do with the wedding. (*Pause.*) Come on, Trisha, you have to tell me.

TRISHA: Meredith, I don't know. Georgeanne and I are not all that close anymore.

MEREDITH (*suddenly, surprised*): It's Tommy Valentine, isn't it. It's because he's here today.

TRISHA: I seriously doubt it.

FRANCES: Tommy Valentine. I have been trying to think of his name all day.

MEREDITH: Georgeanne had a thing with him too?

TRISHA: About a hundred years ago.

MEREDITH (*a whine*): God, is there *anybody* who didn't do it with him? (*Pause.*) I guess when you're as good-looking as he is . . .

TRISHA: He's not *that* good-looking.

MEREDITH: Trisha. He is sweat-out-loud gorgeous. That man is walking sex. Why else would every single one of you go off the deep end over him?

TRISHA: I never went off the deep end over him.

MEREDITH: Right.

TRISHA: I didn't.

FRANCES: I met him once, when Tracy brought him to that family reunion at Uncle Reece and Aunt Kitty's lake house? He was real nice.

MEREDITH (*to Trisha*): You look me in the eye and tell me you did not have a thing with him.

TRISHA: I did not have a thing with him.

MEREDITH: Trisha.

TRISHA: We went out a few times, before he and Tracy ever got together. As a matter of fact, I introduced them to each other.

MEREDITH: I know.

TRISHA: So how do you know everything? You were only a little kid.

MEREDITH: I was a smart little kid. And I also happen to be sisters with Tracy the mouth.

TRISHA: Well, then you probably know more than I do.

MEREDITH: I didn't know about Georgeanne and Tommy Valentine. (*Georgeanne enters. In her early thirties, she wears the same dress and hat as the others and carries an opened bottle of Champagne. Her hat is slightly askew. She bursts through the door, slams it behind her, kicks it once, then leans against it, crying, unaware there is anyone else in the room.*)

GEORGEANNE (*kicking the door again*): You stupid fucker! (*She wipes her nose on part of her dress and takes a swig from the Champagne bottle, then turns and sees the others. An awkward pause.*) Well, hello there.

TRISHA: Hey, hon.

MEREDITH (*sweetly*): Hey, Georgeanne.

GEORGEANNE: Please excuse me. (*She goes into the bathroom and slams the door.*)

MEREDITH (*thrilled*): Whoa. (*Trisha crosses to the window and looks out.*)

TRISHA: They sure are taking their sweet time setting up that bar. Man, I love a good open bar. If I ever get to heaven and there's not an open bar, God is going to have some serious explaining to do to me.

FRANCES: There will most certainly *not* be any liquor in heaven.

TRISHA: Well, thank you for clarifying that for me, Frances. I'll be sure to bring my own.

MEREDITH (*whispering*): Tommy must have said something to Georgeanne to get her that upset, don't you think?

TRISHA: Meredith, why do you even care?

MEREDITH: Maybe it's her husband! I notice he's not here today, I bet he's cheating on her!

TRISHA: Jesus.

MEREDITH (*gleefully*): I bet he's cheating on her and she just found out! You think?

TRISHA: I think it's none of your fucking business. Her life is her life, it's not a source of personal entertainment for you. That's pathetic.

MEREDITH (*stung*): I'm sorry. God.

TRISHA: I suppose you've never been through anything you didn't want the whole world to watch?

MEREDITH: I said I was sorry. You don't have to bite my head off. (*Pause.*)

TRISHA: Well. I'm just a little sensitive about that particular issue, since I am the reigning queen of the bad rep.

MEREDITH (*not quite heartfelt*): Your reputation is fine.

TRISHA: You shouldn't lie, Meredith, if you can't do it any better than that.

MEREDITH: I have never heard anybody say one bad thing about you.

TRISHA: Your mother used to habitually refer to me as "that little whore."

MEREDITH: You're crazy. Mama always loved you.

TRISHA: Meredith. Your mother hated my guts. She still does. She will not look me in the eye to this day.

MEREDITH: Why would she hate you?

TRISHA: Because she thought I was the world's worst influence on Tracy. And I was. But it is just basic human nature to be a real degenerate every now and then. And you ought to be able to do it without the whole world looking down its nose at you and acting like it's anything out of the ordinary. (*Looking out window*) Oh, God. There's the earring.

MEREDITH (*joins her at window*): What?

TRISHA: That cute boy usher, with the earring.

MEREDITH: Oh, him. He's Scott's cousin.

TRISHA: He is a piece of work.

MEREDITH: Ugh, you think?

TRISHA: Uh-huh.

FRANCES (*brightly*): You know, my big sister was dating a boy who had an earring, but Mama and Daddy made her break up with him.

MEREDITH: Frances, your sister is two years older than me.

FRANCES: Is she?

MEREDITH: And she still lets her parents tell her what to do? That is fucked.

FRANCES (*flushed*): Meredith, the Bible says to honor thy father and mother.

MEREDITH: The Bible also says that eating shellfish is an abomination, but that didn't stop you from sucking down that lobster bisque at the rehearsal dinner.

TRISHA: What is his name?

MEREDITH: His name is Tripp Davenport and you know it. (*Trisha looks at her.*) Oh come on, he flirted with you all through the rehearsal dinner.

TRISHA: Yeah, but he never told me his name.

MEREDITH: Well, his real name is Griffin Lyle Davenport the Third.

TRISHA: I think Tripp suits him better. He's got that look, you know?

MEREDITH: What look?

TRISHA: That look that makes you feel like you're at a really boring party and you and he are the only ones with drugs. It's the same look Tommy Valentine has.

MEREDITH: You'll have to point it out to me.

TRISHA: Oh, no. Believe me, you would be better off if you never even saw that look. It always turns out to be more trouble than it is worth.

MEREDITH: Look at all of them, in their tuxes. They look like a bunch of big—birds, you know?

TRISHA: Pigeons. (*Laughs.*) They are *pumped*.

MEREDITH: Why are men so stupid?

TRISHA: Because they're allowed to be.

MEREDITH: They are so weird. They are so weird.

TRISHA: Which one do you want?

MEREDITH: The only one of them that doesn't totally gross me out is Frank.

TRISHA: Frank? Really?

MEREDITH: I still remember what he was wearing the time he came to pick up Tracy for the Valentine's Dance when they were in the eighth grade. A white leisure suit with blue stripes, a navy blue shirt and a white tie. A white belt and white shoes with big silver buckles. I thought he was the most gorgeous thing I had ever seen.

TRISHA: He is handsome.

MEREDITH: He's a fag, isn't he.

TRISHA: Well—

MEREDITH: I knew it. What a waste.

TRISHA: Meredith, that is a terrible thing to say.

MEREDITH: I meant it as a compliment.

TRISHA: Calling somebody a waste is not a compliment. (*Pause.*)

FRANCES: Billy.

TRISHA: What?

FRANCES: He's the one I want.

TRISHA: Scott's little brother?

MEREDITH: Frances, he's fifteen.

FRANCES: I know.

TRISHA: Frances, you are *bad*. You're a wild woman, aren't you? (*Georgeanne enters from the bathroom.*)

GEORGEANNE: Yo.

MEREDITH: Hey, Georgeanne.

TRISHA: Hey, babe. You okay?

GEORGEANNE: No, I'm all fucked up. (*She sits on the edge of the bed, stares at the others, and starts to cry. Pause.*)

MEREDITH (*nosy*): What's wrong, Georgeanne? You can tell us. We won't tell anybody, I swear.

TRISHA: Meredith.

MEREDITH: It might do you some good to talk about it.

TRISHA: Meredith, why don't you and Frances go see if they've set up that bar yet?

MEREDITH: Why don't you just look out the window? (*Trisha makes a "just get out of here" face at Meredith, who makes a "why can't I stay" face back at her.*) Oh, all right. Y'all are going to have to wait for me to put on another pair of shoes, though. I am not wearing those peach-colored Chinese torture devices one minute longer. (*She goes into her closet. An awkward moment.*)

GEORGEANNE: Hey, Frances.

FRANCES: Hi there.

GEORGEANNE: Look. I know we don't know each other at all, but I am sorry you have to see me like this.

FRANCES: It's okay. Jesus wept. (*Meredith emerges from the closet carrying a pair of men's athletic shoes, sits on the bed and puts them on.*)

GEORGEANNE: One of those bartenders, the bald-headed one? If you flirt with him, he'll give you a bottle of Champagne.

MEREDITH: I can't do that.

FRANCES: I can. You'll have to drink the Champagne, though, because—

MEREDITH: You're a Christian. I know. How do I look? (*Checks herself in the mirror.*) Hideous.

TRISHA: You look fine.

MEREDITH: Yeah, right. (*Grabs Frances.*) Come on, Frances.

FRANCES (*sweetly*): Bye-bye now!

MEREDITH (*mimicking Frances*): Bye-bye, now! (*Meredith and Frances exit. Trisha shuts the door behind them but remains standing.*)

TRISHA: Please do not tell me this is about Tommy Valentine. (*Georgeanne nods, ashamed.*)

GEORGEANNE: I was walking down the aisle, first thing I saw was the back of his head. It just jumped right out at me. I recognized that little hair pattern on the back of his neck, where his hair starts? You know where it comes to those two little points, and it's darker than the rest? I always thought that was so sexy. Then I looked at him during the ceremony, and something about the way the light hit his face . . . I swear, it just broke my heart. And then outside, I saw him talking to this total bitch in a navy blue linen dress with absolutely no back, I mean you could almost see her butt. And he was smiling at her with that smile, that same smile that used to make me feel like I really meant something to him. And then it all came back, just bang, all those times I sat waiting for his phone call, me going out of my way to make things convenient for him. Having to take a fucking taxicab to the Women's Health Center that day because it was so cold my car wouldn't start. And later that awful, awful night I sat out in front of his apartment building staring at Tracy's burgundy Cutlass in the driveway, just wishing I was dead. You know, I started smoking cigarettes that night. And if I ever die of cancer I swear it's going to be Tommy Valentine's fault. (*She lights a cigarette, stands, and wanders around listlessly.*) God! I feel like I am going crazy! My cousin George, he's a nurse, he says I am the perfect type to get some weird disease because I'm so emotional.

TRISHA: You're not going crazy. You're just being really dramatic and self-indulgent.

GEORGEANNE: Self-indulgent! You think I want to feel like this?

TRISHA: Nobody's making you. (*Pause. Georgeanne stares at her, then takes a swig from the Champagne bottle.*)

GEORGEANNE: All right. Enough about me, more about my *dress*. Can you believe Tracy made us wear these things?

TRISHA: Yes.

GEORGEANNE: Of course, I can't believe she asked me to be in her wedding—

TRISHA: I can't believe you accepted.

GEORGEANNE: Well, I didn't have any choice, Trisha. What was I supposed to say? Tracy, I don't think I can be in your wedding, because you remember when I had that nervous breakdown my junior year of college? That was because your boyfriend knocked me up and I had to have an abortion all by myself while he was taking you to the Kappa Sig Luau, and things have been just a little, well, *strained* between you and me ever since.

TRISHA: Have you ever talked to her about that?

GEORGEANNE: Oh. No, neither one of us has ever mentioned it. (*Looking out window*) And now here she is, getting married to Scott McClure, the biggest piece of wet toast I ever saw in my life. 'Course I married Chuck Darby, the *second* biggest piece of wet toast I ever saw, because I thought I wanted some *stability*. And there's Tommy Valentine, getting ready to rip that little bitch's backless linen dress off of her scrawny little body and fuck her brains out. God, I wish I was her.

TRISHA (*exasperated*): Oh, please. You do not.

GEORGEANNE: Oh, yes I do. I am wearing over a hundred dollars' worth of extremely uncomfortable lingerie from Victoria's Secret that I bought specifically for him to rip off of *me*.

TRISHA (*staring at her*): You honestly thought you were going to sleep with Tommy Valentine today?

GEORGEANNE: Well. Yeah, I mean, why not? Remember page sixty-seven of *The Godfather?*

TRISHA: I think your memories of him might be just a little rosy, I mean it has been almost, what, ten years?

GEORGEANNE: Three months.

TRISHA: Excuse me? (*Georgeanne nods guiltily.*) Georgeanne, you better spill your guts to me right now.

GEORGEANNE: I ran into him at this sleazy bar that only plays fifties and sixties music? I hate those places but at least I'm not the oldest one there. He seemed really happy to see me, and then we started flirting, but it wasn't gross, it was real sweet— (*Trisha laughs.*) I'm serious, it was.

TRISHA: I'm so sure.

GEORGEANNE: You weren't there!

TRISHA: I've been there. So then what happened?

GEORGEANNE: Well, we closed that bar, and he asked me if I wanted to go somewhere where we could be alone. I said, look, this not a good idea, I'm married, I have a little boy. And once I said that? It's like I didn't have to worry about it.

I had said it, so it was out of the way. And I just went nuts, we ended up doing it in the parking lot, on the concrete, right behind a Dempsey Dumpster. (*Pause.*)

TRISHA (*impressed*): Wow. That's pretty good.

GEORGEANNE: Trisha, it was the best sex I ever had in my entire life. I will never, ever be able to smell garbage again without thinking about it. So my memories of Tommy are pretty recent and pretty accurate, I think.

TRISHA: Yeah, but Georgeanne. Did he call you after that?

GEORGEANNE: No.

TRISHA: Okay, so here's this guy who totally bagged out on his responsibility to you, left you to go through an abortion all by yourself. Ten years later, he fucks you in a parking lot and then he ignores you. And you still want him.

GEORGEANNE: I can't help it. I love him.

TRISHA: That's not love, that's addiction.

GEORGEANNE: Well, I'm sorry, but I hadn't had sex in over a year. And I wouldn't mind making a habit of it.

TRISHA: What? (*Pause.*)

GEORGEANNE: Chuck and I don't even sleep in the same bed anymore. He sleeps in the guest room.

TRISHA: Why?

GEORGEANNE: I don't know.

TRISHA: You have some idea. You have to.

GEORGEANNE: He doesn't talk to me, Trisha. It's like I'm not even there. I told Chuck about Tommy, the next day. He just looked at me with this fish face, and then he said, "You don't have to tell me everything you do." (*She starts to cry.*)

TRISHA (*irritated*): Georgeanne!

GEORGEANNE: What can I do?

TRISHA: *Make* Chuck talk to you. Make him go to a counselor.

GEORGEANNE: No.

TRISHA: Do you want to save your marriage?

GEORGEANNE: No! I *don't!* I never should have married him in the first place, just like you said. I don't love him. I don't even like him! (*Suddenly, the door opens and Mindy enters. She is an attractive, slender woman in her mid to late thirties. She is dressed exactly like the others.*)

MINDY: Y'all, am I bleeding?

TRISHA: Not that I can see.

MINDY (*goes to the mirror*): I will be. I am having one of those days where I just can't stop running into things? Do you ever have those? I am usually a very graceful woman, but something about this dress, it makes me feel like Bigfoot. I just ran smack dab into a cabinet in the kitchen, just walked right straight into it. Like there was a big magnet in that cabinet and I had a steel plate in my head. Ka-BOOM. I will probably need stitches by the time this reception is over. (*Turns to them.*) I am terrified. Terrified I am going to do something to ruin this wedding, and Scott will never forgive me. Just like that time I ralphed right in the middle of his Eagle Scout induction ceremony. My therapist thinks I was jealous that I couldn't be an Eagle Scout, but I don't think that was it. I mean, I was nineteen. I think I had just had a bad tuna salad sandwich. (*Notices Georgeanne's tears.*) Oh, this is a bad time, isn't it? I'm so sorry. I'll leave. (*She exits, knocking something over in the process.*) See what I mean? (*Pause.*)

GEORGEANNE: Are they all like that?

TRISHA: Who?

GEORGEANNE: You know. Lesbians.

TRISHA: What, clumsy?

GEORGEANNE: She's just so, I don't know. Blunt. Are they all like that?

TRISHA: Why are you asking me?

GEORGEANNE (*evasively*): Well, you know . . .

TRISHA: No, what?

GEORGEANNE: Well, haven't . . . I mean, I just remember hearing something about you and . . . oh, forget it.

TRISHA (*smiling*): All the lesbians I have known have not been clumsy. As a matter of fact, Mindy is the first.

GEORGEANNE: She is so strange.

TRISHA: I like her.

GEORGEANNE: Me, too, I guess. She seems to thoroughly detest Tracy, so she can't be all bad. (*Georgeanne crosses to the vanity. Looking in mirror*) God. Look at me. I am totally pathetic. I just don't want to be alone. Is that too much to ask? I mean, I still believe in marriage. I do. (*Trisha laughs ruefully.*) You don't?

TRISHA: To be perfectly honest with you, Georgeanne, I think any woman who chooses marriage in this day and age is out of her fucking mind.

GEORGEANNE: Don't you believe in love?

TRISHA (*turning to her*): I certainly believe in consideration. And respect. And I definitely believe in sex, because it's healthy and necessary. But love, what is that? I have had so many guys tell me they loved me, and not a single one of them has made any difference in my life.

GEORGEANNE: Maybe you haven't met the right one.

TRISHA: Oh, please. I've met him more times than I'd care to admit.

GEORGEANNE: Well, maybe you just haven't given him a chance.

TRISHA: I have given him too many chances.

GEORGEANNE: Oh, come on. What's the longest relationship you ever had, how many hours did that last?

TRISHA: Well, why drag it out? He'll just start trying to run my life or else he'll want me to be his mother.

GEORGEANNE: Not all men are like that.

TRISHA: I have yet to meet one who isn't. And I seriously doubt if I ever will.

GEORGEANNE: Really?

TRISHA: Yeah.

GEORGEANNE: How can you live like that?

TRISHA (*a laugh*): Well, in the first place, it's not a major tragedy. I'm just being honest. (*Pause.*)

GEORGEANNE: Maybe you're right. I'm probably just a hopeless romantic, doomed to go through my life being disappointed. (*At window*) There he goes. Sniffing after little Miss Navy Blue Linen. God. Look at the way he walks . . . he sure can wear a pair of pants.

TRISHA: I mean, what's the payoff? For having had that many women? Does it make him feel accomplished? Wiser? Or has it just become this drug he has to have?

GEORGEANNE: Well, you've slept with just as many guys. What's the payoff for you?

TRISHA: I have not slept with as many guys!

GEORGEANNE: How many guys *have* you slept with?

TRISHA: I don't know. A hundred.

GEORGEANNE: A hundred!

TRISHA: I haven't kept *count*.

GEORGEANNE: Trisha! That's a lot.

TRISHA: Yeah, but Tommy Valentine is like Wilt Chamberlain, he's probably had sex with a *thousand* women.

GEORGEANNE: God, I wonder if he's ever had an AIDS test.

TRISHA: You better hope so. Did he use a condom in the parking lot?

GEORGEANNE: No.

TRISHA: Georgeanne.

GEORGEANNE: I know. (*Pause.*) You think he's ever done it with another man?

TRISHA: A guy like Tommy, as good-looking as he is? I'm sure he's had opportunities.

GEORGEANNE: Yeah, but he's way too good in bed to be a queer.

TRISHA: That doesn't mean a thing. I knew this lifeguard once, talk about good in bed, this boy could have taught old Tommy Valentine a trick or two. He was a total animal, he loved sex. Loved it. Then one day I showed up at his apartment and found him in bed with the telephone repairman, which is obviously why I hadn't been able to call to tell him I was on my way.

GEORGEANNE: Oh my God. What did you do?

TRISHA: I went to happy hour at Bennigan's and picked up a busboy. (*Pause.*)

GEORGEANNE: Have *you* ever had an AIDS test?

TRISHA: Yep.

GEORGEANNE: I'm too scared to take it. I mean, I know the chances are slim, but with *my* luck. Weren't you scared?

TRISHA: Yeah, I was.

GEORGEANNE: What made you go through with it?

TRISHA: Well, it seemed like the responsible thing to do, and . . . that lifeguard died.

GEORGEANNE: Shit, Trisha. He died of AIDS? (*Trisha nods.*) You're okay, aren't you?

TRISHA: Yes, Georgeanne. I'm fine.

GEORGEANNE: Oh my God. I never knew anybody who actually had it.

TRISHA: You will. (*Pause.*)

GEORGEANNE: Well, I certainly don't want Tommy Valentine to have AIDS. But I tell you one thing. I can't wait for him to lose his looks.

TRISHA: And he will. It's bound to catch up with him. He's going to end up one of those hatchet-faced old men that really handsome guys turn into.

GEORGEANNE: Yes. He'll have one of those big red Ted Kennedy noses from drinking so much his whole life.

TRISHA: And a beer gut.

GEORGEANNE: He'll lose his hair.

TRISHA: He'll wear golf pants.

GEORGEANNE: Green golf pants. That are too tight.

TRISHA: Yes! And he'll unbutton his shirts a couple of buttons more than he should. (*Pause.*)

GEORGEANNE: No. He won't do any of that. He'll just get better-looking as he gets older, he'll never gain any weight, he'll wear a T-shirt and blue jeans and have grey hair and he will be so gorgeous that it hurts just to look at him. *I,* on the other hand, will be as big as a house, I'll wear too much makeup, I won't have any hair left from a lifetime of bad perms, and I'll get skin cancer from going to the lake too much when I was in high school and I'll just wake up one morning and I'll be dead. And Tommy Valentine will read my obituary in the paper and it won't even occur to him that he ever even knew me, much less slept with me. (*She bursts out laughing.*)

TRISHA: You were right. You *are* crazy.

GEORGEANNE: I am one sick ticket. Well, I guess I should give up my fantasy of getting laid by Sonny Corleone today.

TRISHA: Not necessarily. There are lots of cute guys here.

GEORGEANNE: Yeah, I dare you to find one who is straight, single and who has a job.

TRISHA: Maybe you need to lower your expectations.

GEORGEANNE: Maybe I need to have a nervous breakdown. Maybe I need to have a big, loud, nasty, smelly nervous breakdown right when Dr. Marlowe goes to do his father-of-the-bride dance with the new and improved Tracy Marlowe hyphen McClure.

TRISHA: I'll give you twenty bucks if you do.

GEORGEANNE: Do not tempt me, Trisha. I just might.

(*Meredith bursts in.*)

MEREDITH: I will give you a hundred bucks. I will give you anything you want. I will give you this pair of one-carat diamond studs I got for graduation.

TRISHA: Meredith!

MEREDITH (*rummaging through her jewelry box*): I will give you this antique ring that belonged to my grandmother that has been appraised at over five hundred dollars. See that? Isn't it pretty? It's yours.

TRISHA: How long have you been standing out there?

MEREDITH (*innocently*): I just heard that last little bit, I swear.

TRISHA: I cannot *believe* you.

MEREDITH: Please, Georgeanne, please say you will.

GEORGEANNE: No, Meredith. I will not.

MEREDITH: Please?

GEORGEANNE: *No.* I am *not* going to cause a scene.

MEREDITH (*whining*): Why not?

GEORGEANNE: Because this is your sister's wedding day, and that would be a really rotten thing for me to do. I may be a bitch, and I may be a slut, but I do have some standards.

MEREDITH: Shit.

TRISHA: Why are you so intent on something happening today, Meredith?

MEREDITH: I just hate this whole thing. I hate it. It's so goddamn fake it makes me sick. (*She lights a cigarette and crosses to the window, irritated.*)

TRISHA: Where's Frances?

MEREDITH: She's down there sucking up to that bald-headed bartender and he is a complete geek, if you ask me. (*Trisha and Georgeanne join her at the window to watch.*)

TRISHA: Oh, he looks nice.

MEREDITH: Gross. His Adam's apple is as big as my head.

GEORGEANNE: At least he's not wearing a rug. I swear, sometimes I look at my husband and his toupee is sitting up on top of his head like a stale pancake, and my heart just goes out to him. I mean, does he think people don't *know?* A ten-year-old *child* can tell. (*Mindy enters with a plate of finger foods.*)

MINDY: I wish I had one of those lobster bibs, I just know I'm going to be wearing this food any minute now. Of course, it's not like I plan to ever wear this dress again.

MEREDITH (*sarcastically*): Sure you will. Have it taken up, wear it as a cocktail dress. It'll be sweet.

MINDY: I'll probably give it to my friend Leroy, he's the only person I know who can wear this color. Anyway. Mrs. Marlowe sent me up here to tell y'all to come downstairs right this instant. She might have just wanted me out of her dining room, she was looking at me with this frozen smile, I could see every vein in her neck. Like, please God, just keep her away from my crystal. But she said for me to tell you all that it was a poor reflection on Tracy for all her bridesmaids to be avoiding the reception.

MEREDITH: Oh, well, God forbid we should make Tracy look bad.

GEORGEANNE: Why not, she's made every single one of us look perfectly dreadful.

MINDY: I like this dress.

GEORGEANNE: You do not.

MINDY: I do. I am so glamorous in this dress, I am goddamn Leona Helmsley. I am the queen of my own empire with a heavily armed security force. I am woman, hear me fucking roar.

TRISHA: Now do you think Tracy really thought these looked nice, or was it a conscious attempt to surround herself with ridiculous-looking women so that she would look better?

MEREDITH: What do you think?

GEORGEANNE: Like she needs to look better.

TRISHA: She is one beautiful woman.

GEORGEANNE: She is perfect. Perfect.

MEREDITH: She always has been.

MINDY: I hate her.

GEORGEANNE: I have no idea who she is now.

MINDY: I don't want to know.

GEORGEANNE: I'm serious.

MEREDITH: She's a rich white Republican bitch.

GEORGEANNE: Meredith! She's your sister.

MEREDITH: So? Y'all are trashing her, too.

TRISHA: I used to know her. Really well, I thought.

GEORGEANNE: You guys were tight.

TRISHA: For a while. But it was one of those friendships, you know, that's based on giving each other permission to be just totally wild and irresponsible? Those never last.

GEORGEANNE: She is—in *Glamour* magazine, you know the do's and don't's? She is the ultimate "do" girl.

TRISHA: And we're all the "don't" girl.

MEREDITH: Not you, Trisha.

TRISHA: Please.

GEORGEANNE: Oh, please my butt. You're the only friend Tracy ever had who was pretty as she is. You're probably the first girl she ever met who wasn't intimidated by her.

MINDY: No wonder she liked you. What freedom.

TRISHA: We had a lot of fun. That's why it's so weird now. I can barely carry on a conversation with her. We have absolutely nothing in common.

MEREDITH: Except Tommy Valentine.

TRISHA: And we're members of quite a large club in that respect.

GEORGEANNE: Wait a minute. Don't you think this is kind of weird?

MINDY: What?

GEORGEANNE: That we're all in her wedding but not one of us is really her friend?

MEREDITH: She had to dig, too. Look at my dorky cousin Frances.

GEORGEANNE: Good lord. I grew up with Tracy, I was her ugly sidekick all throughout high school and college, but I haven't been close to her in years.

TRISHA: Me neither.

GEORGEANNE: Doesn't she have any real friends?

MINDY: Don't look at me. Tracy and I move in very different circles.

GEORGEANNE: Meredith?

MEREDITH: I don't know. Seems like she hangs out with Mama an awful lot.

GEORGEANNE: I don't believe it. Here she is, the perfect woman, the ultimate do girl. She's beautiful, she has a great body, she has a fancy career, now she's got herself a rich husband who worships the ground she walks on. But she doesn't have any friends, does she.

MINDY: Can't have everything.

GEORGEANNE: This makes me feel so much better, I can't tell you. (*The phone begins to ring. As the other women watch, Meredith crosses to it, picks up the receiver, and then puts it back down again. Pause.*)

TRISHA (*looking out window*): Well, finally, that bar looks like it's running smoothly, and I see a bottle of Beefeaters that has my name on it. Okay, ladies. Let's get this show on the road.

GEORGEANNE (*groaning*): Do we have to?

TRISHA: It'll be fun.

GEORGEANNE: Yeah, compared to a triple bypass.

TRISHA: Don't even think about him, Georgeanne, he is scum.

GEORGEANNE: He is. He is slime.

TRISHA: He is garbage. (*Georgeanne winces.*) Oh, I'm sorry. I for-got.

GEORGEANNE: I need about another bottle of Champagne.

TRISHA: Anyone care to join us?

MEREDITH: In a minute.

TRISHA: Mindy?

MINDY: Why would I want to go out there? It's just the same old relatives who have been embarrassed by me my entire life.

TRISHA: Okay, we'll see you two later.

GEORGEANNE: Trisha, if I start acting like a real asshole, if you will just take me aside and smack me, I would greatly appreciate it.

TRISHA: Babe, it's going to take everything I have to keep myself in check, so I'm afraid you are on your own.

GEORGEANNE: God help us. (*They exit. Meredith stands looking out the window, an inscrutable expression on her face. Pause.*)

MINDY (*her mouth full*): Mm. You should try one of these little bacon wrap jobbies, Meredith, they are delicious.

MEREDITH (*not turning to her*): No thanks, I'm not hungry. (*Pause.*)

MINDY: Well, now that Scott and Tracy are officially married, I guess that makes you and me sisters. (*Meredith turns and looks at her, blankly.*) I always wanted a sister.

MEREDITH: It's not all it's cracked up to be. (*She turns back towards the window. Pause.*)

MINDY: Are you glad to finally be done with school?

MEREDITH: Yeah, Mindy, I'm just thrilled to be back at home, living with my fascist parents.

MINDY: Well, have you thought about what you want to do?

MEREDITH: No.

MINDY: What is your degree in?

MEREDITH: English. It's completely worthless.

MINDY: No, it isn't. You can do a lot with that. You can teach, you can write copy, you can edit, you can go to law school—

MEREDITH: Oh, *yeah*. That's just what I want to do, become a hired gun for the ruling class. (*Pause.*)

MINDY: All I'm saying is you don't have to do what you studied for. My degree is in behavioral psychology, and I sell real estate. Which, I suppose, it's completely appropriate when you think about it. But you really should let me introduce you to some people I know, Meredith, I bet they could—

MEREDITH: I just want to move.

MINDY: Move into town? Well, shoot, I can help you find a great place, this is the perfect time to be looking, too—

MEREDITH: God, no. I want to get as far away from Knoxville as I possibly can. I hate this town, I hate everything about it. I want to go somewhere where I don't know a single person. Where nobody will bother me. Where people will just leave me alone. (*Pause.*)

MINDY: Well, I guess I'll go . . . see if they have any of these meatballs left. . . .

MEREDITH: Uh-huh.

MINDY: We'll see you down there.

MEREDITH: Okay.

MINDY: Bye-bye. (*She exits. Meredith stands at the window, watching something—or someone—below, a blank, impassive expression on her face. The phone begins to ring again, startling her. She does her best to ignore it, and after a moment, she begins to cry quietly, as lights fade.*)

ACT TWO

The scene is the same as before; it is a couple of hours later. From outside can be heard the sounds of the wedding reception in full swing: people talking and laughing, a band playing dance music, etc.

Trisha and Georgeanne are seated on either side of Frances, who sits in front of the vanity. They are performing a makeover on her. Trisha applies makeup; Georgeanne is preparing to apply nail polish. She has partially unfastened the back of her dress to get comfortable, revealing the back of an elaborate black-lace bustier. Mindy is seated on the edge of the bed, holding a plate of food. Everyone except Frances has a cocktail. Most have removed their hats; they have all removed their shoes.

GEORGEANNE: Okay, Frances, which do you want, Maple Melon Mist, or Cha-cha Chinaberry?

MINDY (*her mouth full*): How come makeup is always named after food?

GEORGEANNE: What do you mean?

MINDY: Well, like Cha-cha Chinaberry, Maple Melon Mist. Raspberry Whip. Tangerine Dream. Simply Strawberry—

TRISHA (*picks up lipstick, reads label*): She's right. Guess what this is called.

GEORGEANNE: What color is it?

TRISHA: Kind of an orangey pink.

GEORGEANNE: Peaches and Cream.

MINDY: Pumpkin Chiffon.

TRISHA: Nope.

MINDY: Wait, let me guess. Ah . . . Nectarine Nights. No? Canteloupe! Canteloupe Cascade—

GEORGEANNE: Kickass Carrot Cake.

TRISHA: Nope.

MINDY: Cha-cha Cheez Whiz!

GEORGEANNE: Oh hell, what is it?

TRISHA: Absolutely Apricot.

MINDY: See? They *are* all named after food.

TRISHA: Well, what else are they going to name it after, Mindy?
What are they going to say, Bleeding Wound Red?

GEORGEANNE: Did you decide which nail polish you wanted,
Frances?

FRANCES: Uhm, I'll take the red.

GEORGEANNE: Good answer. Trisha, be sure and give her red lips,
too.

TRISHA: Well, now wait. Do you want to look fresh and natural,
or do you want to look like a woman with a past?

FRANCES: Oh, fresh and natural, I think.

TRISHA: Hmm. I think we'll go for a more neutral lipstick color.

FRANCES: I don't want to be too made up, now. I don't want him
to think I look trashy.

TRISHA: Don't you worry. When I get through with you, he
won't stand a chance.

GEORGEANNE: What's his name?

FRANCES: Bradford.

GEORGEANNE: Bradford what?

FRANCES: He didn't tell me.

GEORGEANNE: Bradford. Brad. Brad and Frances.

MINDY: Only Brad I ever knew was my orthodontist Brad Rosenblum. He had the hairiest hands. And he was always sticking them in my mouth.

GEORGEANNE: Brad and Fran. Brad and Frannie.

FRANCES: I hate being called that.

GEORGEANNE: It's cute.

FRANCES: It sounds too much like fanny.

TRISHA: What does he do?

GEORGEANNE: Trisha. He's a bartender.

FRANCES: No, he's in law school.

GEORGEANNE: Really?

FRANCES: He only bartends part time, thank goodness.

TRISHA: Well, you tell him he makes a superior martini.

GEORGEANNE: Law school! Frances, you have scored. How old is he?

FRANCES: Thirty-six.

GEORGEANNE: Thirty-six and he's never been married? That's not a good sign.

FRANCES: He's been married once before. No kids, although he says he wants to.

TRISHA: Divorced?

FRANCES: No, she died.

GEORGEANNE: Ugh.

TRISHA: Poor thing.

FRANCES: Four years ago.

GEORGEANNE: Well, in a way, that's kind of—*attractive*. I mean, it makes him kind of tragic and mysterious.

FRANCES: He feels like he's just now getting over it.

TRISHA: Frances, your timing is impeccable.

MINDY: I just had a horrible thought.

GEORGEANNE: What?

MINDY: What if he killed her?

TRISHA: Mindy.

MINDY: I'm serious. What if he goes around the country, marrying women and then killing them. Didn't you ever see that movie?

GEORGEANNE: Yes! And you know what? He kind of looks like that guy.

MINDY: Doesn't he?

GEORGEANNE: He's got those shark eyes.

MINDY: How did she die, Frances?

FRANCES: He didn't say. (*Pause.*)

GEORGEANNE: My cousin George works for the state patrol, I could get him to run a security check for you.

TRISHA: I thought your cousin George was a nurse.

GEORGEANNE: That's my other cousin George. I have three cousins named George, one named Georgette and one named Georgina. And my Aunt Georgia. We're all named after my grandfather.

MINDY: What was his name?

GEORGEANNE (*staring at her*):   George.

FRANCES: Bradford is too nice to be a killer.

GEORGEANNE: Uh-uh. Those are the ones you need to watch out for.

MINDY: Wouldn't that be gross?

FRANCES: What?

MINDY: If you fell in love with a real psycho killer? And you really loved him, and you married him and all, and then you found out what he was? What would you do? (*Pause.*)

GEORGEANNE: Well, first thing, I would find a good support group for the wives of psycho killers, because I think I would need to talk to some people who really understood what I was going through.

MINDY: Would you tell the police?

GEORGEANNE: Come to think of it, I guess I would be kind of scared of him. (*Meredith enters, holding a cocktail. She locks the door behind her.*)

MEREDITH: Y'all, I have got to get out of this dress. It is completely unnatural. Georgeanne, will you unzip me?

GEORGEANNE (*doing so*): What are you going to do?

MEREDITH: I am going to be comfortable for the first time today, damn it. (*She maneuvers her way out of the dress, leaving it in a pile on the floor. Underneath she wears a strapless bra and a pair of boxer shorts. She is still wearing boy's athletic shoes.*)

TRISHA: Meredith, you can't go out there and not be wearing that dress. You just can't.

MEREDITH: Don't worry. I am not going out there again. It's a fucking zoo out there. (*She retrieves a T-shirt from the bathroom and puts it on, then begins to dig through a box of CDs.*) My crazy old Great Aunt Rosalie just came up to me and screamed in my ear, "Well! I guess we'll be seeing you get married next, honey!" You know what I said to her? I said, "Fat chance. You will be dead long before I am ready to put myself through this shit."

TRISHA: You did not. (*Meredith puts a CD in the CD player.*)

MEREDITH: Well, no, I didn't. But I had to bite my tongue to keep from doing it. God! I am so sick of listening to that cheesy band. (*Screaming, nihilistic rock and roll blasts over the speakers.*)

TRISHA: What are you in such a bad mood about now?

MEREDITH: First Tracy yells at me because I took that thing off my head. "It's not optional," she says. "It's part of the uniform." Then Mama has to join in about how I have gotten too much sun on my shoulders and they're all freckled and just ruined. "It's not ladylike," she says, whispering to me like she was telling me I had B.O. Ladylike! Of course, to her, there are two types of women, debutantes and dykes, and guess which category I fall into. No offense, Mindy. Then poor Scott starts having a sneezing fit—

MINDY: He always does that when he gets nervous.

MEREDITH: —and the band is playing "Tie a Yellow Ribbon." You know that hostage song? And all the old farts are dancing— Is there any of that joint left?

MINDY: Meredith, what *is* this music?

MEREDITH: You don't like it?

MINDY: It's really . . . intense. Don't you have anything a little . . . *less* intense?

MEREDITH: Sure, let me see if I can find something bland enough for you. (*She pulls the CD out and starts rummaging around.*) What are all y'all doing up here?

TRISHA: Frances has a date, and so we're giving her a makeover.

MEREDITH: A date? With who?

GEORGEANNE: Bradford the Bartender.

MINDY: And part-time psycho killer.

MEREDITH: What are you going to do?

FRANCES: Well, he said he knew of this place right outside town that was real pretty, and maybe we could just drive there and have some beers. (*The other women exchange looks.*) But then I told him I didn't drink beer, that I was a Christian, and he said, well shoot, we could go to McDonald's, that he just enjoyed talking to me. I thought that was real sweet.

TRISHA: That is.

FRANCES: He comes from a real small town too, we were talking about how scary a place like Knoxville can be. And he said as soon as he gets his degree he's going back to the country. Not to where he came, he doesn't think he can ever go back there, since his wife died—

MEREDITH: She died?

MINDY: Yes, and under very mysterious circumstances.

FRANCES: He said he felt like he had to shut the door on that part of his life, and start all over with a clean slate. (*Mindy and Georgeanne trade looks.*)

GEORGEANNE: Just like the guy in that movie.

MINDY: Uh-oh. You better get him to show you some pictures of himself when he was younger, Frances. For all we know, he might not really be bald, he might have shaved his head to change his identity.

GEORGEANNE: I bet Bradford is not even his real name.

MINDY: You know what you do? Go to McDonald's with him, and then when he's not looking, you take something that he's touched, pick it up with a napkin, though, and just slip it in your purse, and then tomorrow you take it to the FBI.

GEORGEANNE: If she's alive tomorrow.

MINDY: Oh, I don't think he would kill her on the first date.

TRISHA (*laughs*): You two are horrible.

FRANCES: He can't be a killer. He's a Christian. (*Pause.*) Of course, he's a different kind of Christian than I am, since he believes in drinking beers. I told him that was wrong and he said he didn't think so, but that he would be willing to talk about it. That's the main reason I decided to go out with him.

GEORGEANNE: Really.

FRANCES: A good Christian man is hard to find these days. There isn't a single one in my church group, except for the ones who are younger than me, but they don't count. I think the man should be older than the woman. (*Pause.*)

MINDY: And taller, too, I bet.

FRANCES: Well, sure. (*The other women avoid each other's eyes, trying not to laugh. Meredith has found the joint.*)

MEREDITH (*holding up the joint*): Anybody want to smoke any pot?

TRISHA: I'll take some.

MINDY: I don't usually, but I think I'll make an exception today.

GEORGEANNE: Oh, well, twist my arm. (*Sits next to Mindy on the bed.*) You are going to have to promise to keep me away from that food table, though. I dropped ten pounds for this wedding, I intend to keep it off for at least a week or two.

MEREDITH: Ten pounds, how did you do it?

GEORGEANNE (*dryly*): I was motivated. (*As they pass the joint around, Frances coughs dramatically.*) Hey, how old were you when you first smoked pot?

MINDY: Twenty-one. I was a late bloomer.

GEORGEANNE: I was eighteen.

TRISHA: Fifteen.

FRANCES: I don't take drugs. I'm a Christian.

GEORGEANNE: What about you, Meredith?

MEREDITH: I was twelve.

GEORGEANNE: Twelve!

MEREDITH: You remember when I was in junior high, Trisha, you and Tracy let me spend the night at your apartment on campus? We drank black Russians and got high.

TRISHA: Meredith, I am so sorry I corrupted you like that.

MEREDITH: No, I loved it! I couldn't believe how cool you were. I thought you were *it*.

TRISHA: Oh, hon. If you only knew how fucked up I was back then. (*Meredith puts a reggae CD on the stereo and begins dancing loosely; Mindy watches her.*)

MEREDITH: So, Trisha, what's up with you and Tripp Davenport?

TRISHA: Nothing.

MEREDITH: Come on. I saw you talking to him for about an hour out there.

TRISHA: Yeah?

MEREDITH: You two seemed to really hit it off.

TRISHA: I wouldn't know, I was on automatic pilot.

MEREDITH: But you said he had that look.

TRISHA: I'm sick of that look. It always leads to trouble.

GEORGEANNE: I don't know, Trisha. He's pretty cute.

TRISHA: Believe me, he's quite aware of that.

MEREDITH: He's not *that* cute.

TRISHA: He's pretty cute.

MEREDITH: He's no Tommy Valentine.

TRISHA: Thank God. I will say one thing about him, he has the best hands.

GEORGEANNE: Hands?

TRISHA: Yeah. You can tell a lot about a guy by his hands. They are just so amazingly beautiful. And also— Oh, y'all are going to make fun of me.

GEORGEANNE: No, we won't.

MEREDITH: We promise.

TRISHA: Well. It's not a man's feet. And it's not his shoes either, you know those big black wing tip shoes like businessmen wear?

GEORGEANNE (*not sure she wants to hear this*): Yeah?

TRISHA: It's a man's feet . . . *in* those shoes. (*Pause.*)

MEREDITH: That's really weird, Trisha.

MINDY: My therapist would have a field day with that.

GEORGEANNE: I like a good neck, myself.

MEREDITH: Shoulders.

FRANCES: Rear ends.

MINDY: Well, personally, I prefer a nice set of hooters. (*Everyone laughs.*)

MEREDITH: So, Trisha, do you like him or don't you?

GEORGEANNE: She likes him a lot.

TRISHA: How do you know?

GEORGEANNE: Because I know you, Trisha, and I know how you get when you really like somebody. You light up like a god-damn Christmas tree and then you get all shy. And that is exactly what you have done today.

MEREDITH: How old is he?

MINDY: He's—(*thinks*)—twenty-nine.

GEORGEANNE: Twenty-nine! Trisha, you old dog. (*Trisha looks at her.*) No, that's great. Go for the young meat.

TRISHA: Georgeanne! That's only—three years younger than me.

GEORGEANNE: Three strong, limber, and highly energetic years.

MEREDITH: What does he do?

TRISHA: I forgot to ask for his resume.

MINDY: He works for a bank, telling other people where to put their money.

GEORGEANNE: Way to go, Trisha, that means he's probably rich.

MEREDITH: Is he single?

MINDY: He just broke up with his girlfriend a couple of months ago.

GEORGEANNE: How do you know so much about him?

MINDY: He's my cousin, and he's the only one who never got weird when I came out, so I keep in touch.

GEORGEANNE: Is there anything wrong with him?

MINDY: No, he's a really nice guy.

GEORGEANNE: Damn. Trisha, you have the best luck of any woman I know.

TRISHA: I don't believe this. I have a simple conversation with him and now I'm supposed to be picking out my china pattern? What century are you women living in?

GEORGEANNE: Oh, right, I forgot. You're through with men.

TRISHA: No, I'm through with being disappointed. I have never met a man who could look at me and see anything but his own ego, and Tripp Davenport is no different. No offense to your cousin, Mindy, but I think I'll pass.

GEORGEANNE: He really got to you, didn't he?

TRISHA: I'm sick of it. I am. I quit. I'll just be an old maid. (*Pause.*)

FRANCES: Don't you want babies?

TRISHA: You don't need a man to have a baby.

MINDY: Well, actually you do, technically.

TRISHA: Yeah, but you don't have to cement yourself to him. Hell, he doesn't even have to know about it.

FRANCES: But that's so wrong.

MINDY: I don't think so. All the movie stars are doing it.

FRANCES: God wants you to be married if you have a baby.

TRISHA: How do *you* know what God wants?

FRANCES: Because the Bible says so.

TRISHA: Frances, has it ever occurred to you that the Bible is a book that was written by men?

FRANCES: The Bible is the holy word of God, Trisha.

TRISHA: Well, I will grant you that it is the history of one culture's *quest* for God, but—

FRANCES (*hotly*): *That* is secular humanism talking, and *that* is the kind of talk that has got us into the mess we are in today, causing the collapse of family values and all decent morality. *That* is why there is so much crime and violence and licentiousness in this world, and that is why we are living in the end times and the rapture could happen at any minute. Any minute! (*Pause. Everyone is a little surprised by this outburst.*)

MEREDITH (*a laugh*): Get serious.

FRANCES (*upset*): I *am* serious. Now, I will sit here and watch you all drink liquor and take drugs, every other word F this and G-D that, honestly, you ought to be ashamed, you are *ladies*. But I will *not* tolerate you making fun of the Bible.

TRISHA: Nobody's making fun of anything. Am I not allowed to have an opinion?

FRANCES: Not if it is disrespectful to my religion, no, ma'am, you are not. (*A pause.*)

TRISHA: I'm afraid I have a little problem with that.

FRANCES: This is America. I have a right to my beliefs.

TRISHA (*evenly*): Listen, Frances, I wholeheartedly support your right to live your life however you see fit. But you cannot exercise that right without extending the same courtesy to other people who might think differently than you do.

FRANCES: My religion happens to be very important to me, and I don't want to listen to you criticize it.

TRISHA: Then leave. (*Pause.*)

GEORGEANNE: Trisha.

TRISHA: I mean it. Go on, get out of here.

FRANCES (*shocked*): What?

TRISHA: Go someplace where people don't have ideas. Where everybody is willing to trade their God-given intelligence for any old blind set of rules just because they don't want the responsibility of making their own decisions. I'm sure you won't have to go very far.

FRANCES: I—

TRISHA: But don't you *dare* tell me what I can and cannot talk about. You do *not* have the right to do that. (*A pause. Frances backs down completely.*)

FRANCES (*looking at her half-made-up face in the mirror, weakly*): But I can't go out there looking like this. I'm only half done! What would people think? (*She turns to Trisha, terrified. Tearfully*) I don't look right!

TRISHA: Oh, good grief, Frances. Don't cry, your mascara will run.

FRANCES: I'm sorry.

TRISHA: Hon, I'm not mad at you, I just—oh, now look. Hm. Well, maybe we'll go for the woman with a past look instead of the fresh and natural, that way we can do a smudged charcoal thing around your eyes. Okay?

FRANCES: Thank you. I'm sorry. (*Trisha resumes the makeover on Frances. A pause, as the others exchange surreptitious glances. Georgeanne mounts stair-climbing machine.*)

MEREDITH (*a stoned laugh*): Look at my dress. Doesn't it look like a big old cake, just sitting there? My mother told me there is an art to wearing a gown, that I should just float down that aisle like a swan. I wanted to say, Mama, have you ever seen a swan walk? Anybody can float on a lake.

MINDY: She meant like this. (*Mindy puts down her plate, stands, and swoops across the room in a hyper, ultragraceful manner.*)

GEORGEANNE: Hey, do that again.

MINDY: Okay. (*Mindy repeats the move. It is stunning and absurd.*)

GEORGEANNE: Where'd you learn how to do that?

MINDY: Miss Amelia's Charm School.

TRISHA: You're kidding. You went to charm school?

MINDY: My mother *made* me go when I was in sixth grade, I think she was dimly aware of my dyke potential and was hoping Miss Amelia would nip it in the bud.

GEORGEANNE: What else did she teach you?

MINDY: She taught us how to choose the right haircut for our face and how to avoid shooting a beaver when we sat down. We had our own beauty pageant for graduation. The Princess Charming Pageant.

GEORGEANNE: Oh my God.

MEREDITH: That must have been so humiliating.

MINDY: Are you kidding? I loved it. I wore a nautical bathing suit with a little skirt attached, and high heels, and I played "Crimson and Clover" on my bassoon for the talent competition and I won.

GEORGEANNE: You did not.

MINDY: It was the high point of my life. I'm serious. It's been all downhill ever since.

GEORGEANNE: I would have thought you hated beauty pageants.

MINDY: Why? Because I'm a lesbian? Hell, no. I haven't missed a Miss America pageant in twenty years. Those girls are better than drag queens. Hell, they *are* drag queens. (*She performs another dramatic swoop and then stands on the bed.*) "I am just so thrilled to be poised on the brink of a fabulous career combining broadcast journalism and teaching handicapped children but most importantly being a good wife and mother and a good American. (*Turning*) Here's my tits, here's my butt, here's my tits again. Thank you!" (*She waves insanely. The other women crack up laughing. Meredith gets up on the window seat and yells out the window to the guests below.*)

MEREDITH: Hey everybody! Here's my tits! (*Pulls down her bra and flashes her breasts, then waves insanely.*) Thank you! (*A shocked pause, then Georgeanne and Mindy cross to Meredith and pull her away from the window, as Trisha attempts to calm Frances, who appears to be hyperventilating.*)

TRISHA: Meredith.

MEREDITH (*laughing hysterically*): I just flashed my *mother—*

MINDY: Meredith, you're drunk.

MEREDITH: Duh.

GEORGEANNE: Come on. You need to sit down. (*They seat her on the bed*.)

MEREDITH: I just flashed my mother. I couldn't help it. I saw her look up here with her face all pinched and I don't know, I just flashed my tits at her.

GEORGEANNE: Did anybody else see you?

MEREDITH: I don't know. Probably. I don't care. I'll just say that I didn't do it, and then she'll get confused. I'm sure she's heavily sedated by now, anyway. (*Suddenly serious*.) I'm glad I did it. It was fun.

GEORGEANNE: There *is* a certain amount of freedom in letting your tits fly, isn't there?

MINDY: I remember this one baby-sitter me and Scott had, she would look at us real sweet and say, "Do you all want to see my titties?" Well, of course we did. So we would sit there on the edge of my bed, and she would slowly pull up her blouse. And we would just look at them. (*She retrieves her plate and resumes eating*.)

GEORGEANNE: How old was she?

MINDY: Oh, I don't know, twelve, thirteen.

MEREDITH: That's child abuse.

MINDY: Please. A young girl who is proud of her new breasts is hardly child abuse. It was completely innocent.

GEORGEANNE: Hey, I want to know something. Do you always eat like this?

MINDY: Yes.

GEORGEANNE: Then how the hell do you stay so skinny?

MINDY: I'm extremely neurotic and high-strung.

GEORGEANNE: You don't like pig out and barf, do you?

MINDY: No. I just have a really high metabolism and burn every-thing off.

GEORGEANNE: God. I hate your guts.

MINDY: You do not. You love me.

GEORGEANNE: In your dreams.

MINDY (*mouth full of food*): Kiss me.

GEORGEANNE: Get away.

MINDY: Kiss me.

GEORGEANNE (*laughing*): You are the grossest person alive.

MINDY: Thank you.

GEORGEANNE: Let me have some of that.

MINDY: Oh please. Take it away from me.

GEORGEANNE: I'm starting to miss those ten pounds I lost. (*Mindy hands Georgeanne her plate, then notices a demure little sundress in a floral print in Meredith's closet.*)

MINDY: This is so cute. Meredith, is this yours?

MEREDITH: It used to be. Back when my biggest goal in life was to be in the Junior League.

MINDY: I bet you looked real sweet in this.

MEREDITH: You would.

MINDY: What is that supposed to mean?

MEREDITH: Nothing. (*Pause.*) Just what I'd expect from a coun-try club socialite like you.

MINDY (*a laugh*): I am hardly a socialite, Meredith.

MEREDITH: A little white girl dress like that.

MINDY: You know, that's about the third time I've heard you say something about white people. I hate to point this out to you, hon, but you aren't exactly Queen Latifah.

MEREDITH: Yeah, well at least I am not a hypocrite.

MINDY: Neither am I.

MEREDITH: So?

MINDY (*amused*): You think just because you put a picture of Malcolm X up on your wall, that proves something? If you really cared about injustice as much as you let on, you'd be out doing something about it, instead of sitting up here with your portable CD player and your StairMaster and your five-hundred-dollar motorcycle jacket, complaining about how unfair things are. (*Meredith stares at her, then turns to Trisha.*)

MEREDITH: So, Trisha. Tripp Davenport looks like he—

TRISHA: Don't start. Okay, Frances, all done. (*She turns Frances around so she can look in the mirror.*)

FRANCES: Oh, my.

TRISHA: What do you think?

FRANCES: I never knew I could look like this! (*She turns to face the others. She looks quite glamorous.*)

GEORGEANNE: Frances, you look *hot*.

MEREDITH: Trisha! You should do this for a living.

MINDY: God. She looks fabulous.

FRANCES: I don't even look like myself.

GEORGEANNE: Trisha, where did you learn to do that?

TRISHA: *Years* of practice.

MINDY: Will you do me next?

TRISHA: Well—

MEREDITH: And then me?

TRISHA: I'll do one more and then I have to get back out there.

MINDY: Hot damn! (*She sits down in front of the mirror.*)

TRISHA: What do you want to look like?

MINDY: A truck stop whore. (*The telephone rings. Meredith answers it.*)

MEREDITH: What, Mother? (*Meredith suddenly erupts, and screams into the receiver.*) Bitch! Would you just shut up and leave me the fuck alone, for *once*? (*She slams the receiver down. The other women stare at Meredith, a bit taken aback. She looks at them, scowling, then suddenly bursts into laughter. Mimics*) "Everybody could see your dinners, honey, plain as day." Dinners! That is totally Appalachian. (*The other women exchange looks. Meredith wanders over to the stair-climbing machine, mounts it, and begins to tread lazily.*)

GEORGEANNE: That's what my mother calls them too.

MEREDITH: Those two are in rare form today.

GEORGEANNE: I can just hear them. "Kitty, I want to tell you, Tracy just looked radiant at her wedding. Just radiant. Why thank you, Eleanor, you know, Georgeanne looked radiant herself. Is she expecting another child? Heavens no, Kitty, Georgeanne just needs to lose about twenty pounds, she's a fat pig."

MINDY: You are not fat.

GEORGEANNE: Well, I certainly ain't skinny.

MINDY: I think you look fabulous.

GEORGEANNE (*unbelieving*): Thanks.

MINDY: And I think it's high time women let themselves just be women for a change, and stopped trying to look like all these anorexic models that, face it, they look like men. Every time I turn on the TV, there's some high-attitude fashion bitch stomping around like she's such hot shit and I think, *this* is what I'm supposed to want to be? I would rather eat glass. (*To Trisha*) No that's not right. I want something sluttier. Like dime-store blue.

TRISHA: Meredith, do you have any blue eye shadow?

MEREDITH: I sincerely hope not. But check in that top drawer.

GEORGEANNE: I don't think there's anything wrong with wanting to look *pretty*—

MINDY: Good grief, neither do I. But these women who are willing to have their lips poofed up and their tits inflated and their ribs removed? I mean, come on. That sounds like a Nazi war experiment. Those ribs are there for a reason. And that fat-sucking thing? I'm sorry. There is something desperately wrong with a culture which encourages people to go to such extremes. We think we are so civilized. But we're just as barbaric as those Aztec guys who played soccer with human heads. Look at this whole ritual today. Here's your sister in this white monstrosity, meant to symbolize that she is undamaged goods, it's like a sacrifice! And I mean, who in this day and age is a virgin when she gets married?

FRANCES: *I* will be a virgin when *I* get married. (*Pause.*)

TRISHA: Frances, really?

FRANCES: Yes ma'am.

GEORGEANNE: Get out of here.

FRANCES: I am saving myself for the man that I get married to. (*Pause.*)

GEORGEANNE: Frances. That is whacked. Because believe me, he ain't saving himself for you.

MINDY: I think that's admirable. You hold out for Mr. Right, Frances.

TRISHA: Hon, you are selling yourself up for a major letdown.

FRANCES: What is wrong with wanting to be a virgin when you get married?

GEORGEANNE: How old are you?

FRANCES: Twenty-one.

TRISHA: Haven't you ever been in love?

FRANCES: Not that way.

TRISHA: Haven't you ever had the hots for somebody?

FRANCES: I have more respect for myself than that.

TRISHA: Okay, forget about the sex. Don't you ever get lonely?

FRANCES: No. I don't, because I have Jesus in my heart. He is always there for me, ready to give me strength when I feel weak. To show me compassion when I feel anger. And to embrace me completely, in the deepest, purest love that there is. Whenever I need it. (*Pause.*)

GEORGEANNE: I think I might like a date with Jesus.

FRANCES: That's not funny.

GEORGEANNE: I'm serious.

FRANCES: Jesus didn't date.

GEORGEANNE: Are you kidding? He was the biggest rock star of his day. I bet he had groupies coming out the wazoo.

MINDY: I think it's rather interesting that he had twelve men in dresses follow him wherever he went.

FRANCES: Those were *robes*. Jesus and his disciples did not wear dresses. (*Pause.*) Except on very formal occasions. (*She giggles briefly, then casts her eyes upward and mouths the word "Sorry."*)

TRISHA: Meredith?

MEREDITH: Uh-huh?

TRISHA: Why do you have all these pictures of Tommy Valentine? (*Pause.*)

MEREDITH: Where?

TRISHA: Here, in this drawer.

MEREDITH: Tracy must have left him there. This used to be her room, you know.

TRISHA: Yeah, about ten years ago.

MEREDITH: Well, I don't know how they got in there.

TRISHA: Look at this one of him water-skiing. He must be all of nineteen.

GEORGEANNE (*grabs photo and looks at it*): Oh, would you just look at that stomach? God, how I hate him.

TRISHA: He sure was beautiful, wasn't he?

GEORGEANNE: Still is.

MINDY: Let me see. (*Looks at photo.*) Yeah, he's okay. If you like that sort of thing. Wait a minute. This guy's here today.

GEORGEANNE: Yep. He still is.

MINDY: This guy made a pass at me.

GEORGEANNE: What?

MINDY: Yeah, I was standing around at the food table and he came up to me and said, we haven't met, but I feel like I know you. I said, you must be mistaken, because you do not know me. And he said, well, I would like to. How do I go about it? I just laughed and said, whoa, buddy, you are barking up the wrong tree.

TRISHA: He is so shameless.

FRANCES: That's the same thing he said to me.

GEORGEANNE: What?

FRANCES: Yeah, he remembered me from the first time I ever met him, up at Uncle Reece and Aunt Kitty's lake house? He said he always wished he'd gotten to know me better.

GEORGEANNE: No.

FRANCES: Uh-huh. He was real sweet. He suggested that we go out after the reception, but I told him I was already spoken for today.

GEORGEANNE: That son of a bitch!

FRANCES: I'm sure he just meant for us to, you know, talk.

GEORGEANNE: Oh, I'm sure.

TRISHA: Good grief. That boy should have the word "trouble" tattooed right across his forehead, just as a common courtesy. I mean, imagine. Here he is at his old girlfriend's wedding, and he has either slept with or made a pass at every one of her bridesmaids. Well, all except one. That is so incredibly rude.

GEORGEANNE: Yeah, Meredith, you better be prepared for him to try to jump your bones next, you're the only one left. (*Pause.*)

TRISHA: Oh, please. Don't tell me. (*Laughs.*) Somebody needs to put him on a leash. (*Pause. Meredith is silent.*) Meredith? What's wrong?

MEREDITH: Nothing. (*She sits on the bed and starts to cry. A stunned moment, then they all gather around her.*)

TRISHA: Honey, what is it? Are you okay?

MEREDITH: I'm fine. I'm fine, I don't know why I'm crying, I'm so stupid.

TRISHA: No, you're not stupid.

GEORGEANNE: Did he do something to you?

MEREDITH: No, he—I just—I had a—a thing with him, too. We had a thing.

GEORGEANNE: What?

MINDY: When?

MEREDITH: A long time ago. It was—it was okay, he didn't rape me or anything. Please don't ever tell anybody. Promise me you won't ever tell anybody. Especially Tracy.

TRISHA: I promise.

MEREDITH: We just . . . we had a thing. Not for long. It's okay. It was okay.

MINDY: How old were you? (*Pause.*)

MEREDITH: I don't know. Twelve, thirteen. (*Pause. Georgeanne grabs her shoes and hat.*)

GEORGEANNE: That does it. I am going to find that sleazy fuckwad and tell him just what—

MEREDITH: Don't!

TRISHA: Georgeanne—

GEORGEANNE: He has it coming, Trisha!

MEREDITH: Don't! Please! (*Georgeanne exits.*) Trisha, don't let her!

TRISHA: Frances, you go after her, and do *not* let her make a scene.

FRANCES: But what can I do?

MINDY: Get that psycho killer boyfriend of yours to help. Go on. Stop her.

FRANCES: Okay. (*She finds her shoes and exits.*)

MEREDITH: She can't say anything to him, Trisha. She can't.

TRISHA: She won't, Meredith, they won't let her.

MEREDITH: I would die if anybody ever knew.

TRISHA: It's okay. You don't have to tell anybody.

MINDY: Yes, she does.

MEREDITH: He really liked me, Trisha. He really did. And now he won't even look at me. I went up to him outside, I was nervous as shit, and I said hey, Tommy. Remember me? And he said, "Well, sure I remember you. Hey there." But he wasn't looking me in the eye. And he *wouldn't*. He wouldn't even *look* at me.

TRISHA: Oh, hon. (*Pause.*)

MINDY: What did he do to you, Meredith?

MEREDITH: It's not like it sounds, he was really nice, he really— he really liked me. He did. He was always bringing me little presents whenever he came home with Tracy. Telling me how pretty I was getting to be. He came to my junior high swim meet when I won first place for the freestyle, it was one of the happiest days of my life.

TRISHA: I remember that.

MINDY: Tell me what he did. (*Pause.*)

MEREDITH: He was here one Christmas, it was Christmas Eve, and everybody had gone to sleep. I was laying in bed. I was thinking about him. I was imagining what it would feel like. I had never even kissed a boy. (*Barely audible*) And there was a knock on my door, real soft. It was like a dream. He said he thought it was time we got to know each other a little better. And Trisha, I wanted it. I wanted it to happen.

TRISHA: That's only natural, Meredith. Everybody is curious about sex—

MEREDITH: No, I wanted him. I wanted Tommy Valentine. I wanted him to fuck me.

TRISHA: And there is nothing wrong with that. He is a good-looking, charming, sexy man. Of course you would want that. But there *is* something very wrong with him actually doing it. Very wrong with *him*.

MEREDITH: I loved him.

MINDY: That wasn't love, Meredith. That was abuse.

MEREDITH (*angry*): No it wasn't!

MINDY: How long did it go on?

MEREDITH: Just a few more times, then he said he thought we should quit, I mean, after all, he was engaged to my sister.

MINDY: Listen to me. You need to talk to somebody about all this.

MEREDITH: I can't tell—

MINDY: I'm not talking about Tracy, or your parents. I'm talking about somebody who can help. What happened, Meredith, was not harmless. It was abuse. You were sexually abused.

MEREDITH (*upset*): Stop saying that.

MINDY: And it happens to a lot of women. You're not the only one. I know a lot of people it happened to. (*Meredith looks at her uneasily.*) You need to realize exactly what did happen, and how it affected you. And you need to be with people who have been through it. They can help.

MEREDITH: I could never tell anybody.

TRISHA: You told us.

MEREDITH: Yeah, and obviously that was a mistake.

MINDY: I have a number you can call, I'm going to give it to you. I want you to promise—

MEREDITH (*angry*): I'm okay.

MINDY: Just promise you'll think about it.

MEREDITH: It's not a big deal. God. You're trying to make it into this big thing, it *wasn't*—

MINDY: I'm going to leave it right here on your dresser, okay?

MEREDITH: Do whatever you want, I don't care.

MINDY: And I'm putting the names of a couple of people you can speak to directly on here, they're friends of mine, and they will—

MEREDITH: Look. Get this straight, Mindy. I am not interested in meeting any of your friends. I'm not.

MINDY: But they can help—

MEREDITH: Oh, I *bet*. (*Pause.*) What do you think, I'm an idiot, Mindy? I am not blind, I see the way you look at me. But I am not like you. I'm just *not*, okay? So it really wouldn't do much good for me to meet any of your friends. (*Pause.*)

MINDY: Meredith, I—

MEREDITH: What? Nobody asked you to butt into my life, did they? I don't recall anybody asking you to butt into my life. (*She removes her bathrobe, retrieves her dress from the floor, and maneuvers herself into it.*) If you all will excuse me, I think I am needed outside. Trisha, can you zip me up?

TRISHA (*doing so*): Are you okay, hon?

MEREDITH (*irritable*): I'm fine. I wish everybody would stop acting like I was falling apart. I am not a child, you know! I am fine.

TRISHA: Well, I just want to tell you, if you ever need me, I'm here.

MEREDITH: Excuse me. (*She exits.*)

MINDY: Well, great. That's just great. Anything I can offer is going to get thrown back in my face as being some perverted seduction attempt. Meanwhile, a man can actually molest her while she's still a child and she calls it love. (*A burst of anger*) That *fucking* son of a *bitch!* I swear to God, Trisha . . . sometimes, I just can't believe how fucking . . . how incredibly fucked up men are. They've fucked up the economy, they've fucked up the environment, and what the hell do they do about it? They fuck little girls! You don't mind if I rant, do you?

TRISHA: As long as you don't expect it to change anything.

MINDY: God knows, I don't want to be one of those dykes who hates men. I don't hate men, some of my best friends are men. I just hate them right now.

TRISHA: What on earth goes through a man's head while he fucks his fiancée's twelve-year-old sister? (*Pause.*) I wonder if it's too late for me to become a nun. I mean, I don't believe in God, and I've partaken of just about every sin there is, but I tell you what, that life is starting to look pretty good. (*Pause.*)

MINDY: I knew this day was doomed, from the moment when Scott first told me he was going to marry Tracy. (*Mockingly*) *Tracy,* who requested that I not bring Deb who is my lover of *nine years* to the rehearsal dinner because they wanted to keep it just *family.* And I acquiesced because I didn't want another big scene, and now Deb is boycotting the wedding which *Tracy* has gone out of her way to let me know she is *very hurt* by. Bitch. (*Pause.*) She will never love my little brother the way he deserves to be loved. She will never *honor* him and *cherish* him, like she said she would today, in front of God and everybody. It just makes me so sad. And now here I am in this ridiculous dress, with a fucking pin cushion on my head, I look like a hooker from the Twilight Zone, and if I blow chunks, I'm going to be really upset. (*Georgeanne has entered during this tirade.*) I hate throwing up. You are totally alone when you throw up.

GEORGEANNE: It's so humiliating.

TRISHA: It's good for you.

GEORGEANNE: Last time I threw up, I felt terrible, Chuck and I had been drinking tequila all night long in a totally misguided attempt to have *fun* together, and I just barfed all over the place, and felt so bad, and instead of trying to make me feel better, he just looked at it and said, "God, Georgeanne, I could reconstruct your entire meal. Don't you ever chew your food?" And then he poured a beer on my head.

MINDY: I haven't thrown up in almost twenty years.

GEORGEANNE: Twenty years? Really?

MINDY: Really. Not since Scott became an Eagle Scout.

TRISHA: Are you serious?

MINDY: Yep. I'm too repressed.

TRISHA: Oh, please. You're the least repressed person I've ever met.

GEORGEANNE: You don't *not* throw up because you're *repressed*.

TRISHA: You should throw up, Mindy, you really should. It's completely primal, you would feel so much better.

MINDY: Maybe I will.

TRISHA: You should throw up on Tommy Valentine.

MINDY (*with resolve*): I will.

GEORGEANNE: I got bad news for you guys. Tommy Valentine has already left.

TRISHA: Oh, he's such a chickenshit.

GEORGEANNE: No, I think he made a *friend*.

TRISHA: You're kidding!

MINDY: Why should that surprise you?

TRISHA: Who?

GEORGEANNE: Blonde hair, navy blue linen dress.

TRISHA: The backless?

GEORGEANNE: Yep. Who was that, do you know?

TRISHA: Karen Murdoch. Tracy's boss at Pepsi.

GEORGEANNE: Well, *that's* perfect.

TRISHA: Now Tracy and Tommy can run into each other at business functions and be tense and peculiar together.

GEORGEANNE: Ten to one she has an affair with him now that she's married.

TRISHA: Who knows?

GEORGEANNE: Who cares? (*Pause.*)

TRISHA (*to Georgeanne*): So how are you doing, babe?

GEORGEANNE: Trisha, I am fabulous. I am so drunk I can barely walk. And I have my eyes set on a certain saxophone player who shall remain nameless. Mainly because I have no idea what his name is, nor do I want to know. I just want to get him drunk, have my way with him, and then leave him stranded on the side of the interstate without any pants. Naturally, he doesn't even know I'm alive.

TRISHA: His loss.

GEORGEANNE: Aw, that is so sweet, Trisha. (*She hugs Trisha warmly.*) Listen, I am really sorry for the way I just kind of blew you off after I got married. I did, didn't I?

TRISHA: Yeah, you did. But it's okay. You were so weird to be around, I was actually relieved.

GEORGEANNE: But I should have been there when you were going through all that with that lifeguard.

TRISHA: Don't worry about it.

GEORGEANNE: And as soon as I unload that deadbeat piece of wet toast that I married, and I think that may be real soon, I am going to have a lot more free time to spend with the people that I really care about like you.

TRISHA: You're on.

GEORGEANNE: I've missed you. (*She hugs Trisha again; she is getting sentimental.*)

TRISHA: Georgeanne, your dress is still undone.

GEORGEANNE: Oh, my lord. And I was just walking around outside with it like this! Well, hell, at least *somebody* got to see my new sixty-dollar bustier. (*She twists her body around in an attempt to refasten her dress, much to the amusement of Trisha and Mindy.*)

MINDY: You look like a dog trying to chase its own tail.

GEORGEANNE: Well, I can't help it, I am being held hostage by my underwear— (*She wobbles toward the window, with Mindy right behind her, still attempting to refasten her dress. Trisha already stands at the window, gazing out, searching. Teasing*) Who are you looking for, Trisha?

TRISHA: I was trying to find Meredith—

GEORGEANNE: Yeah, right. (*Looking out*) Look at Frances, stuck to the bar, drooling over Ted Bundy.

MINDY: Good grief. You straight women, throwing yourselves away on mass murderers and child molesters. It's such a waste. (*Tripp appears at the door. He is in his late twenties, charming, dressed in a tuxedo. He shouldn't be overly handsome, but definitely sexy. This man enjoys a good time.*)

TRIPP: Well, what the hell are you all doing up here? There's a party trying to happen outside.

GEORGEANNE: We were just trashing your sex, Tripp Davenport.

MINDY: I'm fixing to puke my guts out.

TRIPP: And I'm just in time.

GEORGEANNE: Some guys have all the luck.

TRIPP (*to Trisha*): Hi.

TRISHA: Hi.

TRIPP: I've been looking all over for you.

TRISHA: I can be hard to find, sometimes.

TRIPP: So I've noticed. (*Pause.*) Mind if I join you?

MINDY: No.

GEORGEANNE: Pull up a chair.

TRIPP: I have been cutting up the rug with your mother for the past half hour, Mindy. I had no idea she could dance like that.

MINDY: Are you kidding? She danced for the U.S.O. in Korea.

TRIPP: Get out of here. Aunt Betty?

MINDY: That's where she met Daddy. And that's where I was conceived out of wedlock and my entire dysfunctional family began.

GEORGEANNE: That is so romantic.

MINDY: She was nineteen years old. Barely.

TRIPP: God. Isn't that weird to think about? When my dad was my age, he already had three kids.

GEORGEANNE: I'll tell you what's really weird to think about. There are some things that we are already too old for. Some things that have just passed us by, that we will never get a chance for.

MINDY: Like what?

GEORGEANNE: Like I will never be a stewardess. (*Pause. Trisha laughs.*)

TRIPP: You would have been a great stewardess.

GEORGEANNE: I would have.

TRIPP: What did you want to be when you were growing up?

MINDY: I wanted to be a nurse.

GEORGEANNE: You and my Cousin George.

MINDY: A nurse! I am so sure. Can't you just see me giving some old coot a sponge bath?

GEORGEANNE: I always wanted to be a teacher. Well, I wanted to be Miss Crenshaw, because her fiancé would come pick her up in a blue Chevy Malibu with a white vinyl top and he was so cute, he had a blond crew cut and his sideburns were darker than the rest.

TRIPP: What about you, Trisha?

TRISHA: I wanted to be that lady on *Mission: Impossible,* the one who had to pretend to be in love with dictators so she could double-cross them and then go back to her husband who always wore the mask so he could turn into that week's guest star? I thought that would be a great life.

MINDY (*To Tripp*): What about you?

TRIPP: Well, mine's kind of similar, actually. I wanted to be Ilya Kuryakin on *The Man from U.N.C.L.E.*

GEORGEANNE: God, remember him? In fifth grade, every girl in my class was totally hot for him.

TRIPP: And that's exactly why I wanted to be him.

GEORGEANNE: I bet you wore a lot of turtlenecks.

TRIPP: Would you all be totally grossed out if I took off my shoes?

MINDY: I couldn't possibly be any sicker than I already am.

TRIPP (*untying his shoes*): I have the hardest time with shoes, I've got this one pair of wing tips I wear to work, it took me forever to break them in but now they are the most comfortable shoes I own. I begged Scott just to let me wear them today because nobody would know, but you know what he did? He said he had to ask Tracy, and of course *she* said no, I had to wear the same stiff patent leather shoes as the rest of the ushers, and now my feet are about to kill me. (*Pause.*)

GEORGEANNE (*sneaking a glance at Trisha*): Wing tips?

TRIPP: Yeah. (*Pause.*) What?

GEORGEANNE: Well, I guess I'll go see what's happening outside. Mindy, would you care to join me?

MINDY: No, but I will.

GEORGEANNE: I'm kind of hungry.

MINDY: Oh, please. Do not even mention food, or I will throw up on *you*.

GEORGEANNE: At this point, I probably wouldn't even notice.

MINDY: That makes you the perfect date. (*They exit.*)

TRIPP: Hi.

TRISHA: Hi.

TRIPP: How are you?

TRISHA: Well, it's been a day.

TRIPP: How so?

TRISHA: Oh, I don't know. This is a very weird wedding.

TRIPP: They always are.

TRISHA: They always start out fine, but everybody has such high expectations, and then gradually they just disintegrate, and things get . . .

TRIPP: Hallucinatory.

TRISHA: Exactly. (*Pause.*) What about you?

TRIPP: What about me?

TRISHA: Are you having fun?

TRIPP: I always have fun.

TRISHA: Really?

TRIPP: Just about.

TRISHA: And why is that?

TRIPP: I'm not sure. But I kind of like it that way, so I try not to question it too much.

TRISHA: You're just an easy-going kind of guy, I guess.

TRIPP: I guess.

TRISHA: I would imagine you get into a lot of trouble that way.

TRIPP: It's happened.

TRISHA: And will happen again.

TRIPP: We can hope.

TRISHA: Why are we talking like this?

TRIPP: Like what?

TRISHA: Like a cheap version of Humphrey Bogart and Lauren Bacall in *The Big Sleep.*

TRIPP: I don't know. Maybe we're possessed.

TRISHA: I don't get possessed.

TRIPP: Maybe we're nervous around each other.

TRISHA: Why would we be nervous?

TRIPP: Maybe we like each other.

TRISHA: *Like* each other?

TRIPP: Well, sure. What else are we going to do at this point?

TRISHA: Liking each other just sounds so—I don't know, it sounds so innocent.

TRIPP: Maybe it is.

TRISHA: What are you going to do now, give me your I.D. bracelet?

TRIPP: If you really liked me, you would carve my initials in your arm.

TRISHA: What?

TRIPP: My next-door neighbor in seventh grade did that, so she would have a scar in the shape of her boyfriend's initials. I thought that was so—*ultimate,* to have a girl like you so much she would mutilate herself for you.

TRISHA: I will never like you that much.

TRIPP: Damn.

TRISHA: A tattoo would be much easier.

TRIPP: Don't get a tattoo.

TRISHA: Why not?

TRIPP: I hate tattoos on women.

TRISHA: Oh, but you love them on men? Is there something you need to tell me, Tripp?

TRIPP: You don't need a tattoo.

TRISHA: Well, nobody *needs* a tattoo. People get them because they want them.

TRIPP: I don't want you to have a tattoo.

TRISHA: A minute ago we just liked each other, and already you're trying to run my life. This is a bad idea.

TRIPP: So you're admitting that we do like each other.

TRISHA: I'm saying we did a minute ago.

TRIPP: At one point in time, we liked each other.

TRISHA: I think we can agree on that.

TRIPP: Good. (*Pause.*) Now what do we do?

TRISHA: Who says we have to do anything?

TRIPP: You know, you have this way of answering every question with a question—

TRISHA: Do I?

TRIPP: As if you have to challenge everything I say.

TRISHA: Does that bother you?

TRIPP: No, it doesn't bother me.

TRISHA: Good.

TRIPP: I like it. I need to be challenged. Sometimes I can be full of shit.

TRISHA: No. I don't believe it. You?

TRIPP: It's true.

TRISHA: I'm shocked.

TRIPP: It's hard to imagine you being shocked, somehow.

TRISHA: Oh, I get shocked.

TRIPP: By what?

TRISHA: By how stupid people can be. How selfish. How people are so willing to add to other people's suffering.

TRIPP: Wait a minute, are we going to have a real conversation now?

TRISHA: I don't know, what do you think?

TRIPP: I'm not opposed to it, I just need to shift gears a little bit.

TRISHA: We don't have to, if you're not up to it.

TRIPP: No, let's do it. Okay. Do you believe in God? Do you ever think about Death? When was the first time you had sex? When was the first time you really *liked* it? Do you ever feel guilty, just because your life isn't too terribly difficult?

TRISHA: Never.

TRIPP: Good, me neither. Let's go to the mall.

TRISHA: The *mall?*

TRIPP: Yeah. It's Saturday, we could go the mall, hang out with the teenagers at the multiplex, chow down on some Chick-fil-A? Shop for hours in the tape and record store without buying anything?

TRISHA: We're not dressed for it.

TRIPP: Why not?

TRISHA: Oh, I couldn't.

TRIPP: Trisha, this is uncharacteristically gutless of you, I'm surprised.

TRISHA: I am thirty-four years old, I am not about to traipse around a mall looking like I just came from my prom. The only way I would do such a thing is with the assistance of major pharmaceuticals.

TRIPP: Well, in that case. (*He produces a packet of cocaine from his pocket.*) Say hello to our surprise guest.

TRISHA (*obviously pleased*): No! I have a feeling you could be a bad influence on me.

TRIPP: I have a feeling nobody is ever a bad influence on you.

TRISHA (*suddenly nervous*): Tripp, I really like you.

TRIPP: Oh, I bring out the drugs and suddenly I'm Mr. Wonderful.

TRISHA: You're not a coke head, are you?

TRIPP: No, this is strictly a special occasion thing.

TRISHA: Would you tell me if you were?

TRIPP: Yes, I would tell you if I was. We don't have to do this.

TRISHA: No, I want to.

TRIPP: But now you're nervous, now you don't trust me.

TRISHA: It's not that.

TRIPP: What is it, then? (*Pause.*)

TRISHA: I would really hate for you to be a coke head.

TRIPP: Okay, let's make a deal. You don't get a tattoo, I won't be a coke head.

TRISHA: Deal. (*Pause.*)

TRIPP: We really don't have to do this.

TRISHA: Well, what's the worst thing that could happen?

TRIPP: We could talk a lot and be *really* interesting.

TRISHA: We could have heart attacks.

TRIPP: We don't have to do that much. I have kind of a low threshold, anyway.

TRISHA: We could get arrested.

TRIPP: We could spend the night in jail.

TRISHA: We could just spend the night. (*Pause.*) Are you blushing?

TRIPP: Well—

TRISHA: You are, you're blushing.

TRIPP: Maybe a little.

TRISHA: Did I shock you?

TRIPP: No, I just—

TRISHA (*really enjoying this*): Is that not the direction you were intending to go in?

TRIPP: Well, of course it occurred to me, but . . .

TRISHA: You never expected me to *say* it. You thought it would just kind of happen.

TRIPP: I guess. (*Pause, as they look at each other. Holding up cocaine*) If we do, I don't think I want to do this.

TRISHA: Why not?

TRIPP: Because I think I'd like to have a clear head.

TRISHA: We'll do it after.

TRIPP: Oh, good, because I quit smoking.

TRISHA: Okay, then. No sense hanging around here. Let's go. (*She grabs her purse and turns to him. A bit of a challenge. Pause.*)

TRIPP: Wait a minute. I'm not so sure about this.

TRISHA: Why not? (*Pause.*)

TRIPP: I think I would like to get to know you better.

TRISHA: Oh, brother.

TRIPP: I'm not so sure I want to go to a motel, do drugs and have sex, just for the hell of it, because I think there might be more to you and me than that.

TRISHA: Do you think there's something wrong with going to a motel, doing drugs and having sex, just for the hell of it? Do you think that's bad?

TRIPP: No, I don't.

TRISHA: You're the one who pulled out the cocaine.

TRIPP: You're right. And when I came to this wedding, that's exactly what I was looking for. But now that we're here, now that this is happening, I don't know.

TRISHA: I knew it. Guys like you cannot deal with a woman who takes charge.

TRIPP: Guys like me? I've been reduced to a *category?* Thanks.

TRISHA: You don't want me to be the one who makes the move, do you.

TRIPP: I don't want you to be an easy fuck in a cheap motel. For me, that usually works best when it's with somebody I don't really care one way or the other about.

TRISHA: Why, Mr. Davenport. Are you saying you care for me? I'm touched.

TRIPP (*frank*): I'm saying there's something between the two of us that I don't run into every day. I felt it the first time I met you, and you did too.

TRISHA: I don't think you have any idea what I feel.

TRIPP: I think I do. I think it scares you, and I think that's why you left me in the middle of the reception and came up here to hide.

TRISHA: I did *not* come up here to hide.

TRIPP: Why else would you care if I was a coke head?

TRISHA: I *don't* care if you're a coke head, Tripp. I don't care if you're a liar, a thief, if you're married, I *don't* care if you're a child molester *and* a psycho killer and you're wanted in fifty states by the FBI! I just want to have a good time today. I *want* to go to a motel, do drugs and have sex, just for the hell of it. Okay? Forgive me for being so shallow. (*Pause.*)

TRIPP: I don't buy that for a minute.

TRISHA: I cannot believe how amazingly arrogant you are.

TRIPP: You can't believe somebody's calling your bluff.

TRISHA: Oh, fuck you.

TRIPP: Women like you—

TRISHA: Now *I'm* the category.

TRIPP: —you like to stay one step ahead, just out of reach, but you're always looking back to say, "Don't stop reaching."

TRISHA: Yeah, well, better one step ahead than one step behind.

TRIPP: You think that's where I want you to be? I just broke up with somebody who was perfectly happy to be one step behind me, I don't want that.

TRISHA: See? This is it. This is all about what *you* want. Well, I'm sorry, but I am not here to be who you want me to be. (*Pause.*)

TRIPP: All I know, Trisha, is that I've never met anyone quite like you before. I have fun when I'm with you, more fun than I've had in a long time. So I don't want to blow this chance to see what—to see where we could . . . Okay, if you want to go to a motel, do drugs and have sex, fine. I just want you to know what I'm feeling before we do it, because it's not going to be insignificant. (*Pause.*) I don't want to be just another notch on your belt.

TRISHA: You don't want a lot of things, Tripp. Why don't you tell me what you *do* want?

TRIPP: I want you to promise me something.

TRISHA: Okay, here we go. What?

TRIPP: I want you to promise me that you won't leave your body after we make love. And that you won't completely write me off, because we did. (*Pause.*)

TRISHA: Well, since we're all being so wonderfully honest, thank you, I have to tell you, Tripp. I can't promise that. I know myself, and I know that's what I do sometimes.

TRIPP: I had a feeling.

TRISHA: I *will* promise to try not to let that happen.

TRIPP: And if you feel like it is happening, you'll tell me?

TRISHA: But you have to promise me something in return.

TRIPP: Fair enough.

TRISHA: You have to promise not to get all twitchy on me, and start obsessing about me and turning me into something that I'm not.

TRIPP: I have to promise not to fall in love with you?

TRISHA: You have to promise not to get too intense too fast. I'm serious. You have to promise not to put any pressure on me. Because I have absolutely no patience for that.

TRIPP: I promise.

TRISHA: That was too easy.

TRIPP: I'll be as quiet as a church mouse, you won't even know I'm around.

TRISHA: I'll know. (*Pause.*)

TRIPP: So, we're agreed, here?

TRISHA: Uhm . . . we *understand* each other.

TRIPP: Good. Let's go to the mall.

TRISHA: I am not going to the mall.

TRIPP: Well, where else can we go?

TRISHA (*exasperated*): Where do you *live*, Tripp?

TRIPP: Actually, I live in Atlanta.

TRISHA: You don't live here in Knoxville? (*Pause.*) You don't live here in Knoxville? You just put me through all that and you don't even live in the same *town?*

TRIPP: I have a car.

TRISHA (*laughing in spite of herself*): You are such an asshole.

TRIPP: Is this a problem, me not living here?

TRISHA: Actually, it makes you infinitely more attractive to me.

TRIPP: Well, that's a backhanded compliment. You really think I'd be so hard to deal with on a regular basis?

TRISHA: Probably. I am.

TRIPP: You can always come visit.

TRISHA: We'll see.

TRIPP: I'm a great cook. I make the best toast in three states.

TRISHA: I do need to ask you something.

TRIPP: What?

TRISHA: Are you averse to latex?

TRIPP: Not at all. I just bought a variety pack. (*There is a commotion heard from below. They cross to the window and look out.*)

TRISHA: Whoops. I guess I'm supposed to be out there.

TRIPP: Oh, shit, I haven't missed that garter thing, have I? I love that, it's so stupid.

TRISHA: Look at Georgeanne, waving her hands in the back like a wide receiver. She can't catch the bouquet, she's already married.

TRIPP: Everybody else looks afraid of it. (*Pause. Cheers from below.*) Oh, her. Good.

TRISHA: Frances. That's perfect.

TRIPP: Are you sad because you didn't get it?

TRISHA: Oh, right.

TRIPP: Always a bridesmaid.

TRISHA: Never a schmuck. So. Tripp. Where are you staying? With Scott's family?

TRIPP: No way. I'm slaying at a really nice hotel downtown.

TRISHA: The Regency?

TRIPP: No, the Quality Inn.

TRISHA: Oh, yeah, that's a *real* nice place.

TRIPP: You've been there?

TRISHA: No, but I've always wanted to, I've heard such fine things about it.

TRIPP: Well, perhaps you would allow me to be your escort.

TRISHA: God. I've dreamed of this.

TRIPP: We'll dine in the Lamplighter Room. Later, we'll take a moonlight stroll around the parking lot, before ducking inside Chuckie's Hideaway, where we'll sip Mai Tais and boogie to the disco beat of the Rhythm Rascals. Then we'll retire to my suite, order nachos and Cheez Whiz from room service, and watch *Pretty Woman* on HBO. How does that sound?

TRISHA: Sounds suspiciously like going to a motel, doing drugs and having sex just for the hell of it.

TRIPP: How can you take something so beautiful and turn it into something so sleazy and cheap?

TRISHA: I am sorry. It sounds heavenly. I can't possibly imagine a more perfect evening.

TRIPP: Tracy and Scott won't be having nearly as much fun.

TRISHA: Really, they're going to be stuck in Jamaica. Look at her, she looks like a hot-air balloon from this perspective, doesn't she?

TRIPP: She sure knows how to work a crowd.

TRISHA: Promise me something.

TRIPP: Anything.

TRISHA: If you ever see me dressed in something that ridiculous, please shoot me.

TRIPP: Uhm . . .

TRISHA: If you really like me, you will promise.

TRIPP (*surveying her dress*): Trisha, if I make that promise, I'm going to have to shoot you right now. (*He turns her to him and puts his arms around her. They study each other for a moment, then she places her arms on his shoulders and they kiss.*)

TRISHA: You are either a total con artist or the most naive man in America. Either way, I'm in trouble.

TRIPP: That makes two of us. (*They kiss again. Suddenly, the door bursts open and in walk Georgeanne, Mindy, and Frances in quick succession, all holding Champagne glasses, with Meredith lagging slightly behind. Georgeanne also carries several tiny tulle bags, filled with rice, tied with ribbons.*)

GEORGEANNE: Hey. Quit it, you two.

MINDY: Gross.

GEORGEANNE: Trisha, we want to take a picture.

TRISHA: Of what?

GEORGEANNE: Of all of us. And we have to hurry, because I don't want to miss the chance to throw these bags of rice right at Tracy's head.

MINDY: I'm going to throw some of those little cocktail weenies at her.

GEORGEANNE: Everybody get on the bed. Meredith, go get that camera. (*Meredith goes into her closet.*)

TRISHA: Frances, what is that you have in your hand?

FRANCES (*beaming*): I caught the bouquet!

TRISHA: In your other hand.

FRANCES (*sheepishly*): Oh, that's Champagne. I just wanted to taste it. I'm sorry.

TRISHA: Hell, don't apologize. Here's to it. (*She raises her own glass in a toast; Frances does likewise.*)

FRANCES (*glowing*): To holy matrimony! (*Trisha stares at her.*)

TRISHA: Can't we just drink to love?

MINDY: Hear, hear.

FRANCES: I'm sorry. To love.

GEORGEANNE: Oh, please. You guys make me sick. (*Raises her own glass.*) To mindless sex in public places. Okay, Frances, you get down in front. And we'll be, like, your court. Meredith! I just had a great idea!

MEREDITH (*comes out of closet holding Polaroid camera*): What?

GEORGEANNE: Do you know where Tracy's homecoming queen crown is?

MEREDITH: Yeah, it's in here.

GEORGEANNE: Get it!

MEREDITH (*handing camera to Tripp*): Here you go, Griffin Lyle Davenport the Third. You know how to use this?

TRIPP: Isn't this the kind of camera that any idiot can use?

MEREDITH: Uh-huh.

TRIPP: Yeah, I know how to use it. (*Meredith goes back into the closet; Georgeanne steps back, directing everyone else.*)

GEORGEANNE: Mindy, move a little to your left. Y'all leave a space for Meredith. (*Studies the tableau.*) We need sunglasses. (*Everyone goes for their purse.*)

FRANCES: I don't have any.

GEORGEANNE: Meredith! (*Meredith emerges from the closet holding a crown in front of her.*)

MEREDITH: What?

GEORGEANNE (*taking crown*): Perfect. Do you have an extra pair of sunglasses?

MEREDITH: I'm sure I do somewhere.

GEORGEANNE: For Frances.

TRISHA: Everybody still have their bouquets?

GEORGEANNE: Here, Frances, let's get that hat off your head.

FRANCES: Why?

GEORGEANNE: Because you were born to wear a crown, babe. (*She places the crown on Frances's head. Mindy arranges herself seductively, pulling the shoulders of her dress daringly low. Meredith finds a pair of sunglasses in one of her drawers.*)

MEREDITH: What about these? They're kind of Jackie O.

GEORGEANNE: Excellent. Oh, good, Mindy.

MINDY: I want a cigarette.

MEREDITH (*grabs her pack and offers her one*): Here. (*Mindy looks at her, taking the cigarette tentatively.*)

MINDY: Thanks.

MEREDITH (*flatly*): Sure. (*They are all on the bed now, decked out in sunglasses, arranged around Frances, who wears the crown.*) Wait, I want to wear my leather jacket.

GEORGEANNE: I'm missing my bouquet!

MINDY (*grabs Tripp's shoes off the floor*): Hold these. (*Pause.*)

GEORGEANNE: No, I think Trisha should hold these.

TRISHA: Shut up.

MEREDITH: Come on, Trisha.

TRISHA: I hate you all. (*Trying not to laugh, she trades her bouquet for the shoes. Meredith, having donned her jacket, rejoins the others on the bed.*)

MINDY: We. Look. Fabulous.

GEORGEANNE: We *are* fabulous.

TRISHA: Okay, Tripp. Tell us when.

FRANCES: Oh, wait!

TRISHA: What?

FRANCES: I know I shouldn't, but . . . Meredith, would it be okay if I wore your diamond bracelet?

MEREDITH: Frances, I don't have a diamond bracelet.

FRANCES: Well, I know I saw one. It's right over here— (*She crosses to the open jewelry box and retrieves the bracelet she tried on at the beginning of the play.*) If you say no, of course I will understand.

MEREDITH: Frances. Those aren't diamonds.

FRANCES: They're not?

MEREDITH: No, who do you think I am, Liz Taylor? Those are dime-store rhinestones.

FRANCES: Oh.

MEREDITH: That whole thing cost me about six bucks. You can have it.

FRANCES: Oh, no, I couldn't.

MEREDITH: Sure you can, it's my present, since you caught the bouquet.

FRANCES: It's so *nice,* though.

MEREDITH: It's junk.

FRANCES: But—

TRISHA: Frances, some things in life are gifts. You can accept them. You are allowed. (*Pause.*)

FRANCES: Oh, my. Well, thank you so much.

MEREDITH: You are so welcome.

GEORGEANNE: Okay, Tripp. Tell us when.

TRIPP: Everybody squeeze in. Good. This is some major babe action happening here.

MINDY: Hell, yes.

TRIPP: Now, when I count to three, say—

GEORGEANNE: Cha Cha Cheez Whiz.

TRIPP: One . . .

FRANCES (*beside herself*): I feel so glamorous!

GEORGEANNE: You *are* glamorous, damn it.

TRIPP: Two . . .

MINDY: I just know I have something stuck in my teeth.

TRIPP: Three— (*All the women shout "Cha Cha Cheez Whiz" as they are illuminated by the flash from the camera. Simultaneously, there is a general blackout except for a couple of specials, leaving the women momentarily in tableau, before the remaining lights fade.*)

SMOKING LESSON

by Julia Jordan

CHARACTERS

TARE:	fifteen years old
MARY KATE:	fifteen years old
LISA ANN:	fifteen years old
TOM:	twenty-seven years old

The time is the present and the place, under a railroad bridge on the edge of the Mississippi River, St. Paul, Minnesota. The river lies in a steep valley and is set off from the community by its inaccessibility. A railroad bridge nearly covers the stage and arches up to the ceiling of the theater over the audience. The bridge is a series of iron girders and pilings. The bridge is active with trains. There is a rope hanging from a high girder which the girls swing on. The base of the bridge can be used as a jungle gym. The girls sit on it, hang from it, and do gymnastics off it.

Prologue

In the dark.

We hear clapping sounds, rhythmic.

A dim light comes up on the three girls. They are playing "Say, say oh playmate" without the words. Gradually they break their circle as if an invisible fourth has joined them. The claps that connected them are now incomplete, only two sets instead of three, when there should be four.

The three separate slowly till all connecting slaps are silent and they are each in their own separate spotlight.

The three girls are slowly turning around, arms outstretched. They are perfectly in sync with one another's movements and increase and decrease their speed at exact increments so that all are facing the same direction at the same time.

MARY KATE: Fast. (*Beat. Beat. Beat.*)

LISA ANN: *Faster.* (*Beat. Beat. Beat.*)

TARE: *FASTER!* (*Beat. Beat. Beat.*)

MARY KATE: STOP! (*Beat. Beat. Beat. They freeze, dizzy.*) Again. (*Beat. Beat. Beat. They start spinning.*) Slow. (*Beat. Beat. Beat.*)

LISA ANN: S l o w e r. (*Beat. Beat. Beat.*)

TARE: S l o w e r. (*Beat. Beat. Beat.*)

MARY KATE: Stop. (*Beat. Beat. Beat. They freeze.*) Again. (*Beat. Beat. Beat. They start turning.*) Fast. (*Beat. Beat. Beat.*)

LISA ANN: *Faster.* (*Beat. Beat. Beat.*)

TARE: *FASTER!* (*Beat. Beat. Beat.*)

MARY KATE: STOP!

(*Simultaneous lights out on Mary Kate and Lisa Ann. Spotlight stays up on Tare.*

Tare continues spinning faster and faster. Lights slow fade. Sound of a train overhead. Headlights flashing between the rails as it passes from the stage over the audience's heads. Lights out.)

Scene 1

It is night. The three girls are under the bridge at the edge of the water in the dark.

LISA ANN: I brought candles.

TARE: No candles.

LISA ANN: Candles would be nice.

TARE: No candles! We didn't find candles the first time. We found matches, wooden matches. We used wooden matches. We kept on using wooden matches and we're gonna use wooden matches this time too.

MARY KATE: Think you own it or somethin'?

TARE: Just want it done right.

MARY KATE: Well, let's just get it over with. 'Cause the whole thing's getting embarrassing.

TARE: It's not s'posed to be a drag.

LISA ANN: Let's just start.

TARE: Start.

(They gather downstage facing each other.)

LISA ANN: Once a year, on this day, we tell the story.

MARY KATE: For seven years we've told this story.

TARE: And this is the last time we'll tell it. And we'll tell it *right*.

(The three strike matches simultaneously and watch them burn in silence. One by one they strike matches and speak. They can only speak while the flame is alive. Mary Kate and Lisa Ann speak more quickly

and shake out their matches before the flames can reach their skin. Tare
allows hers to burn itself out and shows no fear at all. The flames light
their faces.)

LISA ANN: Once upon a time, in this same place in the world,
there lived a girl like us who was fifteen but only eight years
old in her mind. And on this day she jumped from this railroad bridge and fell, falling all the way down to our playground. And the Mississippi River held her in the leaves and
branches of an also-fallen tree. Held her here for us to find.

MARY KATE: And every year on this day we tell the story and do
the thing. 'Cause . . . Why?

TARE: I wrote it out. Didn't you practice?

MARY KATE: I'm askin' why.

LISA ANN: 'Cause we promised.

MARY KATE (*beat*): 'Cause the sirens rang out for a dead girl. And
a mother screamed for a lost girl. And the fingers pointed
and the blame fell for a gone girl. And there was crying.

TARE: Because there was crying, but not from us. Because she
was not dead to us. She was not lost to us. She was not gone
from us. Her name was Pearl and she's been here under this
bridge, ever since and all along, with us. Theresa Louise
McCauley . . .

LISA ANN: Lisa Ann Manley . . .

MARY KATE: Mary Kate Riley . . .

TARE: And now we're, all four of us, fifteen years old inside and
out.

LISA ANN: And on that night she crawled under the fence and
the sign that says "Stay Out." Just like we did on this very
same day, seven years later. Just like we did tonight.

MARY KATE: And she climbed up this bridge hand over hand, too
scared to try before. And she walked these girders, arms out-

stretched like a bird for balance, though she had clung to the
ground before. And there was a wind that night. Just like
tonight.

TARE: Once I heard a person say a wind can hold you up, just as
soon as push you over, if you lean into it. But she wanted
the air, a split second, falling through a piece of a minute all
alone, with plenty of life left to go. All this life left over trying to push itself into that moment. She fell overflowing and
left it here to wait for someone to take it.

(*Tom enters. He sees the girls and does not disturb them. He listens.
They remain focused on their story and do not notice his presence.*)

LISA ANN: And the also fallen tree held her here for us to find. I
saw her first. With her face hiding in the water, her mother's
slip floating and her hair waving at us. Come find me. Here
I am, looking like a cloud. Like a perfect cloud in a greenish
sky at your feet.

MARY KATE: And we three had braided hair. And I said she should
have a braid too. So you could say we were a team. And my
ribbon was red and Lisa Ann's was green and Theresa's was
blue. And blue looks best with wet blonde hair.

TARE: My hands were best for braiding and the water was touching her body, but it felt like regular water. And Pearl was
dead, but when you looked around it looked like a regular
day. But she was never regular and now she looked like a
cloud, and I wanted to touch her like that, when she was
like a cloud. I tied the blue ribbon in a bow.

LISA ANN: And they tried to send us away. Told us to run along
home 'cause we were small and we were only girls. But it
was us that found her and it was one of us who went in the
water and touched her. 'Cause she was *our* friend and we
wanted to see her face.

MARY KATE: So we hid in the trees and watched as they pulled
her onto land. They had all laughed before but no one

laughed when they pulled her from the arms of the Mississippi. Pulled her from the embrace of the also fallen tree and placed her here, right here where we're standing.

TARE: They put her on her back with her arms and legs stickin straight up in the air. The cops said they just froze like that from hanging down in the water all night long, even though it was August and a hot one. But Pearl didn't care 'bout that. And it looked to me like even though she was dead she still had enough life left over to be reachin out for somethin. Life enough to still be wantin somethin.

LISA ANN: And they took her away and they all went away and we were still here. We came down from the trees and everything looked like the day before. Like they had all never come. Like we had never found her. And Mary Kate saw the matches. A box of matches under that girder there.

MARY KATE: And I lit a match and Lisa started in on the story, and we all knew it back to front, and that's how we knew that it was true. It was us that found her. It was us that braided her hair. And they took off the blue ribbon but it was Theresa who touched her first when she tied it.

TARE: And we looked at the flames and we smelled the burning and we told the story again.

LISA ANN: The matches and the story.

MARY KATE: The matches and the story. And we all held hands like a three-way tie.

(*They hold hands.*)

TARE: And somethin, some part of Pearl, the eight-year-old part, the part that didn't play with girls her own age. The part that chose us. That part was still here. With us. Under the bridge. And we crossed-our-hearts-hoped-to-die promised to take care and hold on and not tell a soul. So she could grow up with us and be fifteen inside like the body they buried. And every year we give her what she needs for that year. The best things of each year.

LISA ANN: I saw a woman in the park sit so still the birds came to her without an offering of crumbs. I give that to you.

MARY KATE: I waved to an old man in a parade who had walked on the moon. I give that to you.

TARE: I heard a woman sing shudders into that space inside you. I felt the red velvet on a chair in a museum with a sign that said "Do not touch." And I saw a guy climb this bridge and walk all the way to Minneapolis, walk the girders like a balance beam, pole to pole and nothin to hold onto in between. And the wind was blowin hard and that was some-thin to see. That is somethin to do. And these are all good things and I give these to you. (*Tare lights another match.*) Once I touched a girl who died of her own free will. That's mine. That's just for me. (*Blows out the match.*)

LISA ANN: That's the last time. The last year to tell the story and say the prayer. So, if there ever really was a ghost of Pearl, like we used to play, you can go now.

MARY KATE: Now you fit together, fifteen inside and out. You can go and we can stop playing with imaginary ghosts. We kept our promise.

TARE: And no one will ever know. No one else will ever know you've been right here all along.

LISA ANN: First.

MARY KATE: Second.

TARE: Third. (*Tare holds up a blue ribbon, and the three touch their matches to the bottom. The flame crawls up and Tare drops it reluc-tantly.*) Bye.

MARY KATE: The end.

LISA ANN: Amen. (*Lisa Ann makes the sign of the cross, Mary Kate follows. Tare just stares.*)

MARY KATE: Father, Son, Holy Spirit.

TARE: Up, down, left, right. (*Tare starts spinning slowly. The other two join her, perfectly in sync.*)

MARY KATE: Fast.

LISA ANN: *Faster.*

TARE: *FASTER!*

MARY KATE: STOP! (*Beat.*) Slow.

LISA ANN: S l o w e r.

TARE: *FASTER!*

(*Mary Kate and Lisa Ann stop and stare at Tare spinning as fast and furiously as she can.*)

MARY KATE: What happened to "slower"?

LISA ANN: You're s'posed to be the third "slower."

TARE: I felt like a "faster."

MARY KATE: It's not what you feel like. It doesn't go that way. You can't just change it. That's not the way it goes.

LISA ANN: Faster, faster, faster. Slower, slower, slower. Like that. Not just any old way. Right?

MARY KATE: Right.

TARE: I just felt like a "faster." It just happened like that.

LISA ANN: I was all ready to go slower and you said "faster" and I went slower 'cause I already started sorta, and you threw me off and got me all discombobled.

MARY KATE: Bobulated.

LISA ANN: What?

TARE: The word is discombobulated.

LISA ANN: Same difference.

(*Tare picks up a broken bottle and smashes it. Then another.*)

MARY KATE: What are you doin'?

TARE: Smashin' things.

LISA ANN: What for?

TARE: I feel like it.

LISA ANN: We were talkin'.

TARE: I don't feel like talkin'.

MARY KATE: You're doin' an awful lot of feelin' all the time.

(*Tare stops what she's doing.*)

TARE: I feel like it.

MARY KATE: Well, stop it.

TARE: Why?

LISA ANN: What do you feel like doin' now?

TARE: Screamin'.

LISA ANN: What for?

TARE (*to Mary Kate*): You wanna?

MARY KATE: Yeah.

LISA ANN: Why?

TARE: Naked?

LISA ANN: WHAT?

MARY KATE: Yeah.

TARE: Do it then.

LISA ANN: Okay. I'll scream. But why do we gotta be naked?
     (*Mary Kate and Tare have their T-shirts half over their heads when*

they see Tom step out from his hiding place and start walking, laughing, toward them. Lisa Ann has her back to Tom and is removing her clothes. She is talking to herself, expecting the other two to ignore her, and so for a moment or two she doesn't notice that they have stopped and are staring in shock over her shoulder.) We always have to do this stuff. Why huh? Why? My mother would . . .

(*Tare and Mary Kate pull their shirts back down. Tom half jumps, half slides down the ravine. Lisa Ann screams for all she's worth and scrambles for her clothes. Tom laughs. He grabs Lisa Ann by the hand and spins her around.*)

TOM: Lisa Ann, what would your Momma say? Screamin' with no shirt on!

MARY KATE: Shut up, Tom.

TARE: Let's go, you guys.

MARY KATE: You've got no business comin' down here Thomas Delaney.

TOM: I've been comin' here since you were in diapers.

MARY KATE: This place is ours.

TOM: You own this river little girl?

MARY KATE: As a matter of fact yeah, I do.

LISA ANN: Yeah, we do.

TOM: That so?

TARE: We should go.

MARY KATE: Matter of fact it is so.

LISA ANN: Bought it yesterday.

TOM: Baby-sitting money?

MARY KATE: None of your business.

LISA ANN: But the answer is no.

TARE: We're just here.

TOM: So where'd you get the money to buy a piece of the Mississippi River? From that dancin' you were doin'? Nobody's gonna pay good money to see that.

LISA ANN: We can dance. It just so happens we're plannin' on being professional dancers.

TOM: I wasn't puttin down your dancin'. I was puttin' down your chest. Or the lack thereof.

MARY KATE: Thought that's the way you liked 'em.

TOM: You got somethin' to say, Katie? Spit it out.

LISA ANN: You're nothin.

MARY KATE: All you do is smoke cigarettes and work on a belly.

TOM: Says who?

LISA ANN: Says everybody.

(*Tom pulls up his shirt and looks at his stomach.*)

TOM: I don't see a belly.

MARY KATE: Well, I do.

TOM: Where?

LISA ANN: Right there.

(*Tom slaps his stomach.*)

TOM: Hard as a rock. Feel. Here, feel it. (*All three step back.*) C'mon, Mary Kate.

MARY KATE: No.

TOM: Miss Lisa Ann?

LISA ANN: I wouldn't touch you with a ten-foot pole.

TOM: Oh, sure you would. How 'bout you? (*To Tare*) You scared too?

TARE: I'm not scared.

TOM: Go ahead then. Touch it.

TARE: I wouldn't touch you with a ten-foot pole.

TOM: Now where have I heard that before? Don't you have a mouth of your own?

TARE: Yeah.

TOM: Then speak for yourself.

MARY KATE: Don't you talk to her like that.

TOM: What are you gonna do about it? I'm not talking mean to you, am I?

TARE: I don't know.

TOM: What do you think?

TARE: I've got to think about it.

TOM: See? You've got your own mouth. A pretty mouth too. I do believe you have the prettiest mouth. The prettiest mouth of the three. (*Beat.*) Do you think you have the prettiest mouth?

TARE: I don't know.

TOM: Do you think I'm getting a belly?

TARE: I don't know.

TOM: Want me to tell you what I know?

MARY KATE: No.

TARE: What do you know?

TOM: I know you're not stupid. You're probably the smartest girl standing on the banks of the Mississippi River today. I don't know what's going on down in St. Louis or New Orleans but all in all, chances are you probably are, the smartest that is. I can tell. I've got an eye for smarts. And I know that a smart girl like yourself doesn't draw any conclusions until she has been given all the information. You're not a jump in and guess kind of person are you? Am I right? Tell me I'm right.

TARE: I'm not a jump in and guess kinda person.

TOM: 'Cause that's how a smart girl makes decisions.

MARY KATE: You're an ass, Thomas Delaney.

LISA ANN: Can we go?

TARE: I guess you're right.

TOM: So maybe you'd reassure me, 'cause these two have got me mighty worried I'm going to pot and that would be an awful shame, young as I am. Between you and me . . . What is your name again?

LISA ANN: Theresa.

TARE: It's Tare. Everyone calls me Tare.

LISA ANN: They do not.

TARE: They're gonna.

MARY KATE: I'm not.

TOM: Tare, between you and me, a young man's self-esteem is very important to his future—

MARY KATE (*overlap*): You're not young.

TOM: —and my future is resting in your hands. (*To Mary Kate*) I'm not thirty. You understand don't you, Tare? I know you understand.

TARE: Sure . . .

(*Tom lifts his shirt.*)

TOM: So I need some reassurance.

TARE: You look fine to me.

TOM: Well, thank you, but the blow these two dealt my manhood, well—

MARY KATE: Jesus Christ.

TOM: —it's deeper than you imagine. Would you lead me to believe that what you said before is true, Tare? That you wouldn't touch me with a ten-foot pole? Am I that disgusting a creature?

MARY KATE: Yes.

LISA ANN: And you're an ass.

TOM: I was asking Tare.

MARY KATE: Don't answer him, Trese.

TARE: You're not disgusting.

TOM: Tare's got a gorgeous little mouth of her own. Go ahead then Tare, reassure me. I need some reassurance. (*Tare reaches out and* quickly *brushes her fingertips across his stomach*.) Ahhh, never has reassurance felt so soft.

MARY KATE: Tom Delaney . . .

TOM: Yes, Mary Kate Riley?

MARY KATE: You're an ass.

LISA ANN: A number one jackass. Everybody says so.

TOM: Where Mary Kate Riley goes, Lisa Ann Manley is sure to follow.

LISA ANN: Even my brother says so.

TOM: Your brother is an ass.

LISA ANN: My brother is a lawyer.

TOM: I rest my case.

MARY KATE: And you're nothin.

TOM: And I like it like that. Tare here, Tare's like me. Two of a kind. We got our own minds.

MARY KATE: Theresa isn't like you.

TOM: Ask her.

LISA ANN: Theresa wouldn't hurt a fly.

MARY KATE: Everybody knows what you did.

TOM: Did what? Did what Mary Kate? What did I do?

(*Mary Kate lies down with her arms and legs in the air and rocks, emulating the corpse of Pearl.*)

MARY KATE: 'Member?

TARE: Let's get outta here.

TOM: You're a sick girl Mary Kate.

MARY KATE: Yeah?

TARE: C'mon let's go.

TOM: What's that supposed to mean?

TARE: Nothin'. Let's go.

(*The three girls start heading for the slope.*)

TOM: Hey Tare! You want a cigarette?

TARE: I don't smoke.

TOM: I didn't ask if you smoked. I asked if you want a cigarette.

TARE: I don't think so.

MARY KATE: I'll take one.

TOM: Mary Kate, I'm shocked.

MARY KATE: Just give me one.

TOM: Do you smoke, Mary Katharine?

MARY KATE: Are you gonna make me beg?

(*Tom presents the package, one cigarette extended. Mary Kate takes one.*)

TOM: Lisa Ann? (*He presents the package in the same way, and Lisa Ann takes one.*) Where Mary Kate goes . . .

LISA ANN: Ass.

TOM: Tare? Don't leave me hanging. You know you're my favorite. (*Tare pulls a cigarette from the pack. Tom brandishes the flame of his lighter. Mary Kate leans in to light hers. Tom pulls the lighter away.*) Ladies, ladies . . . Have you all smoked before?

TARE: No.

TOM: When you read you begin with A-B-C, when you smoke you begin with (*sings do-re-mi*) Tom light me.

MARY KATE: Just give me the light.

TOM: Now Mary Katharine, if you say it that way it doesn't rhyme.

MARY KATE (*monotone*): Tom light me.

TOM: No musicality! But a sport all the same. Lisa Ann?

LISA ANN (*monotone*): Tom light me.

TOM: Mary Kate did, so we had faith Lisa Ann would too. But again no musicality. Moving right along to the talented Tare. I feel a musical vibe coming my way.

TARE (*equally monotone*): Tom light me.

TOM: Not to worry folks, that was just a warm-up. C'mon Tare make me proud. (*She hesitates.*) C'mon let's hear those bell-like tones come bubbling out of that nightingale of a perfect little throat. *(Tom waits again, all eyes on Tare's indecision.)* Two of a kind, Tare, two of a kind.

TARE *(sings)*: Tom light me.

(Tom clutches his heart and keels over.)

TOM: Shot me with a beautiful bullet right through the heart. It hurts me deep inside. It does. It hurts. *(Tom on one knee lights her cigarette. Tare coughs violently.)* Shit, you never did smoke before. Why'd you inhale like that?

MARY KATE: 'Cause she never smoked before.

LISA ANN: Ever in her life.

TARE: It just went down the wrong way is all.

TOM: Don't you worry. Those two aren't even inhaling.

MARY KATE: Fuck you, Tom.

TOM: Now don't you go teaching Lisa Ann bad words.

LISA ANN: Fuck off.

TOM: See! See!

(Mary Kate grabs Tare's hand.)

MARY KATE: We're leaving.

(The three head toward the path up the back plane. Tom bounds ahead and blocks their path.)

TOM: But ladies, ladies, I haven't yet shown you the finer points.

MARY KATE: What finer points?

TOM: The finer points of smoking.

LISA ANN: There are no finer points of smoking. You just stick it in your mouth and suck.

TOM: Oh no, no, no. Don't be a girl. A woman should know better. There are subtleties, things, special things. *(Tom backs them down the slope almost without their knowing.*) Maybe some-day, you three will be unwinding, in say Paris, after a partic-ularly riveting dancing girl extravaganza, elegantly crossing your legs at some cafe out on the street like they got there. Will you pull out cigarettes stick 'em in your mouths and suck?! No, no, no! It's wrong! IT'S WRONG! **IT'S WRONG I SAY!** Repaint this picture for me Tare.

TARE: What do you want me to say?

TOM: What brand of cigarettes will you smoke for instance? Will you follow the collegiate crowd and smoke French cig-arettes? Gauloise? You are in France after all. Or American? Marlboro.

LISA ANN: The French ones.

TOM: WRONG! You are Americans. From the heartland. The bread basket of the world. God's Country. Land of ten thousand lakes and the origin of the Mississippi River! You are standing on the banks of the Mississippi River! (*Beat.*)

TARE: Marlboros.

TOM: Tare darlin, you are like a private star shining on my heart. Marlboros is right. Marlboros or Camels but not Winstons. Only crazy people smoke Winstons.

MARY KATE: My Mom used to smoke Winstons and she's wacko.

TOM: They're all wacko. Winston smokers. All Winston smokers are wacko. A rule to live by. Okay, you're still at the cafe and your American cigarette is lonely for a match. Alas, you lit the last one an hour ago. Some Jacques or Pierre recognizes your distress and offers his flame. What do you do?

(*Mary Kate makes a little curtsy.*)

MARY KATE: *Merci.*

(*Lisa Ann curtsies.*)

LISA ANN: *Merci* very much.

TOM: WRONG! Tare?

TARE: He wants to light my cigarette?

MARY KATE: Don't inhale, Trese.

LISA ANN: Might go down the wrong way.

TARE: Shut up!

TOM: Touch his hand, girl. Touch his hand. Like this. (*Tom places her fingertips on his hand holding the lit lighter.*) Guide him to your perfection of a mouth. Your touch is the sweetest thanks.

TARE: You're welcome?

(*Mary Kate and Lisa Ann look at Tare, appalled. Tom smiles.*)

TOM: There's something so intriguing about a woman with fire at her fingertips.

TARE: Fire at her fingertips?

TOM: Fire at her fingertips and smoke at her mouth.

MARY KATE: Jesus.

LISA ANN: Yeah, Jesus Christ.

(*Tare shoots Mary Kate and Lisa Ann her most threatening look. Tom focuses on Tare.*)

TOM: The burning orange ember, the white paper, blue smoke curling across red-painted lips, and red-painted nails wrapped ever so lightly around. Now, that is a heaven.

TARE: I'd like to go to Paris.

TOM: Maybe I'll take you someday, and then again, maybe I won't. . . .

MARY KATE: Tom Delaney, you've never been farther than Wisconsin.

TOM: That doesn't mean I'm not going.

MARY KATE: You're going nowhere.

LISA ANN: And fast.

TOM: I can go anywhere, anytime. I could start walking right now. I could follow this river all the way down to New Orleans. (*To Tare*) New Orleans is like Paris right here at home in the U.S.A. and it stays warm there the whole year round. I could start walking right now. I've got nothing keeping me here.

MARY KATE: Sure you do.

TOM: Like what?

MARY KATE: Like money. You don't have any.

TOM: Walking is free.

LISA ANN: Food isn't. You can't bring your momma and her kitchen with you.

TOM: I'll hunt.

MARY KATE: Hunt what? There's nothing down here.

TOM: Squirrels and fish.

LISA ANN: You don't have a fishing pole. I bet you don't even own a fishing pole.

MARY KATE: Nevermind a gun.

TOM: I'll catch 'em with my bare hands and eat 'em raw.

TARE: There's only carp. Carp aren't good eating fish.

MARY KATE: What'll you drink?

TOM: I got the whole Mississippi River.

LISA ANN: You can get cancer just by touching it.

TOM: I've been swimming in it my whole life.

TARE: I never saw you swimming in it.

TOM: You've been watching me, Tare?

MARY KATE: There's a big difference between swimming in it and drinking it.

TOM: I'll like the dew at dawn and suck juice from wild strawberries I find growing peacefully in the moss.

MARY KATE: Puh-leeze . . .

TARE: What about cigarettes? You only have four left.

TOM: Now there's the catch.

MARY KATE: Guess you're staying right here.

LISA ANN: Not going anywhere.

MARY KATE: Nothing and staying nothin till you die of lung cancer with a big ole fat belly—

LISA ANN: —at your Mom's house!

TARE: How will you buy cigarettes?

TOM: Lend me a few bucks Tare? (*He smiles.*) Aw, try that smoke again, girl. Just drag it out lightly this time. (*Beat.*) Here, hold it like this. (*Tom adjusts her fingers around the cigarette. They all watch as she awkwardly puts it to her lips.*) Damn. You're green.

LISA ANN: Blow it out Trese.

MARY KATE: You're makin' an ass of yourself, Trese.

TOM: Don't be stupid. Blow it out.

(*Tare coughs it out uncontrollably. Lisa Ann pounds her on the back.*)

LISA ANN: You okay?

MARY KATE: Tryin' to act all grown up all of a sudden. Wonder why?

TOM: Is she gonna be sick? I'm leavin' if she's gonna be sick.

TARE: I'm not gonna be sick.

LISA ANN: That was real dumb, Trese.

TOM: God, what a stupid kid. She okay?

TARE: I'm okay!

MARY KATE: She's okay. She's just not the fire-at-the-fingertips type.

TARE: Am too.

TOM: Naw, you're a sweet one. Christ, Lisa Ann's got more fire than you.

TARE: I'm not sweet.

TOM: Bet you still go to church.

TARE: Do not.

TOM: Sure you do, in your mind.

TARE: You said we were two of a kind.

TOM: Where'd you find this one anyway, Katie?

TARE: She didn't find me.

TOM: Ain't exactly your style.

TARE: She didn't find me. I've always been here. Just 'cause you couldn't see me. Can't you see me at all?

LISA ANN: Don't get mad.

MARY KATE: What're you going on about?

TARE: D'ij'ever think I was invisible because I wanted to be? Ever think of that?

LISA ANN: Calm down, Trese.

TARE: 'Cause I've got fire at my fingertips all right. I've got it all over me. I've got so much fire in my hands I've got to hold it tight so it won't burn you.

MARY KATE: Theresa?

TARE: I hafta hold it so tight you don't even know it's there. Ever think of that? Ever think I had so much fire I could burn you all down? You never did 'cause I can turn my fire into anything I want. Birthday candles and Roman candles, color fireworks to dazzle you. Campfires and bonfires and brushfires and wildfires and towering infernos. I can control it and I can do whatever I want with it. I've got all kinds of fire you can't see. I've got all kinds of fire at my fingertips. I've got fire all over me. I'm not afraid of fire. (*She takes the cigarette and presses the lit end into her palm, extinguishing it.*) We're two of a kind Tom Delaney. I've been watchin you and we're two of a kind. Remember that.

(*A silence. Lisa Ann takes Tare by the wrist and drags her up the hill. Mary Kate turns to face Tom.*)

MARY KATE: You stay away from us, Thomas Delaney. Or, I swear to God, I'll tell everyone I know you did that to her yourself.

TOM: I didn't do anything.

MARY KATE: Now where have I heard that before?

TOM: Scram.

MARY KATE: Everybody knows. You can deny it till kingdom come. Everybody knows.

TOM: Are you gearing up to say somethin'?

MARY KATE: It's you that should do the talkin.

(*Lisa Ann returns alone. She comes halfway down and beckons for Mary Kate.*)

TOM: Have I been accused of somethin?

LISA ANN: Katie, c'mon.

TOM: Yeah. Run on home little Lisa girl and ask your big-shot lawyer brother a question. Ask him, have I been accused of somethin'? I mean legally accused of somethin'? 'Cause I don't see no judge and jury 'less that's s'posed to be you two.

LISA ANN: You need twelve. My brother says you need twelve for a jury.

TOM: Well, what d'you know? Law school pays off. The boy knows you need twelve.

MARY KATE: Twelve? Is that all? Twelve's no problem. I could find you thirty-two without raising my pinky. The boys up at the park? Why, they were practically eyewitnesses. Shoot, your very own Mother. Deep down in her heart of hearts even your mother knows. You just stay away from Theresa.

TOM: Keep her away from me. You never know, you never know what I'll do when some girl starts hanging on me. You never know 'bout old Tom.

(*Tom starts walking toward Mary Kate.*)

LISA ANN: *C'mon Mary Kate.*

TOM: Why, I could be devisin' some evil plan right now. Hatchin' some evil thoughts concerning two other little girls. I can see it now. . . . (*Tom lunges at Mary Kate.*) Hah!

(*Mary Kate and Lisa Ann scream and run up the hill. Tom chuckles to himself, then lights a cigarette and stares at the water. Lights out.*)

Scene 2

Daylight. Tom is sitting at the edge of the water. Tare creeps down the hill. A train passes above. Tare watches. Tom does not look up. Tare reaches in her pocket and applies some bright-red lipstick without the help of a mirror. She takes her finger and circles her mouth to make sure she stayed within the lines. The train is gone. Tare takes a step toward Tom, then slips on purpose, making a little noise. Tom does not turn around. She gets closer. She picks up a branch and snaps it over her knee. Tom takes a drag off his cigarette and continues to stare at the water.

TOM: That's you, I bet. How's your hand?

TARE: 'S okay.

TOM: Musta hurt like a bitch.

TARE: I got tolerance.

TOM: I noticed.

TARE: How's your belly?

TOM: It's comin' along.

TARE: You're s'posed t'say "hard as a rock."

TOM: Not in the mood.

TARE: What're you doin'?

TOM: Go talk to your girlies.

TARE: We're all talked out. I want to *do* somethin'. What're you doin'?

TOM: Nothin.

TARE: Looks like you're watchin' the river.

TOM: Like I said, nothin.

TARE: You're watchin' the river float down to New Orleans.

TOM (*beat*): When you've been lookin' at somethin', watchin somethin' for almost twenty-seven years, you just seen it all before. You can sit right next to somethin' and see nothin'.

TARE: You're lyin'.

TOM: Go home.

TARE: Sure you are. You're lyin'.

TOM: I've seen this river from every possible angle. I've shimmied up every tree down here worth shimmying up. I've swum this river. I might've been drunk but, stink and all, I swum it. I've slept winter nights by this river and it wasn't pretty. I've seen this river, now I just sit here. I don't see this river anymore.

TARE: You climbed this bridge over this river.

TOM: I climbed that bridge in a clown suit on Halloween half out of my mind on a candy buzz.

TARE: With Pearl screamin'.

TOM: 'Cause I was holdin' up the trick or treating. (*Beat.*) How'd you know she was screamin'?

TARE: You've never seen what this river looks like in New Orleans.

TOM: I don't even know you. And you're tellin' me she was screamin'.

TARE: You're in a bad mood.

TOM: What's your name again?

TARE: A real bad mood.

TOM: Tell you what, let's just start over and say we never met. And then let's keep it that way.

TARE: You got a cigarette?

TOM: Aw, don't be mad. There's a lot of bugs in this world I can't name.

TARE: You got a cigarette?

TOM: I'm not giving you any more cigarettes.

TARE: Why not?

TOM: 'Cause you can't be trusted to smoke 'em.

TARE: I promise I won't burn you. (*She holds out her hand for the smoke.*)

TOM: Jesus Christ. (*He pulls out pack. Gives her one and takes one for himself.*)

TARE: Thank you, Tom.

TOM: Welcome. (*He lights his own cigarette.*)

TARE: I'm—what d'ya call it?—in distress over here.

TOM: What?

TARE: Some Jacques or Pierre should recognize my distress.

TOM: What?

TARE: A light.

TOM: Jesus, Mary and Joseph. (*He holds out his lighter. She touches his hand as he taught her. She doesn't cough. She smokes expertly. He stares.*)

TARE: I've been practicing.

TOM: Don't get in the habit.

TARE: Don't start in tellin' me what do.

TOM: Shit you got mouthy between then and now.

TARE: I've always been mouthy. It was just hiding. (*He doesn't respond, so she holds up the conversation.*) It just has to warm up. My mouth. It just hides till it's good and warmed up. It's gotta get used to new people before it goes. Then it just goes. Where you been anyway?

TOM: I thought you were gonna smoke that.

TARE: You've been away.

TOM: Don't wave it around like that. Just hold it nice. Just hold it. Christ.

TARE: You haven't been down here all week.

TOM: How do you know?

TARE: I live right up there. I can see everyone coming and going.

TOM: Maybe you missed me.

TARE: Nope. Never happened.

TOM: Maybe you did.

TARE: I was watchin' close.

TOM: What for?

TARE: Where you been?

TOM: Around.

TARE: Doing what?

TOM: Stuff.

TARE: Like what?

TOM: Just stuff. This 'n that. Things.

TARE: You're s'posed to be down here just about every Monday, Wednesday and Friday 'round three-thirty. You missed Monday and you missed Wednesday. This is Friday. Where were you?

TOM: Watchin' the grass grow.

TARE: For four days?

TOM: It grows real slow. Are you a spy?

TARE: I've just seen you.

TOM: Are you in the fucking CIA Youth Corps or somethin'?

TARE: I've just seen you. I live across the street.

TOM: How'd you know about Pearl screamin?

TARE: I told you. I live right up there on the River Road.

TOM: I never saw you down here before the other day.

TARE: You didn't look.

TOM: Look where? Behind a tree? Is that what they teach you in the FBI cadets corps, to hide behind a tree? Was that cigarette burn some spy trick? Have you got some double-oh-seven burn protector? Let me see. (*He grabs her hand. It hurts her. She lets out a yelp.*)

TARE: I wasn't spyin'.

TOM: Spyin' on me today.

TARE: I was looking for you. It's not the same. It's just, I look and there it is.

TOM: Spyin' from your lookout tower. You got a lookout tower in your mansion up there on River Road? You followed me down here.

TARE: Maybe I was coming down anyway.

TOM: You're an odd person Tare. You're a freak.

TARE: Knew you knew my name!

TOM: How could I forget the burn victim.

TARE: Not a victim if you do it yourself.

TOM: How come you're spying on me, huh?

TARE: I'm not.

TOM: How come you're puttin' out my cigarettes on your pretty little hands?

TARE: It was my cigarette. You gave it to me.

TOM: How come you're hangin around me right now? Didn't your mother tell you not to talk to strangers? Didn't she tell you what happens to little girls when they talk to strangers?

TARE: I can talk to whoever I want.

TOM: Does the CIA hand out special medals for being an A class, number one pest?

TARE: I'm not a pest.

TOM: Okay, so why're you looking for me?

TARE: We're two of a kind.

TOM: Jesus, girl, I just said that to piss off Mary Kate.

TARE: Why? 'Cause you like her?

TOM: 'Cause I was about to slap her sassy mouth.

TARE: You do though. You like blondes.

TOM: I've got no opinions on the bunch of you.

TARE: 'Cept for me. We're two of a kind.

TOM: I don't know you.

TARE: Trust me.

TOM: You really are a freak. An A class, number one, freak.

TARE: Gimme a cigarette?

TOM: Say please. You're gonna make yourself sick. You just had one.

TARE: I'm a chain-smoker.

TOM: You are, huh? A chain-smoker? (*He tosses her the pack.*)

TARE: Just like you.

TOM: I'm not a chain-smoker.

TARE: Might as well be. Light? (*He extends his lighter. She touches his hand.*)

TOM: Red is your color.

TARE: 'Scuse me?

TOM: The lipstick. Doesn't look half bad. (*Tare stares at him, unsure of how to respond.*) No, it looks good. It does. You have a nice mouth.

TARE: You said that before.

TOM: I did?

TARE: You can kiss it if you want.

TOM: I don't think so. (*Tare quickly leans over and kisses him. She pulls away with a huge grin. He just stares at her.*) Don't do that again, okay? And I'm gonna ask you somethin'. (*Beat.*) 'Bout you all down here with your clothes off . . .

TARE: It's a secret.

TOM: 'Bout all that spinnin' and the matches and all that. She isn't some game for you kids to play, you know.

TARE: You don't know anythin' about it. You weren't s'posed to be there. You never come on that day. You never did.

TOM: It was Friday. I come on Fridays. So why should I let somethin' that happened seven years ago, that I had nothin' to do with ruin my routine? You three been down here every year playin your little game?

TARE: I'm not telling. You have to earn the right to know. You could rip off my toenails *slowly* and I wouldn't breathe a word.

TOM: Shit. What makes you think I'm so interested in your little game anyway? You really are a strange kid.

TARE: I'm not a kid.

TOM: How old are you?

TARE: Old enough.

TOM (*looks her up and down*): Oh, I don't think you are.

TARE (*softly*): I'm the same age as Pearl.

TOM: What did you say?

TARE: I'm old enough to do anything I want.

TOM: And what's that?

TARE: I want to see the river from up there.

TOM: What would you want to do a thing like that for?

TARE: I feel that I want to.

TOM: Why don't you just go look at the river from the Lake Street bridge?

TARE: The Lake Street bridge has a walkway.

TOM: Exactly.

TARE: The river doesn't look the same from a walkway with a guardrail and streetlamps. Do you think I'm stupid? Don't talk to me like you think I'm stupid. It's gotta be this bridge, the railroad bridge. This is the one across from my house. This is the one you climbed.

TOM: Say you climb the bridge and see the river, so, then what?

TARE: I climb down the other side and then I'm thinkin' about takin' a walk.

TOM: Where you think you're walkin to?

TARE: New Orleans.

TOM: That's an ambitious hike.

TARE: I've got a route all planned out.

TOM: Gonna follow the Mississippi?

TARE: All the way down to the Gulf of Mexico.

TOM: Just gonna follow the river.

TARE: Just follow the water.

TOM: That'll take you quite a while.

TARE: I figure the rest of summer.

TOM: You can't just follow it, you know. You can't just follow it like a God-given path. There'll be things in the way. Facto-

ries and sewage plants and vicious dogs and Do Not Enter
signs.

TARE: I've got a way with dogs.

TOM: Electric fences. Touch 'em and you fry.

TARE: I'll walk around 'em.

TOM: You'll lose your way.

TARE: You'd have an awful hard time losin a river as big as the
Mississippi.

TOM: Gonna hunt squirrel and catch fish with your bare hands?

TARE: Naw, silly. I've got a backpack to fill with food from home.

TOM: Water's too heavy to carry and the river . . . filthy here!
Just imagine down south.

TARE: There's fresh streams feeding it all the way down. Just
feeding it. I've got some iodine tablets for purification and
an empty bottle to fill up at gas stations and drinking fountains. And I've got some money for a pop now and then.

TOM: Gonna sleep under the stars?

TARE: Gonna sleep under the moon.

TOM: What if there's a tornado? Could be dangerous.

TARE: Tornado season's over.

TOM: What if you're all alone at night, a girl all alone, and you
run into some lone guy down by the river. Or during the
day even. A beautiful day just like today.

TARE: A lone guy like you?

TOM: Yeah, like me, but not me, someone else, someone you
don't know.

TARE: I'd say, "Hello, sir! Fine day for a walk down the Mississippi River Valley!"

TOM: What if it's a Bad Guy? A killer maybe, a kidnapping rapist abuser maybe, a pornograph-i-an freak who just sits by the river and waits for a little girl to come strolling by on her walk down to New Orleans. Someone who would spot your accent and know—

TARE: I don't have an accent.

TOM: —you were a long way from home. Someone who would follow you for miles and watch you pick flowers and listen to you humming to yourself and, all the time, be thinking of the horrible deviant things he's gonna do to you. *Lovin'* it. What would you do when the Bad Guy stepped out from behind that tree and said, "Hello."

TARE: Just 'cause I don't know him doesn't make him a bad guy. I just officially met you.

TOM: But you've got your house right behind you and Mommy and Daddy. You've got someone to run to. You aren't alone.

TARE: You wouldn't hurt me if I was alone. You wouldn't hurt me.

TOM: Maybe I would. Maybe I'm just not in the mood.

TARE: Lie.

TOM: I could be aching to wring your little neck right now and you'd never know it.

TARE: You like me too much.

TOM: 'Member who you're talkin' to. Tom Delaney here.

TARE: I know who you are. We're the same.

TOM: You think we think alike? You think you have my kind of thoughts? I could take you up there and push you right off. There's some around here say I've done it before. Where've you been? Hiding up in your spy tower watchin' people come and go but not listenin to what they say? I could take you up there on that bridge and give you just a little push.

Nobody'd see. I wouldn't get caught. And this is comin' out of my mouth. So you know it's crossed my brain.

TARE: I could climb up this bridge someday, just a little ways up, and I could wait for you. And then, when you least suspect it, when you've forgotten I said this, I could wait there with a gallon of gasoline. And I could pour it all over you. And then, while you're all shocked-out thinkin, "What is this?" you just might look up and I'd be there droppin' lit matches right on your wonderin' face. Fire and gasoline. It crossed my mind, you know it did, *'cause I just said it*.

TOM: And that's what makes us two of a kind.

TARE: And we're both from here.

TOM: The whole place is from here.

TARE: Some people round here don't know the Mississippi River's running through their front yard or backyard or just around the corner. That's a big thing. We know that.

TOM: And some of 'em do.

TARE: But we know it from this small place here, on this side of the river, under this bridge.

TOM: Not just us. Mary Kate and Lisa Ann were here just the other day.

TARE: They don't count. It's just us three. Us three. You climbin the bridge, Pearl too scared to try and me behind some tree.

TOM: Spyin'.

TARE: I was not spyin'!

TOM: You were hiding behind a tree!

TARE: I don't hide on purpose. It just sorta comes natural to me.

TOM: That's ridiculous.

TARE: It's not ridiculous. It's like the Indians.

TOM: Like what Indians?

TARE: Like the American Indians. Maybe I've got some Indian blood in me. You know, like the Indians.

TOM: I don't know.

TARE: Yeah, you know. Like they tell you in stories.

TOM: What stories?

TARE: Like when you're readin in a story about how the Indians, before the Wild West. How the Indians . . . when it was really wild. How they could walk right through a forest or a valley or wherever, and not make a sound. Walk right through the forest in their moccasins or their bare feet, steppin on twigs and leaves and all sorts of crackling things and not make a sound. Invisible 'cause no one would look for something they didn't hear. And they could stand so still the animals would just go about their business right in front of them. And not just squirrels, but foxes and deer and wolves even. I'm not that quiet. People don't hear as good as foxes and wolves though. You probably know that. (*Tom looks confused. Tare gives him a moment to catch up.*) Well, I learned about it in the stories and it sounded good. You know? Real good. So I tried it out. I got some Minnetonka moccasins. But I had better luck barefoot. I was born with leathery feet, so I've got all the equipment necessary, if you know what I mean. And I just tried it out. I was a kid and it was somethin to do. Just walk softly and play Indian and I'm telling you, it's easy when you put your mind to it. You just think like your body's got water in the legs and you just pour that water slowly from one leg to the other. So slowly. And if you keep it smooth and still and not crashin and sloshin around, you're cool. If you keep it smooth it's silent. Easy, see? And you get to like the feeling of it. I liked it so much I did it all the time. Till I did it natural without even thinkin about it sometimes. It's not sneaky. Spying sounds sneaky. It's not sneaky, it's quiet. It's hiding, but if you looked I'd be right there. If you listened, you'd hear me. You just didn't. You were busy being another way. You were too busy with Pearl to notice me.

TOM: You followed us down.

TARE: Sometimes.

TOM: What did you see?

TARE: I saw you put up the tire swing. (*Tare goes to the rope hanging from the bridge.*) Why don't you get another tire for it? I'd use it. (*She swings on the rope.*)

TOM: How often?

TARE: All the time. I love swingin'.

TOM: *How often, SOMETIMES, did you follow us? How often did you watch us?*

TARE: Maybe, sometimes I was comin' for myself but you two were here and you seemed private.

TOM: I never did anything private to her.

TARE: Private, like quiet, not like that! Like sometimes the water is still and some person throws a rock in to see the break of it, see the ripples, and it pisses you off but you can't think of a reason that makes sense when you say it? That kind of private. I didn't want to be the asshole with the rock. I'd of rather been Pearl. I'd rather be her.

TOM: Why would you want to be a dead girl?

TARE: Then you'd want to teach me how to climb the bridge, and I wouldn't be scared like she was. I wouldn't be scared to climb it.

TOM: I never made her climb it.

TARE: I know.

TOM: I never hurt her.

TARE: You don't have to tell me.

TOM: I used to wash her hair under the garden hose, for God's sake.

TARE: You kissed her once. On the mouth.

TOM: I never messed with a retard.

TARE: *She wasn't retarded!* She was just different.

TOM: She was retarded.

TARE: And I didn't say you messed with her. I said you kissed her. Once. And, anyway, it was nice 'cause she wanted you to.

TOM: How would you know? You didn't live next door to her. You didn't know her.

TARE: I know. I saw it.

TOM: You think you know everything. See everything.

TARE: I eat carrots.

TOM: Carrots?

TARE: For my eyesight. My Gramma says carrots make you see in the dark like a cat.

TOM: That so?

TARE: It's a proven fact.

TOM: Says who?

TARE: My Gramma. And me. I say so. I'm living proof. I eat carrots and I can see in the dark.

TOM: Think with your carrot-powered eyesight you can see through lies?

TARE: Think I can.

TOM: You sure I didn't mess with her?

TARE: I'd've seen you.

TOM: Only when we were here. Maybe we were somewhere else. She'd go anywhere with me.

TARE: Never happened.

TOM: Maybe I toyed with her eight-year-old mind and fifteen-year-old body in my very own room and then I told her to go jump off a bridge. She'd do anything I said. Anything.

TARE: No, she wouldn't.

TOM: If I told her to take off all her clothes and fuck the dogs while the neighborhood threw confetti, she would've done it. She loved me.

TARE: She wouldn't climb the bridge for you. She was afraid of falling.

TOM: And you're not?

TARE: I'm not afraid of falling.

TOM: Go ahead and climb it then.

TARE: You have to come with me.

TOM: I won't do that.

TARE: You have to.

TOM: Why?

TARE: Didn't someone show you?

TOM: I didn't need anyone to hold my hand.

TARE: Well, I do. (*She picks up his hand. He shakes her off.*)

TOM: Hold somebody else's.

TARE: Does somebody else know what to do if a train comes along?

TOM: Don't walk on the tracks.

TARE: What if it shakes?

TOM: Hold on tight.

TARE: And if a wind comes along?

TOM: A wind can hold you—

TARE and TOM: —up just as soon as push you over if you lean into it.

TOM: You're so weird.

TARE: You're so cool. (*She beams at him.*)

TOM: What?

TARE: I'm gonna teach you how to walk like an Indian.

TOM: Huh? (*She tugs at his arm, trying to get him to stand.*)

TARE: C'mon it's easy. Anyone can do it. (*She pulls him to his feet.*) YAY! I WON!

TOM: Don't be yayin' and winnin' or I'll sit back down. (*He drops her hand. She picks his up again.*)

TARE: Okay, okay. Imagine that your legs are filled with the warm waters of the Mississippi. The Mississippi River. But from before, when it was still clean. Filled with fishes. Deer lappin at the sides. No beer cans. You got it?

TOM: I don't remember that.

TARE: I said imagine not remember. Now pour that smooth warm water from one leg to the other. Same time as me. Together. (*Tom closes his eyes.*) Don't close your eyes. Look at me. (*Tom opens his eyes and steps on a stick. A loud cracking sound.*) That's okay. Shit happens when you're a beginner. (*Tom drops her hand and stamps all over the place, whooping up a mock-Indian rain dance. Tare considers being hurt, then joins in. They fall down laughing.*) You've got Indian blood too!

TOM: That why everyone treats me like shit?

TARE: Oh, don't do that.

TOM: Do what?

TARE: Go away in your mind again. You owe me now. I showed you somethin, show me, and I'll walk you all the way to New Orleans. And we'll sit at an outdoor cafe in a Paris right here in the U.S.A., and chain-smoke cigarettes while the Mississippi River floats on by.

TOM: You've got money for a pop, now and then?

TARE: Coke or Pepsi?

TOM: You've got money for cigarettes? I'm a chain-smoker.

TARE: I've got money for Marlboros. No French cigarettes, we're from the heartland. And no Winstons. 'Cause only wackos smoke Winstons.

TOM: It is dangerous. A girl alone. You'll need protection.

TARE: Let's smoke on it.

(*Tom gives her a cigarette and lights it. Tare touches his hand. Tom stares at her mouth. He doesn't smoke.*)

TOM: You really shouldn't wear lipstick.

TARE: Red's my color.

TOM: No. (*Tom swipes her cigarette and holds it in front of her face.*) That was a lie. (*Tom crushes the lit end into his palm. He shows no pain.*) Ouch. (*Tare just beams.*)

TARE: So cool. (*She runs up the hill.*) Tonight!

(*Lights out.*)

Scene 3

It is night. Tare is waiting. There are night sounds amplified by her loneliness. She has her back to us, searching the hill for Tom's arrival. She has a backpack and an old cotton sleeping bag, a bottle of water and a flashlight. She turns to the river and brushes dirt out of a scrape on her knee. She winces.

Tom creeps down the slope. He steps on a twig and it crackles. He hides.

Tare jerks her head around and scans the trees. She listens. Nothing.

A train approaches. Rumbles and screeches, lights crashing through the rails. It passes.

A cloud moves from in front of the moon, and the bridge glows for a moment. She waits. The crickets start in on their humming. She lights a cigarette. She waits. She crouches next to the bridge, wraps the sleeping bag round her shoulders, points the flashlight at the trees and waits.

Tom watches her.

She falls asleep.

Tom stands guard.

Lights out.

Scene 4

Morning, bird sounds. Tare is asleep, crouched by the bridge. The flashlight has fallen out of her hands. Mary Kate and Lisa Ann enter. They walk right over to her and start shaking her.

MARY KATE: Rise and FUCKIN' SHINE! (*Tare pulls up the covers for warmth, still half asleep.*)

TARE: Leave me . . . lone. . . .

LISA ANN: All I got to say is, next time you tell your Mom you're at my house, you better be at my house and I better know you're there. Cause my Mom's yellin' at *me*.

MARY KATE: Brought you somethin'. (*Mary Kate holds up a tube of lipstick. Next few lines overlap as she takes off the top and twists the bottom of the tube.*)

TARE (*waking up*): What time is it?

MARY KATE: All I got to say is, if you're gonna do it, do it right.

LISA ANN: Right. 'Cause my Mom told your Mom that you weren't at my house and I'm tellin' you the phone line started sizzlin' with those girls this and those girls that. . . .

MARY KATE: It only goes one way. You know how it goes. (*Mary Kate grabs Tare's face and starts smearing lipstick all over it. Lisa Ann's startled. Tare fights.*) Don't go thinkin' I don't know what's goin' on, little miss "I've got fire all over me."

LISA ANN: Jesus, Mary and Joseph. Sometimes you are sick Mary Kate. Sometimes you are a very sick girl. (*Tare buries her face in the sleeping bag. Mary Kate climbs on top, trying to get at her.*)

TARE: Get off! Off!

MARY KATE: Isn't that why we can never find you, 'cause you're down here makin' a fool of yourself?

TARE: No. Get off.

MARY KATE: Oh, good.

LISA ANN: What's goin' on?

MARY KATE: Just checking. (*Tare sits up, conscious that another attack may be coming.*) Makin' sure you hadn't lost your mind and fallen in *luv* with the fuckin' perv'. (*Lisa Ann looks at Tare's red-smeared face.*)

LISA ANN: Katie you are sick.

(*Tare tries to rub the lipstick off with her sleeping bag.*)

TARE: Just gettin' some fresh air is all!

MARY KATE: Is that what you're doing?

TARE: I thought I needed some fresh night air and I'm thinkin' 'bout taking a walk.

LISA ANN: Well, next time you start in thinkin', I suggest you tell your Mom what you're thinkin'. For a start, that is.

MARY KATE: And where you thinkin' of walking to?

TARE: Nowhere.

MARY KATE: And who do you think you're walkin' with?

TARE: Can't say.

MARY KATE: Then I'll come with.

TARE: Can't do that.

MARY KATE: Tommy Delaney, himself. Guessed right the first time.

TARE: You see him anywhere round here?

LISA ANN: Nope.

TARE: That's 'cause he's not.

LISA ANN: Good. He's an ass. Let's go home. See your Mom, who is losing her mind and dragging my Mom to the loony bin right along with her?

TARE: Can't do that.

LISA ANN: Why not?

TARE: Can't go home.

LISA ANN: Why?

TARE: Ran away.

LISA ANN: You can't run away. You live across the street. You can't run away to across the street from your very own house. YOU can't do that 'cause MY Mom will kill ME.

MARY KATE: Me too.

LISA ANN: What?!

MARY KATE: I've run away 'cross the street too.

LISA ANN: You don't live 'cross the street.

MARY KATE: I've run away down the hill, make a left, two blocks and cross the street.

LISA ANN: You can't!

MARY KATE: Just did.

TARE: You haven't been invited. You don't have any supplies.

(*Mary Kate picks up Tare's backpack.*)

MARY KATE: Share and share alike.

LISA ANN: Well, I'm not! And don't go thinkin' you can make me. I'm staying right here. All alone with my Mom and Dad and my stupid brother. Fine. Go ahead. (*Turns her back.*) Not very nice to just run off and leave people. Not very nice at all if you ask me.

TARE (*to Mary Kate*): I never said you could come.

LISA ANN (*thinking Tare was addressing her*): I don't want to come. Don't go tryin' that reverse cycle-ology on me. I'm way ahead of you on that one. Way ahead. Miles.

MARY KATE: And we're gonna be miles away.

LISA ANN: You won't get far. And someday you'll thank me for tellin'. 'Cause it's just dangerous. You guys think you can do anything you want but you can't. You hear that? You can't. 'Cause there's plenty of things out there. Plenty. My brother told me all about what goes on down there at the courthouse. The things they do to little girls. *Terrible things.*

MARY KATE: We're not little girls.

(*Lisa Ann starts heading up the hill.*)

LISA ANN: You'll thank me for tellin' on you. Someday, you'll thank me.

(*Tare struggles out of her sleeping bag and runs after Lisa Ann.*)

TARE: I'll thank you now, Lise. You're right. But . . . but see . . . You got it all wrong. I wasn't running anywhere. Did I say I was? I lied. I'm just gonna take a walk, but it'll end up right back here. Promise. Just don't tell. It's not like you think. It's not us runnin away. (*Mary Kate puts on Tare's backpack.*)

MARY KATE: I'm all geared up to get goin'! Say good-bye to everyone for me, Lise.

(*Tare puts her arm around Lisa Ann and leads her back down the hill.*)

TARE: Shut up, Mary Kate. She's just funnin' with you, Lise.

LISA ANN: Then what were you doing here all night long?

MARY KATE: Yeah, then what were you doing? Runnin? Or waitin?

TARE: I wasn't doin' neither.

MARY KATE: Yeah?

TARE: I was climbin' the bridge.

LISA ANN: Looks like you're on the ground to me.

MARY KATE: You're gonna climb the bridge?

TARE: Can I trust you?

MARY KATE: Who else?

TARE: Lise?

LISA ANN: You can't climb the bridge.

TARE: You gonna tell if I say I am?

MARY KATE: She won't say a word.

LISA ANN: Climbin' the bridge is just as bad as runnin' away. More dangerous even.

TARE: Naw. 'Cause I'm goin' with someone who knows how to do it. Someone who's done it a million times. I've seen him do it. It's easy when he does it. And he's gonna teach me. That's all. That's it.

LISA ANN: Then what's all the gear for?

TARE: You think I'd climb over there and come right on back? Staying the night would be like a victory celebration.

MARY KATE: Stayin' the night with him.

TARE: There's only one sleepin' bag. Do you see two?

LISA ANN: That makes it worse.

TARE: I wouldn't touch him with a ten-foot pole.

MARY KATE: Oh, sure you would. What about when you're up there and a little wind comes along. (*Mary Kate mimics Tare walking the bridge.*) "Oh Tom! Tommy! I think I'm gonna fall!" And he wraps his big old arm around you. (*Mimics Tom with a deep voice.*) "Don't worry poor little falling girl. I've got you in my big strong arms." It's embarrassing just thinkin' about it.

LISA ANN (*matter-of-fact*): And then he'd push you off and I'm telling. (*Lisa Ann turns again to leave, but is stopped by the rising argument.*)

TARE: You said it, so you're thinkin' it, 'cause you wishin' it'd happen to you.

MARY KATE: What's that s'posed to mean?

TARE: I'm only gonna say one more word on the subject.

MARY KATE: Go ahead. Say it.

TARE: Fine. Jealous. That's the word and that's all I'm gonna say.

MARY KATE: Jealous? Of you and him? (*Tare shoots her a look of confirmation.*) You touched her body remember? Made you think you owned the whole thing. Well, Lise and I knew her too. And we remember if you don't. We remember very clearly. Don't we Lise?

LISA ANN: I remember.

MARY KATE: Remember, Lise, up at the park, swinging on the swing set? Remember your brother and the other boys sitting on the hood of the old man's car?

LISA ANN: Just like they always did.

MARY KATE: Yep. And remember Pearl walkin' up the hill. Remember seein' her in that white slip? And I was thinkin, I'd never seen her in a dress before, never ever saw her in anything but cutoffs before.

LISA ANN: I remember that. I remember that real clear.

MARY KATE (*pushes Tare*): Look at her Lise. Look at her with that lipstick all over her face. That remind you of anything?

LISA ANN: Oh, yes. It was all over her face. Don't you remember? (*Pushes Tare.*)

MARY KATE: Oh, I remember. (*Pushes her.*) Theresa, here, seems to need a little refreshing though.

LISA ANN: Well, let's see. (*Push.*) She had lipstick smeared all over her face. Kinda like you do now. Thought makeup was makeup, I guess, and put it on her eyelids as well as her lips. She was wearin' her mother's shoes! Remember?

MARY KATE: *I* do. (*Push.*)

LISA ANN (*push*): Too big and trippin' her up every step she took. But surely Theresa remembers that.

MARY KATE: Apparently she doesn't.

TARE: I know what happened.

MARY KATE: Do you? Do you remember how that slip was fallin off her shoulders? Do you remember how she started fallin' on the car, fallin' on the boys? Tryin' to kiss 'em?

TARE: How they were getting lipstick all over their clothes pushin' her around? Laughing at her makeup, laughing at her mother's slip, laughing at her kisses? Yeah, I remember. (*She pushes Mary Kate hard.*) I remember *that*. (*She pushes Lisa Ann hard.*)

LISA ANN: They didn't laugh. My brother didn't laugh.

TARE: He laughed.

MARY KATE: You remember the rest?

TARE: I remember!

MARY KATE: You remember all that? And you remember how we were s'posedly takin' care of her insides so as she could grow up with us? That was your brilliant idea, remember? And it was you that made us do it every year. Even though Lisa and I knew it was completely stupid. No candles! "We found wooden matches. We kept on using wooden matches. And we're gonna use wooden matches this time too." And we kept doin' it just to please you.

TARE: That true, Lise?

LISA ANN: My brother didn't laugh.

MARY KATE: You remember all that, make a big deal every year 'bout it, and here you are waitin' to be with Tom Delaney. All that and you think I'm jealous?

TARE: And you're not?

MARY KATE: Jealous of you and a person who does dirty things to retards and makes 'em jump off this selfsame bridge you're so keen on climbin'? Jealous of you and a fat aging nobody who lives with his mother?

TARE: He's not fat!

MARY KATE: Pfff . . .

LISA ANN: Yeah, pfff . . .

TARE (*mock tempting*): And he has green eyes.

MARY KATE: You are scary, Theresa.

LISA ANN: Scaring me too, Trese.

TARE: Oh! I'm kidding. I swear. I'm just kidding. It's not like that. Don't worry about that. I just got this thing for the bridge and he's the only one who knows how to climb it. You can understand that.

LISA ANN: No. I can't. It's dangerous.

TARE: Come on! It's right in front of your face. Look at it! I know you want to climb it, Katie. Get her not to tell. Just let me get 'cross it and I promise I'll remember every little thing he says, I'll remember every footprint, every hand-hold, everything, so I can show you. So we can go up there together. We could go up whenever we want just sit up there and blow smoke at the moon.

LISA ANN: I don't want to go up there.

TARE: You don't have to! You don't have to do anything you don't want to do. You can be the trip master! You'll watch from the edge and you can run and tell if anything goes wrong. You'll be the safety net. Our protector. We'd be the only girls to ever climb that bridge. We'd be legends.

MARY KATE: You'll listen real hard so you can take me across?

TARE: So hard my ears'll hurt.

MARY KATE: My 'rents'd freak.

TARE: So don't tell 'em.

MARY KATE: I'll tell 'em when I'm forty. They'll freak.

LISA ANN (*to Mary Kate*): You're gonna do it?

MARY KATE: Always wanted to be a legend.

LISA ANN: Okay, fine. I'll be the trip master. And I won't tell on one condition. You guys don't tell that I didn't go up with you. I mean, I'll be the trip master but that's just between us. Far as everyone else is concerned we all three climbed it together.

MARY KATE: Deal.

TARE: Deal.

LISA ANN: And one other thing . . .

MARY KATE: What?

LISA ANN: Mary Kate and I get to be trip masters together when you cross with him.

TARE: He wouldn't like that.

LISA ANN: He's got no choice.

MARY KATE: That's good. We get to watch and make sure all that's happening is climbing instruction.

TARE: No. He's doing this as a big favor to me. He won't go for it.

LISA ANN: It's the only way I'll keep my mouth shut.

TARE: Okay, fine. Deal. But he can't know you're there. If he knew he wouldn't go through with it. I'm sure of that.

MARY KATE: We'll hide in the bushes.

TARE: Just try to be really still. Don't go crunchin around.

MARY KATE: When's this gonna happen? He didn't show last night. How do you know he's gonna show at all?

TARE: He promised.

MARY KATE: He lies.

TARE: Who doesn't.

LISA ANN: I don't.

MARY KATE: You're boring. (*Tare elbows Mary Kate hard.*) Sorry.

LISA ANN: That's okay. 'Citing things just don't come natural to me.

TARE: Everything's gonna change. Everything's gonna get real exciting real soon.

LISA ANN: For me too?

TARE: You're the trip master, aren't ya?

(*Lights out.*)

Scene 5

Afternoon, two days later. Tare waits on a girder ten feet off the ground with a red gasoline can. Tom arrives and walks beneath her. She pours the can over his head.

TARE: You're late.

TOM: Shit! (*Tom scoots out from underneath as Tare lights a match.*)

TARE: Two *days* late. (*Tare throws it at him.*)

TOM: What the hell are you doin'?!

TARE: It's water. S'posed to be here two nights ago.

TOM: It's called avoidance. I'm avoiding you.

TARE: Not doing a very good job, showin' up.

TOM: This is my place, not yours.

TARE: Ours. Where you been?

TOM: You're like some evil fungus invading my pores.

TARE: Watchin' the grass grow? I hear it grows real slow.

(*Tom advances toward her.*)

TOM: Go!

(*Tare stands her ground.*)

TARE: I've been thinkin' about what it's gonna take to get you to come with me.

TOM: I'm not goin' anywhere with you. Get that through your head. Or I'll push it through.

TARE: Yeah, yeah, yeah. So. I've been thinkin' and thinkin'. . . .

TOM: Arrrgghhh!

TARE: Are you listenin'? I've been thinkin'.

TOM: And what do you think?

TARE: This. (*Tare jumps down and kisses him hard. Tom throws her off.*)

TOM: Go home to your mother.

TARE: I'm not the go home to your mother type, you are.

TOM: Please leave me alone. Or I'll make you.

TARE: Can't do that.

TOM: Don't make me do somethin' I don't want to do.

TARE: Haven't you figured it out yet?

TOM: Look how big my hands are. (*Tom holds his open palm against her face.*)

TARE: Don't you know who I am?

TOM: Look how breakable you are. (*She shakes his hand off and takes it in hers.*)

TARE: You've been waitin' seven years for me. Stand over here. (*She pulls him to the base of the bridge.*)

TOM: What for?

TARE: So I can look you in the eye. (*Tare stands on the bottom girder so she is as tall as him.*)

TOM: Then you'll leave me alone?

TARE: If you still want me to. (*She puts her arms around his neck. He quickly steps out of reach.*)

TOM: Don't touch.

TARE: Don't move then. Gotta look you in the eye when I tell you. Stand still.

TOM: Tell me what?

TARE: The reason for comin' with me.

TOM: Jesus. (*Turns to walk away.*) Why do I keep fallin' for this crap?

TARE: 'Cause it's not crap! I'm gonna tell you what you wanted to know! About the matches and the spinning and the day you caught us and everything you wanted to know.

TOM: I'm not interested in your little games. I'm not interested in you. I just want my place back. I want my peace and quiet back.

TARE: I'm your best friend. I'm your only friend. I'm your favorite thing.

TOM: You go on thinkin' that.

TARE: It's true. I'm the only one.

TOM: How old are you?

TARE: It's a secret.

TOM: Every female has the same stupid secret.

TARE: I'm gonna tell you a secret. When was the last time anybody ever told you a secret? (*Tom turns. Tare grabs his shirt.*) Don't you wanna know what it is? C'mon everybody wants to know a secret. Specially one about you and me. Why are you lookin' at me like that?

TOM: Like what?

TARE: Like that.

TOM: Sometimes you're cute.

TARE: I was tryin' to be mysterious.

TOM: Secret?

TARE: Don't laugh.

TOM: Okay.

TARE: 'Cause if you believe me, things'll be so wonderful.

TOM: What is it?

TARE: For you and me. Things'll be so wonderful.

TOM: Spit it out.

(*Tare takes a deep breath.*)

TARE: I touched her.

TOM: Who?

TARE: Pearl. We three found her but I was the one who touched her. Not them. Just me.

(*Tom takes out a cigarette.*)

TOM: That it?

TARE: I *touched* her. We found her floating facedown in the water. My brain felt half asleep. I thought the water might wake me up. I felt it on my foot and I thought this water is touching her. The water touching me is touching Pearl. But I wanted to touch her for myself. I wanted to know what it was to touch. Mary Kate and Lisa Ann were screaming, just screaming and screaming. And I was in up to my waist when I just put my hand on her pretty neck. So soft and slippery. Just placed my hand there, not pushing or grabbing, just touching. No one's gonna believe me but you.

TOM: Believe what? You touched her.

TARE: And I felt somethin! I felt this little something inside of her sit up and take notice. Just pop up and pay attention.

And that little something, that little something, slipped into my fingertips, pulsed through my hand and ran up my arm. And I've got it inside of me. And I've been takin' care of it, see? That little somethin, I think, was the eight-year-old part. And I've been lettin' it grow up with me 'cause it wanted to so bad. It couldn't just die 'cause her body did. It wanted to be fifteen so bad. Understand? Maybe it's just a memory, like a church thing, or maybe it's somethin else, somethin stronger. But it's somethin'. An active thing. Life left over, I think. And now it is. It is fifteen, that little some-thin'. Both of us. Fifteen years old, inside and out.

TOM: She's inside you?

TARE: Yeah. (*Tom turns to go. Tare grabs his shirt again.*) I'm not done. You promised.

TOM: Didn't promise anything.

TARE: Did. (*Tare takes Tom's hand and opens his palm, then opens hers, comparing scars.*) See? It's a promise. And there's more and it's good. It's real good. She's ready to go now. Ready to leave us alone.

TOM: So send her away.

TARE: I tried. That's what it was, the matches and the spinning. I was trying to send her on her way. But I was s'posed to not feel her anymore and I felt her stronger than ever! It's her that put those cigarettes out on our hands. That's why. See?

TOM: That was just some kiddie church. You all were brought up lighting candles. . . .

TARE: She wants the bridge. She wants to go all the way across. She's not scared anymore. She's fifteen. We get her across and she can go and we can get on with it. 'Cause I'm believin' I'm two times over alive. It's *fire* and it's pushin' me. I've got plenty of my own, see? I can't hold on to hers much longer. And you need some. So there's somethin for everyone. You'll be the guy who up and walked to New Orleans, and I'll be the girl who went with you.

TOM: Why would you want to be with me?

TARE: 'Cause when I look at you the back of my neck sweats.

(*Tom touches the back of her neck.*)

TOM: Dry as a desert.

TARE: In my mind it's sweatin. (*Beat.*) You're lookin' at me that way again. I can see it. I'm wearin' this lipstick for you. I'm ready to take you there, just say when.

TOM: Tell me why again.

TARE: 'Cause I need you to.

TOM: Catch fish with our bare hands?

TARE: Tornado season is over. We could sleep under the stars.

TOM: Sleep under the moon.

(*They kiss. He runs his hand down her back and scoops her up a little to lay her down. Tare starts to unbutton her blouse. Tom pulls back and looks at her. He sits up. She reaches her arms up to him. She is in the same spot Mary Kate was in when she imitated the corpse; the pose is identical. He stops entirely.*)

TOM: Why are you doing this to me?

TARE: It's okay.

(*Tom gets to his feet.*)

TOM: WHAT ARE YOU DOING?

TARE: Don't do that.

TOM: *I'm* not doing anything!

TARE: Don't yell.

TOM: Why are you doing this to me?

TARE: You said I was a private star shining on your heart.

TOM: I don't mess with kids. Put on your clothes.

TARE: No. (*Tare takes off her shirt. She is left wearing a white cotton bra.*)

TOM: Here I am thinkin' you had some sweet thoughts when they were nothing but trash all along. You win. It's all yours. Pearl. Bridge. New Orleans. Yours. (*Tom starts climbing up the hill.*)

TARE: You leave me here all alone and I'll climb right up that bridge and jump. Don't go thinkin I won't.

TOM: Here! (*Tom picks up a heavy rock and lobs it up to her.*) Hold on to this.

TARE: When I'm dead you'll be sorry and I'll be laughin. I'll be shakin' with laughter, you'll be so sorry. I'm goin' up there. . . . I'm climbin. . . . (*Tare throws the rock back at his head. She misses.*)

TOM: You want me to *fuck* you? Is that it? All this 'bout Pearl and New Orleans and you just wanna get ***fucked?*** Fine. (*He takes off his belt and runs up the bridge grabs her and half drops her on the ground.*) All right. Strip. (*Beat.*) Take off your clothes. Don't you know anything?

TARE: Doesn't go like this.

TOM: Oh, yeah. This is it. This is exactly how it goes.

TARE: I know how it's s'posed to be.

(*Tom is kneeling over her, grabbing at her jeans. Tare fights him.*)

TOM: You think you know everything don't you?

TARE: I know somethin' you don't.

TOM: Stop. Start. Make up your mind. This time, Tare darlin', I know somethin'. I know what's gonna happen next!

TARE: Stop!

(*He unzips his fly.*)

TOM: You're gettin exactly what you want.

TARE: They're all right about you!

TOM: They will be.

TARE: They always were. It was always your fault!

TOM: See? You're nothin' special. You're just like 'em. You don't know nothin'.

TARE: I KNOW WHY SHE JUMPED!

(*Tom doesn't loosen his grip.*)

TOM: Go on tell everyone you saw me do her. Don't make it true. Take everything else. That's still mine.

TARE: You left her! And she and I'd walk round playin Indian. Shit, you're slow. She was even better at it than me. We saw everything. And that girl you were with wasn't any older than fifteen herself. She wasn't any older than Pearl.

TOM: Who?

TARE: THAT GIRL. We saw you taking off her clothes and kissin' her and not kissin' Pearl and not kissin' me. And that girl wore makeup and dresses—

TOM: *Who are you?*

TARE: —and all that stuff we didn't have. All that stuff we didn't wear. And you didn't see Pearl cryin' 'cause you didn't look! You didn't listen.

TOM: She was home.

TARE: She was right here. We were right here the whole time.

TOM: I washed her hair in my own backyard and I left her *at home.*

TARE: *You want to know what you did after? 'Cause I can tell you. You took **that girl** up the bridge and her shirt was still open and was* *doin' fake fear for ya, "Oh no, Tommy. I'm scared to go up so high!" all the while she was climbin'. And you were laughin. And Pearl was cryin' even harder. Like you were makin' fun of her on purpose, 'cause she was scared to climb the bridge and she wasn't a regular girl you'd ever want to kiss like that.*

TOM: SHE WAS AT HOME!

TARE: *Kiss with everything you got.*

TOM: Shut up.

TARE: *She went up to the park wearing her mother's slip 'cause she didn't know any better. She put lipstick on her eyelids 'cause she didn't know any better. She went up there to show you she could kiss. But they laughed. They all laughed at her. (He raises his hand to hit her. He stops himself mid-swing.)* Who'd of thought those stupid boys'd get it right. They thought it was your fault and she was actin strange, 'cause it was. *All your fault.*

TOM: No.

TARE: You left us for that girl. Might as well have been one of them pushin her and laughin'.

TOM: Don't even remember her name.

TARE: 'Cause she's nobody. She doesn't have a name. Where were you? Still with her? Or watching TV at your Mom's house?

TOM: All I remember is them pullin her out.

TARE: You didn't see that.

TOM: I was standing right here.

TARE: She was hiding up in the trees with me.

TOM: Oh right. The little somethin' inside of you. Evil little somethin'.

TARE: No.

TOM: Yes, she was. Splattered herself all over everything I ever want to touch.

TARE: What's the point of going through life without ever being kissed like that?

TOM: She jumped from this bridge.

TARE: This is the only bridge.

TOM: Because it's mine. She did it to me. She coulda walked out farther over the open water. So her body coulda floated away. She did it to me. She wanted me to see her like that.

TARE: She didn't think that way.

TOM: Oh yeah she did.

TARE: You're not remembering her right. She was alive till she hit the water. And when she was alive she was scared of the bridge. Too scared to walk out any farther. She must of been so scared.

TOM: Never gonna die in water. May be whole, no important bits missing, no blood. But nobody looks so dead as when they've been dead for a while in water.

TARE: I touched her.

TOM: And you got her inside of you. Well, I got her too. I'm tryin' to breathe, I'm needing to vomit and I got her steppin on my throat so I can't do either. (*Silence.*)

TARE: I'd bleach my hair for you. (*Beat.*) I promise I won't be bad anymore. I won't go kissin' you if you don't like it.

TOM: I liked your kisses.

TARE (*beat*): Maybe when I get real good you'll let me kiss you again.

TOM: You'll be kissin' somebody better than me.

TARE: Ain't no such animal. C'mon. You got to. She's gonna crush your throat and burn me up if she stays and I'm scared it's gonna feel like holding a kitten.

TOM (*softly*): I'm not gonna leave her again.

TARE: Don't you want to know what that means? 'Bout holding the kitten?

TOM: Did you hear what I said?

TARE: What'd you say?

TOM (*beat*): You're scared you feel like you're holding a kitten.

TARE: Yeah. You know how kittens are.

TOM: Don't like cats.

TARE: Not cats. Kittens. Little kitten paws, little kitten nose and their eyes looking up at you. And you want to hold them so tight 'cause they're so . . . soft! But you can't. You got to let them float in your hands, so light. So sweet. 'Cause there's a tiny glass skull inside, a tiny glass skeleton. Gotta be care-ful . . . 'cause you just want to *smush* 'em. 'Fraid that space between bridge and water is gonna be a like a kitten. What would it be like to just do it! Thought of it just spins out of your reach doesn't it? Just tickles your brain.

TOM: No.

TARE: Lie! What would it be like in that instant before you hit? Think your head could even work fast enough to know?

TOM: It doesn't matter.

TARE: 'Cause maybe it can. Maybe when your brain is working that fast it's the most alive a person can be. Maybe grabbing that millisecond between bridge and river would feel better than anything you can imagine in this world. Like scratchin' the most tickle-y itch in the world.

TOM: Feel like shit.

TARE: Never thought about it?

TOM: Never.

TARE: God, you lie. Feet flat on the ground and a burning ember in my hand and it felt good to feel somethin' so strong. Nothin' else is enough. I feel that maybe I can do that millisecond of time with her inside. But I also got this scratchy little thing that's sayin' I could be wrong.

TOM: Listen to that one. That's the one to listen to.

TARE: We can't just sit here for the rest of our lives and not do nothin'. Not feel nothin'. We owe her.

TOM: You don't owe her nothin'. You been holdin' on to her real good.

TARE: I'm goin' tonight.

TOM: Don't think about kittens. Think about cats. Dead cats splattered on a highway. Think bloody fur. Think about the smell.

TARE: Come with, so I don't tempt it. (*Beat.*) I think maybe you need somebody to hold onto. Somebody to take care of. Hold onto me and cross my heart and hope to die, we'll all be fine. She'll be on her way and we'll be on ours. Feelin' fine and trampin down this river all the way to New Orleans.

TOM: They don't even call it a river down there it's so green. They call it sewage.

TARE: Green is my most favorite color, on account of your eyes. (*Tom smiles.*) C'mon, Tom. Kittens . . . (*Tare waits for him.*)

TOM: All right. Let's go.

TARE: Really?

TOM: Let's go. Right now.

TARE: I got everything packed. I'll go get—

TOM: No. Now. (*Tom goes to the bridge. Tare doesn't move.*) C'mon. Right now. (*Tom starts up.*)

TARE: We need our stuff. Water bottle. Money.

TOM: Get up here.

TARE: We gotta do this right.

TOM: NOW.

TARE: We're gonna need our supplies.

TOM: I'm askin' *you* for somethin' this time.

TARE: We're gonna need money. We can't get halfway down there and hafta come back. Everyone'll laugh. They'll laugh at us. (*Beat.*) Money. For cigarettes? Remember?

TOM: You're gonna buy my cigarettes?

TARE: Right.

TOM: Can't even buy my own cigarettes.

TARE: So tonight. We'll go tonight. I got everything we need.

(*Tom climbs down.*)

TOM: I'm not taking you anywhere.

TARE: What?

TOM: You're taking me, aren't you?

TARE: Yeah! (*Tare hugs and kisses him. Then remembers her promise to lay off the affection.*) Sorry. Won't happen again. This is so great. I'm gonna make you so happy. We're gonna be so happy.

TOM: Hurry home. Get some sleep.

TARE: I'll take good care of you. I promise. You'll be fine.

TOM: Don't worry 'bout me.

TARE: Worry? No more worries.

TOM: Go on then.

TARE: Tonight.

TOM: I'll be here.

(*Tare runs up the hill, eager to please him.*)

TARE: Okay, tonight! (*Tare leaves. Tom goes to the rope that was the tire swing and pulls on it, testing its strength. Lights out.*)

Scene 6

Past midnight. Pitch-black. Three flashlights come crashing down the hill. Tare is in front with Lisa Ann and Mary Kate coming up behind her. They cannot be seen, except when a flashlight crosses their bodies.

TARE: Shhh!

MARY KATE: We made a deal. You were supposed to call us.

LISA ANN: You were s'posed to tell us when.

TARE: You're here aren't you.

LISA ANN: No thanks to you.

MARY KATE: Thanks to our knowing all about your sneaky nature.

TARE: I was gonna tell you.

MARY KATE: But you didn't.

TARE: I was just comin' down to check the weather conditions. Make sure the show was goin' on. Then I was gonna run right back home and call you guys.

MARY KATE: Uh huh.

TARE: I was. Precautions are precautions and every expedition needs them.

LISA ANN: Trip masters are key.

TARE: Safety first. That's what I always say.

MARY KATE: You never said that before in your whole life.

TARE: Never climbed a bridge before either, now did I? Just you wait till the night you climb it. You'll be sayin stupid things too and goin' about things backwards. Like comin' down here to look around before you call your friends.

MARY KATE: Don't buy it.

TARE: I'm nervous okay! Maybe even a little bit scared.

MARY KATE: Sorry.

TARE: 'S okay. Just try to understand what it's like. Listen I don't want you losin' your minds if I don't come running straight home afterwards.

LISA ANN: I don't like the sound of this.

TARE: Just do me a favor and let me have my victory celebration on the other side, let me spend the night.

MARY KATE: No way.

TARE: I'm gonna be so exhausted I'll need to rest awhile anyways. Probably fall right asleep without even trying.

LISA ANN: And he'll be wide awake.

TARE: I'd be alone. I'll make him cross back on the Lake Street bridge. You can walk up there and check to make sure.

LISA ANN: That's a mile and a half in pitch-black.

TARE: You've got flashlights.

LISA ANN: It's dangerous.

TARE: There's two of you.

LISA ANN: What if he isn't there?

TARE: Then run on home and tell your Mom. Tell my Mom. I want you to. But give him an extra hour. It'll take him longer to get up to Lake Street due to his being tired from climbin'. Give him an hour and a half 'cause he has to cross back. You won't see him till he's half back across on account of the arch. An extra hour and a half.

LISA ANN: I've got a watch.

MARY KATE: An hour and a half.

(*Short silence.*)

LISA ANN: Hafta call it off anyway. It's too dark. You won't be able to see where you're going.

TARE: The trees make it seem dark. Out there it's fine. The water's reflecting the moon.

MARY KATE: That's not the moon. That's my flashlight.

LISA ANN: It's too cloudy out for a moon. Maybe you should wait till tomorrow.

TARE: I can see in the dark. Tonight.

MARY KATE: We might not be able to see you.

TARE: Tonight.

LISA ANN: Do you think he'll come?

TARE: I think he will.

MARY KATE: What if he doesn't?

TARE: He's comin'.

LISA ANN: You really think so?

TARE: He's comin'. You better get in the trees.

MARY KATE: He's not known for showin up is all.

TARE: He promised.

MARY KATE: He said, "I promise"?

TARE: Yes.

MARY KATE: In those very words? "I" and "promise"?

TARE: We've got an understanding. Hide.

LISA ANN: What does that mean?

TARE: I believe him. Keep your voice down.

MARY KATE: We'll hear him coming. Big thing like that.

LISA ANN: Believe what?

TARE: He'll show.

(*Long silence.*)

MARY KATE: All right. All this waitin around is making me lose interest. I'm not sure if I care about being legends anymore. I don't believe I care if he shows or not.

LISA ANN: I hope he doesn't. I don't know why you'd want to climb that bridge anyway.

(*Silence.*)

MARY KATE: If he doesn't show in the next ten minutes let's just forget it.

TARE: No.

(*Silence.*)

LISA ANN: You could die.

TARE: I won't.

MARY KATE: People did die on that bridge.

TARE: Pearl was alive when she was on the bridge.

LISA ANN: She wasn't alive when she fell off it.

TARE: She was alive till she hit the water.

MARY KATE: What's the difference?

TARE: Nothing. (*Tare starts spinning.*) Nothing at all.

(*Lisa Ann and Mary Kate follow. They keep their flashlight beams on the ground, slowly raising them as they go faster and faster, allowing the momentum to lift their arms involuntarily. They whisper.*)

MARY KATE: Fast.

LISA ANN: FASTER.

TARE: *FASTER!*

MARY KATE: STOP. (*They freeze with their beams shining stage right. A train rumbles, approaching.*) Slow.

LISA ANN: *Slower.*

TARE: *S l o w e r.* (*The flashlight beams are now passing slowly across the body of Tom hanging from the rope that held the tire swing.*) Stop.

(*The train passes above them. Noise and lights. The next section in italics is nearly inaudible due to the train. The three beams converge on Tom's body. Mary Kate and Lisa Ann walk away. Tare walks into the beams of light and toward him.*)

MARY KATE: *We gotta get outta here. Now. Let's go.*

TARE: *What is he doing?*

MARY KATE: *Trese. Get away from him, Trese. We gotta go!*

(*Tare reaches her hand out.*)

LISA ANN: *Don't touch him, Trese!*

TARE: *What is he doing down here?*

LISA ANN: *DON'T TOUCH HIM!*

TARE (*turns her head*): *Why not?*

MARY KATE: *We can't be here.*

(*Tare touches Tom's forehead.*)

TARE: What is he doing? (*She steps closer.*) His eyes are all messed up. (*Mary Kate lunges for her and pulls her away. Lisa Ann starts wailing. Tare is fighting hard.*) LEAVE ME ALONE.

MARY KATE (*to Lisa Ann*): GO UP TO HER HOUSE. GET HER MOM. GET SOMEBODY. (*Lisa Ann runs up the hill. Tare is still fighting.*) Theresa!

TARE: LEAVE ME ALONE.

MARY KATE: TRESE!

TARE: ALONE.

MARY KATE: Stop it, Trese.

TARE: ALONE!

MARY KATE: THERESA! STOP!

TARE: **MY NAME IS TARE!** (*Tare pushes away from Mary Kate. Mary Kate falls.*)

MARY KATE: It's okay, Trese. Your Mom is coming. Lise went to get her. It's okay.

(*Tare walks back to Tom. She reaches in his pocket and pulls out his matches. She lights one and throws it in his face. Mary Kate gets up and runs up the hill to get help. Tare continues throwing lit matches in his face.*)

TARE: The first . . . the second . . . All you needed was a little reassurance. (*Lisa Ann and Mary Kate reappear.*) The third. You couldn't even jump off it. (*Tare lays her hand on his face and pushes. The corpse swings.*)

MARY KATE: Theresa, your parents are coming.

(*Mary Kate and Lisa Ann start edging closer to her.*)

LISA ANN: They'll be here in a second, Trese.

(*Tare turns and sees them closing in on her. Tom's corpse is spinning behind her from her push. Tare bolts for the bridge. Tare climbs up, out of her friends' reach and above Tom's body. Mary Kate follows her up for about fifteen feet. Lisa Ann is stuck on the bottom girders.)* WHAT ARE YOU DOING, TRESE?

(*Tare climbs.*)

MARY KATE: THERESA . . . TARE! (*Tare stops and looks at Mary Kate.*) Tare? Please don't do this.

(*Sirens can be heard in the distance. Tare climbs higher.*)

LISA ANN: Tare. Everything's gonna be okay.

(*Tare turns her head to look at them.*)

TARE: Where are the words "I" and "promise"?

MARY KATE: Please?

TARE: When you read you begin with A–B–C. . . .

LISA ANN: Oh God . . .

(*Tare climbs higher, then stops and looks down. Lisa Ann is crying.*)

TARE: Mississippi River.

MARY KATE: Don't.

TARE: New Orleans.

MARY KATE: Don't jump.

TARE: Paris. (*Tare climbs higher, almost out of view.*)

LISA ANN: Don't jump.

MARY KATE: YOU JUMP, I'M NOT LIGHTIN' ANY FUCKIN' CANDLES. (*Stops and looks down over the edge.*)

TARE: Jump? (*Beat.*) Shit. How would we ever get to Paris? How'd I ever get anywhere like that? I'm still basically 'cross the street from my very own house. (*Tare climbs. She stops and pulls out a cigarette, lights it.*) I've never been anywhere. We never do anything. (*Tare climbs up and up and out of sight.*)

STOP KISS

by Diana Son

for Mom, Dad,
and Michael

Stop Kiss premiered at the Joseph Papp Public Theater/New York Shakespeare Festival in New York on December 6, 1998. It was produced by George C. Wolfe and directed by Jo Bonney, with the following cast:

CALLIE	Jessica Hecht
SARA	Sandra Oh
DETECTIVE COLE	Saul Stein
MRS. WINSLEY	Saundra McClain
GEORGE	Kevin Carroll
PETER	Rick Holmes
NURSE	Saundra McClain

Scenic design was by Narelle Sissons, costume design by Kaye Voyce, lighting design by James Vermeulen, and sound design by David Van Tieghem.

Stop Kiss was written with support from Playwrights Horizons made possible in part by funds granted to the author through a program sponsored by Amblin Entertainment.

CHARACTERS

CALLIE:	late twenties to early thirties
SARA:	mid-twenties to early thirties
GEORGE:	late twenties to early thirties
PETER:	mid-twenties to early thirties
MRS. WINSLEY:	late thirties to mid-forties
DETECTIVE COLE:	late thirties to mid-forties
NURSE:	late thirties to mid-forties. Can be doubled with Mrs. Winsley

SETTING

New York City

TIME

Current

Scene 1

Callie's apartment. Callie puts on a CD: The Emotions' Best of My Love.

She ceremoniously closes all the blinds in her apartment, making sure each blade is turned over. She locks the front door and puts a piece of black tape over the peephole.

As the vocals begin, Callie lip-syncs to the song with the polish of someone who has her own private karaoke often.

The phone rings. Callie turns off the CD like a busted teenager, and picks up the phone.

CALLIE: Hi George . . . yeah I know I'm late, I forgot this person is coming to my house at—(*Callie checks her watch*)—shit! . . . Well I would bring her along but I don't even know her. She's some friend of an old friend of someone I used to be frie— She just moved to New York and I said that I'd— I can't, what if she's some big dud and we all have a miserable time. . . . Exactly, you'll all blame me. Give me half an hour, tops. (*She sets the phone down. Her buzzer buzzes.*) Yes?

SARA (*offstage, tentative*): It's Sara and—

CALLIE: Come on up!

(*Callie buzzes her in and looks at all the junk on her sofa: newspapers, several pairs of dirty socks, a box of Kleenex, mail, a couple videotapes, and a bra. She picks up the bra and heads for the bedroom.*

The doorbell rings. Callie hides the bra and opens the door. Sara is holding a pet carrier.)

CALLIE: Hi.

SARA: You're Callie.

CALLIE: Yes.

SARA: I'm Sara— (*She looks at the pet carrier.*) This is Caesar and I
can't believe you're doing this.

(*Callie gestures at the couch, notices it's a mess.*)

CALLIE: Please uh sit—

SARA: Some apartment.

CALLIE: I was cleaning.

SARA: It's huge—and the neighborhood— (*Sara sits on a pile of
books.*)

CALLIE: You can't be comfortable.

SARA: Oh I am.

CALLIE: Are you sure?

SARA: Very.

CALLIE: —Just . . . let me get rid of this stuff. (*Callie gathers an
armful of junk and heads toward her bedroom. As soon as she turns
her back, Sara sits up and pulls out a large key ring full of sharp
pointy keys and a candlestick from under her as she silently mouths
"ow." She moves the objects to another part of the sofa, covers them
with leftover junk—pulling out the keys so that they show—and
makes a space for Callie. Callie reenters.*)

CALLIE: Coffee!

SARA: —would be great. Listen, this is so nice of you—

CALLIE: I was thinking about getting a cat anyway. Oh, my keys!
This'll give me a chance to see if I can hack it.

SARA: That's how I feel about New York.

CALLIE (*sounds familiar*): Oh yes.

(*Sara hops up and approaches Callie.*)

SARA: How long have you been here?

CALLIE: Eleven years.

SARA: I've lived in St. Louis my whole life. My parents live like, half an hour away. I go there for dinner when it's not even anybody's birthday. Things there—it's been, it is so—

CALLIE: Easy?

SARA: So easy.

CALLIE: It's hard here.

SARA: Good—*great,* I can't wait.

CALLIE: Yeah, you uh—what do you . . . do?

SARA: I teach. Third grade.

CALLIE: Well it won't be hard finding a job.

SARA: I already have one.

CALLIE: Where?

SARA: P.S. 32 in the Bronx.

CALLIE: What was the school like that you came from?

SARA: Society of Friends, a Quaker school.

(*Callie bursts into laughter.*)

CALLIE: I'm not—I'm not laughing at you, I'm laughing . . . *around* . . .

SARA: It's obviously—it's *very* . . . but I can do good work there.

CALLIE: I'm sure you're a good teacher.

SARA: No you don't know, but I am.

(*Pause.*)

CALLIE: Where in the Bronx?

SARA: Tremont.

CALLIE: Is that where . . . Taft, is it Taft?

SARA: Taft High School?

CALLIE: You've heard of it?

SARA: Mm hm.

CALLIE: You know there was a guy who taught there, this rich white guy—

SARA: Yes I know.

(*Pause.*)

CALLIE: He got killed—

SARA: By a student. I'm here on a fellowship set up in his name.

CALLIE: How long is the fellowship?

SARA: Two years.

(*Callie offers Sara a coffee mug and raises hers in a toast.*)

CALLIE: Well, congratulations—

SARA: Thank you.

CALLIE: *Best* of luck—

(*Sara nods.*)

CALLIE: And . . . if it gets too rough—go home.

(*Callie touches her mug to Sara's, but Sara doesn't reciprocate.*)

SARA: What brought you to New York?

(*Callie inhales to prepare for her long and interesting answer then realizes she has none.*)

CALLIE: College.

SARA: And what keeps you?

CALLIE: Keeps me from what?

SARA: What do you *do?*

CALLIE: I . . . ruin things for everyone else.

SARA: You're Rudolph Giuliani?

CALLIE: I'm a traffic reporter for a twenty-four-hour news radio station.

SARA (*impressed*): Helicopters!

CALLIE: "The inbound lane at the Holland Tunnel is closed due to a car accident. The Brooklyn-bound lane of the Williamsburg Bridge is under construction through 1999. The D train is not running due to a track fire. You can't get in. You can't get out. You can't get around. I'll be back in ten minutes to tell you that nothing has changed."

SARA: Does that get to you?

(*Callie shrugs.*)

CALLIE: It's a living.

(*Sara checks out the apartment.*)

SARA: How long have you lived in this apartment?

CALLIE: Five years—well, two by myself—it's a funny—not haha—story.

SARA: It's okay. (*In other words, you don't have to tell me.*)

CALLIE: I moved in here with my boyfriend Tom. This was his aunt's apartment, she lived here for twenty years.

SARA: Your rent must be—

CALLIE: Lucky.

SARA: *You* are.

CALLIE: Well, I got the apartment, he got . . . my sister.

SARA: Oh.

CALLIE: They live in LA now. It's perfect.

SARA: Well at least I don't mean to be crass but—

CALLIE: Yes, no, well I . . . like the apartment.

SARA: It's as big as mine and I'm sharing it with two other people.

CALLIE: Are they— Did you . . . move here with any of them?

SARA: No, they came with the apartment. They're a couple. It's kind of awkward but, he's sweet, she's sweet, they seem to have a—

CALLIE: —sweet?

SARA: —relationshipthey'refine.

CALLIE (*nods*): It's awkward.

SARA: Rents are so— Everything is—

CALLIE: It's impossible to live here. (*Pause. Sara studies Callie.*)

SARA: *You love it.*

CALLIE: You know, Sara, I've actually been to St. Louis and it's a quaint, pretty city but—what's the point of that? Everyone's still got their cars all geared up with Clubs and car alarms and computerized keys. And you have to drive all the way across town to get to the good cheap places to eat. And *drive*, I mean you're in a city and you have to *drive* to get around?

SARA: Where did you grow up?

CALLIE: Tiny town upstate.

SARA: Industrial?

CALLIE: Countrified suburb. Tractor display in the middle of the mall.

SARA: Pretty, though?

CALLIE: I can't connect with mountains, trees, the little animals—they snub me. You know how you can be with two other people and you're all having a great time. Then the person sitting next to you says something in French and the two of them burst into laughter, best laugh anyone's had all night. And you're left out because you took Spanish in the seventh grade, not French. That's what nature does to me. Speaks French to the other people at the table.

(*Slight pause.*)

SARA: I hate jazz.

CALLIE: *You do?*

SARA: I don't usually say that out loud because then people think I don't have a soul or something but I don't like the way it sounds. I don't like saxophones.

CALLIE: My sister played the saxophone.

SARA: I'm sorry—

CALLIE: I hate my sister.

SARA: The one who—

CALLIE: Yeah.

SARA: I hate your sister too.

(*Callie gives up a surprised smile; Sara does too. They hold it just a beat longer than normal, then Sara looks away.*)

CALLIE: So, do your friends think you're crazy?

SARA: Pff. Forget it. And my *parents* and Peter?

CALLIE: Huh?

SARA: —my ex. I mean I've never lived away from them. Even when I was in college I came home every weekend.

CALLIE: Close family.

SARA: It's . . . a cult. It's embarrassing. I should've moved. . . . I mean, you were what, eighteen?

CALLIE: Don't look at me. I was going to go to one of those colleges that advertise on matchbook covers. My guidance counselor filled out my application to NYU.

SARA: I had to interview five times to get this fellowship. By the fourth one I had a rabbit's foot, rosary beads, crystals, a tiger's tooth and a Polynesian *tiki* all in my purse—now that I got this fellowship I have every god to pay.

(*Callie hands Sara a Magic 8 Ball.*)

SARA: What should I ask it?

CALLIE: Something whose answer you won't take too seriously.

SARA (*addressing the ball*): Was moving to New York a good idea? (*She shakes the ball, then looks at it.*) It's sort of in between two of them.

CALLIE: That means yes.

(*Another shared smile. Sara stands up.*)

SARA: I should go, I'm taking up too much of your—

(*Callie looks at her watch.*)

CALLIE: I told some friends I would meet them, otherwise I wish—

SARA: You should've said—

CALLIE: No—no—

SARA: I didn't mean to keep—

CALLIE: What're you doing this weekend?

SARA: I don't know. Unpacking. But then I gotta do something New Yorky, don't I?

CALLIE: Do you want to come over and I'll take you around the neighborhood? Show you some fun places to go to and eat—

SARA: Yes!

CALLIE: And you can hang out here, spend some time with . . . is it Caesar?

(*Sara rushes to the pet carrier.*)

SARA: Caesar, forgive me. He hates being in this thing.

CALLIE: Let him out.

(*Sara does.*)

SARA: He may be a little shy at first, in a new place with a new person—

CALLIE: You could come and visit him. Just let me know. I hope you'll feel—

SARA: Thanks, Callie.

CALLIE: For nothing, for what.

Scene 2

A hospital examination room. Callie is sitting on an exam table buttoning the top button of her shirt. Detective Cole stands in front of her.

DETECTIVE COLE: Was he coming on to you, trying to pick you up?

CALLIE: He was just saying stuff, guy stuff, stupid kind of—

DETECTIVE COLE: What did you do?

(*She folds her arms protectively across her stomach like it was tender.*)

CALLIE: I—I wanted to leave—

DETECTIVE COLE: Your girlfriend?

CALLIE: My friend—Sara . . . said . . . something—

DETECTIVE COLE: What.

CALLIE: "Leave us alone" or something.

DETECTIVE COLE: And that's what set him off?

CALLIE: N—n—yeah. Well, she said—but then he said something back and she told him . . . she said something—upset him.

DETECTIVE COLE: What'd she say?

CALLIE: She sai—I think—

DETECTIVE COLE: What.

CALLIE: She told him to fuck off. Then he hit her.

DETECTIVE COLE: He hit her with his fist?

CALLIE: He hit her in her back then he grabbed her away—

DETECTIVE COLE: Grabbed her from you?

CALLIE: I—I was holding on to her arm with my hand like this—(*She puts her hand on her other elbow.*) I wanted us to leave. But then he grabbed her and started banging her head against the building. And then he smashed her head against his knee—like one of those wrestlers—that's when she lost consciousness—and then he smashed her again. (*Callie refolds her arms across her stomach. Detective Cole looks at his report.*)

DETECTIVE COLE: This was at Bleecker and West 11th—that little park.

CALLIE: Yes.

DETECTIVE COLE: At four-fifteen in the morning?

CALLIE: Yes.

DETECTIVE COLE: What were you doing there?

(*Callie shakes her head.*)

CALLIE: Just . . . walking around.

DETECTIVE COLE: Which bar were you at?

CALLIE: Excuse me?

DETECTIVE COLE: Four-fifteen, honey, that's closing time.

CALLIE: Well we had been . . . we were at the White Horse Tavern.

DETECTIVE COLE: The White Horse. On Hudson Street.

CALLIE: Yes.

DETECTIVE COLE: Was there a good crowd there?

CALLIE: . . . Yeah? Pretty crowded.

DETECTIVE COLE: Did anyone at the White Horse try to pick you up, buy you or your friend a drink?

CALLIE: No.

DETECTIVE COLE: Did you talk to anyone?

CALLIE: Just to each other mostly.

DETECTIVE COLE: What did the bartender look like?

CALLIE: Excuse me?

DETECTIVE COLE: Bartender.

CALLIE: . . . It was a man.

DETECTIVE COLE: Short, stocky guy? Salt and pepper hair?

CALLIE: No.

DETECTIVE COLE: Kind of tall, skinny guy with a receding hair-line? I know a couple of guys there.

CALLIE: I didn't really get a good look at him—Sara ordered the drinks. But I think he was tall.

DETECTIVE COLE: I'll go talk to him. Could be someone followed you from the bar. Maybe there was someone suspicious acting that you didn't notice. Bartender mighta seen something you didn't or talked to someone. What'd the bad guy look like?

CALLIE: He was tall.

DETECTIVE COLE: Like the bartender.

CALLIE: He was big—sort of, like he worked out.

DETECTIVE COLE: Was he black?

(*Callie shakes her head.*)

DETECTIVE COLE: Hispanic?

CALLIE: It was dark, I couldn't—

DETECTIVE COLE: Short hair, long hair—

CALLIE: Short. Wavy, dark brown.

DETECTIVE COLE: You remember what he was wearing?

CALLIE: He had a leather jacket . . . jeans . . . some kind of boots. He was twentysomething, maybe mid.

DETECTIVE COLE: Like a college kid? Frat boy?

CALLIE: No.

DETECTIVE COLE: Like a punk?

CALLIE: No.

DETECTIVE COLE: Like what then?

CALLIE: . . . I don't know.

DETECTIVE COLE: Any markings on the jacket? A name or symbol?

CALLIE: No.

DETECTIVE COLE: So he sees a couple of good-looking girls walking—were you drunk?

CALLIE: Not at all.

DETECTIVE COLE: —he gives 'em a line, one of the women tells him to fuck off and he beats her into a coma. Anything else you want to tell me?

CALLIE: That's—that's what I . . . remember.

DETECTIVE COLE: Doctor done with you?

CALLIE: I think.

DETECTIVE COLE: Allright, I need you to go somewhere with me right now and look at some pictures.

CALLIE: Can you bring them here?

DETECTIVE COLE: I need to take you there.

CALLIE: Because, my friend—if my friend . . .

DETECTIVE COLE: They say she's out of the woods in terms of life or—

CALLIE: But if she wakes up—

Scene 3

Callie's apartment. Callie hangs up her jacket and Sara's. Sara sits on the junk-free couch.

SARA: I mean that's the way I am with the kids.

CALLIE: Sure, with kids it's okay.

SARA: Why just them? Listen, every day when I walk by this park this guy, he's all cracked out, says something to me, you know, something nasty and I just lower my head and walk by.

CALLIE: Yep.

SARA: But yesterday, one of my students, Malik, is waiting for me outside the school and says he wants to walk me to the subway. So I say "sure" thinking maybe he has a problem he wants to tell me about. So we're walking and we pass by the park and I'm worried. "Is this crackhead gonna mention my vagina in front of this eight-year-old boy?" Sure enough, it's "pussy this" and "booty that" and Malik says, "This is my teacher, watch your mouth." And the guy shuts up.

CALLIE: Still—

SARA: Freaking eight-year-old boy. I should be able to do that for myself.

CALLIE: The best thing to do is walk on by.

SARA: But it worked.

(*The phone rings. Sara looks up, but Callie doesn't.*)

CALLIE: Next time, just walk on by.

SARA: Why, what's ever happened to you?

CALLIE: Nothing and that's why.

(*The machine clicks on.*)

GEORGE'S VOICE: Hey Callie, it's George. Your light is on, I know you're there. Jasmine and Lidia and I are at the Sinatra bar, where are you? (*Callie walks toward the phone, then stops.*) Anyway, we'll be here for a while, so come hang out. 'Bye.

(*The machine clicks off.*)

SARA: I should go.

CALLIE: No no, they'll be there for hours.

SARA: I've taken up your whole—

CALLIE: Are you hungry? We could order in something. There's Polish, Indian, Cuban, there's a pretty good Vietnamese—

SARA: Are you sure you don't— I've never had Vietnamese—

CALLIE: I'll show you the menu. (*Callie hops up and goes into the kitchen.*) Something to drink? Beer?

SARA: Yes to beer.

(*Callie returns and hands her a bottle. Sara leans her head toward the phone.*)

SARA: Were those friends from work?

CALLIE: Oh no, the people at my job are a bunch of stiffs—can you imagine? They listen to the same news reports every ten minutes for eight hours a day. They repeat themselves even in regular conversations. No, George—the guy on the phone—Lidia, Jasmine . . . Rico, Sally, Ben—we were all friends in college and now we're stuck to each other. I think we're someone's science experiment, we just don't know it. A study in overdependency.

SARA: Is George your boyfriend?

(*Callie hands a menu to Sara.*)

CALLIE: I like the noodle dishes, they're on the back. (*Sara takes the menu.*) George and I . . . are friends. Who sleep together. But date other people. Sometimes for long periods of time. We've been doing this since we were . . . twenty. Although he never likes anyone I'm dating, he's unabashedly—and I admit I can get jealous when he's—but at least I try to hide it, I'm pretty good at it too. It's only *after* they've broken up that I—Anyway, we'll probably get married. (*Sara gets the 8 ball and shakes it. She looks up at Callie.*) Or not.

SARA: It's stuck between two again.

CALLIE: Why's that keep happening to you?

SARA: Me? I think you have it rigged.

(*Callie takes the ball and shakes it. She looks at the answer [it's between two]. Sara tries to look—*)

CALLIE: Okay, okay.

SARA: All my friends are married or getting engaged, having babies or wishing they were—and lately when I hear about it, I think—why?

CALLIE: Why not?

SARA: Marriage. Why would you say to anyone, "I will stay with you even if I outgrow you."

(*Pause.*)

CALLIE (*remembering*): Peter. (*Sara is unresponsive, then finally nods.*) Did you leave him to come here?

SARA: . . . No.

CALLIE: Mm . . . C-.

SARA: In what.

CALLIE: Acting. (*Sara looks down.*) I'm sorry—

SARA: No no—

CALLIE: I'm prying—

SARA: No, that's not why—

CALLIE: I hope I didn't—

SARA: No, it's okay.

CALLIE: Did you decide what you wanted to order?

SARA: I moved out from our apartment—we lived together—and moved in with my parents about a month ago. I came here from there.

CALLIE: How—how long—?

SARA: Seven years.

CALLIE: *Seven* . . . so you must still be—

SARA: —Finally. Finally where I want to be. I'll stay in New York for two years and then I'm going to take off.

CALLIE: Let me guess: India.

SARA: A for effort, but no. Australia, Malaysia, Indonesia, Micronesia—

CALLIE: All the countries that sound like skin rashes?

SARA: Peter said, "What about Anesthesia?" Mm. Speaking—what time is it?

CALLIE: Almost six.

SARA: Hm.

CALLIE: What?

SARA: Oh, he left a message on my machine saying he was going to call at six. He wants to come visit. He manages a restaurant in St. Louis so he wants to come and check out some of the special places here.

CALLIE: You'd better hurry.

SARA: I couldn't make it in fifteen minutes.

CALLIE: You could if you took a cab.

(*Slight pause.*)

SARA: But then I wouldn't have Vietnamese food.

CALLIE: We could do it another time.

SARA: I just started this beer.

(*Pause.*)

CALLIE: You wouldn't want to waste a beer.

SARA: That's what I was thinking.

CALLIE: Cheers. (*They tap glasses. There is a sudden loud and rhythmic clomping on the ceiling. Callie doesn't respond.*) I always get this. It's not too spicy.

SARA: What is that?

CALLIE: Crispy squid in a little salt and—

SARA: No, what is *that?*

CALLIE: Huh? Oh. Every Thursday and Saturday at six.

SARA: What.

CALLIE: I think he teaches horses how to riverdance.

SARA: Have you complained?

CALLIE: It happens at exactly the same time twice a week for an
hour. I just make sure I'm out or doing something loud.

SARA: Let's go up there.

CALLIE: No, no—

SARA: Why not?

CALLIE: We gotta stay here and wait for the food.

SARA: We haven't ordered it yet.

CALLIE (*about the food*): Yeah so what do you want?

SARA: Chicken.

CALLIE: What kind of chicken?

SARA: You're chicken.

CALLIE: No I'm not, I'm smart.

SARA: Allright, I'll go.

CALLIE: Sara. Come on, don't. Please.

(*Slight pause.*)

SARA: Okay.

CALLIE: I'm gonna order. What do you want?

SARA: Come on, let's go!

Scene 4

Police station house. Mrs. Winsley sits behind a table that Detective Cole is sitting on. She's wearing a sharply tailored business suit.

MRS. WINSLEY: He called them pussy-eating dykes.

DETECTIVE COLE: Come on, why would he call them that?

MRS. WINSLEY: Two women in a West Village park at four in the morning? What's the chance they're *not* dykes.

DETECTIVE COLE: You tell me. You live in the West Village.

MRS. WINSLEY: My husband and I have lived there for eight years.

DETECTIVE COLE: Like the neighborhood?

MRS. WINSLEY: I sure do.

DETECTIVE COLE: Lot of clubs and bars there.

MRS. WINSLEY: They even have ones for straight people.

DETECTIVE COLE: Is that why you live there?

MRS. WINSLEY: My husband and I have a beautiful apartment, Detective Cole. In a safe building on an otherwise quiet street. The fact that it's Graceland for gay people doesn't matter to me.

DETECTIVE COLE: So what were these girls doing?

MRS. WINSLEY: I didn't see—

DETECTIVE COLE: Were they making out, rubbing up against each other?

MRS. WINSLEY: I didn't see anything till I heard the other one screaming. I went to the window then I called nine-one-one.

DETECTIVE COLE: What'd you see then?

MRS. WINSLEY: He was beating on the both of them. I yelled down that I called the cops and I threw a couple flowerpots at him. My spider plants—

DETECTIVE COLE: So the screams woke you up?

MRS. WINSLEY: I was in bed but up. Reading.

DETECTIVE COLE: Four-thirty in the morning?

MRS. WINSLEY: I'm a fitful sleeper.

DETECTIVE COLE: You ever take anything?

MRS. WINSLEY: No.

DETECTIVE COLE: So you weren't groggy or half asleep?

MRS. WINSLEY: No.

DETECTIVE COLE: And you're sure you heard him call them dykes.

MRS. WINSLEY: I'm sure.

DETECTIVE COLE: And your husband? (*No response.*) Your husband?

MRS. WINSLEY: He missed all the excitement.

DETECTIVE COLE: What'd he—sleep right through it?

(*Mrs. Winsley avoids his eyes.*)

DETECTIVE COLE: Oh . . . he wasn't home. Four-thirty in the—is he a doctor?

MRS. WINSLEY: No.

DETECTIVE COLE: . . . Investment banker?

MRS. WINSLEY: Ha!

DETECTIVE COLE: Fire chief?

MRS. WINSLEY: He's a book editor, Detective Cole.

DETECTIVE COLE: I didn't know book editors worked so late.

MRS. WINSLEY: They don't.

DETECTIVE COLE: Was he . . . out having drinks with some buddies?

MRS. WINSLEY: He was obviously out, wasn't he.

DETECTIVE COLE: So you were waiting up for him.

MRS. WINSLEY: I'm a fitful sleeper, Detective. Have been since before I married him and those two girls are lucky that I am and that I was up and that I did something.

DETECTIVE COLE: You called nine-one-one.

MRS. WINSLEY: And my flowerpots.

DETECTIVE COLE: Did you hit him?

MRS. WINSLEY: They fell near him. He stopped and took off.

DETECTIVE COLE: You stopped him.

MRS. WINSLEY: Well it wasn't the cops, took thirty minutes for someone to show up. You'd think it was Harlem, not the West Village.

Scene 5

Callie's apartment. Callie walks on wearing jeans and carrying a fresh bouquet of flowers. She places them in a vase.

She goes into her bedroom and reenters with several hangers of clothes. She looks at herself in the mirror as she holds up a tight blouse in front of her—too slutty—then drops it onto the floor. She picks up a shirt and holds it in front of her—too butch—then drops it onto the floor. She tries on a short skirt which she can't get past her hips. She throws the skirt onto the ground. She puts her jeans back on and puts on a third top—it looks like something Sara would wear.

The front door buzzer buzzes. Callie buzzes without asking who it is. She fusses over the flowers and accidentally knocks the whole thing over.

She gets the disobedient skirt and uses it to wipe up the mess. There is a knock on the door. Before Callie can open it, George walks in and steps in the puddle.

GEORGE: Hey Cal, when did they paint the—whoops!

(Callie is stunned to see George but plays it off like it's about the puddle.)

CALLIE: George!

(George looks down.)

GEORGE: Did you get a puppy?

CALLIE: Yeah, right.

(Callie stands up.)

GEORGE: So you're allright, huh?

CALLIE: Yeah, what?

GEORGE: No, I haven't heard from you in a while.

CALLIE: I'm fine, I'm fine . . . busy.

(Callie goes to the kitchen to throw away the skirt.)

GEORGE: Lidia said she called you about that book you were looking for, you didn't call her back.

CALLIE: . . . I forgot.

GEORGE: She got that job, you know.

CALLIE: No, I didn't!

(George stretches himself out on the couch, stacking a pile of pillows behind his head.)

GEORGE: Yeah, she's really excited.

(Callie looks disapprovingly at his move.)

GEORGE: We're gonna take her out on Friday night, so try not to be "fine but busy" that night, okay?

(He grabs the remote and clicks the TV on.)

CALLIE: I'll remember. Um, George—

(He looks at his watch.)

GEORGE: I know, I know, we can watch your show. I just want to
check to see what the score is.

CALLIE: I have plans for tonight.

GEORGE: Oh yeah, what?

CALLIE: I'm meeting someone for dinner.

(George turns off the TV and sits up.)

GEORGE: You have a date?

CALLIE: No!

GEORGE: With *who?*

CALLIE: It's not a date, I'm just meeting my friend Sara for dinner.

GEORGE: Who the hell is Sara?

CALLIE: I told you, that friend of a friend of a— *(refreshing his
memory)* She's new in town, I'm taking care of her cat—

GEORGE: I thought you said she was a big loser.

CALLIE: I said I didn't know, but now I do—she's not.

GEORGE: So what is she?

CALLIE: What.

GEORGE: What's she do?

CALLIE: She teaches up in the Bronx.

GEORGE: Oh, so she's a nut.

CALLIE: There's something wrong with us.

GEORGE: Why?

CALLIE: Because that's what I thought when she told me.

GEORGE: You have to wonder about people who want to do stuff like that. What does she want to do—save a life? Give a kid a chance? Or just feel good about trying.

CALLIE: She won a fellowship. She *competed* to get this job.

GEORGE: To teach in the Bronx? What'd the losers get? (*The front door buzzer buzzes. Callie buzzes back.*) You don't ask who it is anymore?

CALLIE: It's her.

GEORGE: You thought it was her when you buzzed me in.

CALLIE: You're right, that was a mistake.

(*Sara knocks at the door. Callie holds George's jacket open for him.*)

CALLIE: Okay. Please leave now.

GEORGE: Why?

CALLIE: Because I gotta go.

(*He stands up.*)

GEORGE: I'll walk out with you.

CALLIE: But I'm not leaving yet.

GEORGE: Huh?

(*Callie growls at George, then unlocks the door. Sara walks in.*)

CALLIE: Hey.

SARA: Hi, here, these are . . .

(*Sara shyly hands Callie a small bouquet of baby roses. Callie takes them.*)

CALLIE: Thank you. They're so—

SARA: They're babies.

(*Callie goes to kiss Sara on the cheek, but retreats. Sara takes the cue late, now her head is sticking out. Callie tries to respond, but Sara has already reeled in like a turtle. Callie turns away, takes the other flowers out of the vase and puts the roses in.)*

CALLIE: I was just going to throw these out.

(*She crosses to the kitchen.*)

SARA: Hey, did you see they're filming a movie or something on the next block? Do you think we could stop on our way to the restaurant and watch for a while?

(*George steps out.*)

GEORGE: It's *NYPD Blue*— (*Sara starts. She hadn't noticed him.*) Oop—didn't mean to scare you.

SARA: No no, you didn't.

(*He crosses to her and extends his hand.*)

GEORGE: I'm George.

(*Sara shakes his hand.*)

SARA: Oh, *George,* I heard so much about you!

GEORGE (*can't say the same thing*): . . . Nice to meet you.

(*Callie comes out of the kitchen.*)

CALLIE: Oh, sorry. Sara, this is George. George, this is—

GEORGE: We did this.

CALLIE: Good. (*To Sara*) We should go.

GEORGE: Where're you guys having dinner?

CALLIE (*tries to slip it past him*): Vong.

(*George looks at Callie.*)

GEORGE: Dressed like that?

CALLIE: I didn't have time—

SARA (*consoling*): You look great.

GEORGE: Well, tell me what you get.

SARA: Have you ever been?

GEORGE: Out of my league.

SARA (*to Callie*): Is it expensive? I don't want you to—

CALLIE: It's not expensive.

GEORGE (*to Callie*): You're treating? Then I wanna—

CALLIE (*to George*): You still owe me for my birthday.

SARA: Let's go dutch, Callie.

CALLIE: It's *my* treat.

GEORGE: What's the occasion?

(*Silence. There is none.*)

SARA: Actually, we're celebrating the fact that today LaChandra, one of my students, wrote her name for the very first time.

(*Callie looks down at her clothes.*)

CALLIE: I'm changing.

(*She runs off.*)

GEORGE: That's right, you're a teacher.

SARA: Mm hm.

GEORGE: Kindergarten?

SARA: Third grade.

GEORGE: And this kid wrote her name for the first time?

SARA: Perfectly.

GEORGE: Isn't that—

SARA: Wonderful?

GEORGE: . . . Yeah, isn't it?

(*Callie reenters wearing the blouse she started off wearing.*)

CALLIE (*to Sara*): We should go, our reservation's at 8:00.

SARA: Do we have time to stop by? The *NYPD*—

CALLIE: Sure.

(*Sara starts for the door.*)

GEORGE: Okay, well um, 'bye. Nice to meet you.

SARA: Don't you want to come with us and watch them filming?

(*George flashes Callie a furtive look.*)

GEORGE: Mmm, I think I'll wait until it's on TV.

(*He looks at Callie. She ushers him out the door.*)

CALLIE: Meanie.

GEORGE: Never take *me* to Vong.

(*Callie closes the door and locks it.*)

Scene 6

Police station house. Callie sits in an interview room. Detective Cole enters.

DETECTIVE COLE: Hey, thanks for coming in. You want some coffee?

CALLIE: Thank you, I'm fine.

(*He flips through his report.*)

DETECTIVE COLE: We were talking about the White Horse Tavern last time, right? On Hudson Street?

CALLIE: Yes.

DETECTIVE COLE: That's a famous bar, you know? Has a long literary tradition. They say Dylan Thomas died waiting for a drink there.

CALLIE: . . . I hadn't heard.

DETECTIVE COLE: I talked to the bartender there. I told you I wanted to ask him if he noticed anyone suspicious there that night. Maybe someone paying attention to you and your friend that you didn't notice.

CALLIE: Yes, you said.

DETECTIVE COLE: I went in and talked to Stacy, she said she don't remember you and your friend coming in.

CALLIE: It was pretty crowded.

(*Slight pause.*)

DETECTIVE COLE: Do you remember telling me that the bartender at the White Horse Tavern that night was a tall *guy?*

CALLIE: Sara ordered the drinks.

DETECTIVE COLE: So you didn't get a good look at the bartender.

CALLIE: I didn't.

DETECTIVE COLE: Not even enough to tell if it was a girl or a guy.

CALLIE: I'm sorry.

DETECTIVE COLE: So after you leave the White Horse, you and your friend go for a walk. You end up in that park area outside the playground. And you're . . . doing what?

CALLIE: We were sitting on one of the benches, talking to each other . . . when this guy says something.

DETECTIVE COLE: What'd he say?

CALLIE: Something like, "Hey, you want to party—"

DETECTIVE COLE: What did you say?

CALLIE: I didn't.

DETECTIVE COLE: Sara said something.

CALLIE: Yes.

DETECTIVE COLE: So she provoked him.

CALLIE: What!?

DETECTIVE COLE: She told him to "fuck off," and that's when he hit her, right?

CALLIE: No.

DETECTIVE COLE: I mean, if the two of you had ignored him or walked away, this wouldn't have happened, would it?

CALLIE: If *he* hadn't started—

DETECTIVE COLE: But Sara had to say something and that's what got him pissed, that's why he wanted to hit her. Why did she say something?

CALLIE: He started it, he—

DETECTIVE COLE: Allright. *He* must have said something first— something that upset her. What upset her so much?

CALLIE: He was bothering—

DETECTIVE COLE: What did he say? She said "Leave us alone," and then he said what?

(*Callie doesn't respond.*)

DETECTIVE COLE: Did he call her something?

CALLIE: What?

DETECTIVE COLE: Did he call her something. Like a name?

CALLIE: No.

DETECTIVE COLE: What's a name that might upset her?

CALLIE: I don't know.

DETECTIVE COLE: How about bitch?

CALLIE: No.

DETECTIVE COLE: He didn't call her a bitch?

CALLIE: I don't—

DETECTIVE COLE: A pussy-eating bitch?

(*Callie looks at Detective Cole.*)

CALLIE: No.

DETECTIVE COLE: What'd he say, then—

CALLIE: He shouldn't've—

DETECTIVE COLE: What'd he call her?

CALLIE: He called—

DETECTIVE COLE: What?

CALLIE: A fucking—

DETECTIVE COLE: Say it!

CALLIE: Fucking dyke! Pussy-eating dykes—both of us.

DETECTIVE COLE: Why would he say that, why would he call you that? Two nice girls sitting on a park bench talking, why would he call you dykes.

(*Pause.*)

CALLIE: Because we were kissing.

(*Detective Cole gestures—there it is.*)

CALLIE: It was the first— We didn't know he was there. Until he said something. "Hey, save some of that for me." Sara told him to leave us alone. I couldn't believe she—then he offered to pay us. He said he'd give us fifty bucks if we went to a motel with him and let him watch. He said we could dry hump or whatever we like to do—turns him on just to see it. I grabbed her arm and started walking away. He came after us, called us fucking dykes—pussy-eating dykes. Sara told him to fuck off. I couldn't believe—he came up and punched her in the back, then grabbed her and pulled her away. I yelled for someone to call the police. He pushed her against the building and started banging her head against the building. He told her to watch her cunt-licking mouth. But he had his hand over her jaw, she couldn't—she just made these mangled—she was trying to breathe. I came up behind him and grabbed his hair—he turned around and punched me in the stomach. I threw up, it got on him. Sara tried to get away but he grabbed her and started banging her head against his knee. I tried to hold his arms back but he was stronger—he knocked her out. He pushed me to the ground and started kicking me. Someone yelled something—"Cops are coming"—and he took off in the opposite direction. West. He was limping. He hurt his knee. (*She looks at Detective Cole.*) That's what happened.

Scene 7

Callie's apartment. Sara is sprawled out on the couch holding several giant playing cards in her hand. She places a card on the discard pile and drains a glass of wine.

Callie brings a bottle of red wine from the kitchen; an empty one stands on the table.

SARA: Okay. If you're in someone else's bathroom and they have the toilet paper coming out from the bottom instead of the top—

CALLIE: I hate that.

SARA: Do you change it or leave it the way it is.

CALLIE: What do you mean change it? You'd change somebody else's toilet roll?

SARA: If I was gonna use it a couple times.

CALLIE: Pfff.

SARA: Allright, you go next.

CALLIE: So if you were driving down a highway and saw a pot-hole in the road ahead what would you do, straddle or swerve?

SARA: Mm, straddle. You?

CALLIE: Straddle.

SARA (*about Callie*): Swerve.

CALLIE: Nah ah.

SARA: Yes, you would.

CALLIE (*a second scenario*): Cat in the road.

SARA: Caesar!—say a rabbit.

CALLIE: Okay, a rabbit. Straddle, swerve or brake.

SARA (*like this is an option*): Straddle a rabbit.

CALLIE: Sport utility vehicle—four-wheel drive, you could. (*Callie sits down, picks up her cards, and discards.*)

SARA: Screech to a brake, check the rabbit, then—smoke. You?

CALLIE: Brake.

SARA: *Swerve.*

CALLIE: Why do you keep saying that?

SARA: This is you— (*She grips her hands around an imaginary steering wheel. She fills her eyes with panic, turns the wheel a hard right, then a fast left. Callie puts her cards down.*)

CALLIE: These cards are driving me nuts.

SARA: One more hand, please.

(*Callie picks the cards back up.*)

CALLIE: Can I ask you something about your job?

SARA: Yep.

CALLIE: Why did you want it?

SARA: You mean this fellowship?

CALLIE: Public school, the Bronx—teaching.

SARA: Instead of private school, St. Louis—teaching?

CALLIE: That's what you're used to, right?

SARA: It's where I *worked* for five years, I never got used to it. I mean, I never went to private school. We all went to the cruddy public school—I mean, it was cruddy compared to the private school, it's the Sorbonne compared to where I teach now. But in a private school . . . I mean, what am I giving them? They have more than everything.

CALLIE: And the Bronx?

SARA: These kids—you know who I was when I was their age? I was the kid who had the right answer, knew I had the right answer but would never raise my hand. Hoping the teacher would call on me anyway. Those are my favorite kids to teach. And here? Now? I got a classroom full of them.

(*Callie looks at the discard pile.*)

CALLIE: Did you pick a card? You have to pick a card.

(*Sara does.*)

SARA: You should come and meet them one day.

CALLIE: Yeah, okay.

SARA: I'll bet you've never even been to the Bronx.

CALLIE: I go every day.

SARA: *Fly over.*

CALLIE: That's more than most New Yorkers.

SARA: Can I ask you about your job?

CALLIE (*dread filled*): Go ahead.

SARA: Why the traffic?

CALLIE: Why the traffic indeed.

SARA: I mean, as opposed to news reporting or other kinds of journalism.

CALLIE: I'm not a journalist. I never worked in radio or TV before I got that job.

SARA: So how'd you get it?

CALLIE: My boyfriend Tom's uncle worked at the station.

SARA: Oh.

CALLIE: I mean, it's the traffic, it's not even—*the weather.* You just ride around in a helicopter and tell people what the cars are doing.

SARA: The helicopter part is pretty great, right?

CALLIE: Yeah, how great?

SARA: Well if you don't like it you should get another job.

CALLIE: I can't. (*Sara imitates Callie swerving in her imaginary car again.*) I don't get that.

SARA: What time is it?

(*Callie looks at her watch.*)

CALLIE: Two-thirty.

SARA: Already? Is the subway okay this time of night?

CALLIE: You should take a cab.

SARA: How much will that be?

CALLIE: About ten bucks?

SARA: I'll take the train.

CALLIE: I'll give you the money—

SARA: I have it, it's just too much. It's only four or five stops on
the train.

(*Callie sits up a little.*)

CALLIE: Listen you can . . . you know, you're welcome to stay . . .
this pulls out to be a sofa bed . . . you can take a train in the
morning, when it's safe. I'm not getting up for anything in
particular.

SARA: Maybe Caesar will come sleep with me.

CALLIE: Yes! You can reconcile with your cat!

SARA: He's holding such a grudge. He never comes out when
I'm here.

CALLIE: It took a few days before he started to sleep with me.

SARA: Lucky.

(*Slight pause.*)

CALLIE: I'm sure he'll sleep with you tonight.

SARA: Yeah.

CALLIE: Here, let me just get those— (*She pulls off the cushions;
Sara helps. Together they pull out the bed.*) I think it's comfort-
able, I haven't slept on it myself—because I live here—but if
it's not comfortable enough then I'll switch beds with you.
In fact, should we just do that? You sleep in my room and
I'll sleep out here?

SARA: No, no, this'll be fine.

CALLIE: I think it's comfortable. (*Callie bounces on it once, then gets
up.*) Is there anything else you need?

SARA: I think I'm all set.

CALLIE: Allright. Sleep tight.

SARA: Goodnight.

(*They stand there. Finally, Callie smiles and walks off into her room. Sara takes off her shirt just as Callie reenters with a T-shirt.*)

CALLIE: Do you need a tee—whoop.

(*Callie looks away.*)

SARA: Oh—I have one. (*She pulls one out of her bag.*) We did face painting today so I—

CALLIE: I'm sorry.

(*Sara puts the shirt on. Callie leaves.*)

SARA: It's okay.

CALLIE: Goodnight.

SARA: Sweet dreams. (*Sara gets in bed and shuts out the light. She lies there a minute. Then*) Psss pssss psss psss psss. (*She lifts her head up and looks for Caesar.*) Caeeeesar. (*No sign of him. Sara lies there another minute.*) Come on you grudge holder. Pssss psss psss. (*Nothing. Finally, to Callie in the other room*) Is he in there with you?

CALLIE: Uh uh. He's not out there with you?

SARA: No.

(*Callie walks up to her doorway.*)

CALLIE: Is he under your bed?

(*Sara leans over and looks.*)

SARA: No.

(*Callie shrugs at Sara.*)

SARA: Will you do me a favor? For just like a minute?

CALLIE: Sure.

SARA: Would you just lay in bed here for just a minute to see if he comes.

CALLIE: Okay.

SARA: Since he's been sleeping with you. (*Callie gets in next to Sara and pulls the covers up.*)

CALLIE: I guess we have to convince him we're sleeping.

SARA: Oh, right.

(*They lie down.*)

CALLIE: This bed is comfortable.

SARA: Isn't it?

CALLIE: I never laid on it before.

SARA: It's comfortable.

CALLIE: I got it secondhand.

SARA: Really?

CALLIE: A hundred and fifty bucks.

SARA: That's cheap.

CALLIE: It's comfortable.

(*Pause.*)

SARA: Are your feet hot?

CALLIE: What?

SARA: My feet get hot when I sleep.

CALLIE: Even in winter?

SARA: Yeah.

CALLIE: Take them out.

SARA: I usually move the sheet so that it goes the other way, you
      know, the short way—

CALLIE: Okay.

(*Sara gets up and turns the sheet around so that both pairs of their feet
are exposed. She lies back down. Pause.*)

SARA: Do you see him?

CALLIE: Who?

SARA: Caesar.

CALLIE: Not yet. (*They both lie there staring at the ceiling. After a
      while*) Huh? (*Pause.*) Are you asleep? (*No response. Callie turns
      and looks at Sara.*) You're not asleep already, are you?

(*No response. Callie draws her feet under the covers and turns her back
to Sara. Sara opens her eyes.*)

Scene 8

*Callie's apartment. There's loud banging on her door. Callie enters from
her bedroom, wearing pajamas. She looks through the peephole.*

CALLIE: Allright George, I hear you!

(*She unlocks the door and opens it. George bursts in wearing his bartender uniform.*)

GEORGE: How long have you been home?

CALLIE: Lower your voice.

GEORGE: Why didn't you answer your phone?

CALLIE: I don't know.

GEORGE: You wanna know how fucked up and worried about
      you everyone is right now?

CALLIE: No.

GEORGE: You wanna know how I heard?

CALLIE: No.

GEORGE: You wanna know exactly what drink I was making at the moment I heard your name on the goddamn TV?

CALLIE: No, I don't.

GEORGE: Dirty martini. TV's on in the background. I hear about this gay bashing, two women attacked, and I sort of pay attention, not really. I'm making this drink and thinking about how I gotta run downstairs and get some more peanuts. And then I feel my ears close and my face gets all hot, like I just swallowed a mouthful of hot peppers. So I turn to the TV, but now they're talking about some apartment fire. So I switch the channel and they're just starting the story. Gay bashing. Woman in a coma. Callie Pax.

CALLIE: I'm not in a coma.

GEORGE: What?

CALLIE: Sara's in a coma.

GEORGE: How do I know that?

CALLIE: What was I—

GEORGE: How do I know anything but what I see on the goddamn—

CALLIE: What did you want—me to call you from the hospital?

GEORGE: Yes!

CALLIE: What would I say? On a pay phone. In the hospital. Sara lying in a room swollen and blue, face cracked open, knocked out, not responding to anything but the barest reflex—all because . . . because—

GEORGE: Come and get me. That's what you could've said. (*Pause.*) Are you hurt? (*Callie doesn't respond.*) Did a doctor look at you?

CALLIE: Sara's hurt.

GEORGE: Nothing happened to you? (*Callie doesn't respond. He walks toward her; she walks away.*) Callie—

CALLIE: Bruises.

GEORGE: Where.

CALLIE: Cracked rib.

GEORGE: Let me see.

CALLIE: It's nothing.

GEORGE: Let me see.

CALLIE: There's nothing to see.

(*Pause.*)

GEORGE: Do you want me to call anyone?

CALLIE: No.

(*Slight pause.*)

GEORGE: Do you want me to spend the night?

CALLIE: No.

GEORGE: Do you want me to go?

(*Slight pause.*)

CALLIE: No. (*Pause.*) George, do you remember the first time we kissed?

GEORGE (*thinks about it*): No.

CALLIE: Me either. (*Pause.*) You know, I would stand here at the door with Sara and say "goodnight," "take care," "see ya tomorrow," "get home safe—" When what I *really* wanted to do was plant her a big, fat, wet one. Square on the lips. Nothing confusing about it. She wouldn't have to think "Maybe Callie meant to kiss me on the cheek and . . .

missed." You know, just right there. Not between friends. Not a friendly kiss at all. Bigger. So she'd know. She'd know for sure. That I was answering her. Sara is always asking me, "What do you *want, Callie?*" And finally, I let her know. I answered.

Scene 9

Callie's apartment. Callie walks in from the kitchen carrying a roasting pan in two mittened hands. She pulls the top off and rears her head back as the smell assaults her. She reaches in and pulls out a drumstick; it's fossilized. She bonks it on the table; it sounds like a baseball bat.

There's a knock on the door—Callie starts. She looks out the peephole and sees Sara. She hurries to hide the roasting pan and all signs of cooking.

She opens the door, and Sara steps in.

SARA: The kids talked about you the rest of the day, you were hilarious.

CALLIE (*shady*): How'd you get in?

SARA: Huh? Oh, there was this woman with a baby carriage. I held the door for her, then squeezed in behind her. It smells like something in here.

CALLIE: Like what?

SARA: Like someone vomited in sawdust. Oh—I brought you this— (*She hands her a bottle of wine.*) For coming in and talk-ing to the kids.

(*Callie silently takes it and sets it down.*)

CALLIE: It's a little early for me.

SARA: It's . . . almost six.

CALLIE: Go ahead, you have some.

SARA: Don't open it for me.

CALLIE: Okay.

SARA (*trying to figure her out*): So, what'd you do the rest of the day?

CALLIE: Nothing.

SARA: Nothing?

CALLIE: Nothing.

SARA: You know Michelle, the girl who had the sweater with the puppet on it today? She used to say "nothing" just like that. Until I squeezed an answer out of her.

CALLIE: Those kids adore you.

SARA: Do you think?

CALLIE: You have a knack for them.

SARA (*as if it's the first time she's heard it*): Thank you.

CALLIE: It was humiliating for me.

SARA: Why?

CALLIE: Standing up there talking about my idiotic job.

SARA: You ride in a helicopter, Callie, what could be cooler than that?

CALLIE: Have you noticed? The only thing you ever praise about my job is that I ride in a helicopter? (*Pause.*) But that doesn't even matter. Standing up in front of those kids today telling them about what I do I thought—why should these kids care about traffic, their families don't have cars. I don't have a car. No one I care about has a car. Who am I helping?

SARA (*gently*): People with cars.

CALLIE: Who are they? Why do they live in New York City? Why have a car when you hear every ten minutes on the radio that the traffic is so bad?

SARA: Maybe you should look for another job.

CALLIE: Whose uncle's gonna get it for me this time?

SARA: You could get a job based on your experience.

CALLIE: As a traffic reporter?

SARA: What do you want to do instead?

CALLIE: I don't know.

SARA: Allright. Come on, we can think about this. What do you like?

CALLIE: I don't want to do this.

SARA: You know a lot about food . . . you have a great taste in restaurants—

CALLIE: I don't—I really don't want to do this.

SARA: You should become a chef!

(*The noise from upstairs starts again. Callie goes for her coat.*)

CALLIE: Let's get the hell out of here.

SARA: You could go to cooking school—

CALLIE: Let's see what's playing at the three-dollar movie theatre.

SARA: You obviously have some kind of talent for food—

CALLIE: Come on, put your coat on, let's go.

SARA: God, what is that smell?

CALLIE: I think someone downstairs was trying to cook something.

SARA: Ugh, you think that smell is related to food?

(*Callie opens the door for Sara.*)

CALLIE: Barely.

(*They exit.*)

Scene 10

*Sara's hospital room. Callie walks in and stands at the foot of Sara's bed.
What can she do? She thinks a beat. She remembers.*

*She untucks the sheet and rolls it back so that Sara's feet are exposed.
She tucks the sides of the sheet in so that it'll stay that way.*

Scene 11

*Callie's apartment. Callie, dressed up, is impatiently waiting for Sara.
She refuses to sit—she paces across the apartment, picking up things,
scowling at them, then putting them down.*

*Finally, there's a buzz. She buzzes back and puts on her coat. Sara
knocks, and Callie opens the door—Sara is holding a wet newspaper
over her head.*

SARA: Wow, it's really starting to come down now.

CALLIE: That means it's gonna be hard to get a cab.

(*Sara looks at her watch.*)

SARA: We still have time.

CALLIE: Not really.

SARA: We can be a little late, can't we?

CALLIE: Sara, I asked you to be here by 5:30.

SARA: I know, I'm sorry, I lost track of time. (*Sara takes off her
    coat.*) Let me just stand next to the radiator for a second.

 CALLIE: Is that what you're wearing?

SARA: . . . Yeah. (*She looks at her clothes.*) What?

CALLIE: Nothing.

SARA: I mean, is this a dress-up event? (*Callie shrugs.*) What are
    you wearing?

CALLIE: Just . . . clothes.

SARA: Let me see.

CALLIE: It's just . . . what I wore to my hippie friend's wedding.

SARA: Let me see? (*Callie opens her coat a little bit. Embarrassed*) Oh, you look great. (*Callie shuts her coat.*) I'm underdressed.

CALLIE: We don't have time to stop by your place.

SARA: Can I borrow something of yours?

CALLIE: Let's just forget it, I don't want to go. (*Callie sits with her coat on.*)

SARA: I thought you had to.

CALLIE: Technically.

SARA: Isn't your station getting an award?

CALLIE: They are, I'm not.

SARA: So do you want to go or not?

CALLIE: I have to.

SARA: Okay, let's go. (*Sara makes for the door. Callie remains seated.*) What's going on.

CALLIE: Nothing.

(*Pause.*)

SARA: Why are you still sitting down? (*Callie shrugs.*) Let me see what you've got in your closet. (*Sara goes to Callie's bedroom and comes back holding a dress on a hanger.*) Could I wear this?

CALLIE: I wore that to a reception last week.

SARA: You did, I didn't.

CALLIE: People will recognize it.

SARA: Do you care? (*Callie shrugs.*) Callie, what the hell.

CALLIE: I don't know.

SARA: Okay. Just tell me. What do you want?

CALLIE: I have to go to this thing.

SARA: Do you not want me to go? Is that it?

CALLIE: You don't have to go if you don't want to.

SARA: Callie, will you say what you want?

CALLIE: I have to go, I have to.

SARA: So let's go.

CALLIE: What are you going to wear?

SARA: What?

(*Callie gets up.*)

CALLIE: I have to go to this thing and I want you to go with me but I don't want you to wear what you're wearing and I don't want you to wear my clothes. What will people think if we walk in together and you're wearing my clothes?

(*Sara sits down.*)

SARA: I'm not going.

CALLIE: Now this.

SARA: I'm tired, I'm underdressed. I'm not going to know anyone there except for you—forget it.

CALLIE: Sara, I asked you to go to this thing with me a week ago; I told you it was an awards ceremony, why did you dress like you were going camping?

SARA: You didn't make it sound like it was that big a deal.

CALLIE: An *awards ceremony?*

SARA: If you had wanted me to get dressed up, you should've told me.

CALLIE: I told you to be here at 5:30, you couldn't manage that.

SARA: What's the big deal—you don't even like your job.

CALLIE: I don't like my job the way you love your job but that doesn't mean you shouldn't come at the time I asked you to, wearing something appropriate.

SARA: Obviously this is more important than you—

(*The clomping from upstairs starts again.*)

CALLIE: There's my cue. I'm leaving now, I don't care what you do.

SARA: Yeah go, get chased out of your own apartment again.

CALLIE: What?

SARA: Better to plan your life around someone else's schedule than have to face them and tell them what you have every right—

CALLIE: What do you care? What do you care? This is my apartment—

SARA: You're pathetic, Callie—

(*Callie takes off her coat.*)

CALLIE: Fuck it, I'll stay right here then.

SARA: Perfect.

CALLIE: *You* can leave.

SARA: Glad to.

CALLIE: I'm busy tomorrow so forget about the museum.

SARA: Yeah, I'm busy too.

(*Callie opens the door for Sara. Sara grabs her coat and exits. Callie slams the door behind her.*)

Scene 12

Hospital waiting room. Peter is already sitting; Callie walks in; Peter looks up and forces a smile, as he would to any stranger. Then it hits him. After a beat—

CALLIE: Her parents?

PETER: Anita and Joe are in there now, yeah.

(*Silence.*)

CALLIE: They're strict about that—the hospital. Two at a time.

PETER: Noah's ark.

CALLIE: Excuse me?

PETER: Two at a— (*He shakes his head at himself.*) —stupid.

(*More silence.*)

CALLIE: Did you—was your flight okay?

PETER: There were like six peanuts in the whole— (*He covers his eyes.*) Flight was fine, fine. Thank you.

CALLIE: Her parents, are they—how are they?

PETER: Anita is . . . wrecked, *and* Joe—they're . . . I mean, Sara's their only daughter—

CALLIE: I know.

PETER: They never wanted her to come here—

CALLIE: I know.

PETER: The doctor said she can't be moved until she regains consciousness.

CALLIE: They want to move her?

PETER: Mm hm.

CALLIE: Back to St. Louis?

PETER: To Chesterfield, where Anita and Joe live. It's about twenty minutes outside.

(*Pause.*)

CALLIE: But what—what if she doesn't want to go?

PETER: Why wouldn't she?

CALLIE: Because the fellowship, she wanted—she worked so hard to get, and the kids—

PETER: Her old school would take her back in a heartbeat.

CALLIE: Her old school, but she—

PETER: But—I mean we have no idea when she'll be able to go back to work—or *if.* The doctors can't say. There could be permanent . . . she'll need rehabilitation, maybe home care—

CALLIE: I know.

PETER: She needs her family. And they need to take care of her. (*Silence.*) . . . There was a response.

CALLIE: Excuse me?

PETER: The doctor. He said Sara responded to—he told her to squeeze his hand and she . . . squeezed.

CALLIE: She did?

PETER: Yeah.

CALLIE: She did!

PETER: Fucking A.

CALLIE: Amazing!

PETER: I thought you'd want to know.

(*Callie looks him in the eye.*)

CALLIE: Thank you. (*Pause.*) Sara . . . Sara told me . . . nice things . . . about you—so many . . .

(*Pause.*)

PETER: She didn't tell me about you. (*Callie looks down.*) She said you were a friend.

(*Pause.*)

CALLIE: I am her friend.

(*Pause.*)

PETER: And that you knew good restaurants to go to— (*He looks at Callie.*) That's all Sara told me about you.

CALLIE: I see.

PETER: Sara and I—

CALLIE: She told me.

(*Pause.*)

PETER: We lived together for—

CALLIE: Yes.

(*Pause.*)

PETER: I still—

CALLIE: Yes.

(*Pause.*)

PETER: I'd like—I'd like you to tell me what happened that night. (*Silence. Peter waits long enough to figure out Callie's not going to answer.*) Please.

(*Slight pause.*)

CALLIE: I'm sorry.

PETER: What.

CALLIE: I can't.

PETER: Why can't you?

(*Slight pause.*)

CALLIE: Everything you need to know has been in the papers, on the TV—

PETER: I've seen the newspapers and the TV.

CALLIE: Then you know every—

PETER: No, I don't know everything. I know what *time* it happened, I know *where,* and I know that you were there. And now you're here and *Sara* is in there. That's the part I want to know about. Why is *she* in there?

CALLIE: I wish it was me but it isn't.

PETER: Why isn't it? (*Callie doesn't respond.*) Were *you* hurt?

CALLIE: You don't know what fucking happened.

PETER: Tell me! (*Callie doesn't answer.*) Why couldn't you protect her?

CALLIE: He was big, he was stronger—I tried—

PETER: How big?

CALLIE: I *tried.*

PETER: Bigger than me? (*Callie turns away from him.*) Could I have— (*He turns her back.*) Hey, was he bigger than me?

CALLIE: No!

(*Peter steps back.*)

PETER: Why was she protecting you?

(*Callie holds on his eyes but doesn't answer.*)

Scene 13

Callie's apartment. The phone rings. Her machine picks up. Callie runs in from the bedroom and picks it up.

CALLIE: Hello? (*Dial tone sounds over the speaker. She hangs up. She hovers over the phone for a moment. She jerks the receiver up to her ear, dials three numbers then abruptly hangs up. She stares at the phone. She picks up the phone, dials seven numbers then hangs up. She picks up the phone and places it on the floor in front of the sofa.*) Caesar, please? Come on, you've known her longer than I have. I'll dial her number for you. Tell her I—tell her I thought about—just tell her to come over. (*Caesar doesn't come out.*) If you were a dog you'd do it.

(*Callie picks up the phone and dials seven numbers quickly.*)

Hi George, it's me—what. Did you just call here—why not? Yeah, Vong was great. I got the sea bass with cardamom, Sara got the grilled lamb chops with coriander—yeah she eats meat, why wouldn't she? I don't know what you're talking about— Listen, what are you doing for dinner? 'Cause I just walked by Tomoe and noticed there's no line. Come on, I need a sushi fix. Allright, if you get there first just tell them— I know you know. Okay 'bye.

(*Callie hangs up. She puts the phone back on the floor.*)

Okay Caesar, second chance.

Scene 14

Sara's hospital room. Callie walks in and stands at her bedside.

CALLIE: They're finished building that building across from your apartment.

(*Sara doesn't respond. Conversation volume*) Wake up now.

(*No response. A little stronger*) Sara.

(*No response.*)

Can you hear me? (*Callie looks down. Nothing.*) Open your eyes.

(*No response.*)

Open your eyes.

(*No response.*)

They're gonna start you on physical therapy tomorrow. Just little stuff, range of motion, something to get your blood moving.

(*Pause.*)

You've gotten all these cards and letters, I'll read some to you later.

(*Pause.*)

You know your parents are here. They're doing their best—I think they're doing okay, considering. You getting better makes them feel better—yeah.

They look at me . . . your parents look at me . . . like I'm some dirty old man. (*She waits for a response.*) And the newspapers, the TV, the radio—my station, my own station, when they ran the news about the attack, they identified me—"Traffic reporter for this station." Now everybody—the guy at the deli—I used to be the blueberry muffin lady, now I'm the lesbian traffic reporter whose lover got beat up. And I've gotten letters—from two women—their girlfriends were *killed* during attacks—and they wrote me these heartbreaking letters telling me what they've been through . . . and they tell me to speak truth to power and I don't know what that means, Sara. Do you? Do you know me? (*Callie leans in closer.*)

Do you know who I am?

(*Sara opens her eyes.*)

Oh my God. Hi.

Scene 15

Callie's apartment. Callie walks in from the bedroom in her bare feet, wearing a T-shirt and underwear. She pours two glasses of water and drinks from one. George enters from the bedroom wearing jeans and pulling on a T-shirt. Callie hands him the second glass of water. He takes a sip.

GEORGE: Deer Park?

CALLIE: You can't tell.

GEORGE: Tastes like plastic.

CALLIE: You want Evian, you buy it.

GEORGE: Not Evian, *Vermont Natural Springs.*

CALLIE: It's Deer Park or Dos Equis, George. That's what I've got.

GEORGE: Dos Equis, please.

(*Callie hands him a beer.*)

GEORGE: You got any snacks?

CALLIE: I think I have some wasabi peas.

GEORGE: Those *green*—

CALLIE: Taste like sushi—

GEORGE: Oh, *shit.*

CALLIE: What.

GEORGE: I have to go.

CALLIE: Where?

(*He goes to get the rest of his clothes.*)

GEORGE: It's someone's birthday at work so a bunch of people are going out to that Japanese tapas place on Ninth Street afterwards, I promised I'd meet them.

CALLIE: Blow them off.

GEORGE: I can't.

CALLIE: Come on. We'll go to Aggie's in the morning for breakfast. Banana pancakes.

GEORGE: I'm sorry, Callie. I made these plans before you called.

CALLIE: Whose birthday?

GEORGE: This new girl at work. I don't think you've met her.

CALLIE: Let me guess. She's an actress.

(*He puts on his shoes.*)

GEORGE: She's classically trained.

CALLIE: You gotta get out of the restaurant business, George. Broaden your dating pool.

GEORGE: I'll call— I'll see you on Wednesday, at Jasmine's, right? She's having everyone over for dinner.

CALLIE: Yeah, I put it down.

(*He gives her a quick kiss on the lips.*)

GEORGE: 'Bye.

(*He exits, and Callie closes the door behind him. She pours his beer down the drain. There's a knock on the door.*)

CALLIE (*calling*): I didn't lock it.

(*Sara opens the door halfway and takes a small step in.*)

SARA: I saw your light on—

(*Callie turns around, unconsciously pulling on the bottom of her T-shirt.*)

CALLIE: I—I'm not—I didn't know it was you.

SARA: I saw him—he didn't notice me.

CALLIE: Just . . . just give me a second.

(*Sara steps back into the hallway as Callie pushes the door closed and goes to her bedroom. She comes back out wearing a sweater over her T-shirt and a pair of sweatpants. She opens the door. Sara enters carrying a bottle of wine.*)

SARA: I think—I think you'll like this kind.

(*Callie takes it and gestures toward the couch. Sara steps tentatively in and sits down on the edge of it.*)

CALLIE: I'll get us some glasses.

(*Callie heads for the kitchen.*)

SARA: You don't have to open it now—it's late, I just wanted to—

(*Sara gets up and follows Callie.*)

SARA: Apologize, Callie. You've been so good to me since I came here. I'm embarrassed that I acted, that I said—

CALLIE: That I'm a loser?

SARA: I didn't—

CALLIE: That I'm pathetic.

SARA: You're not pathetic.

CALLIE: I do, I know—I sometimes . . . swerve. I was thinking . . . you know, when I was little, my parents made me take tennis lessons—I'm not an athlete—neither are my parents, I don't know why—because the lessons were free! And it was summer, and my parents didn't want me sitting around the house doing nothing, which is what they thought I was doing—which was . . . true. So, they made me take these lessons, even though I was a klutz. And I tried—but I was a natural klutz. Still, at the end of the summer we all had to play in these championships and compete against the kids from the other classes. So for the first round, I get pitted against this kid who obviously took tennis lessons because she wanted to be a really good tennis player. I can't even return her serves. The match takes like ten minutes. Afterwards, my parents can barely speak, they feel so bad. They take me to Dairy Queen, tell me to order whatever I want—I get the triple banana split, and for the rest of the summer they let me sit around and watch *Love Boat* reruns, which is all I wanted to do anyway.

(*Callie hands Sara a glass of wine.*)

SARA: It was a good show.

CALLIE: But lately, I feel like . . . there's something . . . worth . . . winning.

SARA: Callie, I know that neither you nor I have ever—well at least I know that I haven't, I've never really asked—

CALLIE: By the way, I did get an award.

SARA: What?

CALLIE: An award for traffic reporting—who knew?

SARA: Are you serious?

CALLIE: I'm sorry, I interrupted—

SARA: Did you know?

CALLIE: What.

SARA: You knew you were going to get an award, didn't you?

CALLIE: I swear I didn't.

SARA: Is that why you were so—

CALLIE: Sara, I could never have known. Trust me.

SARA: Did they call you up to the dais and everything?

CALLIE: Just like the Oscars.

SARA: I wish I had seen. (*Sara touches Callie's hand.*)

CALLIE: I wish you'da been there. (*Callie squeezes Sara's hand. Slight pause.*) You want to see it?

SARA: Yes!

(*Callie roots through a pile of papers.*)

CALLIE: I thought I stuck it in here.

(*Sara goes to the sofa and lifts the pillows.*)

SARA (*sotto voce*): Sometimes I find stuff in here. (*Sara pulls out a plaque and holds it in the air.*) I found something.

CALLIE: There it is!

(*Sara looks at it. She walks over to the bookshelf and slides some photographs out of the way.*)

SARA: Put it here, okay?

CALLIE: Not there.

SARA: Why not?

CALLIE: Everyone will see it.

SARA: Just keep it there. (*Callie reaches for it.*) Stop it. (*Callie takes her hand away, but reaches for it again.*) I mean it.

(*Callie takes her hand away. Sara takes the plaque, exhales on it, rubs it on her shirt, then puts it back.*)

Scene 16

Sara's hospital room. A nurse is writing on her chart. Callie walks in.

CALLIE: Any good news?

NURSE: She's stable.

CALLIE: I guess that's good news.

NURSE: Her bruises are healing.

(*Callie looks at Sara's face.*)

CALLIE: Yes.

NURSE: Can tell she's a pretty girl.

CALLIE: Yeah.

NURSE: She's a schoolteacher?

CALLIE: She is.

NURSE: Where?

CALLIE: In the Bronx. (*Makes eye contact with the nurse.*) Third grade. She has thirty-five kids. She knew all of their names by the end of the first day.

NURSE: Takes a lot to be a public school teacher in New York City.

CALLIE: She's got it.

NURSE: Those kids are lucky.

CALLIE: They know it.

NURSE: I'm gonna give her her bath now.

CALLIE: Oh, allright.

(*She starts to leave.*)

NURSE: I'll show you so you can do it.

(*Callie stops. Slight pause.*)

CALLIE: Oh—that's very—but I don't think I should, I've never—

NURSE: You've seen the worst of her. Most of her bruises are on her face. Her body looks fine. There's nothing to be afraid of.

CALLIE: I don't know if she'd want me to.

NURSE: It won't hurt my feelings, you know. I'm sure she'd like it better if you do it.

CALLIE: . . . Right now, though, I have to go. (*She taps on her watch face.*) The time. But . . . thank you.

(*She heads out.*)

Scene 17

Callie's apartment. Callie and Sara walk in. Sara carries groceries; Callie carries a bag from a record store.

CALLIE: Which airport is he flying into?

SARA: JFK.

CALLIE: At eleven in the morning.

SARA: Eleven-thirty.

CALLIE: Have the car service pick you up at around ten-thirty, tell them to take the BQE to the LIE to the Van Wyck—that'll get you to the airport by eleven. But tell the driver to take the Midtown Tunnel back; it'll cost you three-fifty but the Manhattan-bound traffic on the Williamsburg Bridge will be too heavy.

SARA: Check.

(*Sara looks through the CDs.*)

SARA: Do you ever go out dancing?

CALLIE: Sometimes I do—my friend Sheila goes to this club on Wednesday nights, and sometimes she invites a bunch of us girls to go.

SARA: I'd like to go sometime.

CALLIE: . . . Sure . . .

SARA: Will you let me know next time you go?

CALLIE: A bunch of us girl friends go . . . it's fun . . . the music's great, and it's fun, you don't have to worry about guys trying to pick you up . . . 'cause it's all women. I like to go there and dance, there's this kind of warm—like when you go to the bathroom, there's only one line and everyone's really nice and smiles. . . .

SARA: Have you ever . . . asked someone to dance?

CALLIE: We kind of stick to each other—us friends. Sheila usually knows a bunch of women there, and I've met them.

SARA: You ever meet a woman there, that seemed . . . interesting . . . to you?

CALLIE: . . . No. (*Pause.*) Not there. (*Pause.*) Have you—?

SARA: What.

CALLIE: In St. Louis, do they—or have you been to?

SARA: We have a couple places like that but I've never been. My friend Janet says that only college girls go to the clubs and bars; older lesbians just stay home and read. That's what everyone in St. Louis does, stays home and brews their own beer or does their email.

(*Slight pause.*)

CALLIE: But I mean, have you ever . . . ?

SARA: Of course, right? I mean, right? I mean I can't imagine any woman who's never *felt* attracted—

CALLIE: Right!

SARA: It's just, I mean if you've never—

CALLIE: You want a beer?

SARA: Love one.

CALLIE: I hope I have some.

SARA: What time is it?

CALLIE: Just about six.

SARA: Uh oh.

CALLIE: What?

SARA: I promised my roommates I'd clean the apartment by the time they came back from their trip, and they're gonna be home in an hour.

CALLIE: Just—wait here a couple more minutes.

SARA: I really should go.

CALLIE: Just wait one minute.

SARA: Why?

CALLIE: I wanna . . . show you something.

SARA: Callie—

CALLIE: Take my watch. (*Callie takes off her watch and hands it to Sara.*) What time is it now?

SARA: Five fifty-nine.

CALLIE: And how many seconds?

SARA: Thirty-eight seconds.

CALLIE: And what day is today?

SARA: Thursday.

CALLIE: What time is it now?

SARA: Five fifty-nine and fifty seconds.

CALLIE: So count 'em.

SARA: What?

CALLIE: Count 'em down. Five seconds, four—

SARA: Four, three, two, one—what. (*Callie opens her hands toward Sara.*) What? (*Callie points toward the ceiling. Callie gestures—I did it.*) It's quiet. Oh! It's Thursday at six! And it's quiet! (*Sara opens her arms, and they hold each other. They keep holding. Callie lets go.*) I'll call you tomorrow.

CALLIE: Okay.

(*Pause.*)

SARA: Um, see ya.

CALLIE: Okay. 'Bye.

(*Sara opens the door and lets herself out. Callie ambles slowly over to the sofa, looks at the door, buries her head in a pillow and screams.*)

Scene 18

A coffee shop. Mrs. Winsley is sitting at a table. Callie walks in.

CALLIE: Mrs. Winsley?

MRS. WINSLEY: Yes.

(*Callie extends her hand; Mrs. Winsley shakes it.*)

CALLIE: I'm sorry I'm late. I came straight—

MRS. WINSLEY: It's fine, it's fine. I don't have to meet my husband until eight.

(*Mrs. Winsley gestures for Callie to sit.*)

CALLIE: Please.

MRS. WINSLEY: Should we order something? Coffee or tea?

CALLIE: Coffee would be great.

MRS. WINSLEY: How are you doing?

CALLIE: I'm okay.

MRS. WINSLEY: Yeah?

CALLIE: I want to thank you for . . . what you did, Mrs. Winsley.

MRS. WINSLEY: I only did what I should've.

CALLIE: Not everybody—

MRS. WINSLEY: How's your girlfriend?

CALLIE: Sara—she's better. Alert and responding. We just have to wait to see what kind of effect. How much and what.

MRS. WINSLEY: I read in the paper she's from Kansas or something.

CALLIE: St. Louis. Missouri. Kansas City is in Missouri, but Sara's from St. Louis.

MRS. WINSLEY: I'm from outside Cincinnati myself, although I've been here for twenty years. When I first moved here I would smile at strangers on the subway, give quarters to beggars on the street.

CALLIE: Sara gives a dollar.

MRS. WINSLEY: So I can imagine what it must've seemed like to her. Small-town girl in the big city—seeing men dressed as women, women holding hands—must've seemed like gay paradise to her.

(*Slight pause.*)

CALLIE: St. Louis is not a small town.

MRS. WINSLEY: What hospital is she at?

CALLIE: St. Vincent's.

MRS. WINSLEY: How are the doctors there? Are you pleased with them?

CALLIE: It's hard to say. You want them to do everything—you just want them to make her better. But they do what they can. I think they're okay.

MRS. WINSLEY: I know they have limited visiting hours, but a situation like this, they must let you stay all day.

CALLIE: I have to go to my job—

MRS. WINSLEY: Of course. Of course you do.

CALLIE: But I do visit every day.

MRS. WINSLEY: It must be exhausting for you.

CALLIE: Well, her family's here—

MRS. WINSLEY: Are you close with them?

CALLIE: No . . . Not close.

MRS. WINSLEY: I know what it's like with in-laws. It took years before mine . . . Have you and Sara been together long?

CALLIE: Um . . . no.

MRS. WINSLEY: Oh, I'm sorry I thought you two were—

CALLIE: I know.

MRS. WINSLEY: Here I've been going on and on as if—

CALLIE: Yes, you were.

MRS. WINSLEY: So you're not really—

CALLIE: No, like I said I go there every—

MRS. WINSLEY: But you're not really involved.

Scene 19

Callie's apartment. George, wearing jeans and a dress shirt, checks himself out in the full-length mirror. Callie walks in from the bedroom wearing a dress.

GEORGE: I'm a little strapped 'cause business was slow last night.

CALLIE: Just don't worry about it.

GEORGE: I brought fifty bucks.

CALLIE: That'll get you a salad.

GEORGE: How expensive is this place?

CALLIE: Expensive.

GEORGE: Why do we have to go to a place like that? Why can't we just go to Benny's Burritos and drink a bunch of margaritas.

CALLIE: I *told* you, I'm gonna pay for the whole thing so stop stressing about it.

(*She pushes George out of the way with her hip and looks at herself in the mirror.*)

GEORGE: Okay Miss Traffic Reporter of the Universe or whatever you are, I'm gonna get the lobster.

CALLIE: They have venison.

GEORGE (*even better*): Ooo!

(*Callie turns toward him.*)

CALLIE: Does this dress make me look fat?

GEORGE: I *can* not, *will* not, *ever* answer that question.

CALLIE: I'm changing. (*She heads for the bedroom.*)

GEORGE: What are you so uptight about?

CALLIE (*offstage*): I'm not uptight.

GEORGE: That's the third time you've changed. Who is the guy anyway?

CALLIE (*offstage*): Sara's ex.

GEORGE: Why do you need to look so good for him?

(*Callie comes back on wearing a different dress. She stands in front of the mirror.*)

CALLIE: It's a nice restaurant.

GEORGE: Is he gonna be dressed up? You told me I could wear jeans.

CALLIE: Because I knew you'd wear jeans anyway.

GEORGE (*has to admit she's right*): Hm.

(*George stands next to Callie; he looks at their reflection. He puts his arm around her waist.*)

CALLIE: So how was the birthday party the other night?

(*She wriggles away.*)

GEORGE: Fine.

CALLIE: Did the birthday girl get everything she asked for?

GEORGE: You want to talk about this?

CALLIE: No.

GEORGE: Cool.

(*Pause.*)

CALLIE: Did you fuck her before or after midnight?

GEORGE: Nice.

CALLIE: I'm just wondering about the technicality—

GEORGE: Listen, I'm not like you and that guy—

CALLIE: Who?

GEORGE: Who was that guy with the nose ring that you—

CALLIE: Hey—

GEORGE: In the bathroom of the—

CALLIE: Hey—

GEORGE: With no protection.

(*The buzzer buzzes.*)

CALLIE: I told you *that?*

GEORGE: I asked.

CALLIE: We should start keeping more to ourselves.

GEORGE: Too late.

CALLIE: Don't say that.

GEORGE: Why not?

CALLIE: Makes me feel old.

GEORGE: We are old.

CALLIE: You are.

(*There's a knock on the door. Callie opens it. Sara walks in alone. Callie looks behind her.*)

CALLIE: . . . Hi.

GEORGE: Hey, how's it going.

SARA (*small*): Hi.

CALLIE: Where's Peter?

SARA: He . . . uh, left. You look beautiful. You too, George.

CALLIE: He left . . . New York?

SARA: Yeah, he changed his flight. He left a couple of hours ago. I told him to tell the driver to take the Van Wyck.

CALLIE: Something happen at work?

SARA: No it—I asked him to leave.

(*Callie moves closer to her.*)

CALLIE: Oh, um— (*She looks at George, then back at Sara.*) Listen, we don't have to go out—

GEORGE: Yeah, no, if you're upset—

SARA: No, it's fine, I want to go out. I want to get to know George.

CALLIE: Are you—did something happen— (*Again she looks at George: Why can't he disappear?*) I mean, you don't have to—

(*George stands behind Callie and puts his hands on her shoulders. She looks at his hands like they are dead frogs.*)

SARA: He was being so—he was criticizing everything. "Your apartment's too small. It's in a bad neighborhood. Your school is dangerous. It's too far away." All he could talk about was how dirty and dangerous everything is.

CALLIE: . . . Well—

GEORGE: It *is*.

SARA: What? Compared to St. Louis? I don't want to live there. I've started something here, and I—that's what—because it's . . . I love . . . New York!

GEORGE (*nods*): Mm.

CALLIE: Let's go eat.

GEORGE (*to Sara*): Are you sure?

SARA: Yeah.

GEORGE: Great! Let's go!

(*George offers Sara his arm. She takes it. He offers his other arm to Callie.*)

CALLIE: I'll catch up with you.

GEORGE: Okay. (*To Sara, on the way out*) They have venison you know.

SARA: You mean Bambi?

(*George and Sara exit. Callie walks over to the Magic 8 Ball, shuts her eyes a moment, then wiggles the ball. She looks at its answer.*)

CALLIE (*quietly*): Yes!

(*She puts down the ball and hurries to catch up with them.*)

Scene 20

Sara's hospital room. She's sitting in a wheelchair, eyes open. Peter sits next to her reading from a book.

PETER: "And then ninety-eight kilometers—that's sixty-one miles—north of Wilcannia is a lunar landscape." That looks lunar, doesn't it? "Some of the locals don't mind showing off the interiors of their white-walled subterranean settlements"—You'll want to sign up early for *that* tour, gonna be a regular Who concert trying to— (*He looks at Sara, clears his throat, then goes back to the book.*) As I was saying. "Looping around about one hundred and sixty kilometers"—that's a hundred miles to you and me—"a road leads to Moot-

wingee, a surprising patch of greenness in the barren Byn-
guano—" Australia *is* an English-speaking country, isn't it?
(*He fingers the last few chapters of the book.*) You know, I'm
dying to see how this ends but can we—

(*Sara nods. He kisses her hand.*)

PETER: Thank you. We'll save the big finish for after dinner. (*He
puts the book away and picks something up.*) Did you see this?
(*He holds a homemade greeting card in front of her. Callie steps into
the room, then steps back. She watches.*) You got a card from
your old class at Friends. See, there's Matthew and Sophia
and Emily—your favorite, the anti-Christ. She writes, "I
hope you feel bitter and come bark soon." I see your
replacement is letting her spelling skills slip.

(*Sara tentatively takes the card in her hand.*)

Hey! Get you. I've been talking to Jenny and Steve a lot,
keeping them updated. Jenny's been letting everyone know
what's going on. Margaret's called, Jamie, Lisa—it's frustrat-
ing for them not to be able to see you. They picture the
worst, all they have are the images in their heads from reading the newspaper articles. It'll be better for them when
they can see you.

The doctor says we can move you soon. Your parents and I
have been talking. I agree that you should stay with them
after you get out of rehab. You're welcome to stay at our old
place, of course, if you want to, I would take off from work
so that I could—well, I'm going to take off from work anyway. (*Pause.*) Just because you're coming back home I'm not
going to act like everything is going to be the way it was. I
know you went to New York because you wanted to
change things.

(*He touches her face.*) You do want to go home— (*Water drops from
Sara's eyes.*) Don't you?

(*Callie turns, walks toward Sara's nurse, who is standing at her station.*)

CALLIE: Excuse me.

NURSE: You're back.

CALLIE: Do you have time now? To show me how to do it?

Scene 21

Callie's apartment. Callie and Sara enter after having left the restaurant. Callie takes off her coat, Sara doesn't.

CALLIE: Uugggh, I'm so full, it hurts to move. What do you want to do, we could watch a movie if you—

SARA: Let's uh . . . let's go out, let's go somewhere.

CALLIE: Where do you want to go?

SARA: There's a bar. In the West Village. Henrietta's, you ever been?

CALLIE: Once.

SARA: Will you go with me?

CALLIE (*she looks at her dress*): Like this?

SARA: We could change. Friday night, it's supposed to be a good night.

CALLIE: Okay. (*Slight pause.*) Good for what?

SARA: There's supposed to be a lot of people there.

CALLIE (*nods, though she doesn't quite understand*): Okay, let's go.

SARA: You change, and then we can stop by my place, and then we'll go.

CALLIE: We don't—you can borrow some of my clothes.

SARA: Really? That's great. That's *great*.

(*They stand there.*)

SARA: You go ahead and change and I'll . . . change next. I'll wear whatever's left over.

CALLIE: I'll go change.

SARA: Maybe we'll like it there—

(*She looks helplessly at Callie.*)

CALLIE (*trying to be helpful*): Yeah, okay.

SARA: Let's just—

CALLIE: We'll go, we'll hang out, have a drink.

SARA: Yes! You know, maybe meet people.

CALLIE: Are you—I mean, do you . . . want to *meet* people?

SARA: Yes!— No! I want to meet people to—meet people maybe make friends, but, no, I don't want to meet *someone,* some stranger—

CALLIE: We'll just go.

SARA: It's just a bar.

CALLIE: With a whole bunch of lesbians in it.

SARA: And us.

(*They lock eyes, hoping the other will say something perfect. They keep waiting.*)

Scene 22

The hospital. Sara's sitting in a wheelchair. Callie enters carrying a bag.

CALLIE: Sara. (*Sara turns to her.*) I brought you stuff to change into. (*She pulls some clothes out of the bag.*) Don't you think? (*Callie puts them in Sara's lap.*) We're gonna do this. Watch me. You gotta listen to me too. (*She undoes Sara's gown.*) Okay, we're gonna start with the left side because we're taking things off. (*She takes off Sara's left sleeve.*) And now the right. (*She helps Sara pull her arm out of the right sleeve. She takes out a bra.*) This closes in front. Can you . . . go like this? (*She lifts her arms at the elbows. Sara does it.*) Good for you. I should tell— (*She looks around for the nurse.*) Later. (*She puts the bra on.*) So far so good. (*She takes the shirt off Sara's lap.*) Nice shirt, huh? Did I pick out a nice shirt for you? Okay, you're gonna need to sit up a little for me. (*Sara sits up. Callie puts the right sleeve on.*) If I can just—am I hurting you? I'm sorry, Sara—I'm sorry— (*To herself*) Relax. (*She puts the left sleeve on.*) This one you can do. Push—push—keep breathing, and push— (*Sara pushes her arm through the sleeve.*) It's a girl! (*Callie buttons Sara's shirt.*) Let's keep you warm. It's cold in this place. (*Callie takes the pants. She helps Sara's right foot off the footrest.*) We're gonna do this together. I'll do this one. (*She points to her left.*) That one you can do. (*Sara lifts her left leg off; it spasms.*) Oh—Oh. Okay. Okay. (*Callie flips the foot pads up. She scrunches up the right leg of the pants and wrangles it on.*) We gotta work together on this one, okay? (*She scrunches up the left leg. Sara lifts her leg.*) Are you helping me? Yes. You are. (*Callie takes out a pair of shoes.*) Now, the shoes go last. Like this. (*Callie puts her right shoe on.*) And like that. (*Sara slips her left foot in the left shoe. Callie pushes Sara's feet closer to her. Callie stands up.*) Now you're gonna stand up. I'm gonna help. One, two, three— (*She puts her hand under Sara's arms and lifts her up. She pulls her pants up. They sit back down.*) I can do this, you see? (*Sara nods.*) Choose me. (*Sara smiles.*)

Scene 23

Sara and Callie are walking down the street, having just left Henrietta's. Finally, Sara turns to Callie.

SARA: *What*—was I thinking.

CALLIE: That was like—going to a birthday party when you don't know the person whose birthday it is.

SARA: I don't know why I was expecting . . . I don't know what I was expecting. What time is it?

(*Callie checks her watch.*)

CALLIE: Around four.

SARA: So late.

CALLIE: Should we go . . . go somewhere—where do you want
to go?

SARA: I don't know—

CALLIE: Let's just . . . keep walking.

SARA: Sure.

(*They walk a few steps in silence. After a while,*)

CALLIE: How do you eat corn on the cob. Around the world or
typewriter style?

SARA: *Typewriter.*

CALLIE: Me too.

SARA: What kind of person eats around the world?

CALLIE: I don't know.

SARA: I mean, what is that based on? You read left to right,
right?

CALLIE: I do.

SARA: So you should eat your corn that way too.

CALLIE: Do you think in Egypt they eat right to left?

SARA: I don't know.

CALLIE: Fascinating question, though.

SARA: Do you wait *in* line or *on* line?

CALLIE: Oh. Now I wait on line. But I used to wait in.

SARA: But physically, you're *in* a line, not *on* one, right?

CALLIE: Yeah, stick by your guns. I caved in.

SARA: You say on. I say in.

CALLIE: What about this?

(*Callie plants her one. They pull away.*)

SARA: Huh.

CALLIE: What?

SARA: You just did that.

CALLIE: Yes I did.

SARA: Nice.

(*They come at each other, but with their heads angled toward the same side. They bump noses.*)

CALLIE: Whoop—

SARA: Sorry—

(*They back away. Callie puts her arms around Sara's waist and pulls her toward her.*)

SARA: Do you think we should—

CALLIE: I don't want to go anywhere, I don't want to change anything. Let's just—

SARA: Okay.

CALLIE: Try again.

(*They get their heads right, connect lips, put their arms around each other. And kiss.*)

TONGUE OF A BIRD

by Ellen McLaughlin

This play is dedicated to
Jane Lincoln Taylor
and to the memory of Sigrid Wurschmidt,
dear friends who gave me sight and
courage.

Tongue of a Bird was commissioned by the Center Theatre Group/ Mark Taper Forum in Los Angeles, Gordon Davidson, artistic director. It was first produced as a staged reading in July 1996 by New York Stage and Film Company and Powerhouse Theatre at Vasser College in association with Ron Kastner. The play premiered at the Intiman Theatre in Seattle, Washington, Warner Shook, artistic director, in September 1997. This production was supported in part by an AT&T: OnStage award. The play subsequently received its British premiere at the Almeida Theater in London. It also was produced at the Mark Taper Forum in Los Angeles, and at the Joseph Papp Public Theater/NYSF in New York City. Cherry Jones, Sharon Lawrence, Melissa Leo, Julia MacIlvaine and Elizabeth Wilson starred in the NYSF production. Lisa Peterson has directed every workshop, reading and production of the play in the United States. The playwright would like to acknowledge Ms. Peterson's vital contribution to the work. The play owes much of its essence, if not its very existence, to her unique intelligence and support.

CHARACTERS

MAXINE: Mid- to late thirties. A search and rescue pilot.
            Solitary, ironic and guarded.

DESSA: Mid- to late thirties. Charlotte's mother. Tough,
            without self-pity and utterly focused.

ZOFIA: Early to mid-seventies. Maxine's grandmother,
            Evie's mother. A Polish exile, survivor of the
            1939 Nazi invasion. Visionary, difficult and wise.

CHARLOTTE: Twelve. Dessa's daughter. Canny, bold and slightly
            malicious.

EVIE: Roughly Maxine's age. Maxine's dead mother.
            Cool, wry and lucid.

TIME

Mid-winter.

PLACE

The Adirondacks.

NOTE ON THE TEXT:

One speech follows another, unless a speech includes a slash (/),
which indicates that the next speaker interrupts the previous
speaker at this point. As in:

MAXINE: I don't think that had anything / to do with—
DESSA: They were laughing.

In this case, Dessa's cue word is "anything" and she talks over
the end of Maxine's speech.

ACT ONE

Scene I. Globe

In the darkness we hear an unidentifiable sound. Lights reveal a child's large globe, spinning. A small figure appears, dressed in brilliant white, perhaps completely wrapped in gauze. The figure approaches the globe and leans over it, peering at it. The figure then places a finger on the globe, stopping it.

As the figure leans in to look at the place it has pointed to, the globe's colors fade, as if frosting over into white. The figure looks down, looks out and then moves on, batting the globe into motion as it goes. The globe spins again, regaining its colors.

Scene 2. The Buzzing

Maxine stands in a high place. She looks down.

MAXINE: There's a girl, this is me, standing at a high window, looking down. She tells herself: you will remember this. And I do. I remember everything. But I don't remember why I remember this. It is morning and I'm looking down across a vast landscape and I've lost something which I think I will spot from this height. The farther up you are the more you see. This is true. I have learned this since . . . and it's like a flicker of light sometimes, perhaps the glint of a climber's goggles, the quirk, almost indiscernible, of the wrong color, the dropped glove, the upturned shoe. These things, the slight, the rare, I see them as others don't, I am gifted—and here, there's something about this memory, but I can't . . .

A fly, I know, is buzzing up the window, a trapped fly, going up the air, which it finds strangely hard and unyielding, going up when it means to be going out. This is crucial but I don't know why. Perhaps it just tells me the season, which must be late autumn, a time when flies are dying in just this way, going up when they mean to be going out. And it seems to me that all nature is dying on this day. Except me, who stands and watches.

So there's the fly and there's the landscape, dropped like a platter below me.

I see it as if I were above it, looking down over the back of my own blond head. I see most of my past this way, remembered with a detachment which looks coolly down on a child I am, experiencing some dreadful thing, which I experienced but didn't, and experience again in recalling it, but don't.

There is that girl, who is me, so far below me, who might have lived my life if I hadn't left her there and come up here to watch her. (*Smiles.*) I was so terribly good at that. A trick I learned so early.

So I became a flyer.

But she asked me to remember this. So I look down with her on the bald hills of some uncertain autumn, and we hear the fly and we wait.

Scene 3. Dessa

Sound of a fly buzzing becomes the sound of planes droning. An airplane hangar, denoted by the light cast from high windows and a rickety table where Maxine and Dessa sit with their coats on, holding paper cups of coffee.

DESSA: —They told me you were the one who doesn't give up. So I'm asking you.

MAXINE: They haven't given up, they're—

DESSA: —Yes they have. They look at me sideways when I come in—everybody runs, pretends to be doing something—

MAXINE: —I really think—

DESSA: —Look at them, unscrewing engines and shit—that guy, Robbie Something—

MAXINE: —Robbie DaCaprio—

DESSA: —He says he's going to be up all day looking for my daughter. I came in, he's sitting there eating soup—

MAXINE: —They have to eat—

DESSA: —Playing with his Game Boy computer thingie—

MAXINE: —They have to come down occasionally, if only to get / gas—

DESSA: —And they're sitting around the table, all of them, laughing—

MAXINE: —I don't think that had anything / to do with—

DESSA: —They were laughing.

(*Pause.*)

MAXINE: I really don't think they've given up. It's just that it's been more than a week—

DESSA: —Eleven days, four hours (*she looks at her watch*), twenty-five minutes, no, twenty-six, and twelve, thirteen seconds, no, fourteen . . . fifteen . . .

MAXINE: You realize you'd be hiring me. It's not free.

(*Dessa takes out an antique watch.*)

DESSA: That's what I got. Heirloom. I got no more money. I spent it on posters and stuff, this asshole detective, Carl What's-his-face, the milk cartons—

MAXINE: —Do the milk cartons / cost . . . ?—

DESSA: —But I figure it's a plane that's going to—'cause if you could just see her— And the money's just—'cause I don't have time to waste, she's— I've been emptying out my . . . So you can have the, this, there's still some money, I've just got to get it out of the bank, just . . . I got your name and called you and I came here right away so I just picked up the watch . . . *it doesn't matter* . . . I'm sitting in that fucking house all day, all night, I'm looking at all this shit, these *things,* and you can have anything, come over, take a look, in fact, do me a favor, rent a U-Haul, like a huge one, pull it up outside the door and just start loading it up, couch, TV, oven mitts, shampoo bottles, bath mats, clocks, celery sticks, just take it—and then get some suction thing, some super-sonic vacuum thing, park the hose at the front door and get the, the, everything, the air, the dust on the walls, between the cracks, the sounds left over in there, and, while you're at it, *me*—yeah, suck me right up out of that place and then the house itself after me, like in some cartoon, if you can do that, porch, banister, walks and windows, get it all, don't leave anything, just a hole, just nothing, not even a hole, nothing, and drive away. If you can find her, if that would help find her, 'cause I'm telling you, whatever it takes, I don't give a shit anymore.

I just want her back. I just want my daughter back.

(*Pause. Maxine slides the watch back to her across the table.*)

MAXINE: I'll need some money later for gas.

Scene 4. *Babcia*

Zofia's house, denoted by an ancient armchair, a side table, and a small light, covered with dust. Zofia is sitting, staring intently straight ahead. Maxine enters, carrying a laundry bag.

MAXINE: *Babcia?*

(*Maxine drops the bag.*)

ZOFIA (*slightly startled*): I thought you were the bird.

MAXINE: What bird?

ZOFIA: There is a bird down the chimney, oh, such a terrible omen, see the black wing marks? The soot all over every-where? Beat, beat, beat against the walls all night, so fright-ened. I think she maybe broke herself trying to get out.

MAXINE: Do you want me to find her?

ZOFIA: No, no, I got her out. (*Confused*) I thought I did. (*She remembers.*) I did. Yes. I put the blanket (*she makes the gesture*), so like that, she was flapping and beating in there, her black wings, yes, I did, because I remember, yes. I stood at the door and . . . (*Zofia makes the gesture of opening her arms and watching a bird take flight.*)

MAXINE: So she's gone.

ZOFIA: Yes. And here you are. (*She really looks at Maxine for the first time.*) Why?

MAXINE: I told you I was coming. This morning, you remember?

ZOFIA: I don't believe in telephones.

MAXINE: Nevertheless.

ZOFIA: Why have you come back to me?

MAXINE: What do you mean, I told you— (*Zofia nods toward the laundry bag.*) What? You think I could get all of my earthly possessions into a laundry bag?

ZOFIA: Yes.

(*Silence.*)

MAXINE: I'm sort of between places.

ZOFIA: What happened?

MAXINE: Oh . . . (*She makes a gesture.*) I don't know. It didn't work out.

ZOFIA: I don't have room for you here.

MAXINE: What do you mean? That's all you've got—room.

ZOFIA: It's all filled up.

MAXINE (*laughs*): With what? You've never even had furniture / here.

ZOFIA (*furious, slapping the arms of the chair*): I have—!

MAXINE: —Well, yes. There is the *chair*, but nothing, almost
nothing—

ZOFIA: —Space!

MAXINE: What?

ZOFIA: It's all filled up!

MAXINE: What?

ZOFIA: With space!

(*Silence.*)

MAXINE: Look, I won't be staying long. Just a few days. Just for
the search.

ZOFIA: What is this?

MAXINE: I got another search. I'm going to be flying these
mountains for awhile, until we find her of course.

ZOFIA: Who?

MAXINE: A girl.

ZOFIA: How young?

MAXINE: Twelve.

ZOFIA: How long has she been lost?

MAXINE: Eleven days.

ZOFIA: Eleven days? In this weather? Ach. She's frozen already.

MAXINE: Well, actually, I'm looking for a black pickup truck.

ZOFIA (*confused*): She's driving . . . ?

MAXINE: She was kidnapped. A man. She was hiking with some
friends. Girl Scouts. She's standing on the edge of a clearing,
and a truck drives out of nowhere, her friends watch her

have a conversation, they can't see the man inside the truck, pickup truck, we don't know what make. Suddenly he reaches out and grabs her, drags her into the truck, drives away up into the mountains. All the roads out of there have been closed off since then, he can't have gotten out so he must have gone up. The police, the Mountain Rescue, the Civil Air Patrol, it's been a big thing. Her picture is all over the place. But it's been awhile and the weather's too tricky for the helicopters anymore and they're too expensive. So that's where I come in. Her mother heard about me.

ZOFIA: Twelve years old?

MAXINE: Yes.

(*Pause.*)

ZOFIA: *Biedny malutki ptaszek.*

MAXINE: What? (*Zofia shakes her head. Maxine continues, writing in the dust of the table.*) Are there any clean sheets?

ZOFIA: There are always sheets. You know where. What are you doing?

MAXINE: Writing my name in the dust.

(*Zofia slaps at Maxine's hand.*)

ZOFIA: I don't want your name all over my nice table.

MAXINE: It looks like nobody's cleaned since I was here last summer. Why don't you ever let What's-her-name come in and clean this place? She's offered dozens of times.

ZOFIA: That woman. She changes things.

MAXINE: Well, yes, she cleans them.

ZOFIA: Stop *looking* at everything. Who are you to look so much?

MAXINE (*gestures to the room*): I have eyes. It's a problem.

ZOFIA: Ach.

MAXINE: I brought you cake.

ZOFIA: What kind?

MAXINE: *Czekolada.*

(*Maxine takes a slice of cake wrapped in a napkin out of her coat pocket. She unwraps it and hands it to Zofia.*)

ZOFIA: Ah. *Ciastko czekoladowe.* What is that smell in it? That dark smell? How nice.

MAXINE: I remembered, you see? Such a doting granddaughter.

ZOFIA: It was the strangest thing. All the children who arrived in New York off the first boat from Poland. Some rich woman sent cake to us, chocolate cake. And we stood on the dock and ate it. It was the first thing I tasted in America. Some . . . what-do-you-call—eccentric millionaire woman, I forget her name, she sends all the children of the war cake. After that our troubles began. But at that time I thought, so this is what it will always be like here—chocolate cake and the salt air, and the sugar frosting on my wool gloves.

MAXINE: So that's why.

ZOFIA: Someone had thought of us. (*Pause.*) Only until you find her. So long you can stay. No more.

MAXINE: I wasn't planning on staying any longer.

ZOFIA: It's good.

MAXINE: What?

ZOFIA: That you can put your life into a . . . everything you have you can hold in a . . . (*Zofia can't find the word; she snaps her fingers with impatience.*)

MAXINE: Laundry bag?

ZOFIA: No, not "laundry," not "bag" . . . ach, *torebka* . . .

MAXINE: "Sack"?

ZOFIA (*relieved*): *Sak! Sak, sak, sak!* Yes. That you can do that, you learned from me that. Yes. Good.

MAXINE: Oh, I'm not so sure anymore.

ZOFIA: Oh, yes. All you need you have to carry here. (*She taps her head.*) Because everything else they can take from you.

MAXINE: Who?

ZOFIA: Who takes? (*She laughs.*) The world. (*She gestures out.*) That. (*She taps her head.*) This is all you can take. When I was a little girl, walking out of Poland after the bombs . . . the ones of us who were left. Ach. We took all the wrong things . . . little spoons, a duck, a purple table runner . . . We were so stupid. We would be holding all the wrong things for the rest of our lives, no matter where we went . . . Ach. I would hold the little comb to my chest all night long on the boat across the ocean, because I cannot hold my mother's hand, never again. And I think, this will save me. This will be enough. A comb she gave me. Because her hand had been on it. This will save me. This thing.

MAXINE: Where is the comb?

ZOFIA (*smiles*): I threw it in the ocean. It was not enough. The cup my dead father made for me, her glove . . . seven silver buttons . . . (*She makes a gesture of throwing.*) I walked off that boat with nothing in my hands. Like an animal. I made myself do that. Skin and bones and this. (*She touches her head. She gestures to the sack.*) What's in there?

MAXINE: Nothing much. Clothes. Some books.

ZOFIA: Throw it in the ocean!

MAXINE: Right.

ZOFIA: Throw them away! (*She laughs.*) Who needs them? Not even little girls. (*She looks out into the night.*) She was twelve?

MAXINE: Who?

ZOFIA: That little girl?

MAXINE (*not quite sure which girl they are talking about*): Yes.

ZOFIA: She's probably dead by now.

Scene 5. Mama

A very dimly lit bedroom. Maxine's old room in Zofia's house. Something is wrong. Maxine is asleep in bed. She wakes, startled. A pause. She turns on the bedside light. A woman is hanging like a side of meat, her feet perhaps five feet from the ground. She is dressed in a stereotypical flight suit—leather dust coat, goggles and helmet. Maxine gasps and turns off the light. Pause.

MAXINE: Mama?

(*Pause. Maxine turns on the light. The figure is gone.*)

Scene 6. Powder Blue

Airplane hangar. Predawn. Dessa is sifting through some photographs and papers she's brought for Maxine. Maxine enters, already exhausted, surprised to see Dessa.

DESSA: I got another picture for you. It's the sixth grade class picture so it's not . . . I mean, her hair is longer and she doesn't have the braces but still. And it's not really like her, the eyes, I think she's about to blink, she hates it, this picture, see she's standing next to this guy, Neil Kransky, she says he smells or something, see how's she's leaning away a little bit. (*Laughs.*) I never noticed that, she's got these *opinions*, she *hates* this photo. See how tall she is, though? She's the tallest one in the back row. I keep thinking that's . . . I keep thinking that's going to make a difference, you know? It's not . . . it's not *rational* but . . . (*Suddenly*) Oh, Jeez, I almost forgot—the jacket she's wearing—it's *really* light blue—powder blue they call it—I went back to the store to look at it, they still had one—so it's not just light blue, like I told you, it's powder blue like— (*She looks around.*) Shit, I was going to bring in something that color—I could go buy the jacket, it's the same one, how about that?

MAXINE: No, that's O.K., I think I—

DESSA (*pointing*): —Like *that*.

MAXINE: What?

DESSA: The sky right now.

MAXINE (*too quickly*): O.K.

DESSA: No. *Look*. Not near where the sun's coming up. Further up.

MAXINE (*looking*): O.K.

DESSA: Not where you're looking. Where I'm pointing.

MAXINE (*trying to oblige*): Yeah. Right there. Got it.

DESSA: Shit, it's already changing. (*She takes Maxine by the arm and pulls her over, then puts their heads next to each other.*) Where my finger is. Is it the same place for your eyes?

MAXINE: Close enough.

DESSA: Fuck, it's already changing. *That* color. Right there.

MAXINE: I see it. Very light blue.

(*Dessa lets go of her abruptly.*)

DESSA: It's changed. Not that color. What it *was*. Do you remember?

MAXINE: Yes.

DESSA: What it *was*.

MAXINE: Yes.

DESSA: Not what it is now.

MAXINE: Yes.

DESSA: Remember that.

MAXINE: Yes.

DESSA: That's the color of the jacket she has on. It's brand-new. (*Pause.*) Go. It's light enough.

Scene 7. Charlotte

Day. Maxine is in the cockpit of her plane, searching.

MAXINE: Charlotte. Charlotte Hobart. I am looking for you. Serious girl, almost pretty, shy, quiet. A good girl. On your report card, your teacher writes: "She seems to be in love with nature. Rather romantic and solitary." I know the type. Always looking out of windows.

Twelve years old. What goes on in that head of yours?

Sex? What do you know about it? What you read in books? Movies? There is a kid in your class who punches your arm a lot and that does mean something. There is one day when you are alone with him in a barn and you find yourselves discussing religion. You lie on your backs and he lazily tosses a baseball straight up toward the rafters and catches it in his glove. Leather smacks neatly into leather. At that moment you say, "I think God exists in everything— the barn swallows, the straw, the dirt under my fingernails, your sneaker." And it so happens that his investigations into things have led him to the same conclusion. "Everything is sacred," he says. And there is a long silence because what now can be said? You lie there, not looking at each other, not touching each other either.

But then, you don't have to. (*Bang. Something hits the side of the plane.*)

It was as perfect as it gets. (*Bang.*)

What was that? A bird?

Life for you was as simple as a long plank to walk.

And at the end of it, this man. Is that right? (*Pause.*)

Bullshit, Maxine. What do you know about it? (*Pause.*)

Charlotte Hobart. What is being done to you?

What is being done to you—right now? (*Pause. Subdued*) Oh Jesus. (*A final bang, the loudest, on the window. Maxine is startled back to reality. As irritated as she is frightened*) What the fuck *is* that?

Scene 8: Ta Da

Lights flicker. Suddenly, the girl, Charlotte, sits beside Maxine in the cockpit; bloody and dead but unperturbed, she looks out the window. Maxine is surprised and horrified.

CHARLOTTE: You found me. Ta da.

MAXINE: Jesus.

CHARLOTTE: Congratulations. Aren't you something.

MAXINE: Oh God, what's going on?

CHARLOTTE: Well, what *would* you do?

MAXINE: What?

CHARLOTTE: See, you can't even imagine.

MAXINE: Of course I can. This is, this is what I do.

CHARLOTTE: No it isn't. You make the search, you sometimes see something. Then you send the helicopter or whatever, right? *You never land.* It's all pretty pristine. You never have to deal with *this* for instance. (*Charlotte draws a bloody finger down Maxine's face.*)

MAXINE: I hate this.

CHARLOTTE: Some hero.

MAXINE: So all right, since you're here. Maybe you can tell me.

CHARLOTTE: What?

MAXINE: Where are you? What is happening to you?

CHARLOTTE: Sometimes the quiet girls go completely mute. Isn't it provoking? Neither seen *nor* heard. Poof. They just vanish. No one can see them, even when they stand right in front of you. Like your mother.

MAXINE: What about her?

CHARLOTTE: You're so farsighted now maybe you can only read suicide notes when they're printed out in huge stones and felled trees. Look. It says maybe "STOP LOOKING" or "GIVE UP comma I'M ALREADY DEAD."

MAXINE: That's not what's going on. Not this time.

CHARLOTTE: How do you know? Can you imagine what I'm going through?

MAXINE: Yes. I can imagine.

CHARLOTTE (*laughs*): No you can't. Me and that Norman Rockwell boy in the barn? You wish, Honey.

MAXINE: I can imagine. Too well. Better than others. It keeps me up here. Looking longer. Past other people's threshold of hope. That thin line between hope and despair—mine's a longer suspension of disbelief. That's why I'm good.

CHARLOTTE: A tightrope walker after all.

MAXINE: Yes.

CHARLOTTE: Just like you dreamed of being when you were my age.

   Don't you find yourself looking at your feet these days?

MAXINE: You never look at your feet. That's the trick.

CHARLOTTE: You've been looking lately. I've noticed.

MAXINE: Never.

CHARLOTTE: You have. You're stuck in the middle of the rope. Right smack in the middle. No going forward, no going back. Fright. Hits the best of them at your age. So you find yourself looking at your foot, and you know what? You're right. This is exactly, just exactly where your mother's foot slipped.

(*Charlotte disappears.*)

MAXINE: No.

Scene 9. Demon Machine

Maxine is in the airport hangar building. She is leaning against the coffee vending machine, obviously tired and cold.

MAXINE (*beleaguered*): Christ. (*She puts some change into the machine. A cup comes down, but lodges wrong, at an angle.*) No, no, don't do this to me again. (*She starts to try to right the cup but isn't quick enough; the coffee starts pouring down and burns her hand.*) Fucking *demon* machine. (*As the scalding liquid pours down, it runs all over the floor. Maxine stands back to watch.*) Oh, tremendous. Lovely. All over the floor. And *coffee,* yet, not hot chocolate, as I requested. Ah, thank you so much. Are we finished? All done? (*Final spurt.*) All righty, then.

Shall we try again?

(*She fishes in her pockets for change. As she does so, Evie descends, looking as she usually does. She hangs behind Maxine and about a foot above her head. Maxine senses something and slowly turns. This is quite disturbing. She quickly looks around to see if anyone else is in the hangar. No one is. She looks back, then experiments. She puts her hands in front of her eyes for a moment, then looks again. Her mother is still there.*)

All right, Maxine. Just fucking deal. Just fucking— (*down to business*) O.K. Get out of here. Shoo. Vamoose. Or at least—

(*Maxine walks over and reaches up for Evie's foot. Evie begins to ascend; Maxine just barely has grasp of a foot. Evie shakes her off and ascends just out of reach. Maxine jumps. Evie is out of range. She ascends slowly out of sight.*)

(*Calling after Evie*) And you never flew a—YOU NEVER FLEW A PLANE IN YOUR ENTIRE LIFE, SO WHAT IS THIS GETUP SUPPOSED TO . . .

Ma? Mama? (*Evie is gone. Maxine looks around, shaken. She slowly walks to the coffee machine, begins to reach for change, and then suddenly punches it violently, hurting her hand. She holds her hand.*) Ow. I'm sorry. Fuck. (*She leans her face against the machine.*)

I'm sorry.

(*Maxine begins to cry. She embraces the machine, crying.*)

Scene 10. Flight

Night. Maxine draws a chair up to Zofia's.

MAXINE: I think it's quite possible you haven't moved from that chair since I left you there, exactly like that, eighteen hours ago.

ZOFIA: It's possible. I guess it looks so to you. But it is not so simple . . . My grandmother's mother, your, what?

MAXINE: Great-great-great-grandmother.

ZOFIA: Great, great, great . . . She was one of the real, the first. The traveling women. They put henbane, an herb it is, rubbed it on the soles of their feet at night and (*she makes a gesture*) shoop, like a black bird. To the mountain. To dance.

MAXINE: You're saying she was a witch?

ZOFIA (*laughs*): A witch. Yes. Traveling woman. *Czarownica.*

MAXINE: Huh.

ZOFIA (*laughs*): You don't believe me. That's why I never told you. It doesn't matter. But I saw them, the traveling women. Like black swans across the sky one night. I was not supposed to see that. Her husband, he tried to tie her up on those nights, to a chair, to a bed, thick rope. And he would watch her. But always he would fall asleep and when he wakes up there is just this neat circle of the rope on the floor. What could he do? It was not so nice, maybe, what she was doing . . . maybe . . . But she couldn't help it. And then there was your mother. There was nothing I could do. *Masz to ve krwi*. It was the blood in her. Even when Evie was a little girl. Running always out into the night away from me. Me calling and calling for her as the dark came and she never comes until so late, even it was morning sometimes, and when she finally comes in she looks so like an animal, her eyes, ach, her eyes . . . You look like that sometimes.

MAXINE: But I can fly.

ZOFIA: Oh, yes. The first one in a plane, but not the first one to fly, only the last one. It's maybe a disease. We pass it down.

MAXINE: It's the only thing that makes me happy. It's good.

ZOFIA (*nods*): It's the blood. Mother to mother to mother. This (*she stamps her foot*) is not enough for any of us. We travel. Ach. (*She holds her head.*) We can't help it.

MAXINE: *Babcia?*

ZOFIA: Traveling too much

MAXINE: You're traveling?

ZOFIA (*holds her head, as if to keep something in*): Can't stay in. I try, it's very hard. So I think someday you will come here and look in the chair, and, oh, nobody. No more.

MAXINE: Where will you be?

(*Zofia shrugs, smiles.*)

ZOFIA: Away. (*She closes her eyes. She takes Maxine's hand.*) If you could see it. It's here. Just here.

(*Zofia gestures to her closed eyes. She leans back. They hold hands for a moment, Zofia with her eyes still closed. Maxine jerks her hand.*)

MAXINE: Come back.

ZOFIA: No.

MAXINE: Come back.

ZOFIA: Why?

MAXINE: Because I can't go with you.

ZOFIA: Ach. Just let me . . .

(*Maxine takes Zofia by the shoulders and shakes her.*)

MAXINE: No. No. No. Stop it.

ZOFIA (*opens her eyes, irritated*): What's wrong with you?

MAXINE: I'm not going to just *watch* . . . You can't expect me to just *watch* while you . . . I don't want to lose you. Not yet.

ZOFIA: But you will lose me. It's how it happens. There comes a day. No one will find me. (*Pause.*) Some things cannot be found.

MAXINE: And some things can.

(*Pause.*)

ZOFIA: Why do you have to find her?

MAXINE (*at a loss*): Because it's important.

ZOFIA: What if she is only dead?

MAXINE: Even so. There's a difference I can make. Even if she's dead. It's the difference between catastrophe, the chaos of this horrible, senseless event, and something else. Not tragedy exactly, but . . . It's important.' That I do this. Search. I can't explain it to you.

ZOFIA: What's lost is lost. You run out into *that?* (*She gestures.*) You get yourself lost in *that?* (*Another gesture.*) Ach. You cannot expect anyone to come looking for you. These things happen. It's a terrible world.

MAXINE: But you *can* expect that. You *can* expect someone to come looking for you. We owe that to each other. At least that much.

And I'm good at it.

ZOFIA: This world. Ach. This world, I think, wants to lose all her children and forget them. She is so good at losing. She is a mother who puts her children out-of-doors to die and forgets them as she turns to make more. We tap on the windows and call her name but the night is cold and she has turned away. So we run into the darkness and hug our sides and suck our dirty fingers for the memory of food. She will not take us back again no matter how we cry. Time goes by and we get older and we forget the warmth of her house, the taste of her bread, and soon we stop crying for them. Anything, I think, can be borne. "Catastrophe," "tragedy" . . . Whatever you want to call it. It doesn't matter.

We are all put out of house and forgotten.

MAXINE: This one girl. I will find her. I can do that.

Scene 11. Tongues

Maxine's room. Night. Evie, the figure, is hanging above her, as before. Maxine stares at her. Silence.

MAXINE: All right. How does this work? Are you going to talk to me? (*Pause.*) I guess I'll get used to you. Like some absurd empty piñata that everyone forgot to take down.

(*Trying another approach*) Since you're here, Ma, about your mother . . . what gives? I mean she seems to be . . . like she's doing some aerial, imaginary tour of the globe before she . . . I mean it's not really that simple, but she does seem to be going somewhere . . .

EVIE: You know where.

MAXINE: Oh, so it is that simple. (*Pause.*)

How many times did you try to kill yourself?

EVIE: Seven. Eight. Seven. Nine? Does it matter?

MAXINE: Oh, let's say nine. That sounds good. Like a cat.
     Am I making you up?

EVIE: You're asking me?

MAXINE: I guess I didn't realize how obsessed I was with Earhart.

EVIE: That's only the most obvious part of this.

MAXINE: What do you have on under your coat?

EVIE: Cut me open and find out. I'm your piñata.

MAXINE: I can't. I think it's feathers.

EVIE: Could be.

MAXINE: Damp, matted feathers. Go away.

EVIE: You'll never find out anything if you're so afraid. Chicken.

(*Evie begins to ascend, making clucking sounds.*)

MAXINE: I'm not afraid of you. (*Evie halts in her ascent.*) How
     could I be? You're just embarrassing more than anything
     else.

EVIE: You used to be. Afraid.

MAXINE: I'm sure I was. I was a little kid. All I knew was that you
     were mad.

EVIE: "Mad." How you flatter me. Sounds so romantic. Why not
     "crackers," why not "loony tunes"? Why not "My crazy
     fucking mother drove me nuts"?

MAXINE: It's what I was told. "Madwoman." "Sent away."

EVIE: "Away." Lovely. It sounds like a white place, like a plate,
     where all the madwomen lie, waiting for judgment day.
     Mouths open and stopped up, tongues flat and silent . . .

MAXINE: Right, Ma. Cooked meat. Pigs' tongues under apples.

EVIE: Cooked, yes, but not apples on our tongues. Black rubber. It tasted of nightmare factories. And you bite down hard. So that when the electricity courses through your soft brain the scream you scream goes meaningless and tiny into the piece of dull night you hold between your dangerous animal teeth. We bit and bit, grinning like the lit skeletons we became.

MAXINE: So you were one of them.

EVIE: Oh, yes. One of the many. Quite the little unhinged sorority. Lining the cots waiting for the daily execution. In our identical thin gowns. And afterwards, all our open mouths, like holes ripped in sheets and nothing coming out, nothing going in. We would walk up and peer into each other just to make sure. You know what a wild bird's tongue looks like? Not your nice birds, I'm talking about the ones you shoo off the garden, the greasy, sinister types—grackles, starlings—the types who steal from nice birds' nests and shriek and dive at the house cats. Look at their tongues— black, flattened, moving splinters.

And the sounds they make with tongues like that. Horrible. In all of our open mouths. Imagine.

MAXINE: I wanted you to be different.

EVIE: Ah, no. There was never any difference between us. And when the treatments began, we knew for sure. We are all the same woman, that thrashing body on the table, biting rubber. You talk about "madness." No, my darling. Much, much simpler, much less grand. For instance, you're looking up at me now, and let me tell you something: You're right. I'm exactly what you look like.

MAXINE: Family resemblance.

EVIE: Oh. More than that. Just another flight-bound, black-tongued thing.

(Evie ascends out of view.)

MAXINE (*calling after her*): Forget it, Ma. I'm not scared of you anymore. You're just something I made up to spook myself.

EVIE (*out of sight*): Just another greasy-feathered bird.

MAXINE: FUCK YOU! I'm *nothing* like you.

(*Sound of wet wings.*)

Scene 12. Earhart

Maxine in the cockpit, searching.

MAXINE: I dress my mother like you, Amelia. What is that about?

Amelia Earhart. Air Heart. Airheart. (*She laughs.*)

One thing I know, Amelia. I would have found you. Weeks they looked for you, all those air force yahoos, the largest air search in history. Not a trace. Hundreds of square miles of gray slate water and no you. I would have found you. Because I know you. I could see it in those eyes of yours. Photo after photo of you, standing in front of planes as if you were guarding them, that obliging beauty, that squint, that smile, that lovely preoccupied air. You weren't there. The drug is what you see. I know that drug. It's coursing through my veins right now. It's solitude taken to the utmost extreme. You hear a snap and, yes, complete disconnection from the world. What wings do. Abandon.

When I say I remember everything I'm lying. I don't remember my mother. Memories only begin after her death, and then they rear up in Technicolor and just won't quit. But before that, just . . . nothing . . . silence. Blind, aching void. And there is very little evidence to assert that she *did* exist, that woman, except for me, I suppose, who must have come from somewhere. She left no trace, no trail, not a mark on this world apparently, no more than a water bug leaves on the surface of a lake.

It would seem that my mother never wrote a letter in her life, not a grocery list, I have never, in fact, seen her signature.

I have no memory of her voice, her touch, the true color of her eyes, the way she laughed, if she ever laughed . . . I look for memories of her inside me and find nothing, no likeness, no scent, except perhaps here, in the air. Airheart . . .

Because you came here too, didn't you, Mama? Countless times. Shot as if from a cannon out of yourself. Nothing and no one, not even you, could hold you in. Disappeared . . .

The search continues. For you, whoever you were . . .

I have so little to go on. The only thing you bequeathed to this earth was me, Mama. I am your bread crumb trail. (*She looks at her hands.*) My bones, my sinews, every single part of me . . . including this (*she raps her head with her knuckles*), which is what? Just some bomb you set ticking before you stepped off the face of the world? . . . You left no traces on this earth except me, Mama, your unwilling shadow, who can do nothing now but limp down your tracks sniffing the air and wondering what strange woods you have brought me to.

Scene 13. Winter

Airplane hangar. Night. Maxine enters, exhausted, another day gone. Dessa is sitting at the table wearing her coat, waiting for her. They don't have to say anything; Dessa knows. Silence.

DESSA: At least it hasn't rained or something. 'Cause you got to find her before it rains or something. Before the snow melts 'cause the black truck—it'll only show up against the snow. That's what I figure. The black against the white. That shows up well, right? You would see that. The truck.

MAXINE: Yeah. That's what I figure too.

DESSA: It's better if it's white. The snow. It's better. Even though it's cold. She's got that jacket and the snow boots from Christmas, they're good. She'll be warm. I know she took her gloves. All the girls said she was wearing them—the thermal what-do-you-call-it, some kind of warm plastic, they're waterproof and everything. She's always out all day in those. That's what these guys (*gestures around the room vaguely*), they don't understand, I'm always calling to her to come in, she'll freeze to death . . . but she won't until she's good and ready. She's like that. That's the thing I know about her. I'm always calling and calling out the back door. And when she's good and ready she comes in. She always comes in.

MAXINE: That's good to know.

DESSA: I hope spring never comes. I need the snow. Until you find her. I need the snow.

(*Pause.*)

MAXINE: Mrs. Hobart, / I really—

DESSA: —NO. (*Long pause.*) I'm not even going to take her library books back. And they're overdue. Eight days now. She'll kill me when she gets back. She's never had an overdue book in her life. She's just like that.

But I can't . . . do it. She's going to have to come back and return them herself. . . . I can never get across to her—she's so *serious* . . . I keep telling her, keep them if you like them, keep them a few days more, just hang onto them . . . It's such a *little* crime . . . to keep something you love . . . just a few days more.

(*Pause.*)

MAXINE: Have you eaten anything today? (*Dessa shakes her head.*)

You need to eat. Even if you can't feel hunger. I could stand a beer. How about we go out someplace? (*Dessa looks outside.*) It's night. Nothing to see until morning.

(*Pause.*)

DESSA (*quiet, staring out*): Fires.

(*Pause.*)

MAXINE: All right. But I need to eat something first. Then you can come up with me for awhile. (*Dessa tries to contain her surprise and exhilaration.*) We'll look for fires.

(*They leave.*)

Scene 14. That Story

Dessa and Maxine in the cockpit. They look out their respective windows. Night. Dessa is giddy, Maxine amused.

DESSA: Oh, God. Finally. To be *doing* something.

MAXINE: I don't know how much you can *see* . . .

DESSA: I can't see a fucking thing. (*They laugh.*) I mean, how can you even fly? What are you, nuts? Not that I want you to *land* or anything. I mean, please don't, but really, where *is* anything?

MAXINE: You see that ridge there? The stand of trees along the top, it's like a knife edge?

DESSA (*laughing*): Nope.

MAXINE: And then there's a little line, it used to be a logging road, it goes down, I always think it looks like a woman's profile.

DESSA: Yeah, well, whatever. Eagle eyes. I guess that's why you can do this for a living.

MAXINE: Why I get the big bucks.

DESSA: Yeah, right.

(*They laugh.*)

MAXINE: But really, I couldn't do this kind of night flying anywhere else. I know these mountains pretty well. Better than anyplace. I love them.

DESSA: Yeah?

MAXINE: They're like, I don't know, I haven't lived here for years, but whenever I dream, this is the landscape. It goes deep, this place.

DESSA: You grow up out here?

MAXINE: Yeah. My grandmother raised me. I stay with her when I come back.

DESSA (*looking out the window*): And you were happy here?

MAXINE: Actually, I think I was pretty miserable. (*They laugh.*) But I still like the mountains.

DESSA: Where was your mother?

MAXINE: She was kind of . . . around sometimes, but . . . she committed suicide when she was about my age.

DESSA: How old were you when she did that?

MAXINE: Six, I think. Maybe five. Small. Four? Somewhere in there.

DESSA: Uh huh.

MAXINE: A long time ago. I never knew her. She was mostly gone.

(*Pause.*)

DESSA: How did she kill herself?

MAXINE: What? Oh. She tried a lot of times, a lot of ways.

DESSA: Which one worked?

MAXINE: Um. I don't really know. And now my grandmother, the only one who really knows, she doesn't remember—

DESSA: —That doesn't seem likely—

MAXINE: —Or she just doesn't want to tell me.

DESSA: I think pills.

MAXINE: What?

DESSA: I've been thinking about pills. 'Cause I'm chicken and I don't want to make a mess. I don't know why I care, since I wouldn't have to clean it up. For once. But I'm pretty persnickety. Tidy.

MAXINE: You're thinking about killing yourself?

DESSA: Well lately, yeah.

(*Pause.*)

MAXINE: I'm probably not the person to talk to about this.

DESSA: Oh sure. Of course. (*Pause.*)
    I mean, don't worry, or anything. I just *think* about it. I find it, you know, comforting . . . That I could, you know, *do* . . . something—to, uh, express my general, uh, disappointment with . . .

MAXINE: God?

DESSA: Yeah, well . . . Whoever's in charge. (*Pause.*) Thanks.

MAXINE: For what?

DESSA: For not saying (*cheerleader*): "Hey, buck up, Mrs. Hobart. Heck, we'll find her, you bet. Don't get so down in the dumps."

(*Pause.*)

MAXINE: I would like very much to find your daughter.

DESSA: Yeah. Don't want to ruin that perfect record. (*Bad pause.*) You know that's why I hired you.

MAXINE: What?

DESSA: I thought you were lucky. Shiny like a new coin.

MAXINE: Yeah. That's me. Lucky, lucky, lucky . . . so lucky. (*Pause.*)

Don't kill yourself, please.

DESSA: Why not?

MAXINE: I'd be very bummed out. (*They laugh.*) Really. "Hey, buck up, Mrs. Hobart"—

DESSA: —You can call me Dessa—

MAXINE: —"Buck up, Dessa."

DESSA: Yeah? Say it.

MAXINE: Say what?

DESSA: "We're going to . . ."

MAXINE: "We're going to . . ."

DESSA: Go on.

MAXINE: "We're going to find your daughter."

DESSA: Oh, man, you fucking well better.
Go champ. Defend your title. (*Pause.*)
What was wrong with your mother?

MAXINE: She was . . . very, very sad.

DESSA: Sad?

MAXINE: Well, I mean, she was also, I don't know, *sick*. Beyond sad. She was insane.

DESSA: So there's some sort of dividing line?

MAXINE: Between sad and crazy? Yeah. It's chemical. She didn't want it.

DESSA: Well, who wants it?

MAXINE: No, I know, but . . . she would pass a certain point that most people get to and they turn back, she couldn't. It was like watching someone fall off a cliff, looking back as they fall, a hand goes up and there's nothing to hold on to. (*She*

looks at Dessa.) I make a lot up, I think. Stories. To make
sense. Give myself a past. Or change it. There's the story . . .

DESSA: What story?

MAXINE: If she'd lived. That story. I think about calling her, like
on her birthday, and it would be . . . so sort of dull and
nice . . . she would let me tell her what I was up to and then
I would listen to what she was up to, you know, how her
cats were doing, getting her gutters cleaned, whether she'd
put her bulbs in early this year . . . you know. And then, this
is the thing, I would hang up, yawn, and forget her. Forget
about her. Because she would just be my mother, the
woman I call once a week. I could take her for granted. I
would love her, certainly, but like the way you love your
hands, or your knees, if you can call that love, since you
don't really think about it. She would just have been my
mother. Known so well that I wouldn't know that I didn't
know her at all. But I could forget her. Because she didn't
forget me.

(*They look out their windows in silence.*)

Scene 15. Open Eyes

*Lights remain on Maxine and Dessa in the cockpit. Lights up on Zofia
in her chair, looking out. Sound of a plane.*

ZOFIA: I hear you Maxine, flying tonight.
That sound, I know that sound.
I have listened all day to it.
It is the sound of your open eyes.
Searching the darkness for your lost girl.

And perhaps she is waiting there. The lost one.
Not the one you think you're looking for.
That child is lost forever.
No.

Someone, something else.

The one in the darkness.

She sees you now.

Her face is white with the moon.

She maybe reaches up,

as if she could draw a finger down your shining belly as you pass above her, raking your beautiful lights across her open eyes.

Turn back, Maxine.

Close your eyes.

What you are looking for is not what you are looking for.

Learn to lose what should not be found.

(*Lights intensify on Maxine, looking out. There is the sense of movement and presence in the darkness around her. Perhaps we hear snatches of Charlotte's dialogue ("You're stuck in the middle of the rope, right smack in the middle, no going forward, no going back . . .") and Evie's ("For instance, you're looking up at me right now, and let me tell you something, you're right. I'm exactly what you look like . . ."). The sound of the plane's engine peaks, as if going directly over the audience's heads, then cuts out abruptly.*)

ACT TWO

Scene 16. Another Story

Lights up on Maxine and Dessa in the cockpit. Later that same evening. Silence.

DESSA: Have you ever looked for a child?

MAXINE: No.

DESSA: Not once?

MAXINE: No. It's been mostly hikers—backpackers who get lost. All adults, just barely, some of them, but yeah, no one under eighteen. There have been people, too, who came up to the mountains, came out alone to kill themselves, or said that's what they were going to do.

DESSA: And you found them?

MAXINE: Every single one. Perfect record.

DESSA: Before or after?

MAXINE: What?

DESSA: They killed themselves.

MAXINE: Before. Two different ones. Before.

DESSA: Huh. (*Pause.*)

You know what? The first thing they did with me at the police station, once they'd asked all the questions and shit, the first thing they do is I'm strapped up to this polygraph test, really, I couldn't believe it, across the table from this guy. He's asking me, did *I* kidnap her. My own daughter. Did I kill her. The needle's bouncing around on the paper. He keeps saying, "Lady, Lady, it's standard procedure." Incredible. I wanted to kill . . . somebody, him, somebody, anybody.

MAXINE: Yeah. But he's right, that's the norm. Abductions of children by strangers are incredibly rare. Children almost always know the person who abducts them.

DESSA: Yeah. I've heard that. And it's a great comfort.

MAXINE: I'm sorry.

(*Pause.*)

DESSA: They told me all that. First thing. *Very* interested that I don't know exactly who her father is. My whole, like, completely fucked-up personal life just lying on the police linoleum there like puke. They couldn't really get it, that I'd just run like hell, put this huge distance between me and anybody who could have been her father. Out of maybe six guys. Just came up here. Put my finger on the map. I thought, O.K. where in the world is it, like, completely nowhere and nobody knows me. O.K. Loon Lake, that sounds nice. I thought, she'll like that, the baby. Loons. And around it, green map color. Nothing much. Trees. There was that little picture of the tree on the map. Pine trees. And none of those guys will ever know, not that they would care much, I'm not going to flatter myself here, but they wouldn't be able to find me even if they wanted to. And no one ever knew I was pregnant. That I know. Nobody from my life before.

MAXINE: Do you know which of them, I mean, can you guess now, knowing her, what she looks like, can you guess which one of them was the one?

DESSA: She doesn't look like anyone I've ever known. She's completely different.

And whoever took her, whoever that was, she'd never seen him before. I know that. Whoever the fuck that was.

The night after the polygraph test I fell asleep in the, the police station there. I put my head down on the desk and bam, like I'd been slugged on the head. Had the print of somebody's paper clip on my cheek for like two days. But here's the thing. What I dreamt was that I *did* abduct her like they said. I'm telling you, oh God, what an incredible relief. I'd just *forgotten* that I did. And I'm standing at the sink, doing dishes and I'm looking out the window at this little green garden shed out back, it's like falling over, about the size of an outhouse, tiny, you know, and I'm looking at it and I suddenly remember that Charlotte, I put her out there *myself,* in the shed, it was all so, like, well, *of course,* how stupid of me, causing all this trouble. I just forgot.

MAXINE: "Silly me."

DESSA: Yeah. Like that.

(Maxine slaps her forehead in a gesture of sudden remembrance. Dessa laughs. They begin on a riff that builds, laughing hard and cutting each

other off. The laughter should seem disproportionate to the jokes them-selves.)

MAXINE: "You won't believe this, Officers"—

DESSA: —Yeah. "I'm just such a knucklehead"—

MAXINE: —"I'm hoping you'll see the *humor* in this"—

DESSA: —"Turns out, all along"—

MAXINE: —"My mistake"—

DESSA: —"My daughter has been sitting out / in the *garden shed*"—

MAXINE: —"in the *garden shed*"—

(*They fall apart, laughing.*)

DESSA: —"I can't for the *life* of me think why I put her out there to begin with"—

MAXINE: —"But she's been out there, eating saltines, for, oh, two weeks now." "Oh, / she's fine"—

DESSA: —"Oh, she's *fine*"—"Nothing a couple of decades of therapy can't take care of"—

MAXINE: —"Sorry to bother you"—

DESSA: —"Thousands of dollars in search parties and helicop-ters, is that right?"—

MAXINE: —"What nice dogs. All the way from Quebec, you say?"—

DESSA: —"Thanks so much for everything. We'll just be going home now"—

MAXINE (*the topper*): —"Won't happen again"—

DESSA: Right. "Won't happen again." (*They are exhausted from laughing so hard, and a little stunned. Silence as they look out their respective windows.*) They got dogs from Quebec?

MAXINE: I just made that up.

(*They look out their windows. Silence.*)

DESSA: You know that story? About calling your mother?

MAXINE: Yeah?

DESSA: I got one too.

   See, it's this winter afternoon, a Sunday, right, beautiful day, and Charlotte is getting back from this field trip that she begged me to let her go on, she's got these friends, these girls, and they go on nature walks but I think it's mostly about screaming, you know, the way they laugh, almost peeing their pants from every- thing being so funny. They never see any wildlife on these things, these expeditions, I think 'cause they make so much noise. But, you know, what the hell, right? I remember that. And it's good for me, I got the whole day. I take all our laundry down to the coin-op and I get, like, nine loads done and between times I'm running around, I shop for the whole week and pick up her shoes from the shoe repair, and all during that day, I'm thinking what a good time she's having. I look up at the mountains from the street there and it all looks so gorgeous. She's up there, I think, laughing like that with all her friends. I make her fried chicken, 'cause I kind of missed her all day, and peas. And when she gets dropped off, she's got some sunburn, not a lot, but from the shine off the snow, you know, and she's kind of like privately exhilarated. She pushes her peas around on the plate and tells me her adventures, goofs on everybody, who threw up on the bus, you know, she sings me a song she just learned, and then she goes to bed sort of early, 'cause tomor- row's school . . . And all over the town, the girls are pushing their peas around plates and telling somebody their adventures and then dreaming. They dream about mountains, of their feet stomping snow, about pine trees, about each other. And then they wake up and forget those dreams and their lives just rush past with all the details and daylight until, in this story, they are old, old women who can't remember that song they sang, that trip they took, the names, even, of their first dear friends, or anything at all really except something very vague but good about one afternoon in the bright sun in the snow, when they were all such young, young girls.

(*They look out their respective windows.*)

Scene 17. The Bear

Late night. Maxine comes into Zofia's place, bearing groceries. She sets the bag down and begins unloading it. She opens the refrigerator. It contains nothing except suspicious items balled up in tin foil.

MAXINE (*to herself*): Jesus, Zofia. (*She gingerly takes an item out, unwraps it tentatively, and sniffs it.*) Oh, for goodness sake.

(*Maxine starts throwing items away. Zofia enters, unsteadily, holding a baseball bat.*)

ZOFIA: Oh. I thought it was a bear in the kitchen. I forgot you were here.

MAXINE: So you often have to club bears in the kitchen?

ZOFIA: Only a few times in the summer, but they sleep in the winter, so I was surprised.

MAXINE: I know you're kidding.

ZOFIA: Oh, good for you.

MAXINE: This does not look like a sane person's refrigerator.

ZOFIA: It's not my fault. Everything goes bad faster now.

MAXINE: What do you eat?

ZOFIA: There's some gingersnaps if you want.

MAXINE: What did you eat today?

ZOFIA (*doing American*): I shot me a moose.

MAXINE: Seriously.

ZOFIA (*referring to her body*): Look at this big hot thing. I eat. Don't worry. Let the bears have it. Just tea. I don't need more. When I was a little girl all I did was eat. And it was never enough. You know what they called me? *Krowka. Mawa krowka*. Little Cow. Because I was always chewing. Like that. (*She chews.*) So, what happened, I ate enough for my whole life then. I don't need any more. I'm done eating. At last.

MAXINE: It doesn't work that way. What did you eat today?

ZOFIA: I forget. But you know what I mean? The way things go bad faster? I look the other way, it can't be very long. I look back . . . Such things as this. (*She picks up an apple Maxine has brought.*) Oh, this will be a terrible wrong thing by noon tomorrow. This can't have been true before. You can't trust anything. Maybe they come into the world older. Like you. Oh, you remind me. I saw your girl.

MAXINE: Who?

ZOFIA: The lost girl. Oh, you've got trouble with her, ach. Such a wild thing. She's been around here. I leave her milk outside, she won't come in. Mostly at night she comes. She likes to play outside the bedroom window. She puts her fingers up and makes shadows on the window. Like this. (*She makes frantic hand signals.*) You can come see if you want. Greasy hands all over the window she leaves. She thinks she's funny, to wake up an old woman. Or she runs past the window there, oh, she's a bold thing, she's grinning. She's in the corner of the eye always. Very smart. You look up and whup, she's gone.

MAXINE: What does she look like?

ZOFIA: So dirty, ach. Her big mouth, the jelly stains. I left jelly on a plate. She ate it up. You know I think you're going to have a hard time. She *wants* to be lost like that. She's happy. It was the same with Evie. She knows you're looking for her but every day, every night that goes by she forgets more the ways she used to be. She can't even talk English anymore. Ach. (*She picks up the apple again.*) Maybe she'll like this. Oh, this will be good. I don't know why I care. She's a terrible little girl. You wait. Maybe tonight. I'll call you when she comes.

MAXINE: You do that.

ZOFIA: Look at you. You're too tired. Go to bed.

MAXINE: I go you go, Pogo.

(*Maxine helps Zofia to her feet.*)

ZOFIA (*laughs*): I go you go, Pogo. Who said that?

MAXINE (*they start to exit*): I did.

ZOFIA: Before you.

MAXINE: You did.

ZOFIA: I did?

MAXINE: Someone I know did.

ZOFIA (*she looks out the window*): It was Evie.

Sometimes I see her in that tree.

MAXINE: Who?

ZOFIA (*dismissively*): Ach. Little girls.

You fell out of that tree. Do you remember?

MAXINE: No.

ZOFIA: You broke your arm. But you didn't cry. Not even a little. The doctor, he couldn't believe it.

MAXINE: I can see why he'd be puzzled.

ZOFIA: He called you "a little soldier." (*Laughs.*)

Do you know what your first sentence was?

MAXINE: No. What?

ZOFIA: "Leave me be."

MAXINE (*appalled*): God.

ZOFIA: You said it all the time. I don't know where you heard that. "Leave me be."

MAXINE: Well. Gosh. Good for me, I guess.

ZOFIA (*as she exits*): I thought it was good.

MAXINE (*alone*): Well, it certainly worked.

(*A thump, as of a bird hitting a window. She looks up.*)

Scene 18. Bed

Maxine sleeps. Charlotte sits bolt upright next to her.

CHARLOTTE: Did you ever notice how completely like *obsessed* you are with other people eating? "Did you eat?" "Do you eat?" "Do you have any food in the house?" "What did you eat today?" My mother, your grandmother. It's a mania with you.

MAXINE (*beleaguered*): Oh, God.

CHARLOTTE: *I've* noticed.

MAXINE: No wonder I wake up exhausted.

(*Maxine stirs and sits upright, but avoids looking at Charlotte.*)

CHARLOTTE: What *is* it with you?

MAXINE: Nobody's—everybody's falling apart on me.

CHARLOTTE: Yeah. So you think *eating* is the solution here?

MAXINE: Wouldn't hurt.

CHARLOTTE: How about you? Don't notice you eating much.

MAXINE: I do.

(*A bump against the window.*)

CHARLOTTE: What was that?

MAXINE: Birds. Starlings, I think. They live in the eaves. Some people have mice. My grandmother has starlings, and apparently bears. The occasional bear.

CHARLOTTE: She was kidding.

MAXINE: One hopes.

CHARLOTTE: And me. She sees me.

MAXINE: Oh, yes, you too. There's a lot going on here.

CHARLOTTE: You think she's crazy.

MAXINE: Oh, she's definitely crazy. I know crazy when I see it.

CHARLOTTE: Uh-huh. And what about you?

(*Pause. Another thump.*)

MAXINE: Please go back to your mother. She's in agony. She misses you so.

CHARLOTTE: Me? (*She snickers.*) As if I had anything to do with that poor woman.

Don't you know whose child I am?

(*Another thump.*)

MAXINE: I did know that. I do know that.

CHARLOTTE: I'm all yours, Baby.

MAXINE: In other words, you're useless.

CHARLOTTE: —I wouldn't say *that*—

MAXINE: —The girl I'm looking for—

CHARLOTTE: —Oh, *her*—

MAXINE: —She's nothing like you.

CHARLOTTE: Who knows? (*Pause.*) Poor thing.

MAXINE: Why can't I find her?

CHARLOTTE: Poor thing.

MAXINE (*cries*): Why can't I find her?

CHARLOTTE: Where are you looking? (*Maxine continues to cry. Charlotte examines her. She carefully places a finger in the center of Maxine's chest. Maxine keeps her eyes closed.*) Can you feel that?

MAXINE: Yes.

CHARLOTTE: What does it feel like?

MAXINE: Ice. Dead ice. Deep, hard. Stop.

(*Charlotte takes her finger away. She then leans down, opens her mouth wide and breathes onto Maxine's cheek.*)

CHARLOTTE: Can you feel that?

MAXINE: Yes.

CHARLOTTE: What does it feel like?

MAXINE: The draft from an open door.

CHARLOTTE: What does it smell like?

MAXINE: Terror.

CHARLOTTE: What does it sound like?

MAXINE: A cry that will not be heard.

CHARLOTTE (*leans back*): Hm. Do you have your eyes closed?

MAXINE: Yes.

CHARLOTTE: Why?

MAXINE: So that I can't see you.

CHARLOTTE: What do you see?

MAXINE: You.

(*Charlotte smiles.*)

CHARLOTTE: Let me try. (*She closes her eyes.*) Oh, yeah. My own personal night. It's not so bad, blindness. All alone in here.

(*Charlotte puts her thumb in her mouth.*)

MAXINE: You're too old to be sucking your thumb.

CHARLOTTE: You know I only do it when no one can see me.

MAXINE: You're so cold.

CHARLOTTE: Yeah, well, I'm dying the good death, asleep in a snowdrift somewhere. Long, sweet dreams that carry you to oblivion in stately procession like a princess: horses, carriages, quaint townspeople cheering. I'm still a little girl, you're right, this is how I would die.

MAXINE: Wait. I don't want you to go.

CHARLOTTE: But you think she's gone, don't you? Why not this way? This is the best you can hope for.

MAXINE: I know.

CHARLOTTE: It's almost painless.

MAXINE: Still.

CHARLOTTE: You know it's the best possible fate.

MAXINE: I can't yet.

CHARLOTTE: Look at this. It's really kind of lovely.

MAXINE: Even so. I want her alive.

CHARLOTTE: But, Maxine, you know what she could be going through. Anything would be better. And this is such a *nice* death.

MAXINE: I know. Even so. Wake up.

CHARLOTTE: You'll have to do it. I'm too tired.

MAXINE: Wake up.

(*Maxine comes up to a sitting position. Still keeping her eyes closed.*)

CHARLOTTE: I'm asleep. Good dreams.

(*Maxine opens her eyes and turns and shakes Charlotte.*)

MAXINE: Wake up! Wake up! (*Lights flicker. Charlotte disappears. Maxine is left, sitting upright in bed. She covers her face with her hands.*)

Not yet. (*She sits up, looking out.*)

I'm sorry. Not yet.

(*Maxine looks up.*)

Scene 19. Knock Knock

Evie descends.

EVIE: There was a time—did I tell you?—a time I stole out of my body and slunk up the wall and then in virtuosic escape, up, up, through the corner of that ceiling, through dust and lathing, through a chink in the sliding slate shingles until there . . . my final sky, that color blue, at last. And like you I could look down on the world, my body, which I could see now was just awkward temporary housing with faulty plumbing, rats in the attic and crumbling foundations, merely a loan of a house for the distinct spark to live in, where you peer through grimy windows and cannot make out the view of the distant hills.

A rattling, death-bound house that every storm shakes.

And even as I bobbed in the air, even in that vastness and release, all the while the damaged world tugged at my sleeve saying go back, return, land the plane. It is not time. There is more to be done. And the drag and pull was unmistakable, back to the blind husk of the animal housing.

There was nothing to do but to force the shining divinity of myself through a hole in the rotting bird-nested roof and down the rickety attic steps and I could hear the rusted deadbolts sink themselves behind me. And as I stood in the damp, airless room of my particular life, grace slipped my grasp like the strings of balloons and flew up through the soot-caked chimneys.

And I stood again at my own windows peering in pain
toward the unseeable hills.

That, my darling, I did. (*Maxine looks up at her.*)

For you.

MAXINE: I can't do this anymore. I'm losing it. Everything.
Please, just— (*Loud thump.*) What *is* that?

EVIE: Something trying to get in.

MAXINE: It's—

EVIE: —Or something trying to get out.

MAXINE: It sounds familiar.

EVIE: Well, it would. (*Evie leans down, almost upside down over Maxine, and knocks on the top of her head. We hear it.*) Like that?

MAXINE: Leave me be.

EVIE: As if I could.

MAXINE: Please.

EVIE: Knock knock.

(*Pause.*)

MAXINE: Who's there?

(*Evie straightens, taking her hand away, and ascends quickly. Just a second too late, Maxine grabs for her. Evie ascends out of sight. Three rapid thumps at the window.*)

Scene 20. Blood from a Stone

Before dawn. Maxine enters the living room. Zofia is there.

MAXINE: I need you to tell me what happened in this house.

ZOFIA: It was over a long time ago.

MAXINE: It's not over for me. I need to know what happened to
Evie.

ZOFIA: You don't remember.

MAXINE: No.

ZOFIA: Good for you.

MAXINE: No, *Babcia*, no. Not good for me. I'm sick of it. I can't . . . I can't do it anymore. It's killing me. You're the only one. You've got to tell me.

(*Pause.*)

ZOFIA (*looks at her for the first time*): I don't remember.

MAXINE: Of course you do.

ZOFIA: No. I threw it away. All of it. One by one. Her feet, her hands, the way she walked, tilt of her head, her face, her face . . . (*She makes the gesture of throwing.*) Everything that happened to her, the whole terrible life of hers, everything she did to that body of hers. That body I gave to the world. (*She makes the gesture.*) I threw it all away. It took years. I did that to her. I killed her in my head. I had to. Because of what she did to me. What is left of her? (*She snaps her fingers.*) Just that. It took a long time.

MAXINE: So you can't give me anything.

ZOFIA (*shrugs*): Blood from a stone, you can't get it.

MAXINE: Blood from a stone.

ZOFIA: I don't remember her.

MAXINE (*vehement*): I don't believe you.

(*Maxine leaves.*)

Scene 21. Still Buzzing

Across a vast, white, vacant field, Charlotte stumbles. She is bloody and dirty. A plane is heard buzzing. She looks up. She puts her hands over her face. The buzzing stops. She takes her hands away, the buzzing continues. The plane is still there, louder now. She is looking up.

CHARLOTTE: Ma? Mama?

(*Lights up on Maxine, asleep at the table in the airplane hangar. Dessa stands beside her. Maxine wakes with a jolt. The buzzing stops.*)

MAXINE: I had to come down for gas.

DESSA: Uh huh.

MAXINE: And the snow. I couldn't see anymore.

DESSA: It's coming down.

MAXINE: I couldn't see.

DESSA: I know. I just . . . I couldn't stay in the house anymore. She's not there. She's so absolutely *not . . . there.* (*She sits.*) I started screaming. I thought I'd give that a try. I'm sick of crying. It's just exhausting now. It used to, well, it didn't make me feel *better* exactly, but you know, when you do it four, five hours straight, and it's kind of amazing that you *can,* you know, physically do that, at the end of it, I kind of felt, I used to feel *different* at least, washed out, changed. It was a lot like *do*ing something. But now it just feels like throwing up, it's not . . . So I tried screaming today.

MAXINE: How'd it go?

DESSA (*holds her neck*): I ripped my throat up. (*She laughs, Maxine laughs with her. Silence.*)
There isn't a sound I can make that is up to it. This.
What's killing me . . .

(*Dessa loses her train of thought.*)

MAXINE: What's killing you?

DESSA: What's killing me is I drive this school bus, right, and I was so happy to get this job when I got it. It's a cinch, you pick them up and drive them all there and then you got the whole day until you take them all home again. I think what it is is there are just so many more kids than there used to be, too many, and you see these mothers, all these young mothers and everybody's pregnant now, they're all over the place, the supermarket, on the street . . . there can't have been that many before, and then there are going to be even *more* kids, dropping their mittens and climbing up that high, tough first step onto the bus, and they're all yelling at each other and kicking and punching and running down the aisle and you know that then *those* ones will get together and be breeding more and putting *theirs* on the bus, which I'll still be driving, 'cause what the hell else will ever happen to me, and so I look at these pregnant women, the like, *battalions* of them and I want them, I want to scream at them to just stop, if they'd just *stop*, you know? Basta. No more. This whole fucking planet, this is what it feels like, it's just a fucking *mess*. These whores and assholes and nobody's paying any attention.

MAXINE: To what?

DESSA (*startled to be in the midst of conversation*): The truth.

MAXINE: Which is?

DESSA: There is this, this . . . evil . . . it's waiting, it, you can't, there's nothing you can do about it. I want it, this whole fucking thing, this earth, to just stop. Just stop. Let it snow for awhile. So it's quiet. So I can think. (*Pause.*)

There can be nothing worse than this. Nothing will ever compare to this. My own death? It's gonna be a fucking picnic.

MAXINE: Piece of cake.

DESSA: Right. Compared to this.

MAXINE: Well . . . at least you know that. You know it can't get any worse than this.

DESSA (*looks at Maxine*): Oh. I think it probably can.

Scene 22. The Glint

Maxine in the cockpit.

MAXINE: You can stop that world, the whole of it, flying, howling as you fly, tears and ice freezing to your open eyes, you
can search the globe for that one child and if you are what
you are, which is the great grieving goddess of that creation,
you will stop that world, place a finger on that spinning
globe and all ceases—no more of the reckless movement
and cursed rush of life. The rivers freeze, the trees drop their
distracting, obfuscating leaves and all land and all sea chill to
bone, ash, the color of visibility. And the land betrays its
true contours in death and sleeping. Wait, wait, you say,
nothing will happen until this one thing happens, until this
one precious individual thing, my only thing, the only color
allowed is found. All nature subdued, all sound gone until
you hear the pulse, the only pulse, of that girl.

If you could do that you would.

Time unticked. Years that she isn't getting older, learning
to play an instrument, use a compass, fall in love—those
years would not go by.

That child, that girl is the silent globe itself, locked on its
axis, tilting her head, her eyes glittering, staring at the finally
fixed stars which tell her stories of light that are too ancient
to mean anything. And there in that stopped, hushed place
between stars and their planets, in that perpetual present of
her absence, there, there, you would find her.

Charlotte. Charlotte. My child. Today is the day.

(*A blinding flash. A violent noise. Blackness and then whiteness.
Silence. Maxine stands on that white vastness that Charlotte walked
across and howls, a screaming howl of grief.*)

Scene 23. The Finding

*Dessa waits in the airplane hangar. Maxine enters, looking destroyed
and violently disheveled.*

DESSA: You found her.

MAXINE: Yes. So they told you.

DESSA: Yes.

MAXINE: I'm—

DESSA: —Of course you are. (*Pause. Maxine shifts her weight.*) And I don't want to be touched. (*Pause.*) You can do something for me.

MAXINE: Please.

DESSA: Tell me. How it, what she, what you saw.

MAXINE: I saw it. The glint. It was the upturned window. The truck was rolled on its side so the window, a part of it that wasn't covered with snow, it glinted. I circled it twice, no, three times, it was three times, and I, basically, I crashed the plane is what it amounts to. I was lucky, but I'd gotten too close and the downdraft of the mountain . . . I mean I managed to get it down but it won't be flying again. So I got out of it and I . . . started running . . . for that place. I just wasn't thinking, I did everything wrong. I didn't radio . . . it was stupid . . . I ran, I don't know how long it took, I ran to that place and I got up there. The truck was deep in a gully at an odd angle, it had hit a tree and I stood on the door, there was something in there and I couldn't get the damn thing open, so I think I, yeah, I kicked through the window, broke the glass and he was in there, dead, he must have died on impact. He'd been dead a long time and she wasn't there. Not a trace of her. And I'm standing on the door and I suddenly realize that there are tracks, you can barely make them out, but tracks, and they run, they're small, they run quite precisely in a neat line to the edge of a cliff. Couldn't be more than twenty paces and then . . . So I got on my belly and looked over . . .

DESSA: What did you see?

MAXINE: Your daughter was . . . her body . . . she was lodged in a tree. She had broken down through, in her fall she'd broken down through the first tiers of a very tall pine tree and she was hanging there. Her arms are outstretched and her head is back, tilted up.

DESSA: Are her eyes open?

MAXINE: Yes.

DESSA: Is she bloody?

MAXINE: No. She is not at all bloody.

(*Pause.*)

DESSA: Is that possible?

MAXINE (*she thinks for a moment*): I think it must be.

(*Long pause.*)

DESSA: I waited for you. They didn't want me to come with them to see her. They didn't tell me anything except that she was dead and that you'd found her. They didn't tell me. I knew you would. (*Pause.*)

 And I'm grateful, or something, I guess. But I think, I think I also, very much, um, hate you. (*Surprised that she's identified an emotion.*) Yes. I do. (*Pause.*)

 They're bringing her back.

MAXINE: It's going to take awhile.

(*Pause.*)

DESSA: I think I can wait.

(*Pause.*)

MAXINE: Dessa. Would you mind if I stayed here with you? Until they bring her back?

DESSA: Just don't ask me if I'll be all right.

MAXINE: I won't.

DESSA: I will never be all right. Never again.

And we will not speak. Never again.

(*They wait.*)

Scene 24. The Return

Maxine enters Zofia's. Very late. Zofia sits, as usual, staring out.

ZOFIA: This is the last night, I think.

MAXINE: Yes. I found her. She's dead.

(*Maxine crumples down next to Zofia. Zofia strokes her hair.*)

ZOFIA (*soothing*): Poor little one. Poor little one.

MAXINE: I've lost my plane, *Babcia*. I crashed it. My sweet old
    Cessna. I've lost everything.

ZOFIA: It is possible. To lose everything. It can be done. I looked
    out the window all day and I thought of you. This cold, this
    long winter and it doesn't seem possible that the world can
    ever be returned to us. Life has turned its face away. But
    much is promised.
        Spring, they say. She will come back. And the world will
    be a wild green place again.
        It has been promised. So perhaps it's true.
        And more, even, is promised to us . . .
        I lied to you. I remember everything. I see her now. I see
    her always. My Evie. And always now she is walking up the
    road, coming back to me like she did those mornings. Her
    hair is wet and filled with new torn leaves and she combs
    her red fingers through it and hums, holding her shoes in
    her hand.
        She looks so tired and calm, so thin . . . And she has seen
    too much.
        But she is coming home.
        And so I think somehow I will touch her again, warm
    her hands, and she will tell me of her adventures.
        Perhaps, after all, it is possible.

They say there will be a spring and a returning.
Perhaps all the lost ones will be called to home.
And I would like to believe it. If only for you.
My little soldier. My little Maxine.
Go to sleep.
In the morning you will go back to your life.

(*Maxine embraces Zofia. Maxine exits. Zofia stares, directly ahead.*)

Scene 25. Last

Evie hangs, as at first, over Maxine's bed.

MAXINE: There was someone who was my mother. A hand on my head, doing buttons down my back, nudging shoes onto my feet, she was . . . whoever she was, she was my mother . . . You can tell me . . . You can tell me now. Why. Why she left me.

EVIE: You don't remember.

MAXINE: No.

EVIE: I remember you. Your little eyes, always on me. What terrible luck for you, to have chosen me. As if I could have been your mother, pulled it off.

MAXINE: But you were. You did.

EVIE: Oh, I could fool myself sometimes. Sunny days, one or two, when I would watch other women, mothers hauling their children by their thin arms around the produce sections, and I'd think, oh, *that's* how it's done. I can do that, certainly. No one need know, not even you, about the black nights of sleeplessness, the screaming voices in my ears, the way my face would distort itself into the monster I knew I was when I looked up from bathing you into the fogged light of the bathroom mirror. You see, it was hopeless.

MAXINE: You could have. I loved you enough.

EVIE: It had nothing to do with love. There was not enough of a mother in me to hold you. Plant my feet like roots in dirt though I did, weight my breasts with your milk, the night would come and pluck me by the hair like a farmer rips a weed from the ground and then I was yanked high and howling once again. Even you couldn't save me from it. Circling in my terrible burning plane, oil flames licking the glass as I looked down on that cherished place where there was no landing night after night.

MAXINE: What did you see from your plane?

EVIE: There were two perfect hills, burnished and smooth, seamed with the fringe of two perfect lines: Your closed eyes, nights when I leaned over you, breathing my dragon breath on your curved cheek. The hills shudder and pulse, holding your dreams of milk and blankets. Your lashes quiver like feathers on a sleeping bird. But up above you in the black sky a plane is circling, burning badly, engine exploding, tin and glass shrieking, circling above you, far too close for comfort. Until the pilot finally pulls herself away at last, spins out into the night alone. I thought, keep me from her, God. Let me let her live.

MAXINE: I was dreaming of you.

EVIE: No doubt. And in those dreams you found a mother I could leave you with. Because I could not stay.

MAXINE: So you left me to miss you for the rest of my life.

EVIE: I knew it would be better.

MAXINE: How could you know? How could you possibly know? I have spent myself in yearning. Yearned for you, searched all my life for you without ever finding any trace of you. I have no place in the world. I am an exile, wandering around endlessly, looking for a woman I can't even remember. There is no compensation for the loss you gave me from the very beginning. None. No true comfort. Just searching. And long nights. And when I dream, I dream of you. You have destroyed me. I never had a chance.

EVIE: You have had a chance. I gave it to you. That's the only thing I've ever done. Give you that. And you do remember me. You know what I did for you.

MAXINE: I remember nothing.

EVIE: It was a particular morning. Still before light. A morning. Very much like this one. You remember.

MAXINE: I don't.

EVIE: Bad times had come again. Sleep would never come again. I had walked the floor all night long. You must have heard me.

MAXINE: I didn't.

EVIE: My teeth chattering from terror. Talking to all the others. They were all there. You must have heard us.

MAXINE: I didn't, no.

EVIE: We leaned over you once more. Breathed one last time on your perfect cheek. You must have felt it. We decided, we discussed it amongst us. There had to be a choice. And I did what I thought was the noble thing. I chose you.

(*Long pause.*)

MAXINE: I hate you.

EVIE: So I climbed up all the stairs to the top of this terrible house. Like a mountain climber. Coil of musty rope across my back. You must have heard me. Thump, thump, thump.

(*Maxine puts her hands over her ears.*)

EVIE: Stood on your grandfather's crumbling wooden chair. Threw the rope up, once, twice, at least twice. You must have heard.

MAXINE: Stop.

EVIE: It was ridiculously hard to do. Truly improbable. The chair swaying. That rotten rafter . . .

MAXINE: This isn't what I wanted to know.

EVIE: And those clumsy knots. Who knew?

MAXINE: Not this.

EVIE: Who knew it would work?

MAXINE: This is nowhere in my head.

EVIE (*vehement*): It is the center stone of the whole damn orbiting mess.

MAXINE: I would remember that.

EVIE: *Yes. You would.* Your open, open eyes.

Because you climbed those stairs too. Just like me, on your little short legs. Wearing your torn nightgown, which caught on the splinters. You remember.

MAXINE: I don't.

EVIE: Oh yes. (*Pause.*) Because you found me.

(*Pause.*)

MAXINE: I found you.

(*Pause.*)

EVIE: You found me. Of course.

MAXINE: Of course.

(*Silence.*)

EVIE: There was a window, and you turned to it after. You looked out. And then this, all these years.

(*Evie plucks at her clothes.*)

MAXINE: Look at you.

EVIE: It was the best you could do.

MAXINE (*suddenly fierce*): Go. Go, if you're going. I dressed you for travel years ago and you have gone nowhere.

EVIE: I can't. I am yours.

(*Pause.*)

MAXINE: I wish I didn't love you.

EVIE: If wishes were fishes . . .

MAXINE: Because then I wouldn't keep you anymore.

EVIE: Love?

MAXINE: Always. Still. All right. Enough. (*Maxine climbs up on the headboard of her bed. She gently pulls on her mother's foot, bringing the body slowly down. They finally stand, face-to-face, on the bed.*)

Enough.

Let me get this off you at last.

(*Maxine takes the aviator goggles, helmet and dust coat off her mother, revealing an ordinary woman in a housedress. Evie slowly collapses onto the bed, into Maxine's embrace. Maxine sits, her back against the head-board, cradling her mother in her arms.*)

EVIE: When I died, I died thinking of you. It was just the two of us. We were traveling. But we couldn't hold hands because we were flying, like birds, feathers and all, wide wings pumping through the blue. I couldn't see you, but I knew you were behind me, and I was glad because, my God, the landscape was so beautiful. Mountains like fabric puckered and plucked from a table, the glint of rivers singing their veins through the mottled green. And I knew you were seeing it too. And I was happy. I thought, well, at least I've given her something.

Because you were right behind me, coming along.

(Evie's body goes limp. Her eyes close.)

MAXINE: There is a hole in me, Mama, big as the sky. It's the hole that you made in your passage out of the world. Passage you could not make except through me. I look up and there it is, I recognize it. It's that big, Mama. I think maybe it goes on forever.

But I put you in it, winged. Because I will have you somehow, even there, even so. Even if your natural element can only be the terrible aching vastness which is your absence from me.

(Maxine is holding Evie in her arms. She lays her mother's body out on the bed carefully, then covers it. Lights up on Zofia, staring out. Charlotte, dressed in her own clothes, unbloody, appears. She and Zofia look at each other. Maxine opens her arms in a gesture of release and looks up. At that same moment, Charlotte turns her back to the audience and lifts her arms, as if taking flight. The sound of wings.)

POLISH PRONUNCIATION

Babcia ("Grandmother")
Pronounced: *Bobcha*

biedny malutki ptaszek ("poor little bird")
Pronounced: *biedneh malootki pitashek*

ciastko czekoladowe ("chocolate cake")
Pronounced: *chahstko chekolaoveh*

czarownica ("witch")
Pronounced: *charrovnitza*

masz to ve krwi ("It's in the blood")
Pronounced: *mahsh toh ve krevee*

mawa krowka ("little cow")
Pronounced: *mahwah kroovka*

ONE-ACT PLAYS

HAPPY TALKIN'

by Laura Shaine Cunningham

Happy Talkin' was first performed as a staged reading by Actors & Writers, in Olivebridge, New York, in the fall of 1999. The cast was as follows:

MELISSA	Sarah Chodoff
PHONE SOLICITORS	John Finn, Davis Hall, Shelley Wyant

The slovenly studio apartment of Melissa (Mel) Dupray. Mel is in a coma or maybe just a bad mood. She is lying in front of her TV, which has no reception. She is drinking wine, smoking, crying lightly and clicking her useless remote. On a cassette player, a tape of South Pacific *plays Mary Martin singing "I'm in love with a wonderful guy." Mel holds a cordless phone with a severed antenna. As she sniffles, drinks, smokes, she punches in the number of her best friend, Rhea.*

MEL (*into phone*): You have to re-record that message. You sound depressed. Well, it's me, Mel. I was hoping you were home. (*Gulp*) I didn't get the job. (*Sniffles*) And damn: that man, the one from Santa Fe who actually seemed normal . . . he hasn't called when he said he would, which was an hour ago. Didn't he sound normal to you? He drove a *truck;* he was in *construction* but *creative* construction. He was . . . oh I hate this word but it fit . . . so so *virile.* And so *normal.* He had been married, for five years but now suddenly his wife is brain dead. So there was a *legitimate* reason he was . . . available. He hadn't had sex in three years since she sort of expired, her brain did, anyway, during surgery, routine surgery and you know me, there's been nothing since Brad, . . . so that's four years for me . . . seven years for the two of us. You can't even imagine how great it felt when we . . . I had *forgotten.* (*Sniffs*) We had unsafe sex after the first four times which were sort of safe. . . . (*Struggles for control*) I trusted this one. His eyes. They had a kind of truthful sparkle. It couldn't have been just me. . . .

(*A beep sounds. Mel is cut off.*)

(*To the room.*) So now out of the blue, I don't get the job—and I was the logical choice to take over as instructor. Well. Call me when you get the chance. They hired *a man,* an Inuit Indian with African American roots; he was raised in foster care. He's also slightly handicapped and will have to get to class by using a ramp and the service elevator. So he was a three-for-three—three minorities for the price of one—and I'm only one minority. (*Losing a bit of control*) It's okay. (*She punches in phone number, redials.*)

We were cut off. Do you think, with Santa Fe, it could just be the time difference? That he thinks he's supposed to call me, *my* time, and I'm thinking *his* time? Then he should call any minute now . . . It's been almost two hours. Oh, shit! I hate, hate this! I swore I would never wait for a man to call!

(*She throws the cordless phone at her wall, instantly retrieves it, tries to extract the remains of the broken antenna wand. As she works on the phone, it rings in her hand.*)

(*A smile in her voice*) Hello . . . ? (*Frowns*) No, I'm not dissatisfied with my long distance carrier.

MCI REP: We're offering a special rate in your area. Eight cents a minute, to anywhere in the country, evenings and week-ends.

MEL: Is that better than what I have?

MCI REP: Oh, yes, you're paying ten cents, twenty-four hours a day with AT&T. So may we switch you over to take advantage of these savings?

MEL: Okay.

MCI REP: Very good. I'm going to transfer you to an independent company that will verify this transaction. You understand you will be recorded? Please hold the line . . .

MEL: Look. I changed my mind. I'm expecting an important call. I don't think I want to go through all this to save two cents. . . . I've had a bad day . . .

MCI REP: This will take only a moment. I see you average $346.00 a month in long distance calls, most of that to Santa

Fe . . . Shall I put that number down as your Friend or Family member?

MEL: I don't know. Yes, I guess so.

MCI REP: And your friend Rhea Katz, too? On Broadway? 212-555-4321?

MEL: Oh, yeah, Rhea, for sure. You know a lot about me . . .

MCI REP: We research our prospective customers so we can offer you the best savings. Ooops, here's our independent verifier on the line!

VERIFIER: Is this Melissa Dupray, also known as Mel, at 2234 Grand Avenue in Sunnyside, Queens? Say "yes" not "uh-huh" please.

MEL: Uh-huh. I mean "yes."

VERIFIER: And your father's name is Reginald Dupray? But he abandoned you and the family when you were only two?

MEL: Yes.

VERIFIER: Thank you. That's all we needed to know. Will you want your ex-husband, Gordon Trowbridge included in your Friends and Family?

MEL: No.

MCI REP: Welcome to MCI! You'll be receiving our convenient calling card in the mail.

(**Click.** *Mel slumps backward, still holding her phone. The cassette is now playing "Bali Ha'i."* ("Most people live on a lonely island, lost in the middle of a foggy sea.")

(*Phone* **beeps** *in her hand.*)

MEL: Hello?

AT&T REP (*hurt tone*): Hello, I'm calling from AT&T. We heard you're leaving us. May I ask "why?"

MEL (*not too involved emotionally*): They offered me two cents less per minute . . .

AT&T REP: We'll do that for you . . . Come back to us.

MEL: Eight cents a minute, twenty-four hours a day, weekends included?

AT&T REP: That's right.

MEL: I don't know. I just went to them.

AT&T REP: We'll give you a seventy-five-dollar gift certificate to cover the switchover. . . .

MEL: Okay. Just do it.

AT&T REP: *Terrific.* You've made the right decision. Please hold while I transfer you to our independent verifier.

VERIFIER: Hello, I'm speaking with Melissa Dupray. You understand you are being recorded to guarantee our excellent service. Please answer a few questions so that we may verify your order. Your birth date is . . . (*She gives today's date*) and, so, hey, today, you are thirty . . . !

MEL: Yes.

VERIFIER: And your weight is one hundred and thirty-nine pounds . . .

MEL: At night, in shoes, with clothes.

AT&T VERIFIER: Your bra size is thirty-eight B and your diaphragm is eighty millimeters . . . ?

MEL: Do you really have to know all this?

VERIFIER: We like to assure our service, be certain we know to whom we are speaking. This call is being monitored to assure quality control. You still use the diaphragm? And jelly?

MEL: Look, that's a bit personal. And I'm expecting an important call. This is tying up my line.

AT&T REP: Shall I put you down for Call Waiting? Then you won't miss that important call, while we talk.

MEL: I cannot even begin to tell you how much I loathe Call Waiting. Technical Rudeness, I call it. Everyone I know has it. I prefer to be the one who is put on hold. If I have Call Waiting too, no one will ever complete a conversation.

AT&T: You risk missing important, possibly lifesaving calls. Someone is trying to reach you now, as we speak . . .

MEL: I'll take it! Put him through!

AT&T: Thank you. You now have Call Waiting. Would you also like Star 69 so that if you have missed a call, it will ring back the party?

MEL: Yes! Yes! Just put him through . . . It's from New Mexico, isn't it?

(*A series of beeps sound.*)

SPRINT REP: Hello, we'd like to welcome you to Sprint. We're offering a special discount in your area if you sign up tonight . . .

MEL: Please! I changed twice already tonight! Please just let me alone. I'm expecting an important call . . .

SPRINT REP: Our system will offer you a lower rate than any of our competitors . . . We continually recheck, by computer, so you are always paying the lowest possible rate and we will give you an introductory gift. . . .

MEL: What—a pager?

SPRINT REP: A car. You can't get around in that old Saab much longer—it has car cancer. You think it has a hundred thousand miles on it, it's way more—the odometer was turned back when you bought it. The original owner is serving time in a minimum security prison in Pennsylvania. So less than eight cents a minute and a car?

MEL: I'm sorry, I'm exhausted from switching . . . I don't have the energy to change again and go through with another verification . . .

SPRINT REP: That makes me sad but I understand.

MEL: It's just been . . . a bad day. I swore I would never wait for a man to call again, and now I have. I even ordered Call Waiting and Star 69. I just can't do more tonight. Maybe sometime in the future . . . This has been going on so long now. . . . The first boy whom I ever loved: Larry Gold— He never called when he said, either. . . . What I don't get is— Why do they always say—"it's going to be such a wonderful summer, or such a wonderful winter"? or even "we're going to have such a great life," then they never call again . . . Why is that?

SPRINT REP: Too much at stake, maybe? I can't really answer that. But we have a brand new service, it's just come to Queens an hour ago, let me switch you over and see if they can help. Just hold one second, please . . . It will only take a second.

SPIRIT: Hello, is this Melissa Dupray? Known to her family as Missy and her friends as Mel? We will try to answer your questions. . . . (*In a rush*) Larry Gold really loved you. He just reconsidered—and decided you were too young. You were only fifteen and he was a sophomore in college. He meant every word as he hugged you and promised to call . . . he partially dialed you three times that summer, then stopped . . . You were underage. He wanted sex. He was afraid of the consequences . . . he was scared he would end up marrying you and cutting short his education and exploration of the female sex. He often dreamt of you and even dialed you once and hung up when you answered. . . . We keep records going back to '79. . . . He dialed you on an old rotary phone on June the twelfth, 1985, at 3:45 P.M.

MEL: Wow! I *am* impressed.

SPIRIT: We have access to incredibly detailed records. Do you want to know about your ex-husband Gordon now? About all the years you were married and you suspected he saw other women?

MEL: Maybe. I don't know what was harder—knowing or *not* knowing, the constant suspicion. . . .

SPIRIT: There were four other women in the New York calling area. You may be relieved to know—Gordon was unfaithful even in his infidelity: he was cheating on everyone. He never uttered a true sentence in his life. He had Call Forwarding from his office—he was seldom there. He was actually speaking to you from other women's bedrooms, bathrooms, from restaurants, bars—this went on for eleven years. . . . Shall I go on?

MEL: I'm stunned . . . but I don't know that I want that much service. Can you send it to me in writing? I am waiting for an important call . . .

SPIRIT: From Jake Dysart in Santa Fe, New Mexico? He's not going to call you.

MEL: You can't possibly know that.

SPIRIT: Not only do I know that, I can change it. You want him to call?

MEL: Uh-huh.

SPIRIT: Say "yes" please. "Uh-huh" will not record.

MEL: Yes. But why won't he call? On his own?

SPIRIT: "El Depresso" Guilt over the brain-dead wife. Right now, he's kicked back, drinking Golden Cuervo and deciding not to get involved with you. He loves you a little, enjoyed you a lot but he's afraid he will ultimately feel disloyal to Kathy, that's his wife, even though she can't possibly know. I feel they should pull the plug on Kathy and then he may feel more free . . . So may we sign you up for Spirit?

MEL: You can really do all that? *Make* him call?

SPIRIT: Anyone you want. You just give us your most popular numbers—"frequently needed but usually ungratifying." We offer a Lost Loves plan, too—Would you like to hear from Larry Gold after all these years? He's unhappily married to a dental hygienist—He still thinks of you but he has no idea of how to reach you.

MEL: Well . . . I admit, this is interesting. And how much would I save per minute?

SPIRIT: You don't save, except spiritually and emotionally. Calls from people who had no intention of calling you come in at a hundred dollars a minute. Calls from people from your past are a bit less, late at night and on weekends. I won't try to talk you into this . . . maybe you like things the way they are . . . ?

MEL: No! Sign me up. Switch me over. I don't care what it costs!

SPIRIT: Alright, we'll transfer your service from AT&T; hold for the independent verifier. . . .

VERIFIER: You really can't go on, can you?

MEL: Uh-hunh. I mean—"No"—yes, I need someone, something, I have to connect. . . .

SPIRIT: You're on. You're signing up for Needed Calling. . . .

(*There is an intrusive **clicking** on the line.*)

MEL: I think that's my Call Waiting . . . Someone's trying to get through. . . . (*She presses for Call Waiting.*)

MCI: We offer Friends and Family . . . We can *make* them become Friends and Family, too . . . A hundred dollars to switch back?

(**Click, click,** *another Call Waiting.*)

AT&T: Not if they never called her . . .

(**Click, click,** *another Call Waiting.*)

SPIRIT: Give us a chance. . . .

MEL: Oy, now I don't know. . . .

SPIRIT: We just need to verify it. . . .

VERIFIER: You wake up at 3:00 A.M. and wonder: What's it all
for? Your heart pounds, and aches . . . You're so scared, you
don't know if you want to go on . . . the words "to be or
not to be?" pass through your mind, glowing like the neon
on your alarm clock . . . Why bother? More heartache, after
heartache, disappointment and despair, culminating ultimately and eventually in deterioration and death?

MEL: Uh-huh.

VERIFIER: We need to hear a yes.

OTHER OPERATORS, MCI, AT&T: No! No! Come to me! Come
to me!

(South Pacific *tape plays:* "Here am I, your special island! Come to
me, come to me!" **Click, click,** *as Call Waiting continues to interrupt.*)

MEL: I don't know. . . .

OPERATORS: Come to me! Come to me!

(*Music:* "Happy talk, keep talkin' happy talk, Talk about things you'd
like to do. You gotta have a dream, If you don't have a dream, How you
gonna have a dream come true?" The phone **beeps** in her hand.)

MEL: (*picking up with a beatific smile*) Hello . . . darling!

OPERATORS: Oh, baby.

MEL, OPERATORS: Yes, yes. Yes!

(**Music swells**.)

LOST

by Mary Louise Wilson

Lost was first performed at Actors & Writers, in Olivebridge, New York, on November 11, 2000, with the playwright directing the following cast:

HELEN   Mary Louise Wilson

ALICE   Carol Morley

Two women of uncertain age: Helen and Alice, old, old friends. Helen is on one of her routine weekend visits at Alice's. A bare stage except for two chairs set together stage left or right of center, representing the car.

HELEN: All set?

ALICE: All set.

HELEN: Okay, you lock, I'll ring for the elevator.

ALICE: Wait. I can't find my keys.

HELEN: You just had them in your hand.

ALICE: I had them when I went to get my water bottle.

HELEN: Retrace your steps.

ALICE: I came out of the bedroom. . . .

HELEN: Did you leave them on the bed?

ALICE: . . . Then I went back into the bedroom. . . .

HELEN: Under the bed?

ALICE: . . . I couldn't remember what I had come in there for. . . .

HELEN: Did you check the sofa cushions?

ALICE: . . . So I came back out.

HELEN: Did you look in the john?

ALICE: Now why would I take them in there?

HELEN: I'm sure I wouldn't know.

ALICE: I went to the kitchen to get my water bottle—

HELEN: I always leave my keys in the same place.

ALICE: Here they are! In the fridge!

HELEN: Well of course.

ALICE: OK! All ready. Let's go.

HELEN: Wait a minute, my glasses.

ALICE: Where are they?

HELEN: I had them.

ALICE: You were just wearing them.

HELEN: Was I?

ALICE: I think so.

HELEN: I must have put them down when I was in the bedroom.

ALICE: Did you leave them on the bureau?

HELEN: I wasn't anywhere near the bureau.

ALICE: Why would you take them off?

HELEN: I don't know. I'm blind as a wall without them.

ALICE: That's probably why you can't see where you put them.

HELEN: Oh for heaven's sake! I'm wearing them.

ALICE: Of course. I'm so used to you with them on I didn't notice.

HELEN: I think *you* may need glasses.

ALICE: Shall we?

HELEN: You lock, I'll get the elevator.

ALICE: Righto. All locked.

HELEN: Here comes the elevator.

ALICE: Hold it! My water bottle.

HELEN: We're going to be late.

ALICE: I can't go without my water bottle.

HELEN: Well go get it, but hurry.

ALICE: What did I do with the keys?

HELEN: In your hand.

ALICE: I'll only be a second.

HELEN (*calling*): The elevator's here!

ALICE (*calling*): Okay, okay, keep your shirt on.

HELEN: Get in. I can't hold this door any longer.

ALICE: It's a good thing I went back, someone left the stove on.

HELEN: I'm starving.

ALICE: Me too.

HELEN: Push "G."

ALICE: Do I look overdressed?

HELEN: No. Do I look too casual?

ALICE: No. (*Small pause.*) Although I would not have worn my
house slippers.

HELEN: Oh my God!! We have to go back.

ALICE: We're going to be late.

HELEN: Well, I can't go to lunch in my house slippers, Alice!

ALICE: Okay, but run. Runrunrun.

HELEN: I'll need the keys.

ALICE: Well I don't have them, Helen.

HELEN: Well where are they?

ALICE: I don't know!

HELEN: Look at that! You left the keys in the door.

ALICE: So I did.

HELEN: We could have been robbed!

ALICE: Oh, now—

HELEN: Someone could have waltzed right in and—

ALICE: All right, all right, I'm holding the elevator. Go! Go go go. (*Sings to herself "Embrace me, my sweet—umhummm— umhummm—you."*)

HELEN: Found my shoes!

ALICE: Great. Get in.

HELEN: These are the shoes I got in London.

ALICE: How was London? I forgot to ask you.

HELEN: I forgot to tell you! London was fabulous! And— Oh, Oh, Oh! I saw a *thrilling* production at the National of—that classic, oh you know, that Russian play—

ALICE: I know the one you mean, it's coming to Broadway with whatshername.

HELEN: It was the most *emotional* evening I've ever had in the theatre. It's an incredibly deep play. There's this scene—this man is very unhappy and he has this wrenching speech— God! It was life changing. Devastating!

ALICE: Do you remember what the speech was about?

HELEN: No.

ALICE: The title is something with birds in it.

HELEN: The lead was— Oh, damn—oh that actor—you know who I mean—

ALICE: Not birds. It's something to do with fish.

HELEN: What the hell is that actor's name?

ALICE: Here we are. Garage level.

HELEN: It's on the tip of my brain.

ALICE: Here's the car.

HELEN: He was so brilliant in that movie, oh, you know the one, what was it called. . . . It was so good, it took place in Ireland. Scotland. Ireland. You saw it. We saw it together!

ALICE: No we didn't. I didn't see it.

HELEN: Yes you did! He plays a gay bus driver who lives with his sister and he wants to be like—oh, that fat playwright—you know the famous wit that got arrested—

ALICE: I can't unlock the car.

HELEN: That is so maddening, what was the name of that film?

ALICE: I can't understand it.

HELEN: Have you got the right key?

ALICE: What is all that stuff in the backseat?

HELEN: We're going to be late.

ALICE: Wait a minute, this isn't my car!

HELEN: Oh for pity's sake.

ALICE: Here it is.

(*They sit in the chairs.*)

HELEN: OK, let's go.

ALICE: I was wondering what all that stuff was doing in the backseat.

HELEN: What were we talking about?

ALICE: When?

HELEN: Just now. We were talking about something—

ALICE: You mean in the apartment?

HELEN: No, just now.

ALICE: Keys? Water bottle? Lunch?

HELEN: Something to do with birds.

ALICE: That actor. What is that actor's name? It begins with a "J." John. James.

HELEN: Jeremy.

ALICE: Albert?

HELEN: Not Albert. That's not an actor's name.

ALICE: How do you know?

HELEN: I know theatre.

ALICE: Well I know theatre too. I'm always going to New York.

HELEN: Turn right at the lights and— Right! Right! Turn right!

ALICE: I thought you said left.

HELEN: I said right. Go up here— Did you see that?

ALICE: What?

HELEN: You didn't see that bird fly by?

ALICE: What bird?

HELEN: A big beige bird flew right in front of the window.

ALICE: I didn't see a bird.

HELEN: Well something flew by, a big beige something.

ALICE: What the hell is that man doing?

HELEN: I can't believe you didn't see it.

ALICE: He's pointing, he's running after us.

HELEN: Stop the car. Stop the car.

ALICE: What is he saying?

HELEN: I'm getting out. Oh my God!

ALICE: What?

HELEN: My purse! He's got my purse! I must have left it on the car roof!

ALICE: Oh for heaven's sake! Thank you, sir, thanks so much. Get in.

HELEN: It must have slid off when you made that turn.

ALICE: Right. Now. Which way?

HELEN: That way.

ALICE: Are you sure?

HELEN: What do the directions say?

ALICE: What directions?

HELEN: You had directions, didn't you?

ALICE: I thought you had them.

HELEN: Why would you think that?

ALICE: Because you keep telling me which way to go.

HELEN: Well, I'm pretty sure this is the right way.

ALICE: What were we talking about?

HELEN: I have no idea.

ALICE: Birds. Shoes. London!

HELEN: London!

ALICE: In my opinion, London can't hold a candle to Paris.

HELEN: Paris!

ALICE: The food, the museums . . . I went to the, uh—the, uh—the big one—

HELEN (*incredulous*): The Louvre?

ALICE: The Louvre! The paintings I just fell in love with were the, uh—you know, the—

HELEN: The Renoirs. The Degas.

ALICE: No. No, the—

HELEN: The Cezannes. The Matisses. The Monets. The Manets.

ALICE: The, uh— Oh he does the ladies, with the hats, you know, sitting in bathtubs—

HELEN: I give up.

ALICE: Where are we?

HELEN: Uh—the sign says "Nepenthe."

ALICE: I've never heard of Nepenthe Street.

HELEN: I don't think we're in the city anymore.

ALICE: Where are we going again?

HELEN: I haven't a clue.

ALICE: God it's dark in here.

HELEN: It's spooky. Is it going to rain suddenly?

ALICE: I can hardly see.

HELEN: Look out!

ALICE: Hold on!

HELEN: We're off the road!

(*The car goes over an embankment, rolls over three times before coming to rest on its roof.*)

ALICE and HELEN together: Umphph.
Oomphph.
Uuunhhh.

Anhnhn.
UNNHHN.
OWWWWW!

(*Silence.*)

HELEN: Alice?

ALICE: Yes.

HELEN: We're upside down.

ALICE: I know. (*Pause.*) Helen?

HELEN: Yes?

ALICE: Albert Finney.

HELEN: Albert Finney! (*Pause.*) *A Man of No Importance!*

ALICE: I don't agree.

HELEN: No. *A Man of No Importance.* That was the film he was in.

ALICE: Oh. (*Suddenly remembering*) Oh! The fat wit that got arrested was Oscar Wilde.

HELEN: Oscar Wilde! "Ignorance is like a delicate exotic fruit; touch it and the bloom is gone."

ALICE: "To lose one parent, Mr. Worthing, may be regarded as a misfortune; to lose both looks like carelessness."

(*Brief silence.*)

HELEN: *The Seagull!*

ALICE: *The Seagull!* I knew it had something to do with fish.

HELEN: This is marvelous. Can you name the capital cities of the fifty-two United States?

ALICE: No problemo . . . Albany, Annapolis, Atlanta, Augusta, Austin, Baton Rouge, Bismarck, Boise, Boston— BON-NARD!

HELEN: Bonnard?

ALICE: Ladies in hats and bathtubs. Bonnard.

HELEN: Alice, if Jim is swimming to Saint Louis at thirty minutes a mile against the current which is two miles an hour, and Bob is bicycling alongside at twenty miles a minute and the distance is two miles, who gets there first, Jim or Bob?

ALICE: Bob. He beats Jim by five and three-tenths of a second.

HELEN: (*starts to giggle*): Do you remember the one about the man who comes into the bar and asks for a beer for his kangaroo?

ALICE: Yeah! "I left my wallet in my other pouch." (*They both start to giggle furiously.*)

HELEN: That reminds me of the one about the two nuns who run over a penguin—

ALICE (*huge gasp*): You BITCH! You JUDAS!

HELEN: What? What?

ALICE: You stole Jimmy Felton from me!

HELEN: Jimmy Felton . . . Your boyfriend?

ALICE: It's all coming back to me. I was in the bathroom and when I came out you were sitting on Jimmy's lap—

HELEN: Ohmy. Jimmy had red hair—

ALICE: —and he had his hand on your titty—you didn't think I saw you but I did (*starts to weep*).

HELEN: Alice. That was third grade.

ALICE: I cried myself to sleep for two weeks.

HELEN: Let's get out of here.

ALICE: I felt so betrayed. You were my best friend.

HELEN: Come on. We can crawl out of this window.

ALICE: We had our club, "The Betty Grables"—remember? No one else was allowed to join.

HELEN: Come on, give me your hand. I'm still your friend. We've always been best friends. We always will be.

ALICE: We had matching pompadours, remember?

HELEN (*pulls Alice up to her feet*): Alley-oop!

ALICE: Ah! Boy, it feels good to be right side up. What happened?

HELEN: I haven't the foggiest.

ALICE: Where's my purse? Oh God, did I leave it somewhere?

HELEN: You just had it in your hand.

ALICE: I had it when we were in the elevator—

HELEN: Retrace your steps.

(*They stagger offstage together.*)

ALICE: I went back into the apartment—

HELEN: Wait a minute, my left shoe is missing.

ALICE: I came out of the apartment—

HELEN: Where the hell is my shoe?

MEDEA

by Christopher Durang and
Wendy Wasserstein

Medea was cowritten by Chris Durang and Wendy Wasserstein for the Juilliard School's Drama Division's twenty-fifth anniversary, April 25, 1994, at the Juilliard Theater, New York City. The evening was produced by Margot Harley. It was directed by Gerald Gutierrez; the choreography was by Christopher Chadman; and the musical direction was by Tom Fay. The cast for the evening consisted of many Juilliard graduates. For this particular sketch the cast was as follows:

MEDEA	Harriet Harris
THE CHORUS	Laura Linney, Diane Venora, Denise Woods
JASON	Kevin Spacey
MESSENGER	Randle Mell
ANGEL EX MACHINA	David Schramm

CHARACTERS

MEDEA:	an angry woman
THE CHORUS:	the chorus
JASON:	Medea's husband
MESSENGER	
ANGEL	

The actress who is to play Medea comes out and makes the following introduction.

ACTRESS: Hello. I am she who will be Medea. That is, I shall play the heroine from that famous Greek tragedy by Euripides for you.

I attended a first-rate School of Dramatic Arts. At this wonderful school, I had classical training, which means we start at the very beginning, a very good place to start. Greek tragedy. How many of you in the audience have ever acted in Greek tragedy? How many of your lives are Greek tragedy? Is Olympia Dukakis here this evening?

As an actress who studied the classics, one of the first things you learn in drama school is that there are more roles for men than for women. This is a wonderful thing to learn because it is true of the real world as well. Except for *Thelma and Louise.* At drama school, in order to compensate for this problem, the women every year got to act in either *The Trojan Women* or *The House of Bernarda Alba.* This prepared us for bit parts on *Designing Women* and *Little House on the Prairie.* Although these shows are canceled now, and we have nothing to do.

Tonight, we would like to present to you a selection from one of the most famous Greek tragedies ever written, *The Trojan Women.* Our scene is directed by Michael Cacoyannis and choreographed by June Taylor. And now, translated from the Greek by George Stephanopoulous, here is a scene from this terrifying tragedy. (*Names the cast members*) ———, ——— and ——— will play the Chorus. ——— and ——— will play the men.

(*Dramatically*) And I, ———, will play Medea. (*The actress playing Medea exits with purpose and panache. Enter the three actresses who play the Chorus. They are dressed in togas. Most of the time they speak in unison. Sometimes they speak solo lines. In the style of the piece, they are over-dramatic and over-wrought.*

But most of the time they should act their lines as if they are the words from genuine Greek tragedy, full of intonation and emotional feeling. Don't send them up or wink at the audience. Let the juxta-position of Greek tragedy acting style and the sometimes silly lines be what creates the humor.)

CHORUS (*in unison*):
> So pitiful, so pitiful
> your shame and lamentation.
> No more shall I move the shifting pace
> of the shuttle at the looms of Ida.

CHORUS MEMBER #3 (*echoes*):
> Looms of Ida.

CHORUS:
> Can you not, Queen Hecuba, stop this Bacchanal before her light feet whirl her away into the Argive camp?

CHORUS MEMBER #3 (*echoes*):
> Argive camp.

CHORUS (*in unison*):
> O woe, o woe, o woe,
> We are so upset we speak in unison,
> So pitiful, so wretched, so doomed,
> Women who run with wolves
> Women who love too much,
> Whitewater rapids, how did she turn $1000 into $100,000?
> O woe, o woe, o woe.
> Here she comes now.
> Wooga, wooga, wooga.

(*Enter Medea in a dramatic, bloodred toga. She is in high, excessive grief and fury.*)

MEDEA:
> Come, flame of the sky,
> Pierce through my head!
> What do I, Medea, gain from living any longer?

Oh I hate living! I want
to end my life, leave it behind, and die.

CHORUS (*in unison; chanted seriously*):
But tell us how you're really feeling.

MEDEA: My husband Jason—the Argonaut—has left me for
another woman. Debbie.

CHORUS (*in unison*):
Dreaded Debbie, dreaded Debbie.
Debutante from hell.

MEDEA: She is the daughter of King Creon, who owns a diner
on Fifty-fifth Street and Jamaica Avenue. Fie on her! And
the House of Creon! And the four brothers of the Acropolis.
   I am banished from my husband's bed, and from the
country. A bad predicament all around. But I am skilled in
poison. Today three of my enemies I will strike down dead:
Debbie and Debbie's father and my husband.

CHORUS (*in unison*):
Speaking of your husband, here he comes.

(*Enter Jason, dressed in a toga but also with an armored breastplate and
wearing a soldier's helmet with a nice little red adornment on top. Sort of
like a costume from either* Ben Hur *or* Cleopatra. *He perhaps is not in
the grand style, but sounds more normal and conversational.*)

JASON: Hello, Medea.

MEDEA: Hello, Jason.

JASON: I hear you've been banished to China.

MEDEA (*suddenly Noel Coward brittle*): Very large, China.

JASON: And Japan?

MEDEA: Very small, Japan. And Debbie?

JASON: She's very striking.

MEDEA: Some women should be struck regularly like gongs.

JASON: Medea, even though thou art banished by Creon to foreign shores, the two innocent children of our loins, Lyle and Erik, should remain with me. I will enroll them at the Dalton School. And there they will flourish as citizens of Corinth under the watchful eye of Zeus and his lovely and talented wife Hera.

MEDEA: Fine, walk on me some more! I was born unlucky and a woman.

CHORUS (*in unison*):
Men are from Mars, women are from Venus.

JASON: Well, whatever. I call the gods to witness that I have done my best to help you and the children.

MEDEA: Go! You have spent too long out here. You are consumed with craving for your newly-won bride, Debbie. Go, enjoy Debbie! (*Jason shrugs, exits.*) O woe, o woe. I am in pain for I know what I must do. Debbie, kill for sure.

CHORUS (*in unison*):
Debbie's done, ding dong, Debbie's done.
Done deal, Debbie dead.
Dopey Debbie, Debbie dead.

MEDEA: But also my sons. Never shall their father see them again. I shall kill my children. (*Ferociously, to the Chorus*) How do you like that????

CHORUS (*in unison*):
Aaaaaaagghghghghghghghgghhhhh!
O smart women, foolish choices.
Stop the insanity! Stop the insanity!
You can eat one slice of cheese, or sixteen baked potatoes!
Make up your mind.

MEDEA: Why is there so little *Trojan Women* in this, and so much of me?

CHORUS (*in unison*):

> We don't know *The Trojan Women* as well as we know *Medea*.
> (Spoken, not sung)
> Medea, we just met a girl named Medea.
> And suddenly that name
> Will never be the same.

MEDEA: Bring my children hither.

CHORUS (*in unison*):

> O miserable mother, to destroy your own increase, murder the
> babes of your body. The number you have reached is not in serv-
> ice at this time. Call 777-FILM.

MEDEA (*in a boiling fury*): I want to kill my children. I want to
sleep with my brother. I want to pluck out the eyes of my
father. I want to blow up the Parthenon. I need a creative
outlet for all this anger. (*Enter the Messenger, carrying a head.
He kneels before Medea.*)

MESSENGER: I am a messenger. Caesar is dead.

CHORUS: (*in unison*):

> Caesar is dead. How interesting. Who is Caesar?

MESSENGER: I am sorry. Wrong message. (*Reads from piece of
paper*) Lady Teazle wishes you to know that Lady Winder-
mere and Lady Bracknell are inviting you and Lady The-
Scottish-Play to tea with her cousin Ernest, if he's not
visiting Mr. Bunbury.

MEDEA: Mr. Bunbury? I do not need a messenger. I need a deus
ex machina. (*Elaborate music. Enter an Angel with great big wings.
Descending from the ceiling or revealed on a balcony. Or dragging a
step ladder that he stands on. Very dramatic whatever he does.*)

ANGEL: O Medea, O Medea.

> I am a deus ex machina.
> In a bigger production, I would come down from the sky
> in an angel's outfit, but just use your imagination. Theatre is
> greatly about imagination, is it not.

I am an angel.

I I I I I I I, yi yi yi.

I I I I am the Bird of Greek Tragedy.

Do not kill your children. Do not sleep with your brother. Rein in your rage, and thank Zeus. I come with glad tidings. Debbie is no more a threat. She's been cast in a series. She has a running part on *Home Improvements*.

CHORUS (*in unison*):
Home Improvements.

ANGEL: Jason will return to you. He sees the error of his ways. He has been lobotomized.

CHORUS (*in unison*):
O fortunate woman, to whom Zeus has awarded a docile husband.

MEDEA: O, deus ex machina, o angel:
O Hecuba, oh, looms of Ida.

CHORUS (*in unison*):
Ida Ida Ida Ida.

MEDEA: I am eternally grateful to you.

CHORUS (*in unison*):
The things we thought would happen do not happen.
The unexpected, God makes possible.

(*Spoken, not sung*)

The camptown races sing a song,
Do da, do da.

CHORUS AND MEDEA (*switch to singing now*):
Medea's happy the whole day long.
Oh the do da day!
Things will be just fine.
Things will be just great
No need to kill her children now,
Oh the do da . . .

(*big musical coda:*)

> *Oh the do da,*
> *Zeus and Buddha,*
> *They're as nice as*
> *Dionysus,*
> *Oh the do da*
> *Work it through da*
> *Oh the do da, do da, do da Day!*

(*Medea and the Chorus and the Angel strike a happy and triumphant pose.*)

NO SHOULDER

by Nina Shengold

No Shoulder was first presented as a staged reading at Actors & Writers in October 1999, with Shelley Wyant and Nicole Baptiste Quinn in the cast, and was a finalist for Actors Theatre of Louisville's Heideman Award. The play premiered on May 3, 2000, at Stage Works, Hudson, New York, as part of the Ten By Ten Festival, with Deena Pewtherer directing the following cast:

RUTH   Giulia Pagano
BOBBIE   Danielle Skraastad

CHARACTERS

RUTH DANSON: Thirty-nine, high-strung, haunted eyes
BOBBIE: Unkempt, waifish, startlingly young

SETTING:

Bare stage with four chairs representing the front and back seats of a car. Near-dark, with surrealistic suggestion of dashboard glow, headlights.

A deserted stretch of the Pacific Coast Highway in western Washington, way after midnight. Ruth Danson sips cold take-out coffee, struggling to stay awake by surfing through radio channels. We hear fragments of country and pop, an evangelist, a deejay announcing the "Night-Owl Request Line."

Loud squeal of brakes, angry honk, and the low-angled swoop of twin headlights: an oncoming truck.

RUTH: Jesus!

(*She swerves back into her own lane, then, startled, pulls over. Heart pounding, she snaps off the radio. Bobbie appears from the darkness beside her car. She is dragging a knapsack. Her wet hair clings.*)

BOBBIE: Hey. Where you headed?

RUTH: I almost ran over you.

BOBBIE: Yeah, well. You missed.

RUTH: You shouldn't be hitching at night. It's too dangerous.

BOBBIE: Tell me about it. That how come you stopped?

RUTH: At least get a flashlight. (*Bobbie holds one up.*)

BOBBIE: The battery died. Soaked, probably. Where're you going?

RUTH (*after a beat pause*): Forks.

BOBBIE: Cool, me too! (*Off Ruth's hesitation*) Cut me a break, it is *pouring.*

RUTH: Get in. (*Bobbie starts to climb into the backseat.*) What do I look like, a taxi? You might as well sit with me.

BOBBIE: You sure? 'Cause it's been like a while since I had a bath.

RUTH: I've got the worst allergies ever. Pine pollen. I can't smell a thing.

BOBBIE: We're made for each other. (*She climbs in. Ruth looks at her.*)

RUTH: Seat belt. (*Bobbie rolls her eyes. Ruth doesn't budge. Bobbie sighs, hauls on the shoulder belt.*)

BOBBIE: So how old are *your* kids?

RUTH: I don't have any kids.

BOBBIE: No shit. You sound just like my mom.

RUTH: Is that good or bad?

BOBBIE: Take a wild flying guess.

RUTH: You don't get along.

BOBBIE: She should never've had me and blames her whole fucking life on me, but other than that, we get along fine. (*Beat pause.*) It's her birthday tomorrow. I hope she's not dead.

RUTH (*startled, concerned*): Is she sick?

BOBBIE: No. People die.

RUTH: How long since you've seen her?

BOBBIE: Two years.

RUTH: Two *years?*

BOBBIE: You know something, I'm fucking soaked here. Have you got a cigarette?

RUTH: I just quit.

BOBBIE: Fuck. (*After a beat.*) Would you buy me one?

RUTH: Where? We've got forty miles of nothing but clearcuts and Doug fir ahead of us. Middle of nowhere.

BOBBIE: Tell me about it. I thought I was gonna grow moss. (*Beat.*) When we get to that truck stop in Queets, would you score me a pack?

RUTH: You shouldn't be smoking. How old are you anyway?

BOBBIE: Nineteen.

RUTH: Do I look like a moron?

BOBBIE (*rote, bored with the question*): I just turned eighteen.

RUTH: Quit now while you can. It gets harder.

BOBBIE: You should've had kids. You've got mother all over you.

RUTH: Thank you.

BOBBIE: That wasn't a compliment, coming from me.

(*Pause. Ruth drives.*)

RUTH: I've got two Springers. (*Off Bobbie's look*) Dogs.

BOBBIE: Uh-huh. Dogs you can train.

RUTH: Not *my* dogs.

BOBBIE: Dogs you can leave at the pound. (*She stares out the window.*)

RUTH: What makes you so sure that your mom didn't want you?

BOBBIE: She told me like five times a day. We don't get along so hot 'cause of some shit that went down when I was still living with her and this mill-rat boyfriend she had that month. But now she sounds into it, me coming up for a visit. Things can change in two years, I mean, I don't know, maybe.

RUTH: Where do you live now?

BOBBIE: Your car. (*Off Ruth's look*) Look, can I sit here, okay? Like just sit?

RUTH: Yes, of course you can.

BOBBIE: No offense or nothing. I'm just, I'm burned out. I been up for two days. I would kill for a cigarette.

RUTH: Sorry.

(*They drive on in silence. Bobbie looks over at Ruth, then back at the windshield.*)

BOBBIE: Coos Bay. With my asshole ex-father. Where do *you* live?

RUTH: We don't have to talk.

BOBBIE: Somewhere back east, right?

RUTH: It's fine with me. Really.

BOBBIE: New York.

RUTH (*surprised and pleased*): How'd you know that?

BOBBIE: I'm real good at accents.

RUTH: But I wasn't . . . Have I got a New York accent?

BOBBIE: Just a few words. (*Beat.*) And your luggage tag.

RUTH: Oh.

BOBBIE: Hitching rule number one: Case the car out before you get in.

RUTH: You hitchhike a lot?

BOBBIE: Only when I want to get someplace. My boyfriend, he had a Camaro but it kind of died and besides we broke up, so I, yeah.

RUTH: You shouldn't take that kind of chance.

BOBBIE: *I'm* taking chances? Hey, you're the one stopped. I'm just here. (*She pats her knapsack, menacing.*) I could be packing an Uzi in here. Like that kid who mowed down his whole algebra class. You don't know shit about anyone, ever.

RUTH: No. You don't. (*She drives. Pause.*) God, I forgot how it rains out here. Sideways. Like spit.

BOBBIE: Seattle sunshine.

RUTH: Tacoma tan. Average rainfall: yes. I remember them all.

BOBBIE: So you *are* from around here.

RUTH: Not anymore.

BOBBIE: Where'd you move to New York from?

RUTH (*after a beat*): Forks.

BOBBIE: No kidding. My mom is from Forks.

RUTH: So you told me.

BOBBIE: Small world, huh?

(*Ruth smears at the windshield.*)

RUTH: Petite.

BOBBIE: A petite fucking world. So you just get divorced?

RUTH: How the hell do you know that?

(*Bobbie points at her left hand.*)

BOBBIE: Line where the ring was. Feel-better French manicure
    chewed all to shit. Plus you're driving through Nowhere's
    Ass, Washington, all by yourself on a Saturday night. I don't
    get an image of marital bliss. Am I wrong?

RUTH: Yes. (*Beat.*) I didn't divorce him. He died.

BOBBIE: Shit. I'm sorry.

RUTH: I would have divorced him, though. Sooner or later.
    (*Looks at her.*) Nobody talks about that part. You wish
    they were dead, then they are. Puts your head through the
    wringer.

BOBBIE: I guess.

(*Ruth does a detailed mime of inhaling a cigarette. Bobbie looks at her,
startled.*)

RUTH: My hairdresser taught me this. Air cigarette. It might look
    insane, but it helps.

BOBBIE: Whatever butters your roll.

RUTH: I've tried it all. Ear staples, nicotine gum, the patch. I'm telling you, quit while you're young.

BOBBIE: You're doing your thing again. How come you never had kids?

RUTH (*after a beat*): It was never the right time.

BOBBIE: Hey. Didn't stop *my* mom.

RUTH: I couldn't get pregnant.

BOBBIE: You're not missing much. It's the pits.

(*Ruth looks at her, shocked.*)

RUTH: You've been pregnant?

BOBBIE: It happens.

RUTH: How old did you say you are?

BOBBIE: Old enough.

RUTH: Hardly.

BOBBIE: Yeah, well. Tell the asshole who did me.

RUTH: What happened to the baby?

BOBBIE: What baby? It got taken care of. No biggie.

RUTH (*chilled*): I see.

(*Longish pause. She drives, tense.*)

BOBBIE: You're not Right to Life or like—

RUTH: No.

BOBBIE: Because I got a right to *my* life.

RUTH: I agree.

BOBBIE: I mean why should I have some creep's baby just because he stuck his thing in my body? It's not like I asked him. I did what I had to, got rid of it. Just like my mom should've done to me.

RUTH: Maybe she couldn't.

BOBBIE: Bullshit, it was legal back then.

RUTH: No. Maybe she *couldn't*. Maybe she felt you moving inside her.

BOBBIE: By the time she found out, I'm the size of a lima bean. How's she gonna be feeling that move?

RUTH: Maybe she knew she'd be thinking about you the rest of her life. That she'd live to regret it.

BOBBIE: Regret's ass. You did or you didn't, and don't waste my time. I've been through some serious shit, but I'm not gonna walk around sniveling poor little me. You wipe up the blood and get back on the pavement, you stay on your *feet* if you wanna get by. I was back on the street two hours later. I didn't tell nobody.

RUTH: Neither did I. (*Off Bobbie's look*) I had one. A long time ago.

BOBBIE: You told me you couldn't get pregnant.

RUTH: I can't. That was it. I've never told . . . anyone, actually. I lied to my husband. To all the fertility doctors. I don't know what made me . . .

BOBBIE: Your secret is safe with me. Honest.

RUTH: It feels like a lifetime ago. When I moved to New York, no one knew me. No reason to rake all that up. A clean slate. (*Beat pause.*) Maybe it's being back here, in the dark, in the rain, in the goddamn woods. He was a logger. He said.

BOBBIE: Hit and run?

RUTH: I will think of that man every day till I die. (*She looks over at Bobbie.*) I was twenty-three. She would be, I suppose, around your age now.

BOBBIE: She? You found out the sex?

RUTH: I just knew. (*Pause. She picks up her purse with one hand, fumbles through it, and hauls out a packet of cigarettes.*)

BOBBIE: You quit, huh?

RUTH: Yeah, well. (*She takes out the last cigarette, lights it, takes a deep drag. Then hands it to Bobbie, who drags on it fervently.*)

BOBBIE: Oh man. Nothing like it.

RUTH: I *am* gonna quit, though.

BOBBIE: Uh-huh, right. Next lifetime. (*She exhales, blowing smoke rings.*)

RUTH: Give that back to me.

BOBBIE: Yes, mother.

RUTH: I *could* be your mother.

BOBBIE: No way would my mother be driving this car. Infiniti, right?

RUTH: It's a rental.

BOBBIE: No way would my mother be renting. If she ever got it together to take her ass somewheres, fat chance, you can bet she'd be hogging two seats on the Trailway bus.

RUTH: How old are you really?

BOBBIE: Sixteen in July

(*Ruth looks at her, shaken.*)

RUTH: July what?

BOBBIE: The third of July. I was s'posed to be born on the Fourth, my mom couldn't even get *that* right. I woulda had fireworks every damn birthday.

RUTH: That's when I was . . .

BOBBIE: What?

RUTH: When my baby was due. (*They look at each other, both spooked.*) So I really *could* be . . .

BOBBIE: Weird. Too weird. (*Ruth stubs out the cigarette, staring at her with obsessive intensity.*)

RUTH: I can see him in you. He had reddish-brown hair. Those same flecks of gold in his eyes. (*She reaches a shaky and tentative hand towards Bobbie's face. Bobbie stares back at Ruth's eyes.*)

BOBBIE: My mom, if she hadn't got fat . . . (*Suddenly she jerks forward in terror.*) Watch it!

RUTH: Jesus! (*Angry loud horn, swoop of low-angled headlights. Ruth grabs for the steering wheel, swerving exactly as she did before. Blackout to pin spot on Ruth. She speaks to the audience.*)

RUTH: This rumor you've heard, that the moment before you're about to die, you see your whole life flash in front of your eyes? It's bullshit. I know. I've looked at the front of an eighteen-wheel semi so close that the headlights were jewelry. It isn't the life that you led that you see. It's the life that you missed.

(*A second pin spot illuminates Bobbie, like the glare of two oncoming headlights. Ruth and Bobbie look at each other in full recognition. Ruth offers her hand. Bobbie takes it. They look at each other a moment, then turn toward the windshield. Squeal of brakes. Flash of white light.*)

MONOLOGUES

BLOWN SIDEWAYS THROUGH LIFE

by Claudia Shear

Blown Sideways Through Life premiered at New York Theatre Workshop (James C. Nicola, artistic director) on September 21, 1993. Christopher Ashley directed; the set was by Roy Arcenas; the costumes were by Jess Goldstein; the lighting was by Christopher Akerlind; the sound was by Aural Fixation; original music was by Richard Peaslee; the choreography was by Mafisa Charriff; the production stage manager was Kate Broderick. Claudia Shear starred.

Before writing and starring in this one-woman show, Claudia Shear worked at sixty-four different jobs, including janitor, waitress, nude model, and phone girl in a whorehouse. After describing some of her more memorable day gigs, she offers this credo.

"Pink Doughnut"

I'm standing on line at one of those doughnut places in New York's Penn Station, marking time, waiting for a train, wanting an iced coffee. In front of me is a guy—tall, fair, handsome, so I notice him. He's carrying a Lands' End bag with that tennis-racket-pocket thing. I'm perusing the doughnuts, watching him out of the corner of my eye, amused because I love watching grown-ups order treats, hearing men's deep voices saying things like "Uh, no, I want the pink one with the sprinkles, please." I look up as he suddenly throws money on the counter, half the small change bouncing to the floor. The small Hispanic woman who has been helping him flinches, and that does it for me. That flinch. That blink of fear, the twist of the mouth that is the insult finding its mark.

"Why did you do that?" I can't help myself.

"Do you know how much they charge for coffee and a doughnut here?"

"So? She works here, for godsake! She works here in *Penn Station!* She probably works for minimum wage under the horrible lights of Penn Station and you're catching a train to go away for the weekend with a tennis racket and you're *throwing* money at her?"

"Uh, it's really expensive." He turns his back to me and starts to walk away.

"You overprivileged fat-assed white motherfucker!"

Back he turns. "I don't appreciate your attitude." The muscles in his cheek are twitching.

Quietly, my teeth clicking, I say, "Have you no shame? Have you no perspective?"

He walks away and I'm left, as always, with the adrenaline like pus in my stomach while the people in the place glance at me, then look furtively away. But the woman behind the counter looks directly at me.

"Thanks," she mouths silently.

Leaving, I pass by a table filled with Puerto Rican drug dealers and the white women who love them.

"C'mere!" They call me over. "C'mere. C'mere!"

"What?"

"Hey. Hey, good for you!"

Good for me? Well, this is what I think: You talk to people who serve you the food the same way you talk to the people you eat the food with. You talk to people who work for you the same way you talk to the people you work for. It's a one-size-fits-all proposition. Talk to people. People will show you classical Indian dance, karate katas, equine dressage; explain Hegel, Jung, Iris Murdoch, Prince; tell you about their hometown in Columbia, Sicily, Tasmania, Moscow. And make you laugh.

Once I was waitering in a ritzy restaurant in Chelsea. Those of us on the late shift were starving, so when we spied a busboy heading to the kitchen with an untouched steak we took off. He was a Peruvian Pied Piper and four of us fell in behind him, pushing and shoving and tearing at the steak with our hands. Suddenly the door to the kitchen swung open and we all froze, guilty, afraid it was the manager. But it was just another waiter who said, without missing a beat, "Oh, look! *Dances with Wolves!*"

Sitting on rooftops, desktops, countertops, under counters; perched on milk crates, wine crates, paper cartons, front steps; hanging out in back alleys, deserted cafeterias, spooky hallways, we are all the same: a motley crew of artsy-fartsy types and single mothers and social misfits and immigrants who work six days, double shifts and send all the money home. We are people in recovery, people in denial, gay guys shocking the shit out of pizza guys from Queens—and vice versa. We all fit in because none of us belongs anywhere. And, boy, what you can learn: dirty words in every language and the fact that nobody is just a typist, just a dishwasher, just a cook, just a porter, just a prostitute. That everyone has a story. Everyone has at least one story that will stop your heart.

———————

Is this disjointed? I don't think so. Life doesn't have a topic sentence. There is nothing as clichéd as a story of a road traveled, of
lessons learned, of obstacles overcome. But that's because it's the
only story, the *big* story, simple as reading something in a book as
a child. Something that sounds made up, like the phases of the
moon. Then one night you look at the sky and realize that it's
true, that you can see it for yourself.

And that's all I can say, really. These things are true and I've
seen them for myself.

And this job is number sixty-five.

And now I dance.

(*Music plays.*)

CRUMBS FROM THE TABLE OF JOY

by Lynn Nottage

Crumbs from the Table of Joy received its world premiere at Second Stage Theatre (Carole Rothman, artistic director; Suzanne Schwartz Davidson, producing director) in New York City, in May 1995. It was directed by Joe Morton; the set design was by Myung Hee Cho; the costume design was by Karen Perry; the lighting design was by Donald Holder; the sound design was by Mark Bennett; the production stage manager was Delicia Turner; and the stage manager was David Sugarman. The cast was as follows:

ERNESTINE CRUMP	Kisha Howard
ERMINA CRUMP	Nicole Leach
GODFREY CRUMP	Daryl Edwards
LILY ANN GREEN	Ella Joyce
GERTE SCHULTE	Stephanie Roth

The narrator of this funny, incisive memory play is Ernestine Crump, an African American seventeen-year-old from Florida. In 1950, after the death of their mother, Ernestine and her younger sister move to Brooklyn with their father, a loyal follower of evangelist Father Divine. There, she finds herself pulled between two very different female role models: her new stepmother, a straitlaced German refugee, and her proudly defiant Communist aunt, Lily Ann Green. Lily smokes and drinks too much. She is a nonconformist, a "dangerous woman."

Ernestine tells Lily that nobody wants to be her friend at school. She asks if she can be part of Lily's revolution, "so folks heed when I walk into the room." Lily laughs long and hard, then responds.

LILY: Ernie, I came up here just like you, clothing so worn and shiny folks wouldn't even give me the time of day. I came with so much country in my bags folks got teary eyed and reminiscent as I'd pass. It was the year white folk had burned out old Johnston, and we'd gathered at Reverend Duckett's Church, listening to him preach on the evils of Jim Crow for the umpteenth time, speaking the words as though they alone could purge the demon. He whipped us into a terrible frenzy that wore us out. I'd like to say I caught the spirit, but instead I spoke my mind. . . . A few miscalculated words, not knowing I was intended to remain silent. You know what a miscalculation is? It's saying, "If y'all peasy head Negroes ain't happy, why don't you go up to city hall and demand some respect. I'm tired of praying, Goddamnit!" Mind ya I always wanted to leave. And mind ya I might not have said Goddamn. But those words spoken by a poor colored gal in a small cracker town meant you're morally corrupt. A communist, Ernie. Whole town stared me down, nobody would give me a word. It was finally the stares that drove me North. Stares from folks of our very persuasion, not just the crackers. You want to be part of my revolution? You know what I say to that, get yourself a profession like a nurse or something so no matter where you are or what they say, you can always walk into a room with your head held high, 'cause you'll always be essential. Period. Stop! But you gotta find your own "root" to the truth. That's what I do. Was true, is true, can be true, will be true. You ain't a communist, Ernie!

[ERNESTINE: No?]

LILY: Not yet! You just thinking, chile. A movie star can't have politics. (*Lily laughs.*)

HILLARY AND SOON-YI
SHOP FOR TIES

by Michelle Carter

Hillary and Soon-Yi Shop for Ties premiered at the Magic Theatre in San Francisco, Larry Eilenberg, artistic director, on November 5, 1999. It was directed by Joan Mankin; music composed by Randy Craig and Michelle Carter; music performed by Randy Craig and Hal Richards. The cast was as follows:

HILLARY (et al.)	Lorri Holt
SOON-YI (et al.)	Amy Tung

Hillary and Soon-Yi Shop for Ties is a vaudeville, a series of scenes, songs, and monologues about two women who become fodder for the tabloids: former First Lady Hillary Clinton and Woody Allen's teen bride Soon-Yi Previn. We first see Soon-Yi at age seven, shortly after she has been adopted by Mia Farrow; the journey of the play takes her far afield from that childhood self. In "Prometheus," her final monologue, the rediscovery of a coat she'd worn as an orphan sends her back in time to a night when passing shows of kindness led her to feel a sense of place in the world.

"Prometheus"

(*Soon-Yi walks the stage, testing the feel of the coat she'd worn as a child.*)

SOON-YI: Late March, or early April. Definitely springtime. I'm seven years old and in between orphanages, so walking is what I do with the day. Today I walk myself to the tourist part of the city. I know this part of the city as a network of garbage bins where cooks empty their woks at closing and barmen dump the orange and cherry garnishes people leave in their drinks. But today for no reason I walk the sidewalk like a child with no knowledge of the bins in the alley.

(*Maureen O'Sullivan appears behind Soon-Yi and drops a bill at her feet. She exits.*)

And I look down at my toes and there's a wadded-up bill. Someone else's money from someone else's country, crumpled in a ball at my feet.

(*She picks up the bill. Stuffs it in her pocket, full of new possibility.*)

On the corner there's a restaurant with white tablecloths and portraits on the walls. It's one of my favorites—every night at eleven, the cook dumps a steaming wok of sweet pork cubes that the tourists must like. I have never sat at a table at a restaurant. I have no idea how a restaurant works. I am desperate to know.

I walk in the door and take a seat. (*She sits.*) There's a napkin on the table in the shape of a fan. When I pick it up it goes limp—it's white like the tablecloth so I smooth it out flat so no one will notice. A man stands over me and asks what I want. I set the wadded bill on the table and we watch it uncrumple. Please bring me some food, I say. I see kindness pulling taut his lips and he doesn't ask where the money came from.

I have no idea what to do with myself. There's a newspaper folded on the seat across from me. I pick it up and instantly feel *worthy*. A newspaper in my hand, and money on the table: I understand these to be birthrights of something.

The man brings a pot of tea. It's starting to get dark on the street and dark in the restaurant. I can't actually read a newspaper, but the trouble is, since it's getting dark I can't *pretend* to read the newspaper. My table doesn't have a candle like the others—I don't know how much it costs to have a candle but I'm in no position to squander my money on light. A newspaper open before me and no light to read it by, I'm sure it's clear to everyone that I have no right to be here.

(*Candles are appearing onstage.*)

Suddenly the newspaper fills with light. There's a lady standing over me. "You'll strain your eyes," she says, and she's out the door. An old couple at the table next to me is putting on their coats to leave, and when they see the lady put her candle on my table they put their candle on my table beside it. Everyone in the restaurant must have seen because one by one, as they finish up and stand to leave, they bring their candles over and set them on my table. The newspaper is made of light and the printing is made of light, and the man brings chicken and vegetables and fish in sauces made of the colors of the rainbow.

Soon my table is sizzling with candles and the light becomes something I can hear, and smell, and taste.

I am hot with it. I am breathing light. I will never forget the night I am bright with fire.

MANHATTAN CASANOVA

by Jenny Lyn Bader

Manhattan Casanova was originally presented as a staged reading at the 1998 National Playwrights Conference at the Eugene O'Neill Theater Center.

The cast was as follows:

CHARLOTTE	Margaret Colin
PAM	Angle Phillips
ANNE	Pamela J. Gray
JOHN	Rob Campbell
WAITRESS	Ava Farber
EVA	Heather Goldenhersh

Charlotte is a pragmatic, antiromantic psychiatrist whose female friends and ex-patients all turn out to be dating the same irresistible man. John, the Casanova in question, is smitten with the intelligent, cynical doctor who doesn't fall for his usual lines. Eventually, she falls hard for him. Their affair is passionate and combative. When Charlotte tells John that she loves him, he responds that he needs to go away by himself for a few days. He is coming back, but not to her. Here, Charlotte seeks help from an unexpected source.

Charlotte is alone in her apartment with her address book and the Man-hattan white pages.

CHARLOTTE (*on the phone*): Hello, Pam? Pam, it's Charlotte. I— Pam? Oh don't hang up. (*The line is dead. She dials again.*) Hi, Marie? It's Charlotte. Are you screening? I know you're there. Pick up. C'mon. I'm sorry I said your baby resembled a turnip. Call me back if you want.

(*Hangs up, dials again.*)

Hi, Mom? It's Charlotte. Look, I'm sorry about what I said about your second husband. I know a lot of years have passed, but I'd like to make amends. You're kidding! Mom, I'm so sorry. When did he die? Really. You did? You got a third one? Congratulations, that's wonderful. What does he do? Not that that matters. I'd love to meet him Mom. Oh. Well I'll talk to you soon. 'Bye.

(*Hangs up, dials again.*)

Evan? Hi, it's me. I'm sorry I said we maybe shouldn't see each other anymore. I mean maybe we shouldn't but—god. Forget it. It's over.

(*She hangs up. Speed-dials, sets her watch, hangs up. Stares at the phone. Opens the phone book and dials.*)

Hi. Is this 1-900-Horoscope? It's tomorrow. November twentieth. What? Two P.M.

(*Listens, nods.*)

Yes I realize I'm the worst kind of Scorpio there is. Can you tell me how I'd get along with someone whose birth-day is October twenty-ninth? No, I don't know the time. Can't you approximate? Of course I know it's important to be specific. I'm a scientist. Psychiatrist. What? I know, but astrology isn't really an exact science either! Is it? Well, can you check the general planetary chart or something? Hmmm?

(*Listens to reading.*)

Miserably? We'd get along miserably? Are you sure? In a permanent sense? No hope?

(*Listens, nods.*)

Doomed. You only see doom. Great. Thanks.

(*She hangs up and leafs through the phone book in a manic state. She dials again and sounds a bit nervous.*)

Hi. How are you? Good! Good. I'm fine. Fine. Yeah.

(*Listens.*)

Don't worry, I'm not going to kill myself, I'm just calling to . . . ask about a friend. A friend of mine is feeling suicidal, and I don't know what to say to him. What do you say to people?

(*Listens.*)

What? I don't see that it's any of your business. Why would you want my address? It's not like I'm ordering in.

(*Listens.*)

Well, no, he's not holding a gun to his head, I'm just calling to discuss the *possibility* of his death. Can't we keep it open? Why is everything always so final with you people? What? No, I've never called you before. I just meant, why are people in *general* so final. Why do they cut themselves off from possibility. Why do I say "they"?

(*Nods.*)

Of course I'm a person too. Yes, I mean why do *we* cut ourselves off from possibility. I cut myself off too, yes. Look, are

you a trained professional, or do you just answer the phone?
Did you take a three-hour crash course or something?

(*Amazed.*)

Yes, I am one. How did you know that?

(*Listens.*)

Really? Every psychiatrist who calls asks you about your
training? Do a lot of psychiatrists call? Second only to
artists? When you say artists do you mean painters or—the
whole artist community.

(*Listens.*)

How long? That's a long time to be answering that phone.
Well, of *course* you're depressed. What? Well of course *I'm*
depressed, I have a dear friend who's suicidal! You'll connect
me to what?

(*Listens, alarmed.*)

What do you mean you're only the receptionist? I was on
hold? *This* was hold? *You* are considered the *receptionist*?
No it's just that . . . I didn't know death had a reception
area. . . . Also, not to emphasize this education thing again,
but I do hold several graduate degrees and—

(*Starts crying.*)

I'm a *terrible* psychiatrist. I just make people worse. And
you're this *receptionist,* and you're making me better.

(*Listens, nods.*)

No, I wasn't saying there's anything wrong with being a
receptionist. I'm saying you're great. You're great and I'm
awful. Don't you ever wonder, why go on? You do? But
then you think what?

(*Listens, stunned, as receptionist briefly explains the meaning of life.*)

Wow. (*Nods.*) That's true. That makes a lot of sense, when you put it that way. Sure, that's a reason to live. But then what do you do about men?

(*Listens intently as the receptionist explains relationships.*)

Who taught you how to talk like this? Who are you? I feel everything is so much clearer. Why I called? Broken heart stuff, nothing . . . earth-shattering. What?

(*Listens, profoundly moved.*)

Yes, love is that. (*Smiles.*) You're right. You're really right. You . . . (*sniffling*) are a very gifted receptionist! Transfer me? To . . . oh, yes, one of the counselors . . . yes I should really talk to one of them.

(*The line goes dead.*)

Hello? Hello?

(*She starts having trouble breathing.*)

Did you lose me in the transfer? Hello? Hello? Is someone there? Is anyone there? Please be there.

(*Frantically pressing buttons, she hits the speakerphone button. The sound of a dial tone fills the space.*)

Anyone? Someone?

(*As she hits the phone, she pushes the volume button and the looming dial tone sound gets louder.*)

Hello? (*Pushing buttons frantically, she hits speed dial. The speakerphone blares.*)

VOICEOVER: At the tone, the time will be eleven forty-four and ten seconds.

(*Blackout.*)

MIRIAM'S FLOWERS

by Migdalia Cruz

Miriam's Flowers was nurtured by Maria Irene Fornes' Playwrights' Laboratory at INTAR; Midwest PlayLabs; Mark Taper Forum's New Play Festival; and Playwrights Horizons.

The first production of the play at Latino Chicago Theater Company, directed by William Payne, featured Justina Machado, Consuelo Allen, Frankie Davila, Felipe Camacho, and Daniel Sanchez. Set and costumes by Joel Kiaff. Lights by Juan A. Ramirez.

The first workshop of the play at Playwrights Horizons, directed by Roberta Levitow, featured Monique Cintron, Divina Cook, Ralph Marrero, Peter Jay Fernandez, and Alex Caicedo.

Miriam Nieves is a sixteen-year-old Puerto Rican girl from the South Bronx. Abused by her father in childhood, and mourning her slain younger brother, Puli, she seeks release in promiscuous sex and self-mutilation, etching designs on her body with razor blades. The play is composed of thirty-seven brief scenes (some wordless) and monologues. This speech is Scene 20.

In church, Miriam, talking to the statue of the Virgin holding the crucified Christ.

MIRIAM: I'm the invisible girl, Mary . . . always searching for a hole in the wall to pull myself through to get to the other side. The other side is only for me, I could see myself then. I could feel my fingertips then and the pointy pieces of skin being torn down the sides of my fingers. I could see the scars then, on the bottom of my thumbs from the Wilkinson Swords—I write on myself with them. I carve myself into my hands. And for Lent, Mary, I'll cover them with purple cloth. I keep my gloves on in the church, until everybody leaves and then I come to you. To show you. (*She takes off her gloves.*) See? I show you mine and then I can touch yours. . . . (*She places her hands on the carved wounds of Jesus.*) They feel so fresh, Jesus. Like mine. I can smell the blood on them. Smells like violets and sweet coffee with five sugars, like Ma takes it . . . (*Pause.*) I'm never gonna die—not from my wounds anyway. I never go in deep and I don't make them long. I make little points that add up to a picture, a flower picture. And sometimes they're so pretty they make me cry, and I like that, 'cause when I get those tears on my hands and on my arms, they sting, and then I know I'm alive, 'cause it hurts so bad. Does that happen to you, too? (*Fade out.*)

THE PRINCESS OF BABYLON

by Warren Leight

The Princess of Babylon was commissioned by All Seasons Theater Group, artistic director John McCormack. It was first directed by Merri Milwe and was performed by Rozie Bacchi in August 2000.

The Princess of Babylon is part of an evening of monologues and one-acts about made-for-TV justice called *Channel Surfin' USA*.

Amy, sixteen, going on forty, stands. She is a little nervous, but she speaks with the righteous indignation of someone who knows she has been set up.

OK, first of all—I didn't do it. I was nowhere near the so-called scene of the crime at the time of the gunshot. I have—don't just take my word for it—I have allies. Alibis. People who can place me in three different places at the time of the alleged shotgun attempt. Which, how do we know, wasn't self-inflicted? OK? I mean, from what Prince Charming tells me—she's a few fries short of a Happy Meal. She's done this sort of thing before. She's thrown herself down a staircase. For one. She pukes up her banquets on cue. She's a mess. I'm sorry, but she's a mess. Do you know what she spends, on *gowns?* So now she takes a gunshot wound to the head—blam—and everyone assumes, like, she had nothing to do with it. I am telling you the girl is pathetic. And threatened by me. Which is, like, way paranoid. And delusional.

I mean, yeah yeah yeah I know everyone treats him like he's royalty, but he has got like shit for brains, ears the size of a pita bread, and really bad sinuses. He makes this clearing noise, *cuhh-hhcuuhh cahooh,* all the time. So for her, and every one of her prissant friends to turn around and say like I should be implicated is just a bag of horse shit, excuse my French. And where is he in all this? No one says, Mr. Prince, how come you were having an affair with a sixteen-year-old high school student who's like young enough to be your daughter? No—I'm the one who's called the slut, the whore, the Lethal Lolita. And he's a victim, she's a victim. Give me an f'en break.

What happened, I think, is that I lost my beeper at a movie theater—*Aliens. Three.* Which was another total f'en rip-off. Anyway, me and my girlfriends—and you can check this with any of them—went to see *Aliens Three* at the Mall in Massapequa over the weekend. Maybe someone in the Prince's entourage was there. Found my beeper. 'Cause it fell out of my pocket, those seats are so cheap I swear to God. (and what do they do there, mop the floors with Diet Coke?) So it fell out of my pocket. He finds it. Takes it to the palatial estate. It falls out of *his* pocket. In fact, maybe he was pokin her. Wait a minute: maybe the Prince walks in on them, gets royally pissed; shots are fired, and now they conspiratize to put the blame on me. Boom, I'm implicatable because he has my beeper. My luck. Probably they paid him—the stupid guinea. I mean, he is so easy to manipulate it is pathetic.

So now I'm sitting here for like, three f'en days. I have my PSATs coming up. Which like, forget about studying in prison. It's disgusting in here.

And for the first time in her life, she's getting all this sympathy. Suddenly everyone likes her. I'm some sort of Long Island low-life, and she's a friggen angel. I would hate to be his wife because until you are like, at death's door, he doesn't gives a rat's ass about you.

Then they just cry and cry. Alligator tears.

And his mother is the worst. Crying all her talk-radio tears. Saying quote: "Amy's Horrible-est," her Prince had nothing to do with it, he's a good boy. He would never cheat on his lady.

Bull shit.

I am being set up. The truth is, their marriage is a sham and he's just using me like he always did.

And I would therefore like my bail reduced.

Thank you your honor.

ROSE

by Martin Sherman

Rose was first performed in the Cottesloe Auditorium at the Royal National Theatre on May 19, 1999. The cast was as follows:

ROSE   Olympia Dukakis

Directed by Nancy Meckler
Designed by Stephen Brimson Lewis
Lighting by Johanna Town

Rose is a survivor. Born in a Ukrainian shtetl called Yultishka, she went on to the Warsaw ghetto, on board the ship *Exodus,* through two radically different marriages, a stint in a commune, and a hotel in Miami Beach. Though Rose is eighty when she tells her story, the incident she describes here took place in her early teens. Her father, who'd made a career out of dying, was finally crushed by a wardrobe full of medicine as Cossacks ransacked his home. Rose's mother responded, as always, without any sign of emotion—a characteristic that caused her two children to wonder if "God had dropped a genuine Christian into the middle of this shtetl and didn't tell anyone."

ROSE: Papa's was my first shivah. So many people came we ran out of wooden benches. I think they needed proof that papa had finally died. Mama was in her element, totally impassive. It was God's will.

A few weeks later, on a hot afternoon, I sold the last grapefruit and went for a walk in the woods. I came upon a field covered with lilac trees. I heard a voice. Someone was singing, singing in an unknown tongue—a gypsy melody; no, it was Muslim; no, totally Hebraic; no, wait, I think Spanish, or maybe African—I couldn't tell—or perhaps it was from the moon. It summoned lovers and demons. I crept toward the field. I had to see who was making this delirious sound. Finally, I spotted a fragile figure holding on to a tree; holding, holding and swaying at the same time. I hid behind a bush and listened to the melody and suddenly the figure turned, and I saw its face, covered with sweat and dirt and desire and longing . . . It was mama. I ran. I ran into the woods. I ran away from her song. I ran back to the shtetl. When Mama returned home, she was scrubbed and cool, and she wore her saintly face. She started to cook.

(*Pause.*)

I never thought of her as Christian again.

TIMES OF WAR

by Eric Lane

Times of War premiered at the Adirondack Theatre Festival (Martha Banta, artistic director; David Turner, producing director) in June 1999. It was directed by Martha Banta; the set design was by Eric Renschler; the lighting design was by Matthew Frey; the costume design was by Susan J. Slack; the sound design was by Douglas Graves; the choreography was by Schele Williams; the production stage manager was Gerald Cosgrove. The cast was as follows:

DORIS, ARLENE	Maggie Lowe
YOUNG DORIS, MARY SUE	Jeanne Willcoxon
KARL, TOM, DIAMANTINI	James Georgiades
WARREN, SCOTT	David Gunderman

Times of War tells the story of Doris, a spirited and resilient woman, whose journey takes her from her youth during World War II, through the late 1960s, and into the mid-1990s. In the play's third section, Doris's grandson Kenny has died in a hospital under mysterious circumstances. Doris was the last person seen alone with him before he was discovered dead, with a pillow over his face. She is accused of killing her grandson, who was dying of AIDS and who she loved dearly. Doris claims she is innocent and finds herself at the center of a media frenzy. Detective Diamantini is assigned to investigate the case. In spite of the situation, the two become friendly. He gets a call to pick her up at the local supermarket and brings her to the police precinct. Here, she reveals what just happened.

DORIS: She spit in my face. At the supermarket.

I'm walking down the aisle. My cart in front of me. This woman heads toward me. Her five-year-old son sitting in the cart. (*Enjoys this brief image.*) He's got a big chocolate mustache from a Ring Ding over his nose and mouth. I look at him and smile. She sees me and our eyes meet. Lock for that moment. Time stops. The music. The fluorescent hum it covers. Just her and me. Her son's fingers covered in chocolate. She looks in my eyes, spits in my face, walks down the aisle, turns and leaves.

[DIAMANTINI: You go after her?]

DORIS: I stand there stunned. Like her son must be each time she hauls off and whacks him one. Just stand there between the boxes of Cheerios and Pop-Tarts. Frozen for a moment. Then start to scream. Loud. So loud women start running from other aisles to see what's wrong. Children whose eyes they shield from this crazy woman grabbing at boxes of cereal, Froot Loops, Lucky Charms and tearing open the box. Circles of pink, yellow, moons and stars flying across the aisle and I yell. Loud. "You didn't know him." Grab a woman by the jacket as she backs away. "You didn't know him." The screaming so loud the manager turns off the music. "You didn't know him. You didn't know him. You didn't know him. You didn't know him. Sit with him at three A.M. beside the bed and wipe his shit. Fix his meals so maybe, just maybe he would have an extra bite. You didn't know him. Watch his weight go down to ninety. Watch your grandson, my grandson— You didn't know him. You didn't know him. You didn't know him!"

THE VAGINA MONOLOGUES

by Eve Ensler

The Vagina Monologues premiered October 1996 in New York City at HERE Arts Center in association with Wendy Evans Joseph. Eve Ensler starred.

The Vagina Monologues is compiled from interviews with over two hundred women about the part of their body that they identify as everything from "coochi snorcher" to simply "down there." The monologues, which have been performed by a solo actress, a trio of stars, and larger groups during Ensler's nation-wide "V-Day Project," cover such taboo topics as first menstruation, pubic hair, types of orgasm, lesbian sex, wartime rape victims and—in this monologue—giving birth.

"I Was There in the Room"
For Shiva

I was there when her vagina opened.
We were all there: her mother, her husband, and I,
and the nurse from the Ukraine with her whole hand
up there in her vagina feeling and turning with her rubber
glove as she talked casually to us—like she was turning on a
loaded faucet.

I was there in the room when the contractions made her crawl
on all fours,
made unfamiliar moans leak out of her pores
and still there after hours when she just screamed suddenly
wild, her arms striking at the electric air.

I was there when her vagina changed
from a shy sexual hole
to an archaeological tunnel, a sacred vessel,
a Venetian canal, a deep well with a tiny stuck child inside,
waiting to be rescued.

I saw the colors of her vagina. They changed.
Saw the bruised broken blue
the blistering tomato red
the gray pink, the dark;
saw the blood like perspiration along the edges
saw the yellow, white liquid, the shit, the clots
pushing out all the holes, pushing harder and harder,
saw through the hole, the baby's head
scratches of black hair, saw it just there behind
the bone—a hard round memory,

as the nurse from the Ukraine kept turning and turning
her slippery hand.

I was there when each of us, her mother and I,
held a leg and spread her wide pushing
with all our strength against her pushing
and her husband sternly counting, "One, two, three,"
telling her to focus, harder.
We looked into her then.
We couldn't get our eyes out of that place.

We forget the vagina, all of us
what else would explain
our lack of awe, our lack of wonder.

I was there when the doctor
reached in with Alice in Wonderland spoons
and there as her vagina became a wide operatic mouth
singing with all its strength;
first the little head, then the gray flopping arm, then the fast
swimming body, swimming quickly into our weeping arms.

I was there later when I just turned and faced her vagina.
I stood and let myself see
her all spread, completely exposed
mutilated, swollen, and torn,
bleeding all over the doctor's hands
who was calmly sewing her there.

I stood, and as I stared, her vagina suddenly
became a wide red pulsing heart.

The heart is capable of sacrifice.
So is the vagina.
The heart is able to forgive and repair.
It can change its shape to let us in.

It can expand to let us out.
So can the vagina.
It can ache for us and stretch for us, die for us
and bleed and bleed us into this difficult, wondrous world.
So can the vagina.
I was there in the room.
I remember.

WHAT A MAN WEIGHS

by Sherry Kramer

What a Man Weighs had its first performance at the Second Stage Theater (Robyn Goodman and Carole Rothman, artistic directors) on April 25, 1990. The cast and creative contributors were as follows:

JOAN	Christine Estabrook
RUTH	Harriet Harris
THE DEBBIE	Katherine Hiler
HASELTINE	Richard Cox
Director	Carole Rothman
Set design	Andrew Jackness
Lighting design	Dennis Parichy
Costume design	Susan Hilferty
Sound design	Gary and Timmy Harris
Hair design	Antonio Soddu
Production stage manager	Pamela Eddington

Joan and Ruth, thirty-five, have been best friends since college. They work in the book conservation lab of a large university with Haseltine, a charismatic womanizer whose conquests are all named The Debbie. Smart, guarded, and self-aware, Joan is in love with Haseltine in spite of her much better judgment. She is at that age when the young truths stop making sense. She is good at her job and has a great love of heights. This monologue opens the play.

Spot on Joan, as she places her foot on the first step of the tallest set of stairs—or perhaps the first words are said in darkness, before the spot hits her, already in position.

JOAN: I climb the stairs. (*She begins to climb.*)

I climb the stairs, and I think—oh yes, he'll be there, he'll be there, and I'll walk through him into another world, and none of the things that make me frightened will ever touch me again, and everything that was ever ugly about me will drop away from me like water. I will be free of it all.

I want to fall down on my knees, I'm so goddamn grateful, as I climb the stairs, at the thought of being free, and so I do, in my mind, I fall down on my knees in my mind as I climb the stairs. He is there, and he has freed me from ugliness forever, from the lines around my eyes, the folds beneath my breasts, he has freed me from my thighs, he has freed me from it all. And the longing bucks inside me, and the heat has just kicked in, and I am climbing the stairs, and I am on my knees, and I am so goddamn beautiful, but it's the heat, in the end, that makes me know. That this is true.

Everything else could betray me. Everything else I could just kick aside. But not that heat. That heat doesn't lie, it has never lied, it is my truth, my own, and it does not lie.

(*She is at the very top of the stairs, past the landings leading anywhere.*)

I have climbed the stairs. And I'm filled with him.

(*She faces the audience.*)

I love this daydream.
And I hate myself for dreaming it.
I have climbed the stairs. And I am filled with him.

(*Beat. She smiles.*)

And he isn't there.

(*Blackout.*)

WIT

by Margaret Edson

Wit was produced by MCC Theater, Long Wharf Theatre, and Daryl Roth, with Stanley Shopkorn, Robert G. Bartner, and Stanley Kaufelt, at Union Square Theatre, in New York City, on January 7, 1999. It was directed by Derek Anson Jones; the set design was by Myung Hee Cho; the costume design was by Ilona Somogyi; the lighting design was by Michael Chybowski; the music and sound design were by David Van Tieghem; the wigs were by Paul Huntley; the production manager was Kai Brothers; and the production stage manager was Katherine Lee Boyer. The cast was as follows:

VIVIAN BEARING, PH.D.	Kathleen Chalfant
HARVEY KELEKIAN, M.D., MR. BEARING	Walter Charles
JASON POSNER, M.D.	Alec Phoenix
SUSIE MONAHAN, R.N., B.S.N.	Paula Pizzi
E.M. ASHFORD, D. PHIL.	Helen Stenborg
LAB TECHNICIANS, STUDENTS, RESIDENTS	Brian J. Carter, Daniel Sarnelli, Alli Steinberg, Lisa Tharps

This production of *Wit* was originally produced by Long Wharf Theatre (Doug Hughes, artistic director; Michael Ross, managing director), in New Haven, Connecticut, on October 31, 1997. The production was then produced by MCC (Bernard Telsey and Robert LuPone, executive directors; William Cantler, associate director), in New York City, on September 17, 1998.

Dr. Vivian Bearing is an intellectually brilliant, emotionally out-of-touch professor of seventeenth-century poetry, specializing in the metaphysical sonnets of John Donne. Diagnosed with terminal cancer, she finds that none of her speculations about the nature of mortality have prepared her for facing her own death head-on.

During her treatment, Vivian has taken record-breaking doses of chemotherapy. She has formed a close emotional bond with Susie, her primary nurse. At 4 A.M., in spite of herself, Vivian cries, telling Susie she is scared. They discuss her "code status"—what to do in case Vivian's heart stops beating. Vivian decides that if her heart stops, they should take no further measures to keep her alive. Susie leaves, and Vivian sits upright, full of energy and rage. She speaks to the audience.

VIVIAN: That certainly was a *maudlin* display. Popsicles? "Sweetheart"? I can't believe my life has become so . . . corny.

But it can't be helped. I don't see any other way. We are discussing life and death, and not in the abstract, either; we are discussing *my* life and *my* death, and my brain is dulling, and poor Susie's was never very sharp to begin with, and I can't conceive of any other . . . *tone.*

(*Quickly*) Now is not the time for verbal swordplay, for unlikely flights of imagination and wildly shifting perspectives, for metaphysical conceit, for wit.

And nothing would be worse than a detailed scholarly analysis. Erudition. Interpretation. Complication.

(*Slowly*) Now is a time for simplicity. Now is a time for, dare I say it, kindness.

(*Searchingly*) I thought being extremely smart would take care of it. But I see that I have been found out. Ooohhh.

I'm scared. Oh, God. I want . . . I want . . . No. I want to hide. I just want to curl up in a little ball. (*She dives under the covers. Scene change. Vivian wakes in horrible pain. She is tense, agitated, fearful. Slowly she calms down and addresses the audience. Trying extremely hard.*)

I want to tell you how it feels. I want to explain it, to use *my* words. It's as if . . . I can't . . . There aren't . . . I'm like a student and this is the final exam and I don't know what to put down because I don't understand the question and I'm *running out of time.* (*Pause.*)

The time for extreme measures has come. I am in terrible pain. Susie says that I need to begin aggressive pain management if I am going to stand it.

"It": such a little word. In this case, I think "it" signifies "being alive."

I apologize in advance for what this palliative treatment modality does to the dramatic coherence of my play's last scene. It can't be helped. They have to do something. I'm in terrible pain.

Say it, Vivian. *It hurts like hell. It really does.* (*Susie enters. Vivian is writhing in pain.*)

Oh, God. Oh, God.

CONTRIBUTORS

JENNY LYN BADER's work has been produced at Center Stage, Actors Theatre of Louisville, HERE, New Georges, John Montgomery Theatre, Pulse Ensemble, Lincoln Center Theater Directors Lab, New York International Fringe Festival, among others. Her play *Manhattan Casanova* won the Edith Oliver Award at the O'Neill National Playwrights Conference. She regularly contributes to the Sunday *New York Times Week in Review.*

ALAN BALL received the 2000 Academy Award for his screenplay *American Beauty.* His full-length plays include *Five Women Wearing the Same Dress* and *Cherokee County.* One-acts include *Your Mother's Butt, Bachelor Holiday,* and *The M-Word.* Mr. Ball was supervising producer for the CBS TV series *Cybill,* and wrote for ABC's *Grace Under Fire.* He is creator and executive producer for the HBO series *Six Feet Under.*

MICHELLE CARTER's play *Hillary and Soon-Yi Shop for Ties* received the PEN USA West Literary Award in drama, the Garland Award for playwriting, an American Theatre Critics Circle Award nomination and a Bay Area Theatre Critics Circle nomination for the score, which she co-composed with Randy Craig. It premiered at San Francisco's Magic Theatre and has been published by Dramatic Publishing.

KIA CORTHRON's *Breath, Boom* was originally commissioned and produced by the Royal Court Theatre. Her works include: *Force Continuum, Splash Hatch on the E Going Down, Seeking the Genesis,* and *Life by Asphyxiation.* Honors include the Fadiman Award, Kennedy Fund for New American Plays, NEA/TCG, and the Callaway Award. She is a member of New Dramatists.

MIGDALIA CRUZ has written over thirty plays, operas, and musicals including: *Salt, Fur, Miriam's Flowers, Telling Tales, Another Part of the House,* and *Frida: The Story of Frida Kahlo.* Her work has been produced across the United States and abroad in venues as diverse as Houston Grand Opera, Latino Chicago Theater Company, and Cornerstone. Among her awards: Kennedy Center's Fund for New American Plays, PEW/TCG Residency, and NEA Playwriting Fellowship.

LAURA SHAINE CUNNINGHAM is the author of *Sleeping Arrangements* and *A Place in the Country,* first published in *The New Yorker* magazine, and now in hardcover and paperback editions. Her plays have been produced at Steppenwolf Theatre, in New York and London. Her first play, *Beautiful Bodies,* appears in *Plays for Actresses* and is widely produced.

CHRISTOPHER DURANG was born in Montclair, New Jersey. He is author of *A History of the American Film, Sister Mary Ignatius Explains It All for You, Beyond Therapy, Laughing Wild, The Marriage of Bette and Boo, Betty's Summer Vacation,* and *Durang Durang.* He is one third of the cabaret act "Chris Durang and Dawne."

MARGARET EDSON lives in Atlanta, Georgia, where she is an elementary school teacher. Between earning degrees in history and literature, she worked in the cancer and AIDS unit of a research hospital. Her first play, *Wit,* received the NY Drama Critics Circle, Drama Desk, Outer Critics Circle, Lucille Lortel, and the Oppenheim awards. In addition, Ms. Edson won the John Gossner Playwriting Award and the 1999 Pulitzer Prize for drama.

EVE ENSLER is an award-winning playwright, poet, activist, and screenwriter. *The Vagina Monologues* won an Obie Award and was nominated for a Drama Desk Award. It had a hit off-Broadway run and has toured throughout the United States and internationally. Her plays include *Necessary Targets, Lemonade, Floating Rhoda and the Glue Man,* and *Extraordinary Measures.* Her articles have appeared in *Common Boundary, Ms,* and the *Utne Reader.*

JULIA JORDAN is the author of *Smoking Lesson* and *Tatjana in Color,* which received the Francesca Primus Prize. She is book writer for the one-act musical *The Mice,* which is part of Harold Prince's project *Three.* Ms. Jordan wrote and directed the short film *The Hat,* which sold to Bravo and IFC channels. Her ten-minute play *Mpls./St. Paul* was a joint Heideman Award winner at Actors Theatre of Louisville.

SHERRY KRAMER's plays have been produced at Yale Rep, Soho Rep, EST, Second Stage, Woolly Mammoth, Mixed Blood, and Signature Theatre. She is the recipient of NEA, NYFA, and McKnight fellowships, the Weissberger Playwriting Award (*What a Man Weighs*), the L.A. Women in Theatre New Play Award (*The Wall of Water*), and the Jane Chambers Playwriting Award (*David's Red-haired Death*). She is an alumna of New Dramatists.

ERIC LANE's *Times of War* premiered at the Adirondack Theatre Festival and has won numerous honors including the Berrilla Kerr Playwriting Award. Plays include *Shellac, Dancing on Checkers' Grave,* and *Cater-Waiter.* He wrote, directed, and produced the award-winning short film *Cater-Waiter,* which has screened throughout the world. Honors include a Writers Guild Award, the LaMama Playwright Development Award, and seven Yaddo fellowships.

WARREN LEIGHT is the author of *Side Man,* which won multiple awards, including the 1999 Tony, and was a Pulitzer Prize finalist. His most recent play, *Glimmer, Glimmer and Shine,* received an American Theatre Critics Association nomination for best new play. Mr. Leight is a member of both the Writers Guild of America East and the Dramatists Guild Councils.

DONALD MARGULIES received the 2000 Pulitzer Prize for his play *Dinner with Friends.* His plays include *Collected Stories, The Model Apartment, What's Wrong with This Picture?, The Loman Family Picnic,* and *Found a Peanut.* Honors include an Obie Award, grants from the Guggenheim Foundation, NYFA, and the NEA. Mr. Margulies is an instructor at Yale University and a council member of the Dramatists Guild.

JANE MARTIN is an award-winning and Pulitzer-nominated Kentucky playwright who first came to national attention for *Talking With,* a collection of monologues premiering in Actors Theatre of Louisville's 1981 Humana Festival of New American Plays. Her other work includes: *Vital Signs, Cementville, Keely and Du, Jack and Jill, Mr. Bundy, Anton in Show Business,* and *Flaming Guns of the Purple Sage.*

ELLEN MCLAUGHLIN's plays *Days and Nights Within, A Narrow Bed,* and *Infinity's House* all received their professional premieres at Actors Theatre of Louisville. Awards include the Susan Smith Blackburn Prize, the Great American Play Contest, an NEA playwriting grant, and the Lila Wallace–Reader's Digest Fund Writer's Award. Ms. McLaughlin is an accomplished actress, best known for originating the role of the Angel in Tony Kushner's *Angels in America.*

LYNN NOTTAGE's *Crumbs from the Table of Joy* was nominated for an NAACP Award and a Black Theatre Alliance Award. Plays include *Mud, River, Stone* (finalist, Susan Smith Blackburn Prize), *Poof!* (Heideman Award), *Por 'Knockers,* and *Las Meninas.* Her plays have been produced off-Broadway and across the country. She cowrote the Merchant Ivory film *Side Streets,* directed by Tony Gerber. Ms. Nottage received playwriting fellowships from MTC, New Dramatists, and NYFA.

CLAUDIA SHEAR won an Obie Award for the off-Broadway production of *Blown Sideways Through Life,* which was also filmed for *American Playhouse.* She wrote and starred in *Dirty Blonde,* which was produced off-Broadway, on Broadway, and in London. *Dirty Blonde* received Tony Award nominations for best play and best actress in a play.

NINA SHENGOLD won the ABC Playwright Award for *Homesteaders* and the Writers Guild Award for *Labor of Love,* starring Marcia Gay Harden. Other TV credits include *Blind Spot,* starring Joanne Woodward and Laura Linney, *Unwed Father,* and *Double Platinum.* Her ten-minute plays (including *Finger Food, Lives of the Great Waitresses, Everything Must Go,* and *Emotional Baggage*) have been produced around the world.

MARTIN SHERMAN's plays include *Bent,* first produced in London with Ian McKellen, subsequently on Broadway with Richard Gere and in over thirty-five countries, *Messiah, A Madhouse in Goa, When She Danced, Some Sunny Day,* and *Rose,* produced at the Royal National Theatre and then on Broadway starring Olympia Dukakis. His screenplays include *The Summer House, Alive and Kicking, Bent,* and *Callas Forever.*

DIANA SON's plays have been produced at Actors Theatre of Louisville, EST, LaJolla Playhouse, the Joseph Papp Public Theatre, New Georges, and Soho Rep. She is a member of New Dramatists and a graduate of NYU's dramatic literature program. Her plays include *Stop Kiss, Boy, R.A.W. ('Cause I'm a Woman), Fishes, Stealing Fire,* and *Happy Birthday Jack.*

WENDY WASSERSTEIN is the author of *The Heidi Chronicles, Uncommon Women and Others, Isn't It Romantic, The Sisters Rosensweig, American Daughter,* and *Old Money,* among other plays. Honors include the Pulitzer Prize, Tony Award, and Drama Desk Award. A graduate of Yale School of Drama, she is also author of the children's book *Pamela's First Musical.*

MARY LOUISE WILSON coauthored the play *Full Gallop,* which had a successful run off-Broadway and subsequently in London, France, Italy, Australia, Brazil, and regional theaters in the United States. She has written articles for *The New York Times, American Theatre,* and *The New Yorker.* She is also a veteran actor of stage, television, and film.

ABOUT THE EDITORS

NINA SHENGOLD and ERIC LANE are editors of *Plays for Actresses* and *Take Ten: New 10-Minute Plays* for Vintage Books. For Penguin Books, they edited *Moving Parts: Monologues from Contemporary Plays, The Actor's Book of Scenes from New Plays,* and *The Actor's Book of Gay & Lesbian Plays,* which was nominated for the Lambda Award for excellence in gay and lesbian publications. In addition, Ms. Shengold edited *The Actor's Book of Contemporary Stage Monologues,* and Mr. Lane edited *Telling Tales: New One-Act Plays.*

NINA SHENGOLD received the ABC Playwright Award and the *L.A. Weekly* Award for *Homesteaders,* published by Samuel French; her short plays are widely performed. She won the 1998 Writers Guild Award and a GLAAD Award nomination for her teleplay *Labor of Love,* and the Shine Award for *Unwed Father.* Other teleplays include *Blind Spot,* starring Joanne Woodward and Laura Linney, and *Double Platinum,* starring Diana Ross and Brandy. Her feature screenplay *Good Will,* adapted from Jane Smiley's novella, is currently in pre-production. Ms. Shengold recently served as a teaching adviser at the Equinoxe Screenwriters Workshop in Bordeaux. She is artistic director of the theater company Actors & Writers, and lives in upstate New York with her daughter Maya.

ERIC LANE won the Berrilla Kerr Playwriting Award for *Times of War,* which premiered at the Adirondack Theatre Festival. The play also received grants from the Puffin Foundation, Pilgrim Project, Jonathan Larson Foundation, and was an O'Neill Center finalist. Other plays include *Shellac, Cater-Waiter,* and *Dancing on Checkers' Grave,* which starred Jennifer Aniston. Mr. Lane wrote, directed, and produced the award-winning short film *Cater-Waiter,* which screened in over forty cities worldwide. For his TV work on *Ryan's Hope,* he received a Writers Guild

Award. Additional honors include the LaMama Playwright Development Award and seven Yaddo fellowships. Mr. Lane is an honors graduate of Brown University and is artistic director of Orange Thoughts, a not-for-profit theater and film company in New York City.

PERMISSIONS ACKNOWLEDGMENTS

Permission was secured for the following excerpts of poetry which appear in the selection *Collected Stories* by Donald Margulies:

"Not So Far as the Forest (I)" by Edna St. Vincent Millay from *Collected Poems* (HarperCollins Publishers). Copyright © 1939, 1967 by Edna St. Vincent Millay and Norma Mary Ellis. All rights reserved. Reprinted by permission of Elizabeth Barnett, Literary Executor.

"Calmly We Walk Through This April's Day" by Delmore Schwartz from *Selected Poems: Summer Knowledge*. Copyright © 1959 by Delmore Schwartz; short quotations by Delmore Schwartz from *In Dreams Begin Responsibilities* by Delmore Schwartz. Copyright © 1961 by Delmore Schwartz; short excerpt by Delmore Schwartz from *Delmore Schwartz Poems*. Copyright © 1998 by New Directions Publishing Corp. Reprinted by permission of New Directions Publishing Corp.

Grateful acknowledgment is made for permission to reprint from the following previously published plays:

Anton in Show Business by Jane Martin. Copyright © 2000 by Alexander Speer, Trustee. Reprinted by permission of Alexander Speer, Trustee for Jane Martin.

CAUTION: Professionals and amateurs are hereby warned that ANTON IN SHOW BUSINESS, copyright © 2000, is subject to royalty. It is fully protected under the copyright laws of the United States of America, the British Commonwealth, including Canada, and all other countries of the Copyright Union. All rights, including professional, amateur, motion pictures, recitation, lecturing, public reading, radio broadcasting, television, and the rights of translation into foreign languages are strictly reserved. In its present form the play is dedicated to the reading public only.

Particular emphasis is laid on the question of amateur or professional readings, permission and terms for which must be secured in writing from Samuel French, Inc., 45 West 25th Street, New York, NY 10010.